The Economics of Talent Management and Human Capital

Sharif Uddin Ahmed Rana
Paris Graduate School, France & World Talent Economy Forum, Malaysia

Adrian David Cheok
Imagineering Institute, Malaysia

IGI Global
Publishing Tomorrow's Research Today

Published in the United States of America by
IGI Global
701 E. Chocolate Avenue
Hershey PA, USA 17033
Tel: 717-533-8845
Fax: 717-533-8661
E-mail: cust@igi-global.com
Web site: https://www.igi-global.com

Library of Congress Cataloging-in-Publication Data

CIP PENDING

ISBN13: 9781668466414
Isbn13Softcover: 9781668466421
EISBN13: 9781668466438

Vice President of Editorial: Melissa Wagner
Managing Editor of Acquisitions: Mikaela Felty
Managing Editor of Book Development: Jocelynn Hessler
Production Manager: Mike Brehm
Cover Design: Phillip Shickler

British Cataloguing in Publication Data
A Cataloguing in Publication record for this book is available from the British Library.

All work contributed to this book is new, previously-unpublished material.
The views expressed in this book are those of the authors, but not necessarily of the publisher.

Table of Contents

Detailed Table of Contents

In traditional e-commerce websites, consumers' evaluation of products will affect new customers' decisions on whether to buy the products. Some fraudulent merchants manipulate consumers' online comments for their interests, and multitudes of fake comments abuse consumers' rights and interests and the development of traditional e-commerce. The purpose of the present work is to detect and identify fake comments through user behavior classification. A series of innovative researches are carried out around the user behavior recognition task from four aspects: extraction and description of low-level behavior feature, spatial representation of high-level user behavior, design of behavior classification model, and user behavior detection in unsegmented text. A feature extraction model based on the super-complete independent component analysis algorithm and a behavior classification model via attention mechanism are proposed. Moreover, a feature source discriminator is designed, and adversarial learning is used to optimize discriminator loss and generator loss.

The financial risk management mechanism of enterprises can be more complete through exploration in the application effect of data mining technology combined with K-means clustering algorithm in enterprise risk audit. Hence, K-means clustering algorithm is introduced to study the paperless status of electronic payment in the trading process of e-commerce enterprises. Additionally, a risk audit model of e-commerce enterprises is implemented based on K-means algorithm combined with Random Forest Light Gradient Boosting Machine (RF-LightGBM). In this model, the actual operation process of data preparation, data preprocessing, model construction, model application and evaluation are the payment flow in the transaction process of e-commerce enterprises by using big data analysis technology. Eventually, the performance of the model is evaluated by simulation.

Jute geotextiles have shown a great potential for numerous applications including civil engineering, agriculture, construction, drainage and river bank protection. The samples of jute geotextiles were supplied by Bangladesh Jute Mills Corporation (BJMC). The samples were treated with bitumen, natural additive, chemicals (resin) and copper-sulphate in the Pilot Plant Processing Division of Bangladesh Jute Research Institute (BJRI). Physical and mechanical properties of jute geotextiles (JGT) were measured at the Testing Laboratory of BJRI. It was found that tensile strength of natural additive treated jute geotextiles increased up to 38% whereas the tensile strength of bitumen treated jute geotextiles may increase up to 14% depending on the treatment conditions. It was noted that tensile strength of the copper sulphate and resin treated jute geotextiles was found insignificant. The treated jute geotextiles were used in the river bank protection in five sites of Bangladesh with a view to control soil erosion.

Bangladesh is an Agro-based country. It is a great delta-comprises with hundreds of rivers, plane lands and hills. The length of its coast beside Bay of Bengal is about 1700 km. Due to its geographical location Bangladesh is always disaster prone. Flood, storm, drought, tidal search etc are the part of its existence. On the other hand the country has been ruled by the different outsider resume since long. Resulted, poverty and famine were, the long-lasting feature of the livelihoods of the people of this land. Therefore, the history of introduction of modern agriculture in Bangladesh is not too old. This history is very much related with famine and poverty. After series of famine the British Government took some steps for introducing agricultural services sector. They have established Dhaka farm and Laboratory Building in the early 1900. The Chief Minister of greater Bengal Sher-e-Bangla A K Fazlul Huq established Agriculture college in Dhaka in the year 1937 for equipping our earlier generation with modern agriculture education and research.

Bangladesh has a well-organized National Agricultural Research System under the umbrella of the apex body-Bangladesh Agricultural Research Council (BARC). There are twelve separate agricultural research institutes to conduct research on crops, livestock, fisheries and forestry. A large number of technologies have been developed by those research institutes, and some of them have already been transferred and adopted by the farmers. Ultimate results of those technologies are visible in the farmers' fields; and the production of crops, livestock, fisheries and forestry have been increased in many folds. In one hand, Bangladesh has a number of reputed agricultural research institutes; in the other hand, those organizations have some weaknesses like lack of advanced research facilities, shortage of qualified scientific manpower, inappropriate incentives for the working scientists, limited scope of short and long term foreign training for the scientists, and poor international funding for agricultural research.

Work-life balance is an important factor that not only stimulate the job-satisfaction of employees but also it has a positive impact on employees' productivity. During this covid-19 period, healthcare employees are struggling to maintain proper work-life balance. Therefore, this study aims to investigate the impact of COVID-19 pandemic on the work-life balance of healthcare employees. This study also aims to provide certain suggestions on how to maintain work-life balance of medical staff during this hard time. Data was collected through structured questionnaire from 50 employees who are working in various hospitals in Tripura & Hyderabad. To find out the impact of COVID-19 pandemic on work-life balance of healthcare employees, Chi-square distribution method is used. Also with the same method, this study analyzed is there any association between job satisfaction of healthcare employees and covid-19 crisis. The findings of this study indicate that this pandemic situation has a negative impact on the work-life balance of healthcare employees.

Preface

In the evolving landscape of the 21st century, two pivotal trends have come to shape the contours of talent management and human capital development. Firstly, the rise of artificial intelligence (AI) and automation is radically transforming industries, redefining job roles, and altering the skills required for future success. Secondly, there has been a fundamental shift in how organizations perceive talent as a key strategic asset, moving beyond traditional methods of recruitment and retention to embrace more innovative and inclusive approaches.

The digital revolution has accelerated the pace at which organizations operate, driving the need for agile and adaptive talent strategies. In this new paradigm, organizations are increasingly becoming boundaryless and more reliant on a global talent pool to remain competitive. This necessitates a deep understanding of diverse talent ecosystems and the ability to leverage them effectively. As businesses move away from location-dependent operations, the importance of fostering a culture of continuous learning and development becomes paramount. It is through such a culture that organizations can cultivate a resilient workforce capable of navigating the complexities of a dynamic economic environment.

Moreover, the integration of AI and advanced analytics in talent management processes offers unprecedented opportunities for enhancing decision-making capabilities. These technologies allow organizations to gain deeper insights into employee behaviors, preferences, and potential, thereby enabling more personalized and effective talent management strategies. However, the adoption of such technologies also brings challenges, including ethical considerations, data privacy issues, and the need for a robust framework to govern AI applications in talent management.

THE CHALLENGES

As we delve into the intricacies of managing talent in the age of AI, several challenges emerge:

1. Adapting to Technological Advances: The rapid evolution of AI and automation technologies requires organizations to continuously reskill and upskill their workforce. Developing adaptive learning frameworks and fostering a mindset of lifelong learning among employees are critical to staying ahead.
2. Redefining Talent Acquisition and Retention Strategies: In a globalized world, traditional talent acquisition strategies are no longer sufficient. Organizations must leverage technology to identify, attract, and retain diverse talent from across the globe. This includes understanding cultural nuances and creating inclusive work environments that appeal to a broad spectrum of talent.
3. Ensuring Ethical and Responsible AI Use: As AI becomes more embedded in talent management practices, ensuring its ethical use is crucial. Organizations must develop clear guidelines and policies to govern AI applications, ensuring transparency, fairness, and accountability.
4. Fostering a Culture of Innovation and Agility: In a rapidly changing world, innovation and agility are key to organizational success. Organizations must encourage experimentation and foster a culture where employees feel empowered to innovate and adapt to new challenges.

The following chapters explore these themes in greater detail, offering insights from leading experts and practitioners in the field. The chapters provide a comprehensive guide to navigating the complexities of talent management in the AI-driven era, covering topics such as innovative talent acquisition strategies, the role of AI in shaping future workforces, and the importance of fostering a culture of continuous learning and development.

ORGANIZATION OF THE BOOK

This book is organized into seventeen chapters, each delving into different facets of talent management and human capital in the context of the modern digital economy:

1. Attention Mechanism Model Combined with Adversarial Learning for E-commerce User Behavior Classification and Personality Recommendation
2. Application of Data Mining Combined with K-means Clustering Algorithm in Enterprises' Risk Audit
3. A New Technology of Jute Geotextiles Developed for River Bank Protection in Different Geographical Places of Bangladesh
4. Agribusiness Innovation-A Pathway to Development in Bangladesh
5. Strengths and Weaknesses of National Agricultural Research Systems in Enhancing Agribusiness of Bangladesh

6. A Study on the Impacts of Covid-19 on the Work-Life Balance of Healthcare Employees
7. Computer Intelligence-Based Analysis of Post-Pandemic Future E-Commerce Business
8. Entrepreneurs Solve Economic Problems in Pandemic
9. The Evolution of the Cosmos and Time
10. Factors Influencing Glass Ceiling: Focus on Women Administration in Higher Education in Malaysia
11. Generative Innovation: Leveraging the Power of Large Language Models for Brainstorming
12. A Revolutionary Framework for Transforming National Innovation
13. Quantum Bridge Analytics II: QUBO-Plus Network Optimization and Combinatorial Chaining for Asset Exchange
14. Resonance and The Cosmos
15. Social and Economic Impacts of the Various Elements that Contribute to Women Glass Ceiling in Higher Education and Administration in Malaysia
16. The Barriers to the Career Progression of Women Employees in Malaysian University

This book aims to provide a comprehensive framework for understanding and navigating the challenges of talent management in the digital era. We hope it serves as a valuable resource for academics, practitioners, and policymakers alike.

Sharif Uddin Ahmed Rana
Paris Graduate School, France & World Talent Economy Forum, Malaysia

Adrian David Cheok
Imagineering Institute, Malaysia

Chapter 1
Attention Mechanism Model Combined With Adversarial Learning for E-Commerce User Behavior Classification and Personality Recommendation

Sharif Uddin Ahmed Rana
https://orcid.org/0000-0003-2296-6044
Paris Graduate School, France

ABSTRACT

In traditional e-commerce websites, consumers' evaluation of products will affect new customers' decisions on whether to buy the products. Some fraudulent merchants manipulate consumers' online comments for their interests, and multitudes of fake comments abuse consumers' rights and interests and the development of traditional e-commerce. The purpose of the present work is to detect and identify fake comments through user behavior classification. A series of innovative researches are carried out around the user behavior recognition task from four aspects: extraction and description of low-level behavior feature, spatial representation of high-level user behavior, design of behavior classification model, and user behavior detection in unsegmented text. A feature extraction model based on the super-complete independent component analysis algorithm and a behavior classification model via attention mechanism are proposed. Moreover, a feature source discriminator is designed,

DOI: 10.4018/978-1-6684-6641-4.ch001

and adversarial learning is used to optimize discriminator loss and generator loss.

1. INTRODUCTION

With the deepening of global informatization, the rapid popularization of computer and Internet technology has created favorable conditions for the development of e-commerce. Meanwhile, the huge demand for e-commerce has promoted the growth of related industries in the field of the Internet, (Kwilinski *et al.*, 2020) (Sadeeq *et al.*, 2020) (Leonard & Jones, 2021). In the scenario of e-commerce on the Internet, because the construction of electronic websites does not need realistic sites and equipment, the cost of store expansion is relatively low. Consequently, the number of e-commerce stores began to show an exponential growth trend. With the explosive increase in the number of users, each business platform has formulated the corresponding user classification and product personalized recommendation mechanism. Besides, to optimize the user experience, each platform has formulated the corresponding user online comment and feedback mechanism. The rapidly increasing user feedback comments imply consumer's consumption intention, which has enormous commercial application value.

However, with a proliferation of e-commerce stores, some businesses take unfair measures to expand their competitiveness and product sales. On the one hand, some unscrupulous merchants hire online supporters to publish fake praise for their products and stimulate the purchase desire of potential users through fake comments, (Lawton, 2018) (Sujan, 2018) (Kuroda, 2021). On the other hand, to suppress their competitors, some businesses deliberately hire professional writers to fabricate negative reviews for their competitors and reduce users' desire to buy. All kinds of fake comments can be found on e-commerce platforms. Ordinary users have a low level of recognition of fake comments, (Chang *et al.*, 2019), which brings immense difficulties to user identification and is not conducive to the sound and stable development of e-commerce platforms.

The development of the Internet of Things (Nauman *et al.,* 2020) and adversarial learning algorithm (Qi *et al.*, 2021) provide a new solution to this problem. Based on the attention mechanism, (Yu *et al.,* 2020), the semi-supervised learning method combined with the machine learning model supplements the comment corpus. In view of the text information related to comments, a depth study is conducted here from four aspects, namely the user behavior recognition task from four aspects: extraction and description of low-level behavior feature, spatial representation of high-level user behavior, design of behavior classification model, and user behavior detection in unsegmented text. In addition, independent component analysis (ICA) is utilized to build a feature extraction model, and the attention mechanism is adopted to construct a behavior classification model. These models can carry out natural language processing and recognition for repeated and unrelated texts and perform supervised learning of fake comment corpus via the behavior detection algorithm. The present work has practical application value for the classification of e-commerce users' behavior and the purification and development of the e-commerce website environment.

2. RELATED WORKS

2.1 Recent Studies on the Attention Mechanism Model

Many scholars have conducted studies on the attention mechanism model. Wang *et al.* (2018) studied the credit scoring mechanism of Internet lending by using the attention mechanism and Long Short-Term Memory (LSTM) algorithm. They proposed a consumer credit scoring method based on attention mechanism by using the online operation behavior data of borrowers. They also tested their scheme and found that the proposed consumer credit scoring method based on attention mechanism and LSTM had an obvious improvement effect compared with the traditional artificial feature extraction method. Zhu *et al.* (2019) explored depth sensors with attention mechanism and convolution neural network (CNN) model and analyzed action recognition based on the skeleton as a case. They adopted the attentional mechanism for depth sensors to extract the most relevant features. These sensors could collect human bone data, providing a wealth of information for motion recognition. The authors extracted the most relevant features to analyze deep learning, and the final results verified the effectiveness of the method. Fang *et al.* (2019) used the improved model with a multi-level vector and attention mechanism to detect and study phishing emails. They confirmed that the overall accuracy of the proposed model reached 99. 848%; meanwhile, the false positive rate was 0. 043%. The high accuracy and low error rate ensured that the filter could identify phishing emails with high probability and filter out legitimate emails as little as possible, which verified the effectiveness of the model in detecting phishing emails. Chauhan *et al.* (2020) studied the two-step hybrid unsupervised model of attention mechanism used for aspect extraction. They used rules-based methods to extract the single-word and multi-word aspects and used these aspects as label data to train the attention-based deep learning (DL) model for aspect-term extraction, reducing the cost of manual annotation of text. Finally, they verified the effectiveness and reliability of the proposed method through the experimental evaluation.

Meanwhile, the research on the attention mechanism model has been extended to many fields such as public transportation in recent years. For example, Zhou *et al.* (2020) built a prediction model based on the spatio-temporal attention mechanism for the city's passenger boarding and boarding demand. They finally proved that the spatio-temporal attention model was superior to the traditional method in terms of prediction performance. Li *et al.* (2020) adopted the attention mechanism to construct a click through rate prediction model based on user interest, to study the characteristics of the automatic encoder based on stack height nonlinear interaction. Their experimental results showed that the proposed model achieved higher performance than the most advanced models available. Gao and Ruan (2021) carried out DL modeling of building energy consumption prediction based on attention mechanism. They proposed three interpretable decoders and self-attention models by using the attention mechanism based on hidden layer state and feature-based attention mechanism. They reported that visualization of model attention weight strengthened the interpretability of the model at the hidden state and feature levels. Kang *et al.* (2021) obtained high-resolution root images through scanners and introduced an attention mechanism to refine the segmentation of root edges. The authors employed the Deeplabv3+ model for end-to-end pixel segmentation of cotton root images. Through simulation, they found that the precision value, recall value, and F1-score of the proposed model were 0. 9971, 0. 9984 and 0. 9937, respectively, which could accurately segment different growth states in the cotton growth cycle. Ren *et al.* (2021) introduced the explicable mixed attention mechanism into the concrete dam displacement technology for the applied research on the new DL prediction model. Specifically, they put forward an interpretable mixed attention mechanism model based on encoder-decoder architecture. The comparison results showed that the model was superior to other models in most cases. To sum up, introducing the temporal attention mechanism model into the decoder stage can correctly extract critical periods by identifying the relevant hidden states of all time steps, which has practical reference value for quantification and visualization of temporal attention weight.

2.2 Research Progress of Adversarial Learning and E-Commerce

Many scholars have discussed adversarial learning and e-commerce. For example, Hershcovis *et al.* (2018) explored the influencing factors of uncivilized behaviors in the workplace by means of confrontation and avoidance. They found that confrontation and avoidance were ineffective in preventing the recurrence of uncivilized behaviors, and avoidance also led to increased emotional exhaustion. Brighi *et al.* (2019) investigated the impact of direct confrontation and toughness on the happiness promotion of adolescents. They conducted a questionnaire survey of youth online victimization and built a structural equation model. The survey results indicated that the network victims and confrontational tactics on mood symptoms were mediated by the elasticity, the influence of network victims showed a positive role, and direct confrontation showed negative effects. Ashburn-Nardo *et al.* (2020) predicted whether people would face other people's discriminatory behaviors through the applied research on fighting prejudice and perception. They assessed whether perceived responsibility for bias for people in supervisory roles at work increased as the number of employees they supervised increased. The results suggested that confronting prejudice and learning were key factors in predicting whether bystanders face discrimination. Case *et al.* (2020) studied the cross-mode of fighting prejudice and they concluded that gender socialization and the stereotype that equated femininity with male homosexuality might reduce the alliance behavior between men and increase the resistance against anti-gay prejudice between women. Zaragas (2021) discussed psychodrama and its contribution to children's competition, made an in-depth study of the phenomenon in the psychodrama circle, and then highlighted the results of applying psychodrama technology to young athletes participating in competitions. The findings suggested that psychodrama could be an innovative alternative to schooling.

Different from the study of adversarial learning, e-commerce has always been the focus of scholars' study and attention. Bhattacharyya (2020) explored the factors influencing the purchase and recommendation of goods on e-commerce websites and found that Facebook-driven social commerce benefited from a large number of likes. At the same time, suggestions on Facebook influenced customers' purchases and recommendations on linked e-commerce sites. Vasić *et al.* (2021) studied the satisfaction function of logistics service users in e-commerce and developed a methodology and an original measurement tool with eight dimensions to explore different dimensions of logistics service. The results demonstrated that the proposed measurement function could improve customer satisfaction of e-commerce. In the context of the computer digital marketing era, Wang *et al.* (2021) studied the immersive interactive experience of users of content e-commerce live broadcasting. They explored the characteristics of a panoramic video transmission scheme based on a simple mail transmission protocol that solved the synchronization problem of heterogeneous networks. Liu, Xu, and Yang (2021) proposed a prudent iterative naive Bayes algorithm by analyzing and studying diseases in pharmaceutical e-commerce. Experimental test results showed that the accuracy of the algorithm reached 98. 64% on six diseases and the recall rate reached 90. 90%, which was better than most benchmark algorithms.

3. MIXED ATTENTION MECHANISM MODEL BASED ON CNN AND LSTM

3.1 Analysis of Practical Functions of the Attention Mechanism and Adversarial Learning Algorithm

In the development of e-commerce, attention mechanism and adversarial learning algorithm are the core elements, and their performance is directly related to the application of network and information components. In the human visual system, there are two different attention mechanisms: top-down and bottom-up. In terms of the way of applying attention, (Fang *et al.*, 2019), the spatial attention model can complete the preprocessing of adaptive tasks by learning the deformation of input but fails to take into account the changes in the number of semantic matches between images and sentence descriptions. Therefore, the present work adopts the spatial-temporal stacked cross-attention mechanism and takes multitudes of network devices as the nodes of information exchange through the combination of wired and wireless networks. If network devices such as switches, gateways, and firewalls are attacked, their information and connected devices will be adversely affected. In addition, the operating system primarily uses Windows, VxWorks, and other commercial systems that can timely repair and protect the vulnerability of the e-commerce system. If the system is rarely upgraded or patched, the system may age and have vulnerabilities that cannot be remedied in time, posing great information security risks. Figure 1 displays the framework diagram of user behavior classification and comments discrimination system of e-commerce platforms based on attention mechanism and adversarial learning algorithm.

Figure 1. Framework of the user behavior classification and comment discrimination system of e-commerce platforms

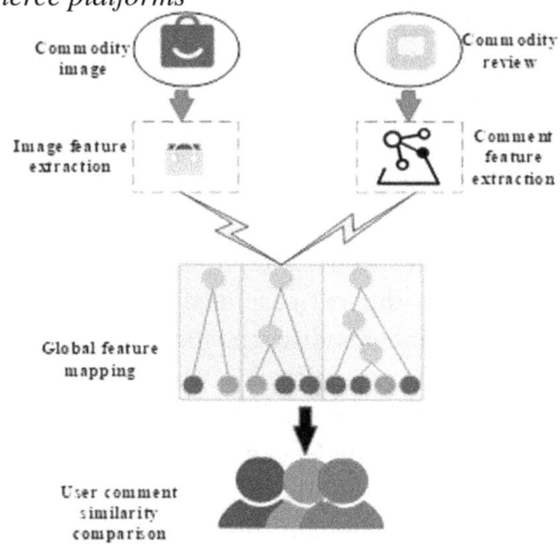

Based on the above analysis of the e-commerce system, as a complex network, the system has security risks in network equipment, operating system, communication protocol, access equipment, and other aspects. Therefore, it is extremely important to use the attention mechanism and adversarial learning algorithm to detect and classify user behaviors.

3.2 Spatial-Temporal Mixed Attention Mechanism Model Based on Super-Complete ICA Algorithm

In the spatio-temporal mixed attention model (Li *et al.*, 2020) based on the adversarial learning algorithm, the generative adversarial network (GAN) needs to be constructed and optimized. GAN composed of the generator G and discriminator D adopts the same calculation method as the gates in the LSTM network. The updating gate information z_t and the resetting gate information $\hbar_t$ are calculated according to:

$$z_t = \sigma\left(W_z \cdot [h_{t-1}, x_t]\right) \tag{1}$$

$$\hbar_t = \tanh\left(W \cdot [r_t * h_{t-1}, x_t]\right) \tag{2}$$

where r_t represents the hidden layer information calculated by multiple gates, and h_{t-1} refers to the amount of information forgotten by the hidden layer at the previous moment. Meanwhile, x_t signifies the demand for hidden layer information $\hbar_t$ at the current moment, and $\sigma()$ denotes the memory hiding function of the network updating gate. The text discrimination model reported here discriminates the comment content through target iteration, to carry out the antagonistic learning and game between text feature recognition generation and feature source discrimination. The objective function of the comment recognition model can be expressed as Equation (3).

$$\max_{D} E_{x \sim Pr}\left[\log D(x)\right] + E_{x \sim Pg}\left[\log\left(1 - D(x)\right)\right] \tag{3}$$

In Equation (3), Pr and Pg respectively represent the distribution of the real text content and the distribution of the text generated by the generator. In the model, the input z of generator G is random noise, and the generator converts this random input into data type and outputs examples.

For text block description, first, each word in the text is represented by an independent coding vector. Then, each independent coding vector is multiplied by an embedding matrix for vector dimension adjustment, and the word embedding vector of the word is adjusted through the bidirectional network. The word embedding vector is averaged from the forward and reverse outputs of each stage, as presented in Equations (4) ~ (6):

$$\overrightarrow{h_i} = \overrightarrow{GRU}(x_i), i \in \left[1, n\right] \tag{4}$$

$$\overleftarrow{h_i} = \overleftarrow{GRU}(x_i), i \in \left[1, n\right] \tag{5}$$

$$e_i = \frac{\overrightarrow{h_i} + \overleftarrow{h_i}}{2}, i \in \left[1, n\right] \tag{6}$$

where $\overrightarrow{GRU}(x_i)$ represents the forward input of each layer of the network, and $\overrightarrow{h_i}$ denotes the forward output of this layer of the network. Besides, $\overleftarrow{GRU}(x_i)$ signifies the reverse input of each layer of the network, $\overleftarrow{h_i}$ refers to the reverse output of this layer of the network, and e_i stands for the unit word embedding vector obtained after averaging.

In the text feature similarity measurement module, after obtaining the predicted global feature V'' of the image through text prediction, its dimension is compared with the global feature V' of the original image. Moreover, the mean square error of the two is used as the loss function of the two, as shown in Equation (7).

$$l_{mse} = (V'' - V')^2 \tag{7}$$

Since the mean square error function treats all data sets equally in training, it cannot solve the problem that the retrieval accuracy of difficult negative samples decreases. Therefore, triplet loss maximization is adopted to calculate the backpropagation gradient based on the most difficult negative samples. By emphasizing the negative sample optimization problem in the loss function, the loss function $l_{MH}(i,c)$ of the matching text (i,c) is defined as:

$$l_{MH}(i,c) = \max_{c'}[\alpha - S(i,c') + S(i,c)] + \max_{i'}(\alpha - S(i',c) + S(i,c)] \quad (8)$$

where c' and i' represent the two sets of the most difficult negative samples, α refers to the batch size of the training set, and $S(i,c)$ denotes the cosine similarity function adopted by coarse-grained hierarchical similarity measurement. Figure 2 reveals the flow of the super-complete ICA algorithm.

Figure 2. Flow of the super-complete ICA algorithm

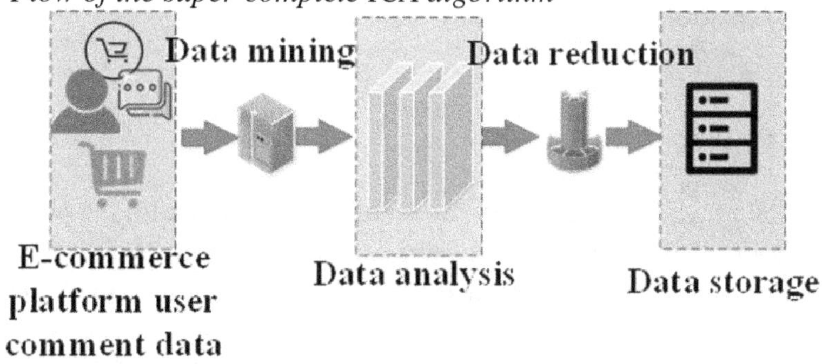

The original attention mechanism is improved as an image-text stacked cross-attention mechanism by combining images and text. Moreover, the aforementioned fine-grained hierarchical feature recognition model of images and statements is used to calculate the image-text similarity between each region in the image and each word in the sentence synthetically. Then, the attention mechanism is used for more accurate recognition and alignment. For the construction of the stacked cross-attention mechanism model, the similarity between image fine-grained hierarchical features V and between text fine-grained hierarchical features E is measured and calculated respectively. Firstly, each local region after image segmentation is used to add the attention mechanism to the experimental text. Denote S_{ij} as the judgment of word similarity between the i-th text region and the j-th text region, which is determined by Equation (9).

$$S_{ij} = \frac{v_i^T e_j}{||v_i|| \, ||e_j||}, i \in \left[i,k\right], j \in \left[1,n\right] \tag{9}$$

In Equation (9), v_i^T represents the vector representation of text description under the image region, e_j denotes the weighted comprehensive value of text represented by the embedded vector. The weighted vector representation can be written as Equation (10).

$$a_i^t = \sum_{j=1}^{n} \alpha_{ij} e_j \tag{10}$$

In Equation (10), $\alpha_{ij} = \frac{\exp(\lambda_1 \overline{s}_{ij})}{\sum_{i=1}^{n} \exp(\lambda_1 \overline{s}_{ij})}$ represents the word vector after text partition, λ_1 denotes the hyperparameter, and $\overline{s}_{ij}$ refers to the result after regularization.

The text description vector defined under the region v_i in the i-th image is calculated by the cosine similarity function of which the vector representation is a_i^t, as shown in Equation (11).

$$\mathrm{R}(v_i, a_i^t) = \frac{v_i^T a_i^t}{||v_i|| \, ||a_i^t||} \tag{11}$$

Finally, the image-text similarity model after average pooling is obtained by integrating the similarity functions between vector representations under each image region and the corresponding attention mechanism, which are calculated according to:

$$S_{LSE}\left(I, T\right) = \log\left(\sum_{i=1}^{k} \exp(\lambda_2 R(v_i, a_i^t))\right)^{(1/\lambda_2)} \tag{12}$$

$$S_{AVG}\left(I, T\right) = \frac{\sum_{i=1}^{k} R(v_i, a_i^t)}{k} \tag{13}$$

where λ_2 is the hyperparameter, $S_{LSE}(I, T)$ represents the image-text similarity error of adding attention to the image in the way of text starting, and $S_{AVG}(I, T)$ denotes the average image-text similarity of adding attention to the image in the way of text starting.

3.3 Model Construction of the Mixed Attention Mechanism Based on CNN and LSTM

To re-add attention mechanism to each word in the text, it is necessary to build a mixed attention mechanism model based on CNN and LSTM algorithm and carry out weighted synthesis by adding image vector features of word attention mechanism. The specific calculation methods are as follows:

$$a_j^v = \sum_{i=1}^{k} \alpha'_{ij} v_i \tag{14}$$

$$\alpha'_{ij} = \frac{\exp(\lambda_1 \bar{s}_{ij})}{\sum_{i=1}^{k} \exp(\lambda_1 \bar{s}_{ij})} \tag{15}$$

where a_j^v represents the weighted value of word text in comments, and α'_{ij} refers to the weighted value of similarity between text statement and image. For each word vector in image matching, the similarity between the vector e_j of the j-th word embedding vector and function value of the image T is also defined as cosine, as shown in Equation (16).

$$\mathrm{R}'(e_j, a_j^v) = \frac{e_j^T a_j^v}{\|e_j\| \|a_j^v\|} \tag{16}$$

The overall similarity between images and texts is calculated according to:

$$S'_{LSE}\left(I, T\right) = \log\left(\sum_{j=1}^{n} \exp(\lambda_2 R'(e_j, a_j^v))\right)^{(1/\lambda_2)} \tag{17}$$

$$S'_{AVG}\left(I, T\right) = \frac{\sum_{j=1}^{n} Rr(e_j, a_j^v)}{n} \tag{18}$$

where λ_2 denotes the hyperparameter, $S'_{LSE}(I, T)$ represents the similarity error between images and texts, and $S_{AVG}(I, T)$ refers to the average similarity between images and texts. The form of emphasizing the most difficult negative sample is adopted for the judgment of similarity of fine-grained level. For matched image-text (I, T), the most difficult negative sample is determined by:

$$\hat{I}_h = \mathrm{argmax}_{m \neq I} S(m, T) \tag{19}$$

$$\hat{T}_h = \mathrm{argmax}_{d \neq T} S(I, d) \tag{20}$$

where $\hat{I}_h$ represents the most difficult negative sample of commodity image data, and $\hat{T}_h$ refers to the most difficult negative sample of comment text data. The loss function $l_{\text{hard}}(I, T)$ of the overall stacked cross-attention mechanism model is defined as follows:

$$l_{\text{hard}}(I,T) = \left[\alpha - S(I,T) + S(I,\hat{T}_h)\right] + \left[\alpha - S(I,T) + S(\hat{I}_h,\mathrm{T})\right] \tag{21}$$

$$l_{\text{adv}}(\theta_D) = -\frac{1}{n}\sum_{i=1}^{n}\left(m_i \cdot \left(\log D(v_i;\theta_D) + \log\left(1 - D(t_i;\theta_D)\right)\right)\right) \tag{22}$$

where $l_{\text{adv}}(\theta_D)$ denotes the cross-entropy loss of modal classification used in each training iteration; meanwhile, m_i stands for the real modal label of each comment instance, which is represented in the form of independent coding vector. Besides, $D(t_i;\theta_D)$ represents the probability that the discriminator of each instance outputs the similar feature. Figure 3 illustrates the framework of the mixed attention mechanism model based on CNN and LSTM.

Figure 3. Framework of the mixed attention mechanism model based on CNN and LSTM

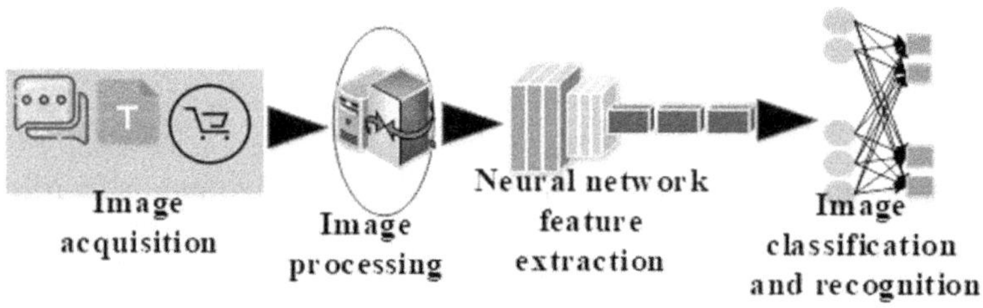

For the overall image feature recognition and prediction network, the loss function optimization process of its generator is shown in Equations (23) and (24).

$$\left(\hat{\theta}_v, \hat{\theta}_t, \hat{\theta}_{imd}\right) = \operatorname{argmin}_{\theta_v,\theta_t,\theta_{imd}}\left(L_{emb}(\theta_v,\theta_t,\theta_{imd}) - L_{adv}(\hat{\theta}_D)\right) \tag{23}$$

$$\hat{\theta}_D = \operatorname{argmax}_{\theta_D}\left(L_{emb}(\hat{\theta}_v,\hat{\theta}_t,\hat{\theta}_{imd}) - L_{adv}(\theta_D)\right) \tag{24}$$

In Equations (23) and (24), $\hat{\theta}$ represents the sample characteristics of text comments, $\hat{\theta}_t$ refers to the minimum sample parameter of text comments, $\hat{\theta}_{imd}$ signifies the maximum sample parameter of text comments, and $\hat{\theta}_D$ denotes the maximum loss function.

The annotated text corpus is limited, and the performance of trained classifier models varies greatly in the initial stage. Therefore, the data accuracy of each initial data set is evaluated by referring to the annotation results of the classifier, as shown in Equation (25).

$$C\left(x\right) = \operatorname{arg}max\frac{\sum_{i=1}^{3}E(y,C_i(x))\times P_i(x)}{\sum_{i=1}^{3}P_i(x)},y \in \text{ Labe} \tag{25}$$

In Equation (25), $C(x)$ refers to the final label of the corpus$x$, $P_i(x)$ represents the accuracy of the classification model in the initial corpus, and y signifies the label of the corpus. Besides, $E(y, C_i(x))$ represents the text classification according to different labels, and the classification method is shown in Equation (26).

$$E(y,C_i(x)) = \begin{cases} 1, C_i(x) = y \\ 0, C_i(x) \neq y \end{cases} \tag{26}$$

For the global text vector, dimension reduction decomposition is carried out through the global word contribution matrix. Then, the final word vector's target loss function$J$ can be presented as:

$$J = \sum_{i,j=1}^{V} f(X_{ij}) \left(w_i^T \widetilde{w}_j + b_i + \widetilde{b}_j - \log X_{ij}\right)^2 \tag{27}$$

where X_{ij} refers to the word contribution matrix, indicating the frequency of occurrence of the word in the statement, b_i denotes the bias term, and $f(x)$ represents the set weight function, which can be described as Equation (28).

$$f\left(x\right) = \begin{cases} (x/x_{max})^{\alpha} \text{ if } x < x_{max} \\ 1 \text{ otherwise} \end{cases} \tag{28}$$

The model is optimized by finding the minimum of the objective loss function to obtain the final word vector. The feedforward attention model after semantic coding can be expressed as:

$$e_t = a(h_t) \tag{29}$$

$$\alpha_t = \frac{\exp(e_t)}{\sum_{k=1}^{T}\exp(e_k)} \tag{30}$$

$$C = \sum_{t=1}^{T} \alpha_t h_t \tag{31}$$

where h_t represents the output result of the encoder, $a(h_t)$ refers to the function with learning ability, α_t stands for the probability of attention distribution, and C represents the semantic encoding format after the probability calculation of attention distribution. In the working process of the feedforward attention mechanism, the input into the hidden layer is sent to $a(h_t)$ function to calculate the probability distribution vector a of attention. Then, the probability distribution vector is multiply accumulated with the hidden layer output of history nodes to get the final semantic coding. Figure 4 illustrates the process of electronic commerce data compression and processing based on product image and the comment text.

Figure 4. Compression and processing process of commodity image and user comment data in the e-commerce system

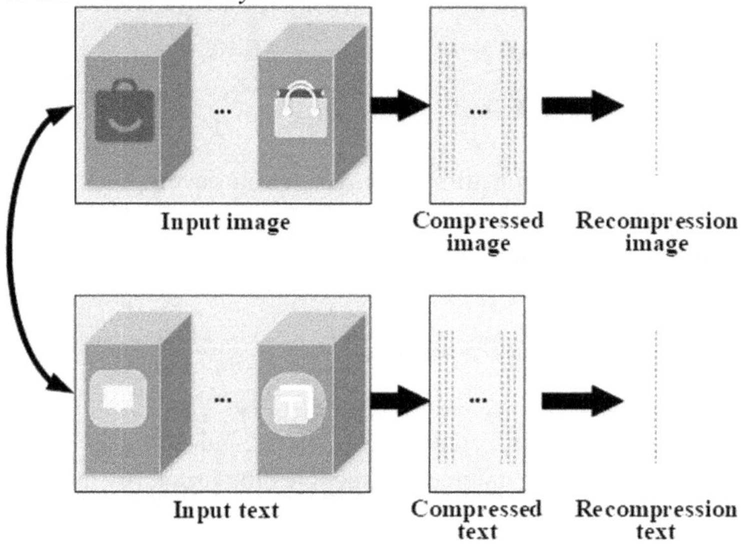

3.4 Case Analysis

To verify the performance of the mixed attention mechanism model based on CNN and LSTM constructed here, the application scenarios of an online e-commerce platform are selected for case analysis. MATLAB is adopted to analyze the user comment data. The user comment data of each commodity on the platform are collected, and the collected data in the data set is divided into a training data set and a test data set by a ratio of 7:3. The proportion of each type of data in the two data sets is consistent. The effects of attentional mechanism and adversarial learning on the text retrieval model are tested and visualized by using mainstream cross-media retrieval data sets Microsoft Common Objects in Context (mS-COCO) and Flickr30K. This test can help the mixed attention mechanism model based on CNN and LSTM achieve the expected prediction results. Besides, the performance of the model reported here is compared with that of traditional algorithms in terms of accuracy, precision, recall, and F1 value. The Alex Network (AlexNet), (Lu, Lu, & Zhang, 2019), Dense Network (DenseNet), (Zhang *et al.,* 2019), Interleaved Group Network (IGCNet), (Zhang *et al.,* 2021), Visual Geometry Group Network (VGG-Net), (Wang *et al.,* 2021), and Residual Network (ResNet) (Hammad *et al.,* 2021) are selected for the comparative analysis. Meanwhile, the training time and test time of these models in mS-COCO and Flickr30K datasets are evaluated respectively.

4. RESULTS AND DISCUSSION

4.1 Comparison of Experimental Performance of Different Models Under the MS-COCO Dataset

With the MS-COCO data set, the performance of the mixed attention mechanism model based on CNN and LSTM is compared with that of the traditional AlexNet, DenseNet, IGCNet, VGGNet, and ResNet models. The accuracy, precision, recall, and F1 value of these models are shown in Figure 5 to Figure 8. Meanwhile, the algorithm training time and testing time under this data set of these models are compared, and the results are shown in Figure 9 and Figure 10.

Figure 5. Comparison of accuracy results of different models

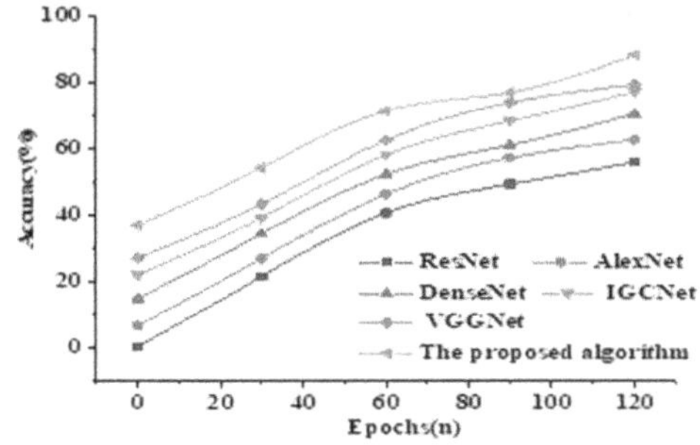

From the comparison of accuracy results of different algorithm models in Figure 5, compared with other models, the model proposed here has the highest accuracy in the test data set. When the number of model iterations is 90, the accuracy of the mixed attention mechanism model based on CNN and LSTM can reach 80%. Subsequently, with the increase in the number of model iterations, the accuracy of each algorithm increases slowly. However, the accuracy performance of other models is not better than that of the mixed attention mechanism reported here, indicating that this model has the highest accuracy performance.

Figure 6. Comparison of precision results of different models

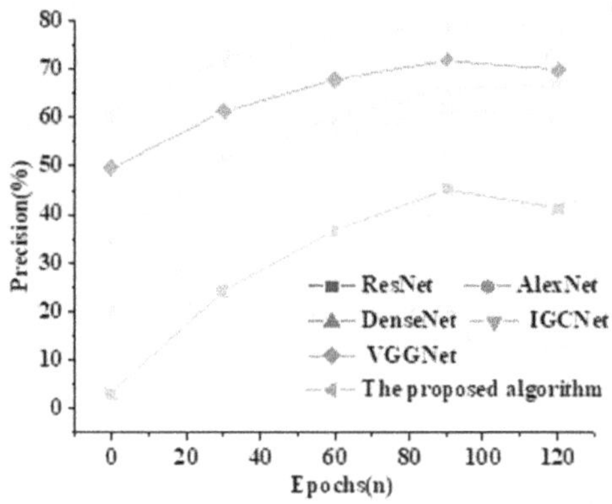

In Figure 6, with the growth of the model number of iterations, the classification precision of each model improves slowly. Among them, the mixed attention mechanism model based on CNN and LSTM always m the optimal precision. After 60 iterations, the classification precision of this attains 75%, which is at least 7. 8% higher than other traditional models. Besides, the classification precision of this model reaches 80% after 120 iterations, which significantly improves the classification accuracy of e-commerce user behavior.

Figure 7. Comparison of recall results of different models

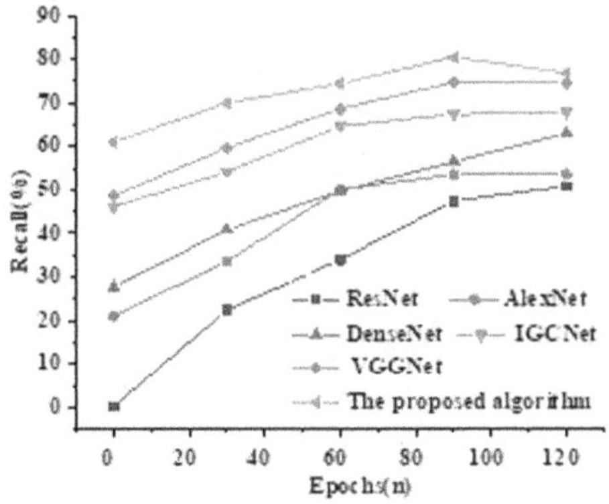

According to the results of recall of different models in Figure 7, the recall of the mixed attention mechanism model based on CNN and LSTM always remains above 60% during the experiment. Compared with other models, although the recall of the VGGNet model is close to that of this model after 120 iterations, there is at least a 6. 8% difference in recall between the two in 30 iterations. This indicates that the model reported here can maintain the optimal recall performance.

Figure 8. Comparison of F1 values of different models

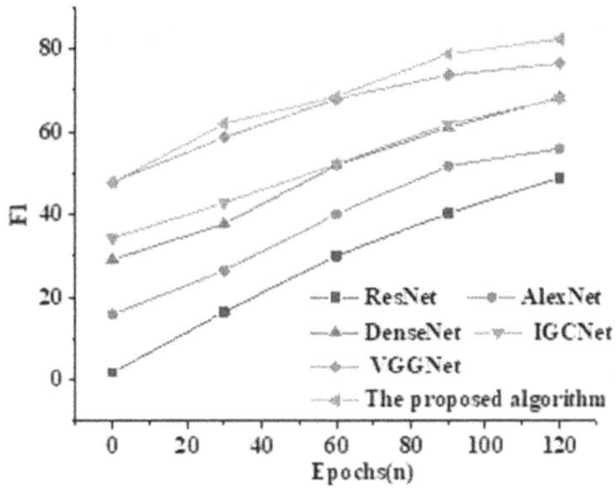

According to the comparison of F1 value results of different models in Figure 8, among the six models, the F1 value curve of the ResNet model always stays at the bottom. Besides, the F1 value performance of the DenseNet model and IGCNet model are relatively close throughout the experiment. In the first 60 iterations of the model, the performance of the VGGNet model is not significantly different from that of the model proposed here in the F1 value. However, with the increase of the number of model iterations, the F1 value of the mixed attention mechanism model becomes increasingly prominent. After 120 iterations, the F1 performance of the model proposed here reach more than 80%, which is at least 3.2% higher than that of other models.

Figure 9. Comparison of the training time of different models

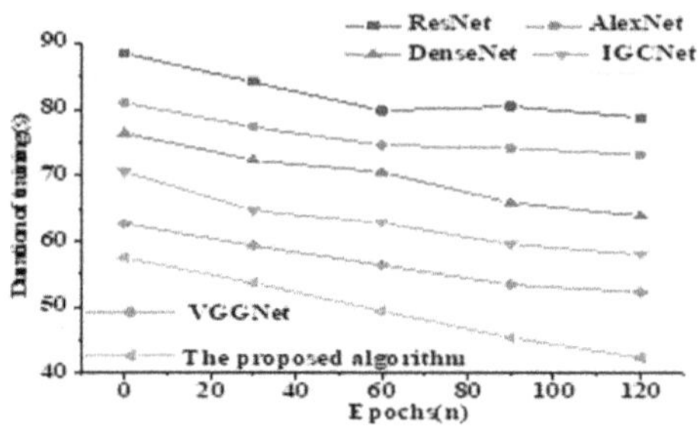

From Figure 9, except for the mixed attention mechanism model, the other comparative models need a long time for training. As the iteration continues, although the training time of each model is shortened, the model proposed here takes the shortest time. At the beginning of the experiment, this model takes about 60 seconds for training. After 120 iterations, the training time is reduced to about 42 seconds, which can save 18 seconds of training time compared with the beginning of the experiment, greatly improving the training efficiency of the model.

Figure 10. Comparison of the testing time of different models

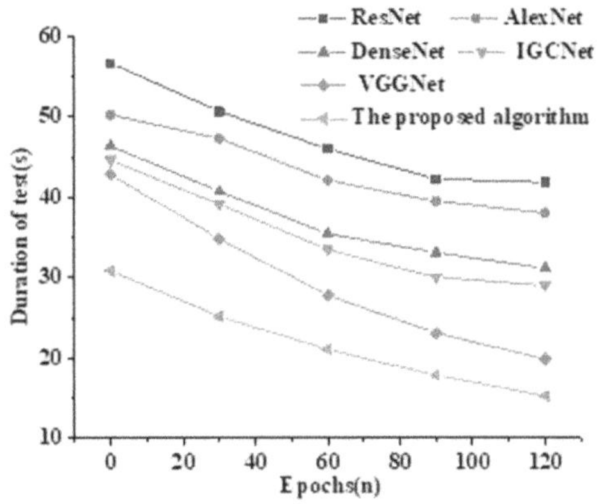

According to Figure 10, the traditional models all take a long testing time. With the increase in the number of iterations, the testing time can be shortened, but the testing time of the model proposed here is the shortest. At the beginning of the experiment, the mixed attention mechanism model requires more than 30 seconds for testing. As the number of model iterations increases, the testing time of this model can be reduced to about 16 seconds after 120 iterations, which decreases by 14 seconds compared with the testing time at the beginning of the experiment. Therefore, the mixed attention mechanism model can achieve outstanding performance in test efficiency.

4.2 Comparison of Experimental Performance of Different Models Under the Flickr30k Data Set

The accuracy, precision, recall, and F1 value of the mixed attention mechanism model based on CNN and LSTM under the Flickr30K data set are compared with the traditional AlexNet, DenseNet, IGCNet, VGGNet, and ResNet models, as shown in Figure 11 to Figure 14. Meanwhile, the algorithm training time and testing time under this data set of these models are compared, and the results are shown in Figure 15 and Figure 16.

Figure 11. Comparison of accuracy results of different models

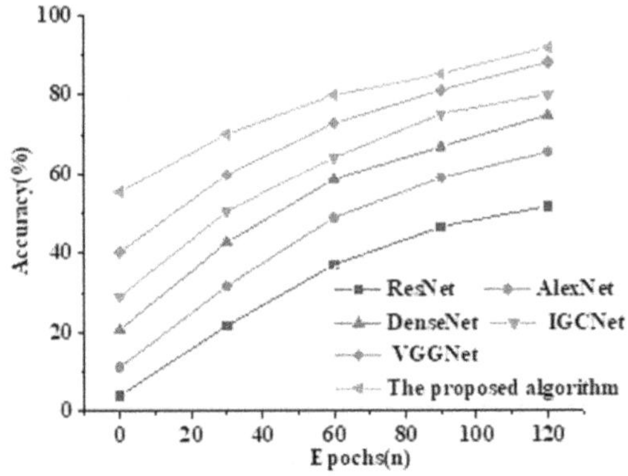

From the comparison of accuracy results of different models in Figure 11, compared with other models, the mixed attention mechanism model based on CNN and LSTM has the highest accuracy on the Flickr30K test data set. After 60iterations, the accuracy of the mixed attention mechanism model can reach 80%. Subsequently, with the increase in the number of iterations, the accuracy of each model increases slowly, but the accuracy performance of other traditional models is still poor than that of the mixed attention mechanism model, indicating that this model has the highest accuracy performance.

Figure 12. Comparison of accuracy results of different models

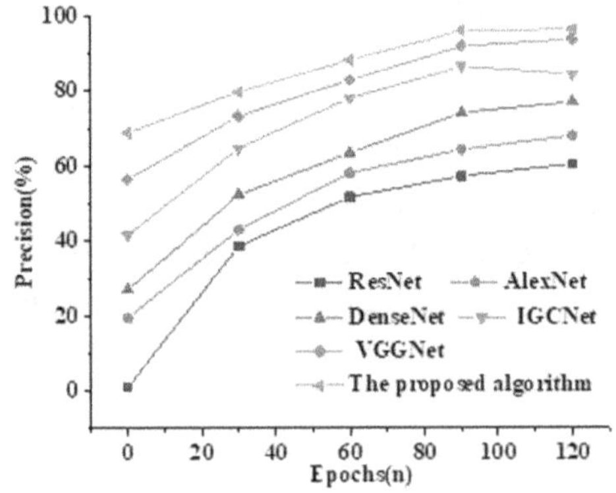

From the comparison of accuracy results of different models in Figure 12, the precision of the mixed attention mechanism model based on CNN and LSTM always maintains above 70%. Compared with other algorithms, this model has significant advantages in precision performance.

Figure 13. Comparison of recall results of different models

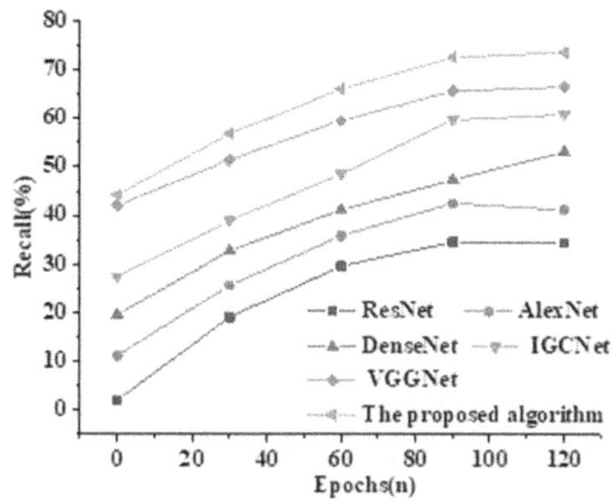

Through the comparison of recall of different models in Figure 13, the recall of the mixed attention mechanism model based on CNN and LSTM always remains above 45% during the experiment. Compared with other models, although the recall of the VGGNet algorithm is close to this model at the beginning of the model iteration, there is a difference of at least 7. 2% between the recall rates of the two at 120 iterations. This demonstrates that the model reported here can maintain the optimal recall.

Figure 14. Comparison of F1 values of different models

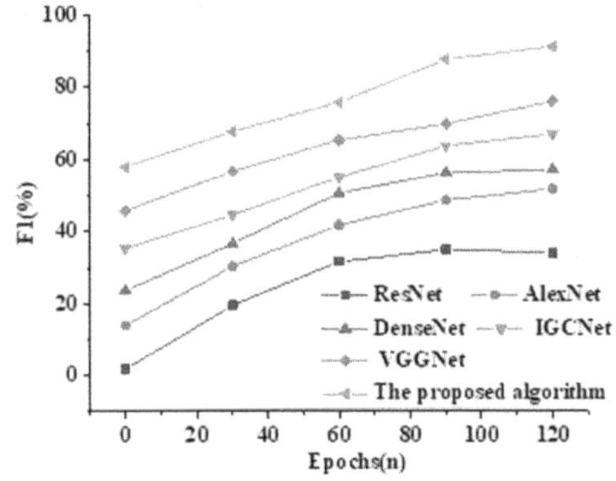

According to the comparison of F1 value results of different models in Figure 14, among the six algorithm models, the F1 value curve of the ResNet model always stays at the bottom. On the contrary, the F1 value performance of the DenseNet model and IGCNet model is relatively close throughout the experiment. With the increase in iterations, the F1 value advantage of the mixed attention mechanism model based on CNN and LSTM becomes increasingly prominent. After 90 iterations, the F1 value of this model can reach more than 90%, which is at least 9. 6% higher than that of other models.

Figure 15. Comparison of the training time of different models

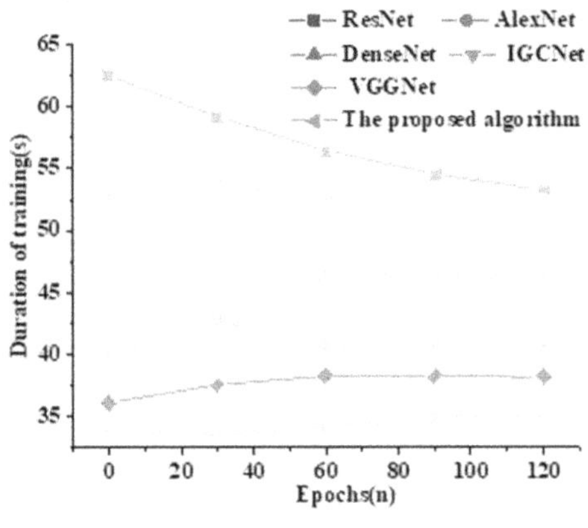

In Figure 15, except for the mixed attention mechanism model based on CNN and LSTM, the rest traditional models take a long time for training. With the increase in the number of iterations, the training time of each model is shortened, but the mixed attention mechanism model takes the shortest time. The overall training time of the model reported here is always maintained under 35 seconds, which can greatly improve the efficiency of model training.

Figure 16. Comparison of the testing time of different models

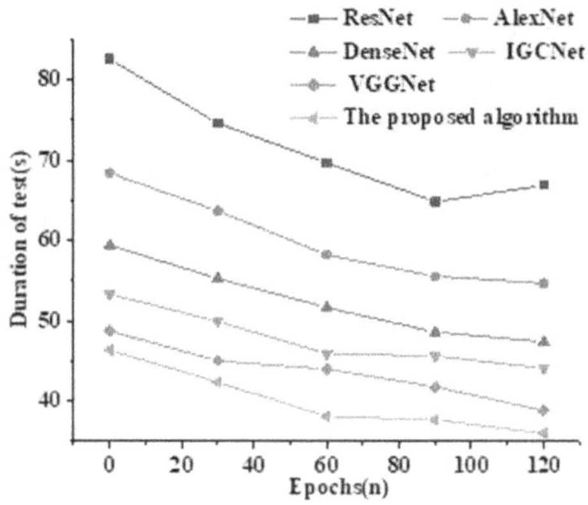

According to Figure 16, the traditional models all take a long testing time. With the increase in the number of iterations, the testing time can be shortened, but the testing time of the model proposed here is the shortest. At the beginning of the experiment, the mixed attention mechanism model requires more than 45 seconds for testing. As the number of model iterations increases, the testing time of this model can be reduced to about 35 seconds after 120 iterations, which decreases by 10 seconds compared with the testing time at the beginning of the experiment. Therefore, the mixed attention mechanism model has a practical application value to improve the efficiency of user behavior classification model.

5. CONCLUSION

With the rapid development of e-commerce platforms, some dishonest merchants manipulate consumers' online comments for their own interests, and a large number of fake comments seriously affect consumers' interests and the development of traditional e-commerce. It is urgent to purify the network environment of e-commerce, promote the healthy development of the platform, and safeguard the rights and interests of consumers. Therefore, an in-depth study is conducted on the user comment data from the extraction and description of the underlying behavior characteristics through case analysis of the application scenario of an online e-commerce platform. Moreover, a spatio-temporal mixed attention mechanism model based on super-complete ICA is proposed. The test results of different models show that stacked cross-attention has a good matching ability of fine-grained hierarchical features. In addition, the recognition accuracy of the mixed attention mechanism algorithm based on CNN and LSTM reported here is above 80% in different test data sets, and the recognition accuracy can be guaranteed at about 95%. The research has certain practical application value for the classification of business users' behavior and the discrimination of true and false comments. However, some disadvantages are inevitable. For example, in the experiment, the optimization effect of adversarial learning on the stacked cross-attention retrieval model is not significant. To strengthen the ability to represent image and text features of the model, future study will improve the word embedding algorithm for comments to extract more effective features.

REFERENCES

Ashburn-Nardo, L., Lindsey, A., Morris, K. A., & Goodwin, S. A. (2020). Who is responsible for confronting prejudice? The role of perceived and conferred authority. *Journal of Business and Psychology*, 35(6), 799–811. DOI: 10.1007/s10869-019-09651-w

Bhattacharyya, S., & Bose, I. (2020). S-commerce: Influence of Facebook likes on purchases and recommendations on a linked e-commerce site. *Decision Support Systems*, 138, 113383. DOI: 10.1016/j.dss.2020.113383

Brighi, A., Mameli, C., Menin, D., Guarini, A., Carpani, F., & Slee, P. T. (2019). Coping with cybervictimization: The role of direct confrontation and resilience on adolescent wellbeing. *International Journal of Environmental Research and Public Health*, 16(24), 4893. DOI: 10.3390/ijerph16244893 PMID: 31817233

Case, K. A., Rios, D., Lucas, A., Braun, K., & Enriquez, C. (2020). Intersectional patterns of prejudice confrontation by White, heterosexual, and cisgender allies. *The Journal of Social Issues*, 76(4), 899–920. DOI: 10.1111/josi.12408

Chang, D., Gui, H. Y., Fan, R., Fan, Z. Z., & Tian, J. (2019). Application of improved collaborative filtering in the recommendation of e-commerce commodities. *International Journal of Computers, Communications & Control*, 14(4), 489–502. DOI: 10.15837/ijccc.2019.4.3594

Chauhan, G. S., Meena, Y. K., & Gopalani, D.. (2020). A two-step hybrid unsupervised model with attention mechanism for aspect extraction. *Expert Systems with Applications*, 161, 113673. DOI: 10.1016/j.eswa.2020.113673

Fang, Y., Zhang, C., Huang, C., Liu, L., & Yang, Y. (2019). Phishing email detection using improved RCNN model with multilevel vectors and attention mechanism. *IEEE Access : Practical Innovations, Open Solutions*, 7, 56329–56340. DOI: 10.1109/ACCESS.2019.2913705

Fang, Y., Zhang, C., Huang, C., Liu, L., & Yang, Y. (2019). Phishing email detection using improved RCNN model with multilevel vectors and attention mechanism. *IEEE Access : Practical Innovations, Open Solutions*, 7, 56329–56340. DOI: 10.1109/ACCESS.2019.2913705

Gao, Y., & Ruan, Y. (2021). Interpretable deep learning model for building energy consumption prediction based on attention mechanism. *Energy and Building*, 252, 111379. DOI: 10.1016/j.enbuild.2021.111379

Hammad, M., Pławiak, P., Wang, K., & Acharya, U. R. (2021). ResNet-Attention model for human authentication using ECG signals. *Expert Systems: International Journal of Knowledge Engineering and Neural Networks*, 38(6), e12547. DOI: 10.1111/exsy.12547

Hershcovis, M. S., Cameron, A. F., Gervais, L., & Bozeman, J. (2018). The effects of confrontation and avoidance coping in response to workplace incivility. *Journal of Occupational Health Psychology*, 23(2), 163–174. DOI: 10.1037/ocp0000078 PMID: 28191998

Kang, J., Liu, L., Zhang, F., Shen, C., Wang, N., & Shao, L. (2021). Semantic segmentation model of cotton roots in-situ image based on attention mechanism. *Computers and Electronics in Agriculture*, 189, 106370. DOI: 10.1016/j.compag.2021.106370

Kuroda, N. (2021). Editorial Comment to False-positive 123 I-metaiodobenzylguanidine scan in a patient with renal cell carcinoma: A case of chromophobe renal cell carcinoma oncocytic variant with a complicated clinical course. *IJU Case Reports*, 4(1), 42–43. DOI: 10.1002/iju5.12244 PMID: 33426496

Kwilinski, A., Volynets, R., & Berdnik, I.. (2019). E-Commerce: Concept and Legal Regulation in Modern Economic Conditions. Journal of Legal. *Ethical and Regulatory Issues*, 22, 1–6.

Lawton, R. (2018). It Ain't What You Do (But the Way That You Do It): Will Safety II Transform the Way We Do Patient Safety?: Comment on" False Dawns and New Horizons in Patient Safety Research and Practice. *International Journal of Health Policy and Management*, 7(7), 659–661. DOI: 10.15171/ijhpm.2018.14 PMID: 29996586

Leonard, L. N., & Jones, K. (2021). Trust in C2C electronic commerce: Ten years later. *Journal of Computer Information Systems*, 61(3), 240–246. DOI: 10.1080/08874417.2019.1598829

Li, H., Duan, H., Zheng, Y., Wang, Q., & Wang, Y. (2020). A CTR prediction model based on user interest via attention mechanism. *Applied Intelligence*, 50(4), 1192–1203. DOI: 10.1007/s10489-019-01571-9

Li, J., Liu, X., Zhang, W., Zhang, M., Song, J., & Sebe, N. (2020). Spatio-temporal attention networks for action recognition and detection. *IEEE Transactions on Multimedia*, 22(11), 2990–3001. DOI: 10.1109/TMM.2020.2965434

Liu, X., Xu, Y. C., & Yang, X. (2021). Disease profiling in pharmaceutical E-commerce. *Expert Systems with Applications*, 178, 115015. DOI: 10.1016/j.eswa.2021.115015

Lu, S., Lu, Z., & Zhang, Y. D. (2019). Pathological brain detection based on AlexNet and transfer learning. *Journal of Computational Science*, 30, 41–47. DOI: 10.1016/j.jocs.2018.11.008

Nauman, A., Qadri, Y. A., Amjad, M., Zikria, Y. B., Afzal, M. K., & Kim, S. W. (2020). Multimedia Internet of Things: A comprehensive survey. *IEEE Access : Practical Innovations, Open Solutions*, 8, 8202–8250. DOI: 10.1109/ACCESS.2020.2964280

Qi, N., Wang, W., Xiao, M., Jia, L., Jin, S., Zhu, Q., & Tsiftsis, T. A. (2021). A learning-based spectrum access Stackelberg game: Friendly jammer-assisted communication confrontation. *IEEE Transactions on Vehicular Technology*, 70(1), 700–713. DOI: 10.1109/TVT.2021.3049653

Ren, Q., Li, M., Li, H., & Shen, Y. (2021). A novel deep learning prediction model for concrete dam displacements using interpretable mixed attention mechanism. *Advanced Engineering Informatics*, 50, 101407. DOI: 10.1016/j.aei.2021.101407

Sadeeq, M., Abdulla, A. I., & Abdulraheem, A. S.. (2020). Impact of electronic commerce on enterprise business. *Technol. Rep. Kansai Univ*, 62(5), 2365–2378.

Sujan, M. (2018). A Safety-II Perspective on Organisational Learning in Healthcare Organisations: Comment on" False Dawns and New Horizons in Patient Safety Research and Practice. *International Journal of Health Policy and Management*, 7(7), 662–666. DOI: 10.15171/ijhpm.2018.16 PMID: 29996587

Vasić, N., Kilibarda, M., Andrejić, M., & Jović, S. (2021). Satisfaction is a function of users of logistics services in e-commerce. *Technology Analysis and Strategic Management*, 33(7), 813–828. DOI: 10.1080/09537325.2020.1849610

Wang, C., Han, D., Liu, Q., & Luo, S. (2018). A deep learning approach for credit scoring of peer-to-peer lending using attention mechanism LSTM. *IEEE Access : Practical Innovations, Open Solutions*, 7, 2161–2168. DOI: 10.1109/ACCESS.2018.2887138

Wang, K., Shawl, R. Q., & Neware, R.. (2021). Research on immersive interactive experience of content e-commerce live users in the era of computer digital marketing. *International Journal of System Assurance Engineering and Management*, •••, 1–11.

Wang, Z., Zheng, X., Li, D., Zhang, H., Yang, Y., & Pan, H. (2021). A VGGNet-like approach for classifying and segmenting coal dust particles with overlapping regions. *Computers in Industry*, 132, 103506. DOI: 10.1016/j.compind.2021.103506

Yu, X., Feng, W., Wang, H., Chu, Q., & Chen, Q. (2020). An attention mechanism and multi-granularity-based Bi-LSTM model for Chinese Q&A system. *Soft Computing*, 24(8), 5831–5845. DOI: 10.1007/s00500-019-04367-8

Zaragas, C. K. (2021). The Psychodrama and its Contribution to The Children's Competitive manifestation. Case Study. *Cultural-historical Psychology*, 17(3), 143–151. DOI: 10.17759/chp.2021170318

Zhang, K., Guo, Y., Wang, X., Yuan, J., & Ding, Q. (2019). Multiple feature re-weight DenseNet for image classification. *IEEE Access : Practical Innovations, Open Solutions*, 7, 9872–9880. DOI: 10.1109/ACCESS.2018.2890127

Zhang, X., Yang, F., & Hu, Y.. (2021). RANet: Network intrusion detection with group-gating convolutional neural network. *Journal of Network and Computer Applications*, •••, 103266.

Zhou, Y., Li, J., Chen, H., Wu, Y., Wu, J., & Chen, L. (2020). A spatiotemporal attention mechanism-based model for multi-step citywide passenger demand prediction. *Information Sciences*, 513, 372–385. DOI: 10.1016/j.ins.2019.10.071

Zhu, K., Wang, R., Zhao, Q., Cheng, J., & Tao, D. (2019). A cuboid CNN model with an attention mechanism for skeleton-based action recognition. *IEEE Transactions on Multimedia*, 22(11), 2977–2989. DOI: 10.1109/TMM.2019.2962304

Chapter 2
Application of Data Mining Combined With K-Means Clustering Algorithm in Enterprises' Risk Audit

Sharif Uddin Ahmed Rana
https://orcid.org/0000-0003-2296-6044
Paris Graduate School, France

ABSTRACT

The financial risk management mechanism of enterprises can be more complete through exploration in the application effect of data mining technology combined with K-means clustering algorithm in enterprise risk audit. Hence, K-means clustering algorithm is introduced to study the paperless status of electronic payment in the trading process of e-commerce enterprises. Additionally, a risk audit model of e-commerce enterprises is implemented based on K-means algorithm combined with Random Forest Light Gradient Boosting Machine (RF-LightGBM). In this model, the actual operation process of data preparation, data preprocessing, model construction, model application and evaluation are the payment flow in the transaction process of e-commerce enterprises by using big data analysis technology. Eventually, the performance of the model is evaluated by simulation.

DOI: 10.4018/978-1-6684-6641-4.ch002

INTRODUCTION

At present, along with the advancing progress of communication technologies such as wireless transmission and mobile equipment, e-commerce enterprises are also developing rapidly. Meanwhile, the emergence of computer technologies like cloud computing, artificial intelligence (AI), and big data (BD) has made e-commerce industries more intelligent. According to statistical analysis, the total volumes of business in e-commerce industries have almost reached 3 billion yuan. The proportion of the online shopping market in the e-commerce market was only about 11% in 2011, and by 2018 it grew to nearly 30%. The rapid popularization of e-commerce in people's lives has also brought new business directions and certain risks to accounting and auditing work, such as paperless transaction processes and electronic payments, (Zhu, 2020) (Jiang & Chen, 2021). Therefore, how to adopt data mining (DM) in the risk audit of e-commerce enterprises has raised a group of relevant scholars' interest.

Compared with the transaction process of traditional enterprises, e-commerce enterprises usually use the Internet, and electronic payments such as Alipay, WeChat payment are mainly taken in the transaction process online. Therefore, this process is also called e-commerce transaction. Online payment makes the transaction process of e-commerce basically paperless, (Huang *et al.,* 2018). The electronic payment process also makes the audit of e-commerce enterprises different from traditional audit in many aspects, such as audit objectives, audit content, audit methods and procedures. Therefore, the audit contents of e-commerce enterprises do not include just enterprises' annual financial reports, but also the analyzation on whether the e-commerce system is still reliable. As the audit content of e-commerce enterprises is more extensive, the audit risk is further increased. Additionally, with the increasing number and scale of e-commerce enterprises, more and more e-commerce servers need certified public accountants to supervise the audit, which also makes the audit inevitably face some risks. DM technology can classify and predict sample data when auditing transaction data information in e-commerce enterprises, (Zhang & Yang, 2021). The advantages of the e-commerce audit risk identification model based on DM technology are that it does not need the tedious conditional assumptions in the traditional statistical model but is suitable for mass data identification without structure and form, and it uses computer to effectively process information and to quickly obtain the identification results. It has the advantages of high identification efficiency and good identification effect.

When auditing the transaction data information of massive e-commerce enterprises, the audit model has also changed from a model based on statistical technology to a model based on intelligent technology, including multivariate analysis, Logistic, AI, support vector machine (SVM), K-means clustering algorithm, decision tree (DT), neural network, random forest (RF), etc., which are all intelligent algorithms that can perform unsupervised learning of multi-level features of data from the original massive data in an unsupervised state. Among them, many studies have shown that the RF algorithm has incomparable advantages over other machine learning (ML) algorithms. It can not only deal with large data sets with high efficiency and high quality, but also maintain excellent prediction accuracy under the condition of high-dimensional feature. It sorts the importance of input variables and has strong adaptive ability and self-learning ability. It is very suitable for nonlinear modeling without the influence of multiple collinearities, (Abd Hamid *et al.,* 2019) (Zhao *et al.,* 2020). Moreover, RF algorithm can overcome the over-fitting problem existing in other models, and has been widely used in many fields, such as bioinformatics, medicine, and social science. K-means algorithm is used to make iterative clustering analysis. When it is carried out, K objects are randomly selected as the clustering center in the first stage. Then, the distance between each object is calculated, and the distance of each seed clustering center is also measured. By these steps, each object is assigned to the nearest clustering center. Clustering centers and their assigned objects refer to clustering. After one more sample is assigned, another calculation should be conducted on the cluster center, according to cluster's existing objects. The process should be repeated until the model meets the termination condition, (Lakshmi *et al*., 2020). Applying it to enterprise audit can effectively classify the transaction process and data, which is of great significance to enterprise risk audit.

To sum up, with the AI algorithms being continuously improved, audit work is facing not only a rare opportunity, but also a big challenge in the widespread popularity of e-commerce companies. It is innovative to introduce the K-means clustering algorithm into the e-commerce industry. Meanwhile, integrated with the improved RF algorithm in the ML algorithm, the Random Forest Light Gradient Boosting Machine (RF-LightGBM) fusion algorithm is designed. And construction is conducted on the risk audit model of e-commerce enterprises based on K-means algorithm combined with RF-LightGBM. Ultimately, through simulation, its performance is evaluated, to provide experimentally referencing values for the later audit risk reduction and quality improvement.

RECENT RELATED WORK

Tendency of the Development of Enterprises' Risk Audit

With the advent of e-commerce, paperless transactions not only affect traditional manufacturing production, but also bring new risks to the accounting and auditing work. Many scholars have studied the risk audit of enterprises. Shad *et al*. (2019)

combined the implementation of enterprise risk management with sustainable development reports to test the influence of risk audit on the enterprises' economic added value. Simultaneously, they proposed to use ordinary least square (OLS) analysis to obtain information about enterprise risk management practices and sustainability reports, (Shad *et al.*, 2019). Hanggraeni *et al.* (2019) displayed significant results of risk management factors by using an offline questionnaire survey. Simultaneously, through the marketing and financial management risk audit assessment, they found that enterprise identification and management activities would have a vital influence on business performance, (Hanggraeni *et al.*, 2019). Cheng *et al.* (2021) proposed a new q-rung othopair fuzzy weighted averaging operator (q-ROFWAO) to rank and evaluate manufacturing small and middle-size enterprises (SMEs). The results show that the method is effective in Sustainability Enterprise Risk Management (SERM) of SMEs, (Cheng *et al.*, 2021). Yang and Liao (2021) introduced the time dimension to describe the dynamic, sudden, and timely evolution characteristics of enterprise risk events in view of the static mapping problem in the knowledge map of existing enterprises. ResNet dynamic knowledge reasoning method was also proposed to improve the loss balance function of multi-network model. Experiments show that the new model can effectively improve the accuracy of entity and relationship prediction, (Yang & Liao, 2021).

Application Status of the DM Technology

With the Internet and information technology being increasingly advanced, the scale of data in all walks of life has been increasing. As one of the AI algorithms, ML has a wide range of applications, which provides a strong guarantee for DM of massive data information and is studied by many scientific researchers. Ping et al. (2019) introduced two ML methods for evaluating the fuel efficiency of driving behavior using natural driving data. Results indicate that this method can be adopted to make effective identification on the relationship between driving behavior and fuel consumption from the macro or micro levels and can effectively predict the driving behavior of vehicles, (Ping *et al.*, 2019). Xu *et al.* (2019) proposed detailed methods rooted in remote sensing, ML, and computer vision, and made full use of existing data to combine convolutional neural networks (CNN) with subtle and scientific observation data of the earth, (Xu *et al.*, 2019). In view of the current situation of flight delays, Gui *et al.* (2019) designed a normalized model using LSTM algorithm and RF algorithm to classify and predict flight conditions. The results show that the proposed model based on random forest can obtain higher prediction accuracy (binary classification is 90.2%) and overcome the overfitting, (Gui *et al.*, 2019). Lv, Qiao, and Singh (2020) constructed a cognitive computing model by context-aware data flow by optimizing the decision tree algorithm in ML. The results show that the application of the model algorithm can ensure the accuracy and stability of behavior classification, which is of great significance for operators to analyze user behavior and develop personalized services, (Ly, Qiao, & Singh, 2020). Kanagaraj, Rajkumar, and Srinivasan (2021) put forward an enhanced multi-class normalized optimal clustering algorithm and applied it to data object grouping and classification. The results outline the needs of different regions in India in terms of energy consumption and show that the proposed method performs significantly better, (Kanagaraj, Rajkumar, & Srinivasan, 2021).

Through the analysis of the research of the above scholars, it is found that in the era of massive data generation, the application field of DM technology is becoming gradually more extensive. In the field of risk audit, most enterprises still adapt the traditional manufacturing audit work. Under the trend of rapid popularization in the field of e-commerce, there are not many studies related to risk audit. Therefore, aiming at the risks existing in the audit process of e-commerce enterprises in the field of e-commerce, the standard algorithm is optimized by the ML algorithm and construction is conducted on risk audit evaluation model of e-commerce enterprises, which are of great significance to the safety improvement and risk control of the audit process in e-commerce enterprises.

CONSTRUCTION AND ANALYSIS OF RISK AUDIT EVALUATION OF E-COMMERCE ENTERPRISES BASED ON DM TECHNOLOGY

Requirements Analysis of Data Sources and Risk Audit of E-Commerce Enterprises

In e-commerce enterprises, data sources are more extensive than financial transactions with traditional supply chain. E-commerce enterprises can improve the real-time update frequency of data through multi-dimensional BD acquisition, thus improving the effectiveness of data audit. Figure 1 illustrates the BD sources of e-commerce enterprises.

Figure 1. BD resource of e-commerce enterprises

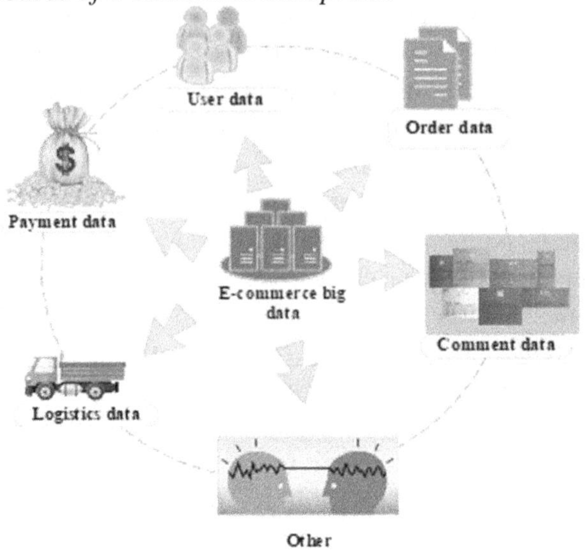

The collection of multi-dimensional data shown in Figure 1 can effectively reduce the information asymmetry and false information, which is conducive to the operation of the BD risk control model in the later stage to avoid the error of the analysis results due to insufficient user information, to better prevent and control various audit risks. Moreover, through the analysis of the credit evaluation model constructed by diversified and deep-seated multidimensional big data, it is conducive to more accurate credit evaluation of users.

The audit mode and method of e-commerce business transactions are also constantly updated with the change of BD technology. The complexity of data types, the expansion of data analysis scope and the increase of audit projects put forward higher requirements for the professional quality of internal auditors. The practical application of BD audit mainly includes the configuration of personnel professional knowledge, the configuration of hardware and software equipment, and the sufficient and accurate data required, (Amani & Fadlalla, 2017) (Nawaiseh, Abbod, & Itagaki, 2020). Primarily, in terms of personnel professional quality, since the BD audit is still in the developing stage, some technical personnel in the audit department still adopt the traditional risk-oriented internal audit work method, which requires the company to increase the introduction of employees and personnel training. There are differences in the development of hardware and software equipment. Moreover, in terms of data preparation, if the business data collected in the audit operations are incomplete, the audit results will be affected. Data, as the basis of audit judgment, will influence the quality of internal audit to a certain degree. If there are information mis-records or missing records and cross-system extraction failures, the audit results will be misleading. Therefore, when auditing the risk of data information in e-commerce enterprises, DM is inevitable. Here, the combination of ML K-means clustering algorithm and RD is used to audit the risk of BD of transactions in e-commerce enterprises, which is significantly practical to the transaction information security and accurate audit of e-commerce enterprises.

Random Forest Algorithm Applied to Big Data Audit Analysis of E-Commerce Enterprises

When auditing the transaction data of e-commerce enterprises, classifying the data is the primary work to be carried out. RF is an improved algorithm based on common decision trees, which has more advanced advantages than common decision trees. It can generate training samples independently in each decision tree, and then form a forest. Ultimately, the results of multiple decision trees are combined by using some strategies. Based on the DT algorithm, a random forest is formed, (Didimo *et al.,* 2020). Figure 2 demonstrates the DT algorithm applied to BD in the e-commerce enterprises.

Figure 2. DT algorithm applied to BD in the e-commerce enterprises

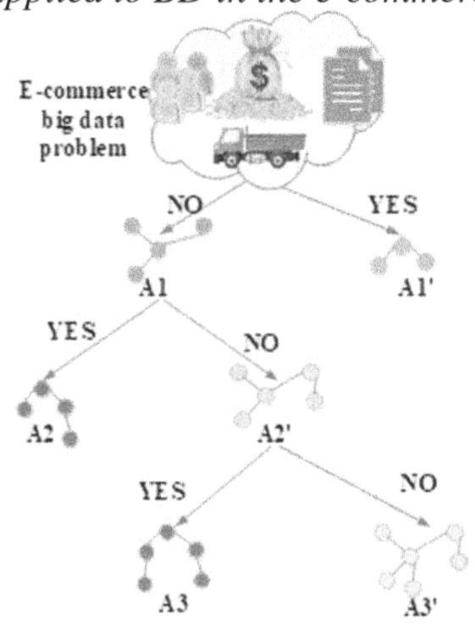

As for the general DT algorithm, the segmented node usually selects an optimal feature attribute from all the sample feature attributes on the node as the basis of the segmented node, (Ashraf, Ahmad, & Ashraf, 2018). However, RF randomly selects some feature attributes on the current node, and then selects an optimal feature attribute as the basis for dividing the node. In this way, RF further enhances the generalization ability of the model. Compared with DT method, RF algorithm is more effective to solve the problem of overfitting in DT. After the establishment of the RF, assuming that there is a new sample, it is put into the RF, and then each DT in the RF enters the sample attribute category for decision-making, each tree has a vote, with a few subordinates to the majority method, the categories with the largest number of DT votes are the final classification results of the sample, (Eremeev & Zakharchuk, 2020). The RF algorithm is applied to DT of e-commerce as shown in Figure 3.

Figure 3. RF algorithm applied to DT of e-commerce

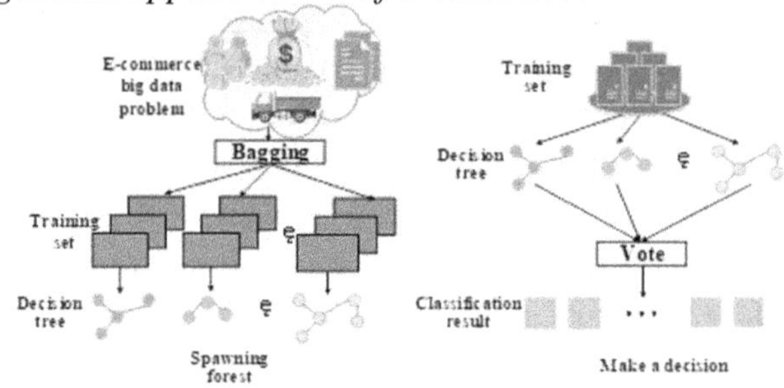

As shown in the right part of Figure 3, the construction of RF algorithm includes three steps: training set generation, decision tree construction, and algorithm formation and implementation. Assuming that the scale of random forest is *N*, the random forest algorithm needs *N* decision trees for training. Hence, a corresponding number of training sets need to be generated. To prevent the DT from producing local optimal solution, the RF generates *N* training sample sets by using the bag random sampling technique with replacement. Besides, this operation will inevitably lead to repetition in the sampling training samples.

Iterative Dichotomiser 3 (ID3 algorithm) (ID3 algorithm refers to a greedy algorithm used to construct decision trees.) is one of the most basic algorithms in RF. The algorithm first calculates the information gain of each attribute, and then compares the information gain of each feature one by one and selects the best attribute for node segmentation, (Zuo *et al.,* 2020). The so-called best attribute refers to the maximum information gained by dividing the sample set according to the characteristics. Information entropy is a basic concept in algorithm operation, which is used to measure uncertainty. Equation (1) indicates the sample set of decision tree at node *m*.

$$X = \{x_1, x_2, \ldots, x_n\} \quad (1)$$

The corresponding sample category can be expressed as:

$$\{c_i|\ i=1,2,\ \ldots,\ N\} \qquad (2)$$

p_i represents the probability for each category and X accords to the information gain obtained by dividing sample by m corresponding to attribute *a*.

$$Gain(a) = Info(X) - Info\ a(X) \qquad (3)$$

In Equation (3), *Info*(*X*) means the information entropy of.

$$Info(X) = -\sum_{i=1}^{c} p_i \log_2 p_i \qquad (4)$$

Info a(*X*) stands for the predicting information required by X.

$$Infoa(X) = \sum_{j=1}^{v} \left[\left(\frac{|X_j|}{|X|} \right) Infoa(X_j) \right] \qquad (5)$$

ID3 algorithm selects the maximum attribute as the test attribute. However, it cannot handle continuous variables and prefers to select properties with more values. Therefore, ID3 algorithm usually leads to that the DT solution is local optimal solution rather than global optimal solution. Scholars have conducted in-depth research and discussion on this issue, and finally proposed the C4.5 algorithm. C4.5 algorithm is based on information gain rate. This algorithm uses the information gain rate to avoid the deviation of segmentation attributes, making it more equitable to select each attribute when dividing nodes, (Liou *et al.*, 2021). Equation (6) illustrates the calculation of information acquisition ratc.

$$GainRatio(a) = \frac{Gain(a)}{splitInfoa(X)} \qquad (6)$$

In Equation (6), *split Info a*(*X*) represents the information segmentation rate, and Equation (7) expresses it in a function.

$$splitInfoa(X) = \sum_{j=1}^{v} \left[\left(\frac{|X_j|}{|X|} \right) \log_2 \left(\frac{X_j}{X} \right) \right] \qquad (7)$$

Although compared with ID3 algorithm, C4.5 algorithm can discreet the original continuous attribute variables, it can handle continuous numerical variables and is also suitable for missing data, (Wu & Moon, 2018). The classification rules generated by C4.5 algorithm are easy to understand and have high precision; however, the algorithm is not dominant in execution time and storage space.

Meanwhile, classification and regression tree (CART) algorithm is also very common in RF algorithm. Different from ID3 algorithm and C4.5 algorithm, CART algorithm uses Gini minimum impurity criterion for node segmentation. Equation (8) displays the calculation process of Gini minimum impurity criterion.

$$Gini(t) = 1 - \sum_{j=1}^{c} [p(j|t)]^2 \quad j = 1, \cdots, c \tag{8}$$

In Equation (8), $p(j|t)$ refers to the probability of type j on node t. When the same category is composed of all the samples of node t, the minimum value is given to the Gini index, namely, 0, and the sample category is the purest. When the Gini index is maximum 1, the purity of the sample category is the lowest, that is, categories are different. The sample set is divided into m branches, and the Equation (9) expresses the Gini index used to split the current node.

$$Gini(X) = \sum_{i=1}^{m} \frac{n_i}{n} Gini(i) \tag{9}$$

In Equation (9), m refers to the number of sub-nodes, n_i accords to the number of samples at sub-node i, and n represents the number of samples at the upper node. Moreover, the application of CART algorithm needs to calculate the Gini index of each attribute in the training process. After the variables with the smallest Gini index are selected to segment the current node, the decision tree needs to be recursively constructed until it reaches the stopping condition.

However, the Light Gradient Boosting Machine (LightGBM) algorithm, as an open source and efficient distributed gradient boosting tree algorithm newly released in recent years, has the characteristics of fast operation, less memory consumption and high accuracy, and is widely used in classification and regression. In the Gradient Boosting Decision Tree (GBDT) iteration, it is assumed that the learner obtained in the previous round is defined as $Z_{t-1}(x)$, whose loss function accords to Equation (10).

$$L(Y, Z_{t-1}(x)) \tag{10}$$

Then, the goal of this training is to find a suitable weak learner to minimize the loss function. Equation (11) defines the loss function.

$$Z_t(x) = \arg\min_{h \in H} \sum L(y, Z_{t-1}(x) + h_t(x)) \tag{11}$$

Then, the negative gradient of the loss function is calculated to fit the approximate value of the current wheel loss function. Equation (12) demonstrates the approximate value of the loss function.

$$f_{ti} = -\frac{\partial(y, Z_{t-1}(x_i))}{\partial Z_{t-1}(x_i)} \tag{12}$$

Square difference is usually used for approximation $h_t(x)$ as shown in Equation (13).

$$h_t(x) = \arg\min_{h \in H} \sum (r_{ti} - h(x))^2 \tag{13}$$

In this round, the strong learner is defined as displayed in Equation (14).

$$F_t(x) = h_t(x) - F_{t-1}(x) \tag{14}$$

Therefore, the LightGBM algorithm is integrated with the RF, namely RF-LightGBM, to reduce the calculation cost of the audit process of e-commerce enterprises, improve the calculation efficiency of the model, and obtain high accuracy while maintaining high calculation efficiency.

Application of K-Means Clustering Algorithm in Big Data Audit Analysis of E-commerce Enterprises

The K-means algorithm can be described as a centroid-based partition technology, that is, the centroid of the cluster C_i is used to represent the cluster. When the K-means algorithm is applied to the data analysis of e-commerce enterprises, the centroid of the cluster is defined as the mean value of the points in the cluster. In the clustering process, n objects are randomly selected with k as the parameter, and each object represents the initial mean value of a cluster. These objects are then divided into k clusters. The remaining objects are placed to the neighbor cluster based on their center distance from each cluster, so that the cluster has higher similarity, (Grover, Bauhoff, & Friedman, 2019) (Li *et al.,* 2018). This time, the mean value of each cluster changes, and the average value is recalculated, and the process is repeated until the result cluster is as independent as possible.

As Equation (15) indicates, a known set of n data samples is defined as Ω.

$$\Omega = \{x_i | x_i = (x_{i1}, x_{i2}, \cdots, x_{id}), i = 1, 2, \cdots, n\} \tag{15}$$

In Equation (15), $x_i = (x_{i1}, x_{i2}, \cdots, x_{id})$ refers to a d-dimensional vector, x_{id} refers to the d_{th} identical attributes of the i_{th} data, n represents the sample size. Equation (16) illustrates the clustering center.

$$C = \left\{ c_j \middle| c_j = (c_{j1}, c_{j2}, \cdots, c_{jd}), c = 1, 2, \cdots, k \right\} \tag{16}$$

In Equation (16), $c_j = (c_{j1}, c_{j2}, \cdots, c_{jd})$ refers to the center point of the j_{th} cluster. There are d attributes in every c_j, and k represents the number of clusters.

Equation (17) expresses the Euclidean Distance $dis(x_i, c_j)$, which is the distance between x_i and c_j.

$$dis(x_i, c_j) = \sqrt{\sum_{l=1}^{d} (x_{il} - c_{jl})^2}, i = 1, 2, \cdots, n; c = 1, 2, \cdots, k \tag{17}$$

In Equation (17), $x_i = (x_{i1}, x_{i2}, \cdots, x_{id})$, $c_j = (c_{j1}, c_{j2}, \cdots, c_{jd})$, k refers to the number of the clusters. Equation (18) accords to the calculation of the center of the same clusters c_j.

$$c_{jl} = \frac{1}{N(\phi_j)} \sum_{x_i \in \phi_j} x_{il}, l = 1, 2, \cdots, d; c = 1, 2, \cdots, k \tag{18}$$

In Equation (18), $N(\phi_j)$ represents the same cluster's amount of data. The criterion function is generally defined by the sum of error squares, which is expressed as Equation (19).

$$E = \sum_{j=1}^{k} \sum_{x_i \in \phi_j} dis(x_i, c_j) \tag{19}$$

In Equation (19), E refers to the total value of the square error of all data objects in the data set of e-commerce enterprise audit, x_i accords to the point in the space, k represents the given e-commerce enterprise audit data object, and c_j stands for the average value of the center point of the j_{th} cluster class. Figure 4 displays the algorithm flow of applying K-means algorithm to BD of e-commerce enterprises.

Figure 4. K-means algorithm applied in the BD of e-commerce enterprises

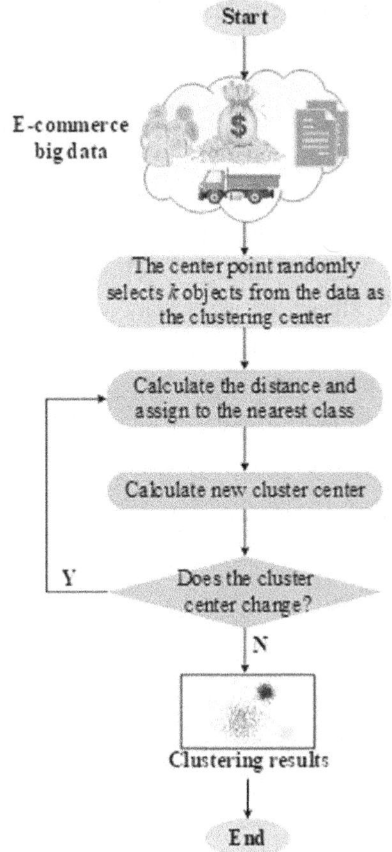

Figure 4 demonstrates the specific steps of when the K-means algorithm is applied to the BD of e-commerce enterprises' audit. Firstly, *k* objects are randomly selected from the BD samples of *n* e-commerce enterprises as the initial clustering center; secondly, the distance from each sample to each cluster centroid is calculated respectively, and the sample is assigned to the neighbor cluster center category; thirdly, after all the samples are allocated, the centers of *k* clusters are recalculated; fourthly, compared with the previous calculated *k* cluster centers, if the cluster center changes, the process turns to the second step, otherwise turns to the fifth step; fifthly, the process stops and the clustering results are output when the centroid does not change.

Construction and Analysis of Risk Audit Model for E-Commerce Enterprises Based on K-Means Algorithm Combined with Random Forest

In view of the diversity and complexity of traffic influencing factors in the road network area of smart city construction, K-means clustering algorithm is introduced here. However, results of K-means clustering algorithm basically depend on initial values, and difference in initial values is the direct reason of the appearance of diverse clustering results. And the number of clusters generated k must be given in advance. Therefore, the RF algorithm is introduced and improved to classify the BD of risk audit in e-commerce enterprises. Finally, construction is conducted on the risk audit model of e-commerce enterprises based on K-means algorithm combined with RF-LightGBM. Figure 5 demonstrates its overall architecture.

Figure 5. risk audit model of e-commerce enterprises based on K-means algorithm combined with RF-LightGBM

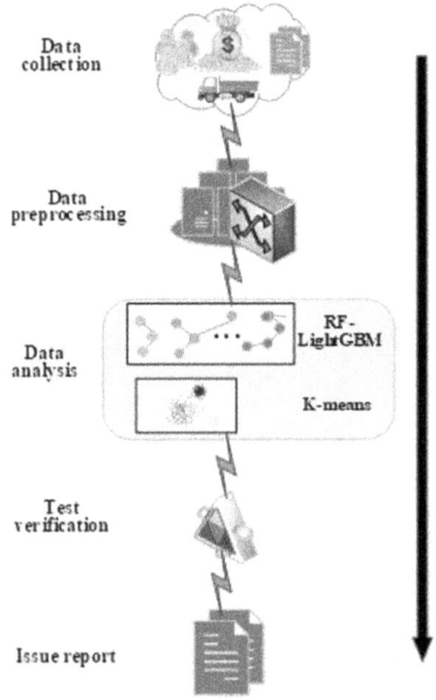

In the risk audit model of e-commerce enterprises, the first step is to collect the audit data required by e-commerce enterprises. The collected data does not only include financial data, but also contains data that covers the business situation of the audited unit and the specific audit rules and regulations. After complete collection, the problems in the same specific direction are integrated and classified.

Secondly, the audited data are extracted and cleaned, such as error data, invalid data and abnormal data found in the audit process during data extraction. Assuming that data is not processed, it is equivalent to predicting future data with the wrong data, which makes the potential link between the data undetectable and makes the wrong direction for the later development of the enterprise. The continuous accumulation of error data will make enterprises face a huge crisis, so data cleaning should not be ignored.

In the data analysis stage, the K-means algorithm is combined with the RF. The construction of this model algorithm can not only avoid the sensitivity to the initial value when using the K-means clustering algorithm alone, but also cause different clustering results for different initial values. The number k of the generated clusters must be given in advance, which can also reduce the calculation cost of the audit process of e-commerce enterprises, improve the calculation efficiency of the model, and obtain high accuracy while maintaining high calculation efficiency. A number of n audit warning indicators are selected from the shared data center of e-commerce enterprises as the object of feature selection, as $X = \{X_1, X_2, \ , X_n\}, X_i = \{X_{i1}, X_{i2}, \cdots, X_{in}\}$. X_{in} indicates the n_{th} character of the i_{th} audit warning indicator. Now, m samples are randomly selected from N samples, and Equation (20) accords to the cumulative weight equation of audit warning features.

$$W_j^{i+1} = W_j^i + \frac{diff(j, x, M(x))}{m} - \frac{diff(j, x, H(x))}{m} \tag{20}$$

In Equation (20), j refers to the audit warning features, which varies from 1 to N; i represents the randomly selected samples; $diff(\bullet)$ means the distance; $M(x)$ stands for the heterogeneous nearest neighbor samples, and $H(x)$ denotes the similar nearest neighbor samples. Table 1 demonstrates the steps of the model based on K-means algorithm combined with RF-LightGBM

Table 1. steps of the model based on K-means algorithm combined with RF-LightGBM

1	**start**
2	**Input:** dataset D, feature set K
3	**Output:** optimal classification of e-commerce enterprise data audit
4	Calculate the feature importance degree I_i of feature f_i using RF respectively
5	The features are sorted in descending order according to the obtained I_i
6	The lightgbm algorithm is used for evaluation. Backward selection is made for the sorted feature subset to calculate the accuracy a_{tmp} after deleting the feature
7	**For** (f_i) do
8	Calculation a_i// Calculates the accuracy of the current feature subset

continued on following page

Table 1. Continued

$C \leftarrow C+f_i$ //delete feature f_i
Calculate a_{tmp} // calculate the accuracy after deleting the feature
if $a_{tmp}>a_i$ then
$a_{best}=a_{tmp}$, C_{best}=C // if the new accuracy rate is greater than the old update feature subset
Else then
$C \leftarrow C+f_i$ // otherwise, the feature just deleted will be recycled
K-means calculates the distance between K cluster centers and samples
end if
end for
end

Stimulation

To verify the performance of the risk audit model of e-commerce enterprises based on K-means algorithm combined with RF-LightGBM constructed here, Matlab software is used to conduct empirical research on the simulation generation of the constructed model. The data set used here comes from the post-desensitization transaction data provided by Jingdong Mall (a Chinese e-commerce plat form). Analyzation is mainly made on the accurate data and fuzzy data from January 17,2020 to February 17, 2020. Accurate data consists of customer consumption records, return and exchange interest, fuzzy data includes user browsing records, commodity comparison records and other information, and the number of all the enterprises behaviors is more than 100 million. Initially, statistical, and visual analyzation are made on the original data, which are then pre-processed. its pretreatment. Afterwards, duplicate values in the data and default values are removed. Finally, the data is divided into a training set and test set in an 8:2 ratio.

In the simulation analysis, the risk audit model based on K-means algorithm combined with RF-LightGBM classification algorithm is compared with the models and algorithms proposed by other scholars in related fields, which mainly refer to RF-LightGBM (Pal *et al.,* 2019), K-means (Yang *et al.,* 2020), LightGBM (Rani, Defit, & Muhammad, 2021), Support Vector Machines (SVM) (Li & Liu, 2017) and Bayesian network (BN) (Alekseeva & Mosentseva, 2020), respectively, from the classification accuracy, data message delivery rate, leakage rate, packet loss rate and average delay of data transmission security. Among them, the model constructed here uses the cluster module of sklearn when designing the K-means clustering algorithm. The parameters are set as follows: *k* for the n_cluster classification cluster setting, valuing 2 ~ 6, maximum number of iterations defaults 120 for max_iter. Specific simulation experiment configuration is mainly considered from both hardware and software. In the software, the operating system is Linux 64bit, Python version is Python 3.6.1, and the development platform is PyCharm; in hardware, the CPU is Intel core i7-7700 @ 4.2GHz 8-core, memory is Kingston ddr4 2400MHz 16G, GPU is Nvidia GeForce 1060 8G.

RESULTS AND DISCUSSION

Comparative Analysis of Classification Accuracy Performance of Each Model and Algorithms

To study the performance of the risk audit model of e-commerce enterprises based on K-means algorithm combined with RF-LightGBM, the system model constructed here is compared in several aspects with the algorithm put forward by other relevant scholars. The classification accuracy is predicted from Accuracy, Recall, Precision and F1 value, and Figure 7 displays the results. Figure 8 presents further acceleration ratio analysis of its classification efficiency.

Figure 6. Curves of influence of iteration on classification accuracy of different algorithms (a. Accuracy; b. Precision; c. Recall; d. F1 value)

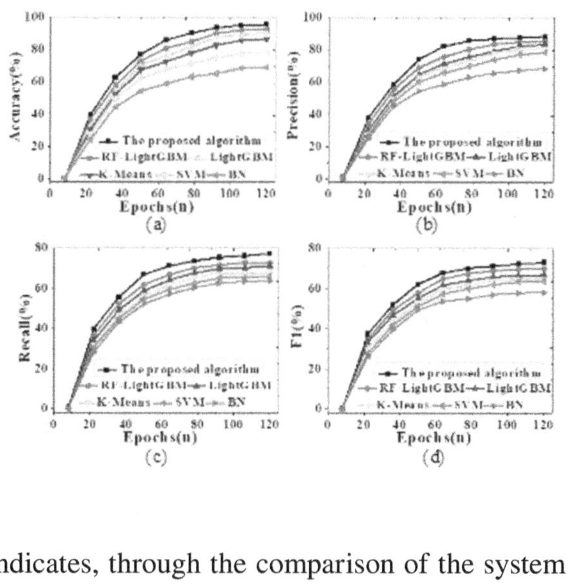

As Figure 6 indicates, through the comparison of the system model proposed here with other DM algorithms from Accuracy, Precision, Recall and F1, results indicate that the recognition accuracy reaches 95.46% of the model proposed here, which is 3.06% higher than that of the models and algorithms proposed by other scholars at least. Further comparison from three angles of Precision, Recall and F1 suggests that the Precision, Recall and F1 of the model algorithm are 88.17%, 77.22% and 73.05%, respectively. Through a comparison between the model with other algorithms, a conclusion can be drawn that the Precision, Recall and F1 of the model algorithm are higher, at least 2.79% higher than those of other algorithms. Furthermore, through a comparison between the model algorithm proposed here with other algorithms proposed by other relevant scholars the K-means algorithm combined with RF-LightGBM algorithm used in the risk audit model of e-commerce enterprises constructed here has better classification accuracy of transaction data of e-commerce enterprises.

Figure 7. Curves of comparison of different algorithms' acceleration ratio (a. pre-processing; b. training; c. test)

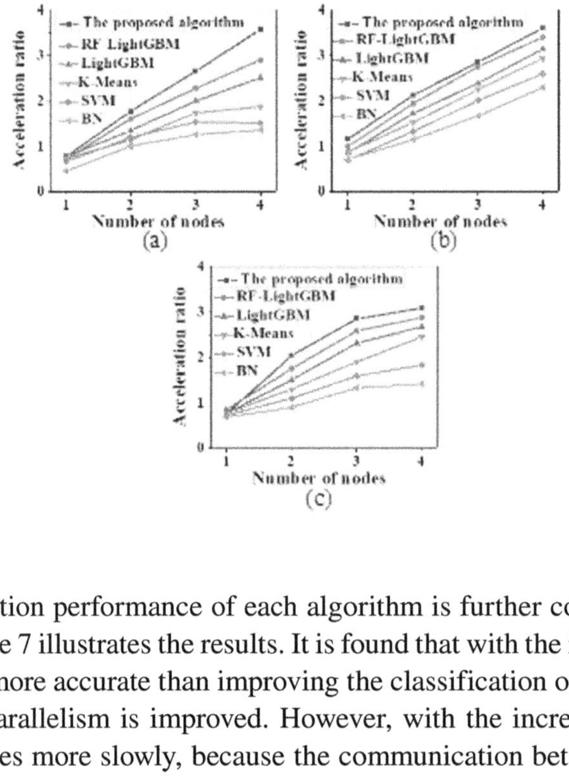

The acceleration performance of each algorithm is further compared and analyzed, and Figure 7 illustrates the results. It is found that with the increase of nodes, acceleration is more accurate than improving the classification of data blocks, and the degree of parallelism is improved. However, with the increase of nodes, the speedup increases more slowly, because the communication between nodes takes up a certain amount of time. Furthermore, it is found that the acceleration ratio of the proposed algorithm is significantly superior to other algorithms, which indicates that the model and the algorithm constructed here can complete the classification of audit data in e-commerce enterprises more quickly.

Analysis of Models' Data Transmission Security Performance Under Different Algorithms

To study the prediction performance model constructed here, analyzation is made from the aspects of RF, LightGBM, K-Means, SVM and BN from the accuracy, precision, Recall and F1 values, respectively. Figure 8 demonstrates the results of the comparison.

Figure 8. Comparative analysis of data transmission security of audit data of e-commerce enterprises under different algorithms (a. average deliver rate; b. average leakage rate; c. average delay; d. average loss rate)

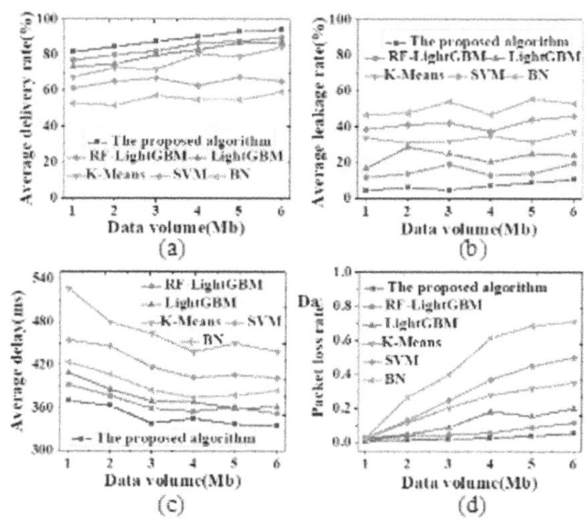

After a further analysis is carried out on each algorithm's data transmission performance. Results show that as the amount of transmitted data increases, the mean of the delivery rate of network audit data shows an upward trend, and the data message delivery rate is not less than 81.54% (Figure 8a) ; the average leakage rate of network data has no obvious change, and the data message leakage rate of this study does not exceed 10.83% (Figure 9b) ; in terms of average delay, when the transmission audit data increases, the average delay decreases, and the mean value of the delay of the model algorithm in this study is basically stable at about 344.39 ms (Figure 8c) ; in the packet loss rate analysis, it is found that BN algorithm has a higher packet loss rate, where there may be hidden terminal problems, namely, packet loss. The algorithm's packet loss rate is the lowest, less than 5.29%, which is due to the balanced processing of the transmitted data (Figure 8d). Therefore, judging by different transmission data, the risk audit model algorithm of e-commerce enterprises based on K-means algorithm combined with RF-LightGBM constructed here has prominent features in higher average delivery rate, lower delay, and lowest average leakage rate. Therefore, it has fantastic performance in data security transmission on the Internet and lowers data transmission risk of the model.

Figure 9. comparative analysis of data transmission security of each algorithm under different survival time of audit data message of e-commerce enterprises (a. average deliver rate; b. average leakage rate; c. average delay)

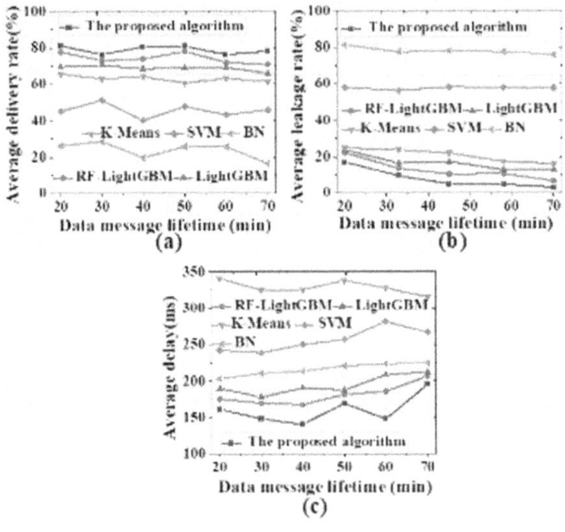

By comparing the network data security transmission performance of each mechanism algorithm under different survival time of audit data message, the results are shown in Figure 9. It can be found that with the increase in the survival time of data messages, the model algorithm in this study shows better average delivery rate and lower message leakage rate, which may be due to the fact that the model algorithm constructed in this study adopts the forwarding strategy of message fragmentation and trusted end users, while other algorithms adopt message fragmentation for security protection of messages, lacking trust evaluation of forwarding nodes or only encrypting. In terms of the average delay, the algorithm in this study shows that with the increase of the survival time of the risk audit data message, the average delay gradually increases, and the average delay of the model algorithm in this study is basically stable at about 148.04 ms.

CONCLUSION

In the era of e-commerce, the traditional methods of risk audit of traditional enterprises cannot meet the need in the face of paperless transactions in e-commerce enterprises. The desensitization transaction data of JD.com is taken as an example. In view of the paperless status of electronic payment in the transaction process of e-commerce enterprises, the K-means clustering algorithm is integrated with the RF algorithm in the ML algorithm to construct the risk audit model of e-commerce enterprises based on K-means algorithm and RF-LightGBM. Finally, through simulation, it is found that the classification accuracy of the model algorithm constructed here reaches 95.46%, and the packet loss rate, data message leakage rate and average delay are lower than those of other model algorithms, which provides experimental accordance for the safety improvement and risk control of the audit process in e-commerce enterprises. The business data of Jingdong Mall is adopted to establish a risk audit model of e-commerce enterprises, indicating that the model is applicable to e-commerce enterprises. However, there is some shortcomings in current research. For example, if the optimized risk audit classification model is directly applied to the risk audit data of insurance companies and other regions, whether it can ensure such a high accuracy remains to be considered. The research is of great significance for the future application of DM in risk audit of e-commerce enterprises.

REFERENCES

Abd Hamid, N., Ibrahim, N. A., Ibrahim, N. A., Ariffin, N., Taharin, R., & Jelani, F. A. (2019). Factors affecting tax compliance among Malaysian SMEs in e-commerce business. *International Journal of Asian Social Science*, 9(1), 74–85. DOI: 10.18488/journal.1.2019.91.74.85

Alekseeva, I. V., & Mosentseva, V. A. (2020). Methodological Approaches to Establishing the System of Internal Control in Agricultural Companies. Accounting. Analysis. *Auditing*, 7(5), 69–79.

Amani, F. A., & Fadlalla, A. M. (2017). Data mining applications in accounting: A review of the literature and organizing framework. *International Journal of Accounting Information Systems*, 24, 32–58. DOI: 10.1016/j.accinf.2016.12.004

Ashraf, N., Ahmad, W., & Ashraf, R. (2018). A comparative study of data mining algorithms for high detection rate in intrusion detection system. Annals of Emerging Technologies in Computing (AETiC), Print ISSN, 2516-0281.

Cheng, S., Jianfu, S., Alrasheedi, M., Saeidi, P., Mishra, A. R., & Rani, P. (2021). A New Extended VIKOR Approach Using q-Rung Orthopair Fuzzy Sets for Sustainable Enterprise Risk Management Assessment in Manufacturing Small and Medium-Sized Enterprises. *International Journal of Fuzzy Systems*, •••, 1–23.

Didimo, W., Grilli, L., Liotta, G., Menconi, L., Montecchiani, F., & Pagliuca, D. (2020). Combining network visualization and data mining for tax risk assessment. *IEEE Access : Practical Innovations, Open Solutions*, 8, 16073–16086. DOI: 10.1109/ACCESS.2020.2967974

Eremeev, M. A., & Zakharchuk, I. I. (2020). A Procedure for Improving Information System Audit Quality by Enhancing Cyberthreat Simulation in Practice. *Automatic Control and Computer Sciences*, 54(8), 854–859. DOI: 10.3103/S0146411620080118

Grover, D., Bauhoff, S., & Friedman, J. (2019). Using supervised learning to select audit targets in performance-based financing in health: An example from Zambia. *PLoS One*, 14(1), e0211262. DOI: 10.1371/journal.pone.0211262 PMID: 30695057

Gui, G., Liu, F., Sun, J., Yang, J., Zhou, Z., & Zhao, D. (2019). Flight delay prediction based on aviation big data and machine learning. *IEEE Transactions on Vehicular Technology*, 69(1), 140–150. DOI: 10.1109/TVT.2019.2954094

Hanggraeni, D., Ślusarczyk, B., Sulung, L. A. K., & Subroto, A. (2019). The impact of internal, external and enterprise risk management on the performance of micro, small and medium enterprises. *Sustainability (Basel)*, 11(7), 2172. DOI: 10.3390/su11072172

Huang, Y., Chai, Y., Liu, Y., & Shen, J. (2018). Architecture of next-generation e-commerce platform. *Tsinghua Science and Technology*, 24(1), 18–29. DOI: 10.26599/TST.2018.9010067

Jiang, J., & Chen, J. (2021). Framework of Blockchain-Supported E-Commerce Platform for Small and Medium Enterprises. *Sustainability (Basel)*, 13(15), 8158. DOI: 10.3390/su13158158

Kanagaraj, R., Rajkumar, N., & Srinivasan, K. (2021). Multiclass normalized clustering and classification model for electricity consumption data analysis in machine learning techniques. *Journal of Ambient Intelligence and Humanized Computing*, 12(5), 5093–5103. DOI: 10.1007/s12652-020-01960-w

Lakshmi, K. N., Neema, N., Muddasir, N. M., & Prashanth, M. V. (2020). Anomaly Detection Techniques in Data Mining—A Review. Inventive Communication and Computational Technologies, 799-804.

Li, Y., Yan, C., Liu, W., & Li, M. (2018). A principle component analysis-based random forest with the potential nearest neighbor method for automobile insurance fraud identification. *Applied Soft Computing*, 70, 1000–1009. DOI: 10.1016/j.asoc.2017.07.027

Li, Z., & Liu, Y. (2017). A differential game-theoretic model of auditing for data storage in cloud computing. *International Journal on Computer Science and Engineering*, 14(4), 341–348.

Liou, J. J., Chang, M. H., Lo, H. W., & Hsu, M. H. (2021). Application of an MCDM model with data mining techniques for green supplier evaluation and selection. *Applied Soft Computing*, 109, 107534. DOI: 10.1016/j.asoc.2021.107534

Lv, Z., Qiao, L., & Singh, A. K. (2020). Advanced machine learning on cognitive computing for human behavior analysis. *IEEE Transactions on Computational Social Systems*, 8(5), 1194–1202. DOI: 10.1109/TCSS.2020.3011158

Nawaiseh, A. K., Abbod, M. F., & Itagaki, T. (2020). Financial Statement Audit using Support Vector Machines, Artificial Neural Networks and K-Nearest Neighbor: An Empirical Study of UK and Ireland. International Journal of Simulation—Systems. *Science & Technology*, 21(2), 1–8.

Pal, A. K., Rawal, P., Ruwala, R., & Patel, V. (2019). Generic disease prediction using symptoms with supervised machine learning. *Int. J Sci. Res. Comput. Sci. Eng. Inf. Technol*, 5(2), 1082–1086. DOI: 10.32628/CSEIT1952297

Ping, P., Qin, W., Xu, Y., Miyajima, C., & Takeda, K. (2019). Impact of driver behavior on fuel consumption: Classification, evaluation and prediction using machine learning. *IEEE Access : Practical Innovations, Open Solutions*, 7, 78515–78532. DOI: 10.1109/ACCESS.2019.2920489

Rani, L. N., Defit, S., & Muhammad, L. J. (2021). Determination of Student Subjects in Higher Education Using Hybrid Data Mining Method with the K-Means Algorithm and FP Growth. *International Journal of Artificial Intelligence Research*, 5(1), 91–101. DOI: 10.29099/ijair.v5i1.223

Shad, M. K., Lai, F. W., Fatt, C. L., Klemeš, J. J., & Bokhari, A. (2019). Integrating sustainability reporting into enterprise risk management and its relationship with business performance: A conceptual framework. *Journal of Cleaner Production*, 208, 415–425. DOI: 10.1016/j.jclepro.2018.10.120

Wu, M., & Moon, Y. (2018). DACDI (Define, Audit, Correlate, Disclose, and Improve) framework to address cyber-manufacturing attacks and intrusions. *Manufacturing Letters*, 15, 155–159. DOI: 10.1016/j.mfglet.2017.12.009

Xu, Y., Du, B., Zhang, L., Cerra, D., Pato, M., Carmona, E., Prasad, S., Yokoya, N., Hansch, R., & Le Saux, B. (2019). Advanced multi-sensor optical remote sensing for urban land use and land cover classification: Outcome of the 2018 IEEE GRSS data fusion contest. *IEEE Journal of Selected Topics in Applied Earth Observations and Remote Sensing*, 12(6), 1709–1724. DOI: 10.1109/JSTARS.2019.2911113

Yang, B., & Liao, Y. M. (2021). Research on enterprise risk knowledge graph based on multi-source data fusion. *Neural Computing & Applications*, •••, 1–14.

Yang, J. C., Chuang, H. C., & Kuan, C. M. (2020). Double machine learning with gradient boosting and its application to the Big N audit quality effect. *Journal of Econometrics*, 216(1), 268–283. DOI: 10.1016/j.jeconom.2020.01.018

Zhang, F., & Yang, Y. (2021). Trust model simulation of cross border e-commerce based on machine learning and Bayesian network. *Journal of Ambient Intelligence and Humanized Computing*, •••, 1–11.

Zhao, J., Lu, Y., Ban, H., & Chen, Y. (2020). E-commerce satisfaction based on synthetic evaluation theory and neural networks. *International Journal on Computer Science and Engineering*, 22(4), 394–403.

Zhu, L. (2020). Analysis and Research of Enterprise Information System Security Based on e-Commerce. *Academic Journal of Computing & Information Science*, 3(3), 1–9.

Zuo, X., Chen, Z., Dong, L., Chang, J., & Hou, B. (2020). Power information network intrusion detection based on data mining algorithm. *The Journal of Supercomputing*, 76(7), 5521–5539. DOI: 10.1007/s11227-019-02899-2

Chapter 3
A New Technology of Jute Geotextiles Developed for River Bank Protection in Different Geographical Places of Bangladesh

Sharif Uddin Ahmed Rana
https://orcid.org/0000-0003-2296-6044
Paris Graduate School, France & World Talent Economy Forum, Malaysia

Adrian David Cheok
https://orcid.org/0000-0001-6316-2339
Imagineering Institute, Australia

ABSTRACT

Jute geotextiles have shown a great potential for numerous applications including civil engineering, agriculture, construction, drainage and river bank protection. The samples of jute geotextiles were supplied by Bangladesh Jute Mills Corporation (BJMC). The samples were treated with bitumen, natural additive, chemicals (resin) and copper-sulphate in the Pilot Plant Processing Division of Bangladesh Jute Research Institute (BJRI). Physical and mechanical properties of jute geotextiles (JGT) were measured at the Testing Laboratory of BJRI. It was found that tensile strength of natural additive treated jute geotextiles increased up to 38% whereas the tensile strength of bitumen treated jute geotextiles may increase up to 14% depending on the treatment conditions. It was noted that tensile strength of the copper sulphate and resin treated jute geotextiles was found insignificant. The treated jute geotextiles were used in the river bank protection in five sites of Bangladesh with a

DOI: 10.4018/978-1-6684-6641-4.ch003

view to control soil erosion.

1 INTRODUCTION

Geotextiles are permeable fabrics, association with soil, have the ability to separate, filter, reinforce, protect, or drainage. Work of geotextiles originally began in the 1950s with R.J. Barrett using geotextiles behind precast concrete seawalls, under precast concrete erosion control blocks and in other erosion control situations. He used different styles of woven monofilament fabrics. BJRI scientist, Dr. A. B.M Abdullah started research work on jute geo-textile from 1986 and jute geo-textiles were treated by bitumen only since 2011.

Geotextiles and related products have many applications and currently support many civil engineering applications including roads, airfields, railway, roads, embankments, retaining structures, canals, dams, bank protection, coastal engineering, and construction site. Usually, geo-textiles are placed at the tension surface to strengthen the soil. Geotextiles are also used for sand dune armoring to protect upland coastal property from storm surge, wave action and flooding. A large sand-filled container (SFC) within the dune system prevents storm erosion from proceeding beyond the SFC. Using a sloped unit rather than a single tube eliminates damaging scour.

Geo-textiles are typically made from polymers (polypropylene or polyester) and may be knitted, woven, or heat-bonded, depending on the application. They are extremely strong and durable, and have permeable traits to allow water to pass.

There are certain associated problems as well. There is slow but sure depletion of the valuable source warranting its controlled use. There is thus an unabated rise in prices of the raw materials as a result which in turn makes geo-textiles expensive. It has been proven through a number of field trials that the DW type Jute geotextiles are applicable for rural road construction and river bank protection (Khan, 2009). Therefore, there is a need to search for eco-friendly, renewable, abundantly available, and economically viable alternatives.

Jute and jute products are not only environmentally friendly but also their wider application protects against environmental degradation and even soil and climate deterioration reducing carbon-foot print and water-foot print. Jute Geotextiles is a green technology currently drawing global attraction as regard rapid climate change and global warming is focused as major challenge of 21st century for sustainable and eco-friendly development (Abdullah, 2016).

1.1 Natural Fiber for Geotextiles

Fiber would be suitable for manufacturing geo-textiles when (a) It possesses suitable mechanical properties and, in some cases, along with good hydraulic properties and (b) It is reasonably resistant to bio-degradation (Basu *et al.,* 2009). Natural fibers can be of vegetable, animal, or mineral origin. Geotextile made if natural fibers can compete with synthetic material in many applications because of their lower price, "environment-friendly" character and superior mechanical properties. The different characteristics of the various natural fibers used in geo-textiles make certain types more suitable than others geo-textiles in specific applications. For instance, geo-textiles made of softer fibers such as jute may have a shorter lifetime than fabrics made of hard fibers such as coir because of a difference in their biodegradable properties. The important vegetable fibers which are either in use or have potential to be used as raw material for geo-textiles are jute, coir, sisal, flax, kenaf, abaca, pineapple etc.

1.2 Jute Geotextiles

Jute is composed of cellulose (63%), hemicelluloses (20-22%), lignin (12-14%), fats and wax (0.4-0.8%), mineral materials (0.6-1.2%), tannin and coloring pigments. Jute is biodegradable natural fiber with high initial strength and excellent drapability, and from a polyfunctional point of view, its application in the form of geo-textile material in various erosion control measures is clearly very significant. From different reports and articles, it is clear that jute has better mechanical properties (desirable for reinforcement application) and more hygroscopic (desirable for drainage) than the conventional polypropylene and polyester fibers (generally prepared from recycled polymers) used for manufacturing geo-textiles. Biodegradability is considered by some as a disadvantage. This is to be borne in mind that all geotextiles act as catalyst the process of improving engineering properties of soil. An effective life span of two season cycles is found to be sufficient for natural consolidation of soil known as "filter cake" formation from extensive laboratory tests by leading academics and field trials. Bioderagadability of jute Geotextiles (JGT) is, therefore, not a discouraging factor.

In this research work, the hessian jute fabrics were collected from Bangladesh Jute Mills Corporation (BJMC). These jute fabrics were treated with different chemical solutions under room temperature in order to increase their mechanical properties. Subsequently, a comparison was made between the physical and mechanical properties of these treated jute fabrics generally known as jute geotextilles (JGT). These jute geotextilles were potentially used to protect the river embankment. Therefore, the main objective of the present article is to find out the suitable chemicals to treat the jute geotextilles and analyze the mechanical properties of the treated jute geotextilles.

2 MATERIALS AND METHODS

2.1 Materials

Double Warp (DW) plain weave Jute Geo-textile of 627 gsm was supplied by Bangladesh Jute Mills Corporation (BJMC) for JGT field trial application. Bitumen, copper sulphate, natural additives (Latex Solution and *Diospyros embryopteris Pers)* and other chemicals (resin) were used in this study. This study was conducted at Hatirjeel project, Dhaka which was implemented by Special Work Organization (SWO) of Bangladesh Army.

2.2 Treatment of Jute geotextiles

The collected jute fabrics were treated with the above-mentioned chemical using suitable material and liquor ratio by using padding machine. Subsequently, the treated samples were dried in open air and packed.

2.3 Thickness and Mass Per Unit Area (g/m^2) Determination of the Treated Jute Geotextiles

The thickness of the treated jute geotextiles was measured by digital thickness gauge. The mass per unit area of the jute geotextiles was measured based on ASTM standards. Sample dimensions of 30 cm $\times$ 30 cm were cut for conditioning and the weight of the conditioned sample was measured on a precision balance. An average of five readings for each sample was taken for determining the mass per unit area (g/m^2) of jute geotextile sample.

2.4 Determination of Tensile Properties of the Treated Jute Geotextiles

Tensile strength and elongation at break of the treated jute geotextiles were determined in both warp and weft directions using tensile strength tester according to ASTM standards. All the samples have been tested in standard atmospheric conditions (21$\pm$2) $^\circ$C and 65 $\pm$ 5% relative humidity. An average of five readings for each sample both in Warp and Weft directions was calculated.

2.5 Location

In this study firstly, natural additive treated JGT sample of 200 meter was implemented at Hatirjeel project, Dhaka by Special Work Organization (SWO) of Bangladesh Army. Bitumen treated woven JGT of 627 gsm was used in Pathoraj river bank, Panchagarh in July, 2011 and in MBR channel river bank, Gopalganj in 2013. Natural additive treated JGT of 627 gsm was used in Gorai river bank, Baliakandi, Rajbari in June 2013 and bitumen, resin, copper sulphate and natural additive treated JGT of 627 gsm were used in Ghagot river bank adjacent to Rangpur Cantonment, Rangpur in May, 2014. Executive Agencies of this JGT are BWDB and Bangladesh Army JGT used in River Bank Protection was designed by Bangladesh Water Development Board (BWDB).

3 RESULTS AND DISCUSSION

The different physical and mechanical properties were tested for untreated and different treated Jute geotextiles. Total amount of jute geotextiles treated in BJRI during last four consecutive years were shown in Table 1.

Table 1. Jute geotextiles processed by BJRI (Various treatments)

Year	Jute fabric processed (yards)
2011	12000
2012-2013	12500
2013-2014	11500
2014-2015	9500
Total	46000

Yarn densities of different jute fabrics used as geotextiles were shown in Figure 1.

Figure 1. Yarn densities of different jute fabrics used as geotextiles

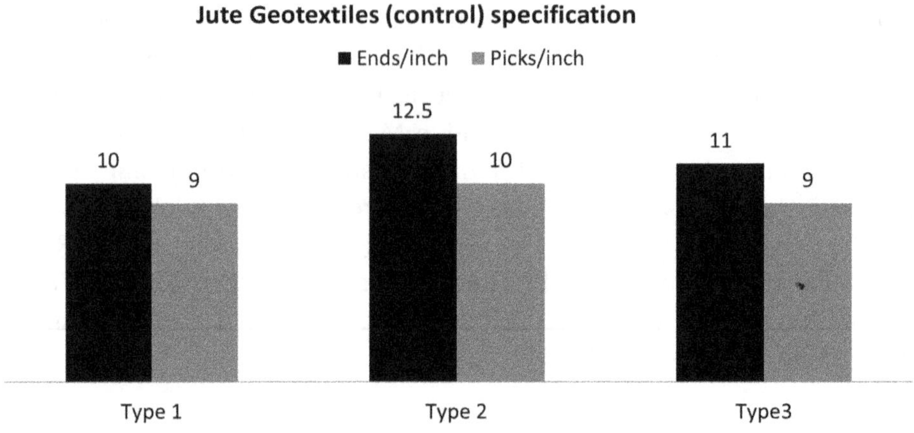

The mass per unit area and thickness of jute geotextiles are shown Table 2. From Table 2, it was revealed that mass per unit area (g/m^2) and thickness has changed significantly after treating the jute geotextiles with different chemicals.

Table 2. Typical gm/square meters and thickness of Jute geotextiles

Samples ID	Gram/square metre (g/m^2)	Thickness (mm)
Untreated/Control	627	1.45
Bitumen treated	950	1.77
Chemical (resin) treated	660	1.69
Natural Additive treated	675	1.69
Copper sulphate treated	665	1.61

Figure 2. Thickness variation of different treated and untreated jute geotextiles

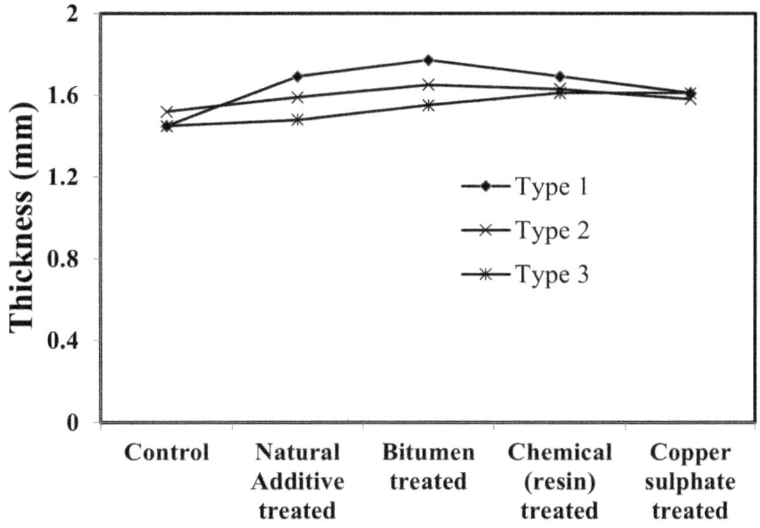

The tensile strength and elongation at break of jute geotextiles in both warp and weft directions are illustrated in Table 3.

Table 3. Typical tensile strength and elongation percentage of Jute geotextiles

Sample ID	Tensile strength (lbs)		Elongation at break (%)	
	Warp wise	Weft wise	Warp wise	Weft wise
Untreated/Control	210	165	17.50	20.85
Bitumen treated	240	180	21.50	20.00
Chemical (resin) treated	212	170	13.75	10.00
Natural Additive treated	290	229	25.75	23.00
Copper sulphate treated	230	160	14.00	23.75

From the Table 3 it was revealed that tensile strength in warp direction of natural additive treated jute geo-textile was increased significantly (up to 38%), whereas the tensile strength of bitumen treated jute geotextile was increased up to 14% depending on the treatment condition. Similarly, the tensile strength in weft direction of natural additive treated jute geo-textile was increased up to 39%, and the tensile strength of bitumen treated jute geotextile was increased up to 9%. It is noted that tensile strength of the copper sulphate and chemicals (resin) treated jute geotextiles has not shown any significant improvement.

The graphical presentation of tensile strength in both warp and weft directions are depicted in Figures 3 and 4.

Figure 3. Warp wise tensile strength of different treated and untreated jute geotextiles

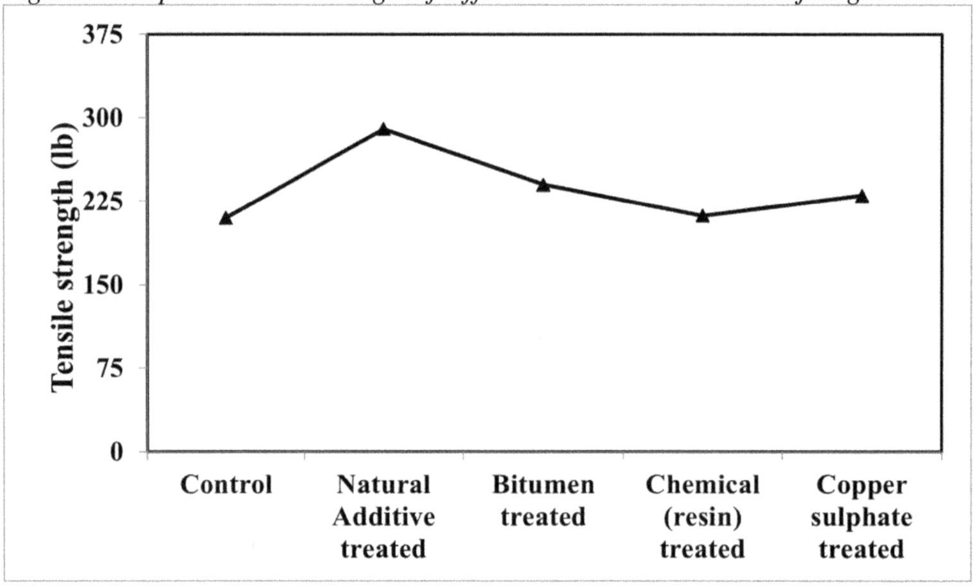

Figure 4. Weft wise tensile strength of different treated and untreated jute geotextiles

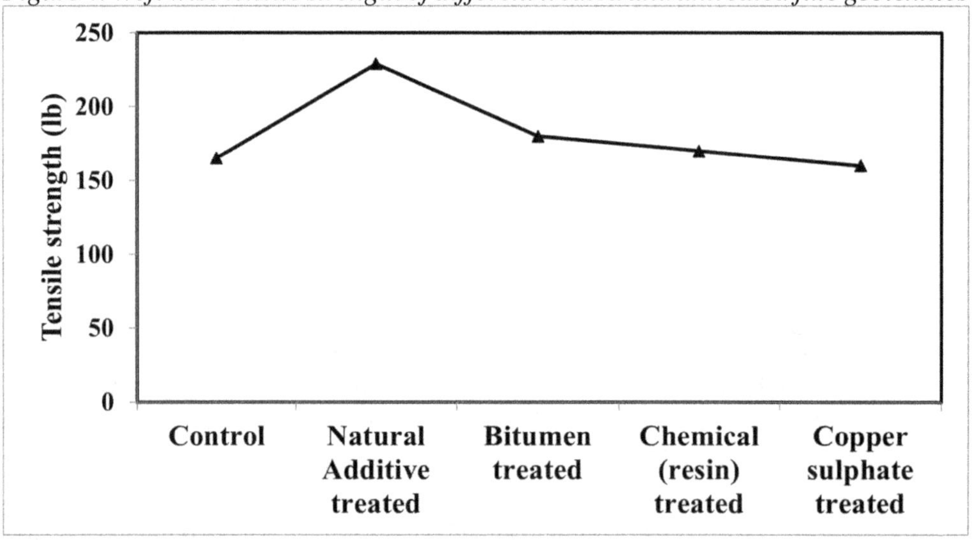

In general, it has been observed that the tensile strength in the warp direction was much higher than the tensile strength in the weft direction due to the better quality yarn used in the geotextle sample. However, the maximum magnitude of the tensile strength in the warp direction was obtained in natural additive treated jute geotextiles. The graphical presentation of elongation at break in both warp and weft directions are also shown in Figures 5 and 6.

Figure 5. Warp wise elongation percentage of different treated and untreated jute geotextiles

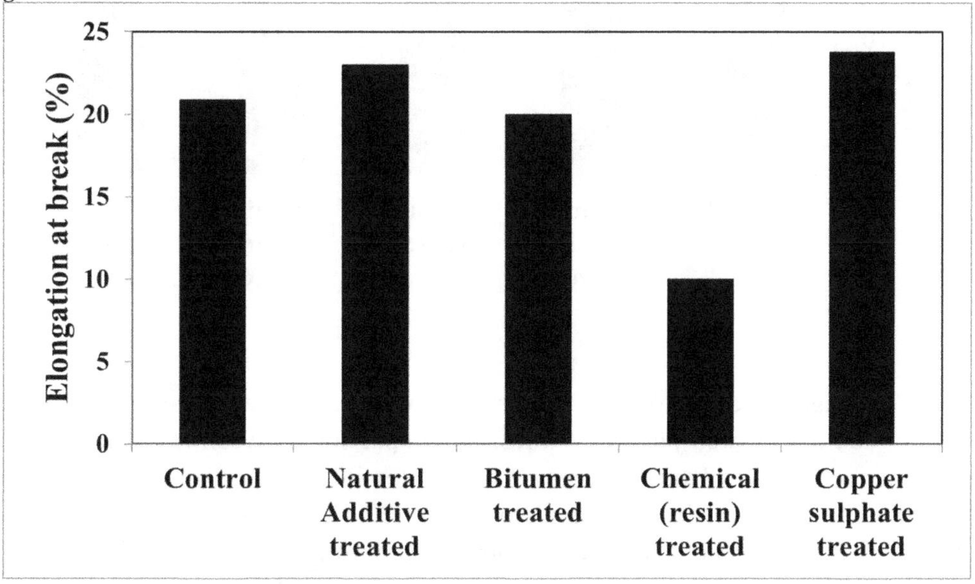

Figure 6. Weft wise elongation percentage of different treated and untreated jute geotextiles

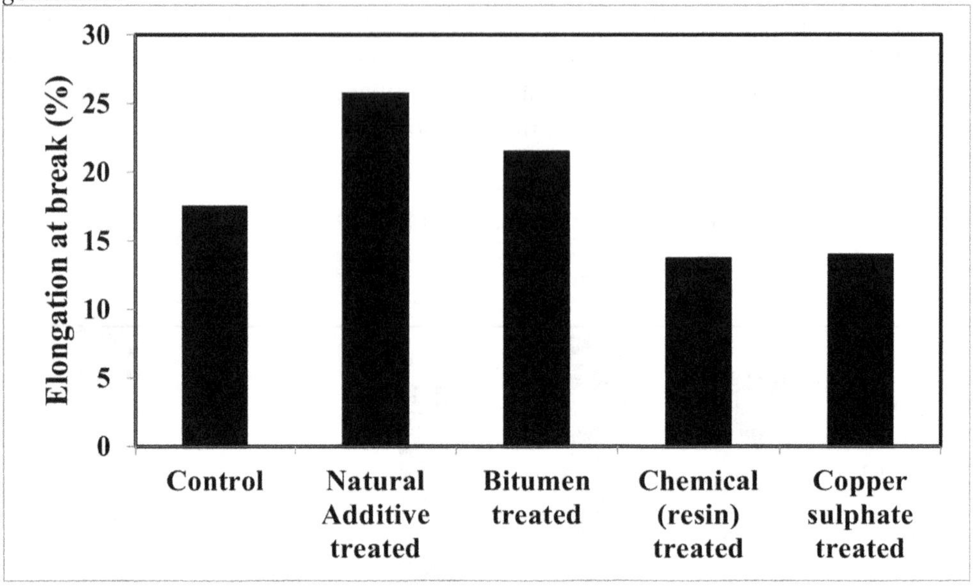

The elongation at break in warp direction was also increased significantly in natural additive treated jute geotextiles. A comparison between the longevity of untreated (control) and different treated Jute geotextiles are shown in Table 4. From the table it is observed that in general, longevity of different treated Jute geotextiles has increased significantly than that of untreated (control) Jute geotextiles. Specially, natural additive treated jute geotextiles exhibit the best performance in comparison to other treated jute geotextiles.

Table 4. Longevity of untreated (control) and different treated Jute geotextiles

Type A	Duration (Months)	Type B	Duration (Months)	Type C	Duration (Months)	Hygienic	Environment friendly
Control 1	3	Control 2	1-3	Control 3	<3	Hygienic	Eco-friendly
Natural Additive A1	36-42	Natural Additive A2	36-42	Natural Additive A3	36-42	Hygienic	Eco-friendly
Bitumen B1	36	Bitumen B2	36	Bitumen B3	36	Non Hygienic	Non Eco-friendly

continued on following page

Table 4. Continued

Type A	Duration (Months)	Type B	Duration (Months)	Type C	Duration (Months)	Hygienic	Environment friendly
Chemical (resin) C1	9-15	Chemical (resin) C2	9-15	Chemical (resin) C3	9-15	Non Hygienic	Non Eco-friendly
Copper sulphate treated D1	6-12	Copper sulphate treated D2	6-12	Copper sulphate treated D3	6-12	Hygienic	Eco-friendly

The evidence of longevity of natural additive treated jute geotextiles has been shown in Figures 7-10.

Figure 7. Various activities of natural additive treated JGT and other types of treated Jute geotextiles at Gorai river bank site, Baliakandi, Rajbari during the year 2013

Figure 8. Application of natural additive treated jute geotextiles at Gorai river bank, Baliakandi, Rajbari (Visited on 30th April 2016)

Figure 9. Application of natural additive treated jute geotextiles at Ghaghot river bank adjacent to Rangpur Cantonment, Rangpur (Visited on 25th May 2016)

Figure 10. Application of natural additive treated jute geotextiles at Ghaghot river bank adjacent to Rangpur Cantonment, Rangpur (Visited on 25th May 2016)

4 CONCLUSIONS

Jute geotextile is one of the most important diversified jute products with a potentially large-scale application. It can have several applications such as: soil erosion control, vegetation consolidation, agro mulching, reinforcement, and protection of riverbanks and embankments, land reclamation and in road pavement construction. The demand for jute geotextiles is increasing in various parts of the world. However, the absence of adequate awareness and standards and specifications seem to be affecting the possible expansion of the market. Jute geotextiles would need to meet to satisfy environmental and geotechnical engineers. The obvious results in erosion control were generally known, but it was interesting to note that composite products involving jute in combination with synthetics, or jute together with coir, can offer optimum solutions in other areas. Some applications are clearly suited to jute, but the material characteristics need more elaboration. Jute geotextiles were treated with bitumen, chemicals (resin), copper sulphate and natural additives. The physical and mechanical properties of untreated and different treated Jute Geotextiles were determined to evaluate the performance of Jute geotextiles.

- From the study it was revealed that tensile strength in warp direction of natural additive treated jute geo-textile were increased up to 38%, whereas the tensile strength of bitumen treated jute geotextile were increased up to 14% depending on the treatment condition.

- It is noted that tensile strength of the copper sulphate and other chemical (resin) treated jute geotextiles has not shown any significant improvement.
- The treated jute geotextiles were used in the construction of river embankment in different places of Bangladesh with a view to control soil erosion.
- The life span of the used jute geotextiles was found satisfactory.
- For river bank protection works 19% reduction in initial cost reduction from Man- made Geotextiles.

REFERENCES

Basu, G., Roy, A. N., Bhattacharyya, S. K., & Ghosh, S. K. (2009). Construction of unpaved rural road using jute–synthetic blended woven geotextile–A case study. *Geotextiles and Geomembranes*, 27(6), 506–512. DOI: 10.1016/j.geotexmem.2009.03.004

Chapter 4
Agribusiness Innovation: A Pathway to Development in Bangladesh

Sharif Uddin Ahmed Rana
https://orcid.org/0000-0003-2296-6044
Paris Graduate School, France & World Talent Economy Forum, Malaysia

Adrian D. Cheok
https://orcid.org/0000-0001-6316-2339
Imagineering Institute, Australia

ABSTRACT

Bangladesh is an Agro-based country. It is a great delta-comprises with hundreds of rivers, plane lands and hills. The length of its coast beside Bay of Bengal is about 1700 km. Due to its geographical location Bangladesh is always disaster prone. Flood, storm, drought, tidal search etc are the part of its existence. On the other hand the country has been ruled by the different outsider resume since long. Resulted, poverty and famine were, the long-lasting feature of the livelihoods of the people of this land. Therefore, the history of introduction of modern agriculture in Bangladesh is not too old. This history is very much related with famine and poverty. After series of famine the British Government took some steps for introducing agricultural services sector. They have established Dhaka farm and Laboratory Building in the early 1900. The Chief Minister of greater Bengal Sher-e-Bangla A K Fazlul Huq established Agriculture college in Dhaka in the year 1937 for equipping our earlier generation with modern agriculture education and research.

DOI: 10.4018/978-1-6684-6641-4.ch004

MODERN AGRICULTURE EDUCATION AND RESEARCH IN BANGLADESH: A HISTORICAL PERSPECTIVE

Historical Background

During the Pakistani era, agricultural education and research in Bangladesh made limited progress. Significant milestones included the establishment of the Agricultural University in Mymensingh in 1961 and the formation of the Directorate of Agriculture (Extension and Management), Bangladesh Agricultural Research Institute (BARI), and Bangladesh Rice Research Institute (BRRI) in 1968, 1969, and 1970, respectively. However, widespread dissemination of agricultural knowledge and technologies to farmers remained inadequate.

The real development of agriculture in Bangladesh began after its independence in 1971. The Father of the Nation, Bangabandhu Sheikh Mujibur Rahman, prioritized rapid agricultural development to ensure prosperous livelihoods for the people. His visionary leadership laid the foundation for most of the agricultural research and extension organizations that are crucial today. Within a short period, he established the essential infrastructure needed for the growth of modern agriculture, making him a pioneer in developing an integrated agricultural system in Bangladesh (Rahman, 2016).

Agricultural Extension in the Agribusiness Sector

Historically, agriculture in Bangladesh was characterized by subsistence farming. Through concerted efforts, it has now transformed into a commercial sector, or agribusiness, with over 200 types of crops being cultivated. The country is also rich in fish and animal resources. In recent decades, under the leadership of Prime Minister Sheikh Hasina, Bangladesh has made significant strides in agricultural production. Education, research, extension services, input and machinery supply systems have all contributed to enhancing agricultural productivity and ensuring food security (Hasina, 2019).

The government has set ambitious Sustainable Development Goals (SDGs), including doubling agricultural production, and ensuring the availability and accessibility of safe and nutritious food for all. However, challenges such as climate change, loss of productive land, population growth, changing food systems, and labor shortages persist. Addressing these issues requires strengthening agricultural education, research, extension, and marketing systems to identify and bridge existing gaps (Ministry of Agriculture, 2020).

Future Directions for Improvement

As subsistence agriculture transitions into agribusiness, there is a need for new extension roles that expedite this transformation. Emphasis should be placed on increasing agricultural productivity, commercialization, climate risk management, production of nutritious and safe food, post-harvest management, and the use of advanced technology and mechanization. Moreover, promoting good agricultural practices, organic agriculture, and increasing women's participation in agriculture are essential for sustainable growth. Utilizing Information and Communication Technology (ICT) in agriculture is another priority area that can enhance the effectiveness of extension systems (Islam & Ahmed, 2018).

Current Status of Agricultural Extension Agencies

Among the various public agricultural extension agencies, only the Department of Agricultural Extension follows the guiding principles of the Agricultural Extension Policy effectively. The Department of Livestock Services and the Department of Fisheries face significant challenges due to weak organizational structures and a shortage of skilled manpower. Despite these limitations, the focus of the agricultural extension system remains on improving the livelihoods of the farming community through project-based group approaches, such as Farmer Field Schools (FFS), Integrated Pest Management (IPM) clubs, and Common Interest Groups (CIGs). However, these initiatives often struggle with sustainability and resource allocation, highlighting the need for more cohesive and long-term strategies (Ministry of Fisheries and Livestock, 2021).

To overcome the challenges facing Bangladesh's agricultural sector, there is a need for a comprehensive strategy that includes strengthening educational, research, and extension systems. By addressing the current gaps and implementing effective policies, Bangladesh can continue to build on its successes and achieve its agricultural development goals.

Among various public agricultural extension agencies, the Department of Agricultural Extension (DAE) is currently the only organization effectively adhering to the guiding principles of the Agricultural Extension Policy in Bangladesh. In contrast, the Department of Livestock Services (DLS) and the Department of Fisheries (DoF) are hindered by weak organizational structures and a persistent shortage of skilled personnel. These limitations significantly impact their ability to deliver effective extension services to the farming community (Islam et al., 2020).

Despite these challenges, the agricultural extension system remains focused on improving the livelihoods of farmers. The current approach relies heavily on project-based group methods, such as Farmer Field Schools (FFS), Integrated Pest

Management (IPM) clubs, Small Farmer Groups (SFG), Common Interest Groups (CIG), and Farmers' Organizations (FO). While these initiatives aim to address diverse goals, they often struggle with sustainability due to fluctuating funding and organizational support. Additionally, the discontinuation of various programs has led to inefficiencies and resource wastage within farming communities (Rahman & Akter, 2019).

Need for Strategic Shifts

Given the current scenario, there is a pressing need to transition from project-based group approaches to more stable and permanent farmers' organizations at the producer level, with robust market linkages. Establishing such structures would serve as the entry point for delivering comprehensive and continuous extension services, ensuring long-term support for farmers (Hossain & Ahmed, 2021).

Furthermore, there is a growing necessity to shift from farmer-centered approaches to product-centered strategies. This change is driven by the increasing demand for mechanized and commercialized agriculture, which requires focusing not just on the producers but also on optimizing the value chain of agricultural products. Adopting such strategies would facilitate better alignment with market needs, enhance productivity, and promote sustainable agricultural development (Hasan et al., 2022).

- ☐ We do not have structured coordination in between education, research, and extension organizations. Which is very needed for sharing and updating the growing issues and the way to solve the issues in the development of agriculture.
- ☐ Still our farming system is almost integrated by nature with crop, livestock, and fisheries. But we do not have formed and regular coordination. Within these disciplines, we have to adequate and effective coordination at central i.e., Ministry and Departments level, district level and upazila level.
- ☐ There are hugest gaps in organization capacities in terms of organization and skilled manpower in educational research and extension organization by introducing a regular human resources recruitment and development plan.
- ☐ We know that the private sector is growing very first in agricultural fields in Bangladesh. They have their own research and development initiatives. But here we do not have a structured coordination system with the private sector. Though our latest Agriculture policy and extension policy have given proper emphasis to working with the private sector by developing effective public private partnership.
- ☐ Many national and international NGOs are also working here in the field of enhancing better livelihoods of rural communities through improved agricul-

tural practices. Unfortunately, we have also coordination gaps. We have to overcome it through development of needful coordination with NGOs.

- ☐ Linkage within agro-processing industries, farmers, researchers and extensionits are not existing significantly. But, for value addition and diversification of processed products this linkage could play effective role which also can contribute to escape farmers from unfair price of their products.
- ☐ Role of women are being increasing in agriculture. Women farmers need to equip with production and nutrition knowledge and skill as they can play outstanding role in establishing improved agriculture in Bangladesh.
- ☐ Use of ICT in agriculture is another area we have to give emphasis for quick dissemination of agricultural information and technologies. Young and educated farmers will be interested in using the ICT for improvement of agricultural practices.
- ☐ Ones educated youth people were not interested in agricultural farming. But, now due to commercialization and mechanization in agriculture the mind set of young, educated people is being changed. Gradually they are coming and getting interested in agro-farming. Therefore, now is the time to encourage them by providing all sorts of incentives.

REFERENCES

Hasan, R., Islam, M. M., & Rahman, M. (2022). Modernizing Agricultural Extension in Bangladesh: Shifting Focus from Farmers to Products. *Journal of Agrarian Studies*, 15(3), 45–60.

Hasina, S. (2019). *Agricultural Development in Bangladesh: Achievements and Future Directions*. Government of Bangladesh Press.

Hossain, M. A., & Ahmed, S. (2021). *Strengthening Agricultural Extension Services in Bangladesh: A Need for Structural Reforms*. Bangladesh Agricultural Research Institute.

Islam, M. M., & Ahmed, S. U. (2018). *Transformation of Agriculture in Bangladesh: Role of Education and Extension*. Bangladesh Agricultural Research Council.

Islam, M. S., Rahman, A., & Khan, M. H. (2020). *Challenges and Opportunities in Agricultural Extension in Bangladesh*. Ministry of Agriculture.

Ministry of Agriculture. (2020). *Agricultural Extension Policy: A Framework for Sustainable Agricultural Development*. Government of Bangladesh.

Ministry of Fisheries and Livestock. (2021). *Annual Report on Agricultural Extension Services*. Government of Bangladesh.

Rahman, M. A. (2016). *Bangabandhu and the Agricultural Revolution of Bangladesh*. University Press Limited.

Rahman, M. A., & Akter, N. (2019). *Assessing the Impact of Project-Based Approaches in Agricultural Extension: A Case Study of Bangladesh*. University Press Limited.

Chapter 5
Strengths and Weaknesses of National Agricultural Research Systems in Enhancing Agribusiness of Bangladesh

Sharif Uddin Ahmed Rana
https://orcid.org/0000-0003-2296-6044
Paris Graduate School, France & World Talent Economy Forum, Malaysia

Adrian D. Cheok
https://orcid.org/0000-0001-6316-2339
Imagineering Institute, Australia

ABSTRACT

Bangladesh has a well-organized National Agricultural Research System under the umbrella of the apex body-Bangladesh Agricultural Research Council (BARC). There are twelve separate agricultural research institutes to conduct research on crops, livestock, fisheries and forestry. A large number of technologies have been developed by those research institutes, and some of them have already been transferred and adopted by the farmers. Ultimate results of those technologies are visible in the farmers' fields; and the production of crops, livestock, fisheries and forestry have been increased in many folds. In one hand, Bangladesh has a number of reputed agricultural research institutes; in the other hand, those organizations have some weaknesses like lack of advanced research facilities, shortage of qualified scientific

DOI: 10.4018/978-1-6684-6641-4.ch005

manpower, inappropriate incentives for the working scientists, limited scope of short and long term foreign training for the scientists, and poor international funding for agricultural research.

I. INTRODUCTION

Agriculture remained the driving force behind the economic growth of Bangladesh during the 20th century and would continue to remain so for years in the 21st century. About 70% of the total population of Bangladesh live in the rural areas and directly or indirectly engaged in a wide range of agricultural activities. The agriculture sector, including crops, livestock, fisheries, and forest sub-sectors contributes a major share to the Gross Domestic Products (GDP), considering the contribution from rural non-farm sector driven by agriculture, the share of agriculture in total GDP is still quite high. In one hand, agriculture being the largest income and employment generating sector, its contribution towards alleviating poverty is significant. On the other hand, its role in meeting the challenge of achieving self-sufficiency in food production and fostering sustainable agricultural development is considered as the key driver for the of pro-growth strategy development is remarkable. Bangladesh is one of the most densely populated countries of the world with more than 160 million people in 147,570 square kilometer having the density of 1100 people per sq.km.

Around 70% of the people in Bangladesh are directly or indirectly employed in agricultural sector. The net cultivable area is 8.52 million hectares out of 14.76 million hectares which reflects 57.72% of the total country's area. The contribution of agricultural sector in GDP is 14.77% (2016), employs 47% of the total labor forces, cropping intensity over 192% approaching to 200%, average farm size is about 0.68 acre and more than 46 economic crops are grown in the country (BBS,2017). The farmers are engaged in crops and as well as fisheries and livestock production with a view to utilize available natural resources and improving their livelihood. Bangladesh has made a considerable achievement in Agriculture Sector especially in food grain production. Over the last four decades, cereal production has increased from about 10 million tons in 1970s to more than 39.68 million tons in 2016-17 i.e. increased about four times, although arable land decreased from 9.8 million hectares to 8.27 million hectares (FAO, 2017). Bangladesh is self- sufficient in rice and potato production but other crops like pulses, oilseeds, spices, fruits, vegetables, and other cereal crops are not sufficient as per need. Agricultural research institutes of Bangladesh have been playing significant role in developing high yielding varieties and improved management practices for different crops grown in Bangladesh.

Agribusiness is one of the most challenging businesses in the world. Bangladesh depends heavily on agriculture, but the prospects and potentials for agribusiness for this country is yet to be adequately understood, studied, and its enormous potential explored. This sector is the best as an emerging stage of development. Bangladesh cannot sustain long-run macro-economic stabilization and economic progress without having a strong agricultural sector accompanied by a dynamic agribusiness sub-sector (Ali and Islam, 2014). From a practical perspective, agribusiness may be defined as various value-adding and synergy-enhancing activities based on agro-based products along with its related upstream and downstream activities ranging from improved seed development, plowing, raising& harvesting various agricultural crops. The products processing, marketing, distribution, storage, transportation, new product development, export promotion, and many other value adding activities are under agribusiness. From this perspective, it would be obvious that agribusiness and agricultural trade may include myriads of activities mentioned above done on a commercial basis and utilizing more modern and scientific production methods and technologies. The term 'agribusiness' is important to visualize based on the following three sub-sectors: the agricultural input sector, the production sector, and the processing-manufacturing-distribution sectors, which are highly interrelated as part of a system in which the success of each part depends heavily on the proper functioning of the other two (Beierlein and Woolverton, 1991), Further, it also argue that the agricultural markets are joined together among various components of the food industry, the supply sector, the farm sector, the food marketing system, among others, within the national economy (Kohls and Uhl, 2002)

II. NATIONAL AGRICULTURAL RESEARCH SYSTEMS IN BANGLADESH

Agricultural research in Bangladesh has a long history. Farmers have been searching for better ways of growing their crops, livestock, fisheries, and forestry since organized cultivation came into existence. National Agricultural Research System of Bangladesh reached the end of the century. It is composed of over 2000 Scientists working at different research organizations. Several educational institutions are also conducting research in some fields of agricultural science. The Bangladesh Agricultural Research Council (BARC) is the apex body of the national agricultural research system. It has the responsibility to strengthen the national agricultural research capability through planning and integration of resources. The growth and development of the national agricultural research system which had taken place since independence had been planned to meet the special needs of this country. After independence, the Father of the Nation Bangobondhu Sheikh Mujibur Rahman in 1973 re-organized Agricultural research system of Bangladesh and established Bangladesh Agricultural Research Council with the aim of coordinating systematic agricultural research in the country. Under the provision of BARC Act 1996, NARS has been reorganized with BARC as the apex body with twelve agricultural research Institutes (BARI, BRRI, BJRI, BINA, BSRI, BFRI (Fisheries), BFRI (Forestry), BTRI, SRDI, BLRI, BSRTI and CDB) are the constituent units. The agricultural universities, NGOs and private sectors though not integrated but linked with NARC in terms of research collaboration.

Crop specific research institutions served the major commodities of rice (BRRI), jute (BJRI), sugar (BSRI), and tea (BTRI). Each of the primary institution under the Bangladesh Agricultural Research System had a specific mandate. Each institution is involved with a wide range of applied and adaptive research activities. Many of the activities are multi-disciplinary and inter-institutional in nature. The Bangladesh Agricultural Research Institute (BARI) is the largest and most diversified. It has primary responsibility for research in oilseeds, pulses, tuber crops, spices, wide range of vegetables, fruits, and flowers. Multidisciplinary research is conducted for different crops. There are a number of crop research centers within BARI i.e., Horticulture Research Centre, Tuber Crops Research Centre, Spices Research Centre, Wheat Research Center, Oilseeds Research Centre, and Pulses Research Centre. Very recently, in 2018 to emphasis more research on wheat and maize, a separate institute i.e., Bangladesh Wheat and Maize Research Institute (BWMRI) have been established with the head quarter in Noshipur, Dinajpur by the present government. Among the twelve research organizations including BARC, six are autonomous bodies under the Ministry of Agriculture and the remainders are under other Ministries; and two institutes BFRI (Forest) and SRDI are government departments.

A list of National Agricultural Research Organizations of Bangladesh is given below:

Figure 1. National Agricultural Research System (NARS) of Bangladesh

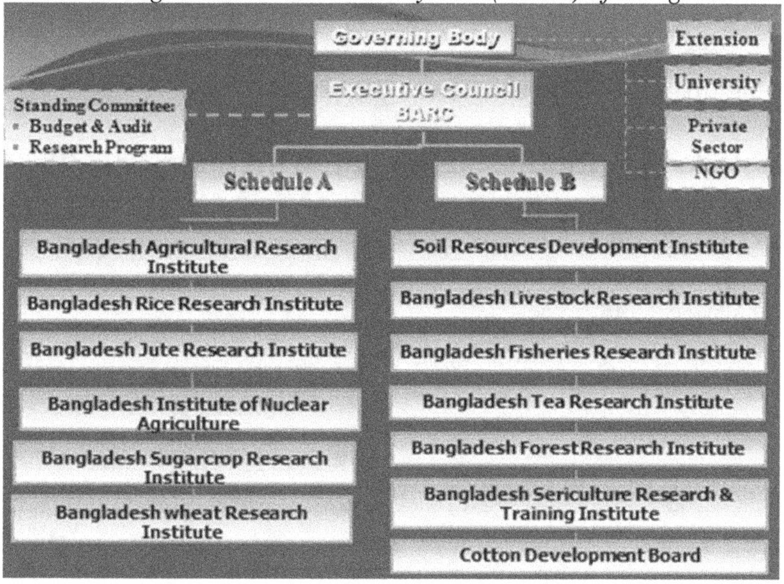

III. RESEARCH ACHIEVEMENTS OF NARS INSTITUTES

Increase of food production during the last four decades has been phenomenal. This was due to the large number of cutting-edge technologies developed by the agricultural research institutes of Bangladesh. A brief description of the developed technologies is highlighted in the following sections:

01. Bangladesh Agricultural Research Council (BARC)

- More than 50 promising technologies e.g., development of aromatic and saline tolerant rice varieties, summer tomato development and dissemination, and irrigation water management in hills etc. are developed under SPGR subprojects etc.
- Agricultural Research Management Information Systems (ARMIS) project was implemented by BARC for management of information on agricultural research conducted by different NARS and other organizations.
- Preparation of Research Priority and Vision Document-2030. This document highlights the priority areas of agricultural research and development.

- Human Research Development Plan 2009 – 2025, has been prepared for skill development of NARS scientists.
- Considering the crop suitability and efficient use of natural resources 'Crop Zoning' map for 17 crops has been developed.

02. Bangladesh Agricultural Research Institute (BARI)

- **BARI Works on 206 Crops**
- BARI Developed Total 1050 Technologies
- Crop Variety: 545
- **Other/ Non-Crop Technology**: 505

Table 1. Variety released so far from BARI

Sl. No.	Name of Crops	Varieties released
01.	Wheat, Maize, Barley etc.	78
02.	Oilseeds (Mustard, Sesame, G.nut, Soybean, inseed, Niger, sunflower)	46
03.	Pulses (lentil, Chickpea, Mungbean, Blackgram, Pigeon pea etc.)	42
04.	Tuber Crops (Potato, St. potato, Seed tubers, different types of aroids)	109
05.	Vegetables (Brinjal, Tomato, Types of gourds and types of leafy veg.).	120
06.	Fruits (Mango, Jack fruit, Banana, litchi, Amra, Papaya, Minor fruits	85
07	Flowers (Tube rose. Zerbera, gladiolus, dahlia, orchids, etc	19
08.	Spices (Onion, Garlic, Dhonia, Chilly, Turmeric, Zinger,etc	39
09.	Other crops (Narcotic, Fibre)	7
10	Total	545

03. Bangladesh Rice Research Institute (BRRI)

- Developed 89 rice varieties (HYV). BRRI dhan-28, 29 are mega varieties.
- These varieties are of different traits, (Short duration; aromatic; salt, pest & disease, drought & submergence tolerant)
- Maintains germplasm of 7000 land races in genebank
- 19 BRRI varieties are grown in 14 different countries
- Total rice Production: 35 Million (BBS: 2017)

04. Bangladesh Institute Nuclear Agriculture (BINA)

- Eighty-seven (87) varieties of different crops (rice: 18) developed.
- Varieties of pulses, oilseeds and production technologies developed using nuclear technique.

05. Bangladesh Sugarcrops Research Institute (BSRI)

- Developed 44 varieties of sugarcane (pest & disease, water logging, short duration, sugar content)
- Developed 02 varieties of sugarbeet

06. Bangladesh Jute Research Institute (BJRI)

- Developed 44 varieties of quality jute and allied crop and other technology (40 Nos.)
- Jute Genome study
- Diversified environment friendly Jute Products

07. Soil Resources Development Institute (SRDI)

- Location specific fertilizer Recommendation
- Soil health service
- Soil & Fertilizer analytical service
- Soil Survey

08. Cotton Development Board (CDB)

- Developed 15 varieties of cotton including 01 hybrid
- Rice-Cotton intercropping in the hilly areas.
- Cotton production in saline soil

09. Bangladesh Tea Research Institute (BTRI)

* 18 improved Tea clone released
    - 05 hybrid tea seed of bi-clonal and polyclonal stocks developed
    - Pruning cycle for optimum crop production determined
    - Developed appropriate pest-management technique

08. Bangladesh Sericulture Research and Training Institute (BSTRI)

- Development of 9 high yielding mulberry varieties
- Development of 28 high yielding silkworm races
- Innovated solar dryer for cocoon drying

09. Bangladesh Forest Research Institute (BFRI)

- Development of bamboo propagation technique through branch cutting.
- Preservative treatment of wood, bamboo and other thatching materials for increasing durability.
- Increment of rubber latex production by optimum fertilizer dose.
- Agar production in agar tree by artificial inoculation and wounding method.

10. Bangladesh Fisheries Research Institute (BFRI)

- Breeding & Hatchery Management of Carps
- Improved seed production & nursery management
- Breeding & seed production of important fish species, GIFT & Monosextalapia, Golda, gulsha, catfish etc.
- Carp polyculture, Cage & Pen Culture

11. Bangladesh Livestock Research Institute (BLRI)

- A total of 65 technologies on improved varieties and Feed for Animal, layer etc. have been developed.

IV. WEAKNESSES OF NATIONAL AGRICULTURAL RESEARCH SYSTEMS

Some problems of National Agricultural Research Systems are given below

1. Until today Scientific establishments (i.e., Advanced research laboratory.) with the requisite physical infrastructures and facilities are very poor. The investment trend in agricultural research in the recent past has been rather erratic. Thus, the situation reveals the lack of realistic, sustainable and systematic supportive investments in the whole agricultural research sub-sector of the country.

2. The qualified scientific manpower in the NARS institutes is very limited. Scientists having a Ph. D degree are around 35%.
3. There is no communication at all between NARS institutes and agribusiness organizations.
4. The quality of the research output has been far below what could be expected in terms of potential capabilities.
5. Inappropriate incentive structure for the working scientists. An acceptable promotion system for the NARS scientists is not yet established. Qualified and well-trained scientists are going to retirement like the other employees. Scientists' retirement age needs to be extended. Brain drain should be stopped.
6. Now- a- days, the scope of short and long term foreign training for the scientists is very limited.
7. Weak collaboration between international agencies and NARS
    7. International funding for agricultural research is much low than the past.
    8. The relationship between NARS institutes and extension agencies (public & private) is also weak.

V. ROLE OF AGRIBUSINESS IN BANGLADESH

Since independence in 1971, the country has been striving to improve economic performance and reduce poverty and to become a middle-income country. In this striving, the agricultural sector in general and agribusiness in particular has the potential to perform a number of critical roles in transforming the country in the desired direction. The sector can provide food for the rising population and the rising urban sector, generating income and employment opportunities for rural population, supplying labor as well as materials for the rising manufacturing and service sectors, providing a market for the country's growing industrial sector, and generating investable surpluses and foreign exchange earnings that could be utilized for developing the country-side as well as the entire economy. On the other hand, the industrial sector of the country can provide critical supports to the agricultural sector in the form of supplying agricultural implements, various other critical inputs (such as fertilizers), improved technology, additional agribusiness-related investments, and providing ready markets for rising agricultural and agribusiness output.

Despite significant structural transformation, the policy frame works would continue to view agriculture as an active and co-equal partner with industry and other sectors during the post-MDGs period (Mujeri, 2014). This is mainly due to two considerations: first, agriculture produces goods that directly satisfy basic human needs, and second, agriculture production combines human effort with natural resources. As such agricultural growth must match with the population growth. Moreover, the later generation dual economy models make it apparent that functions that agriculture and Industry sectors must perform are totally interdependent. The agricultural sector must release resources for industry which in turn must have the absorbing capacity. Growth can occur only if release-cum-absorption of laboratory.

If properly encouraged, promoted, and managed, agribusiness may have the potential to play a strong role in providing rural income, employment, food security, poverty alleviation, and improved external balance position, and thereby contribute to overall industrial and economic development of the country. As Bangladesh suffers from serious employment problems due to over-population and given that food availability is becoming scarcer in the country over time as population increases, income grows, and urbanization takes place, the potentials and prospects for agribusiness in the country should be viewed and explored as critical for the development of the country. As such, strategic management of agricultural business and trade is extremely important so that core competencies can be created and proper supply chain management along with vertical and horizontal integration could be established in the process of promoting and developing agribusiness in the country.

VI. AGRICULTURAL RESEARCH AND AGRIBUSINESS

High yielding varieties of different crops are developed by the Agricultural Research Institutes, but seeds are multiplied and traded by the private seed companies; Farmers collect seeds from seed stores or seed dealers. So, seed business is done by the private businessmen. In a similar way, most of the sapling or seedlings of fruits or other trees are also multiplied and marketed by private nurseries. Nursery business is also an established business in all over Bangladesh. Only a certain portion of seeds and saplings of few selected crops/fruits are multiplied and supplied by BADC. So, there should be good relationship and communication between researchers and seed business men. Fertilizer recommendation for different crops is done by agricultural researchers, but whole fertilizers business is done by private business men.

Methods of irrigation and different irrigation implements are developed by researchers. But these irrigation implements are traded by private businessmen. Other implement for cultivation of soil, intercultural operations, harvesting, threshing, cleaning and processing, packaging, are also developed by the agricultural researchers but the entire implement are also traded by private business men. All agricultural inputs, primary products, processed products and machineries are transported by the businessmen. The input supply and farm products markets are often referred to as agribusiness. Agribusiness is a generic term for the various businesses involved in food production, including farming and contract farming, seed supply, agrochemicals, farm machinery, processing, marketing, wholesale, and retail distribution (Wikepedia 2012)

So, a large number of agribusiness did by the private business men. But the relationship between researchers and agribusiness men is very poor. The relationship and communication should be closer and stronger. One can safely argue that proper development and better management of the agribusiness in the country can also improve the country's scarce natural resource utilization and help to achieve better ecological balance and environmental management. Agricultural researchers and agribusiness men come closer by visiting each other working place, inviting agribusiness men in the seminar/symposium, field day, training program and in technology demonstration program.

VII. CONCLUSION

Agricultural research institutes have been playing a significant role for the generation of new technologies for the development of crops, livestock, fishery and forestry sectors. So, steps should be taken immediately to remove the prevailing weaknesses of the national agricultural research systems. Encouragement, promotion, and management of agribusiness may have the potential to play a strong role in increasing rural income, employment, food security, poverty alleviation, and thereby can contribute to overall agricultural, industrial, and economic development of the country. Close relationship needs to be developed between agri-researchers and agribusiness men.

REFERENCES

Ali, M. M., & Islam, A. M. (2014) Agribusiness potentials for Bangladesh—an Analysis. A paper presented at the biennial Conference on 'Rethinking Political Economy of Development' held on 20-22 November 2014 organized by Bangladesh Economic Association.

BARC. (Bangladesh Agricultural Research Council) 2008.*A Portal of National Agricultural Research System.* New Airport Road, Farm Gate, Dhaka.pp.36

BBS (Bangladesh Bureau of Statistics). (2017) Statistical Year Book of Bangladesh, 36th Edition, Statistics & Informatics Division, Ministry of Planning, Govt. of Bangladesh.

Beierlein, J. G., & Woolverton, M. W. (1991). *Agribusiness Marketing- the Management Perspective*. Prentice Hall.

FAO. (2017) Country Profile-Bangladesh, the Food and Agricultural Organization of the United Nations (FAO), Rome, Italy.

Kohls, R. L., & Uhl, J. N. (2002). *Marketing of Agricultural Products* (9th ed.). Prentice Hall.

MoA. (2016-17) Annual *Report.* Government of Bangladesh (www.moa.gov.bd)

Mujeri, M. K. (2014). Vision 2030: What lies Ahead for Bangladesh in a post-MDGs World. 1st Conference organized by the Bangladesh Economist Forum at RadisonBlu, Water Garden on 21- 23June.

Wadud, M. M., Maniruzzaman, F. M., Satter, M. A., Miah, M. A. A., Paul, S. K., & Haque, K. R. (2001). *Agricultural research in Bangladesh in the 20th century. BARC.* Bangladesh and Bangladesh Academy of Agriculture.

Chapter 6
A Study on the Impacts of COVID-19 on the Work-Life Balance of Healthcare Employees

Sharif Uddin Ahmed Rana
https://orcid.org/0000-0003-2296-6044
Paris Graduate School, France

ABSTRACT

Work-life balance is an important factor that not only stimulate the job-satisfaction of employees but also it has a positive impact on employees' productivity. During this covid-19 period, healthcare employees are struggling to maintain proper work-life balance. Therefore, this study aims to investigate the impact of COVID-19 pandemic on the work-life balance of healthcare employees. This study also aims to provide certain suggestions on how to maintain work-life balance of medical staff during this hard time. Data was collected through structured questionnaire from 50 employees who are working in various hospitals in Tripura & Hyderabad. To find out the impact of COVID-19 pandemic on work-life balance of healthcare employees, Chi-square distribution method is used. Also with the same method, this study analyzed is there any association between job satisfaction of healthcare employees and covid-19 crisis. The findings of this study indicate that this pandemic situation has a negative impact on the work-life balance of healthcare employees.

DOI: 10.4018/978-1-6684-6641-4.ch006

1. INTRODUCTION

The novel corona virus has spread worldwide at a high speed after its outbreak in the month of January 2020 and within a short span of time, it has been stated by WHO that its risk of community transmission is extremely high. The novel corona-virus was formally named as 'SARS-CoV-2' through the International Committee on Taxonomy of Viruses, and sickness inflamed through this virus become known as 'COVID-19'. COVID-19 has been declared as public health emergency of global concern by the world health Organization (WHO), (Wilder-Smith, Chiew, & Lee, 2020). Within only four months after the arrival of COVID-19, more than 2,800,000 confirmed cases and almost 200,000 deaths have been reported due to SARS-CoV-2, (World Health Organization, 2019).

The surge in the number of COVID-19 patients poses an increasing demand for health workers. In these circumstances, it is expected of health workers to work for long hours while they are under huge working pressure. It has been observed that nursing staff from all parts of the world are doing overtime to tackle the COVID-19 crisis. According to statistics of Canada, nursing staffs who worked overtime, usually worked up to 5 more extra hours in every week during April & May of 2020 than 2019, (Carrière *et al.,* 2020). Indian nurses are struggling to cope up with the huge workload and spending extra time in the hospitals treating covid-19 patients (Hindustan Times, May 13, 2021). The healthcare workers are giving extra hours of service in the hospitals throughout the world. Working for longer hours than the standard hour of working sometimes poses a negative impact on the work-life balance. Work-life balance is nothing but investigates how employees manage time at work and outside work. It is an important aspect to take care of because if an employee is unable to maintain work-life balance then he or she might become unhappy and dissatisfied with his or her job.

Moreover, there is a risk of being infected when healthcare employees are dealing with COVID-19 patients. On the flip side of the coin, they are exposed to many inaccurate news, all these contribute to their increasing level of anxiety, (Schwartz, King, & Yen, 2020). There are many reports which claim that healthcare workers, who were in close contact with COVID-19 patients, became infected with corona virus, (Zhu *et al.,* 2020). Working under these circumstances broadens psychological and mental health issues, likewise emotional distress among the healthcare professionals, (Lai, Ma, & Wang, 2020) (Xiao *et al.,* 2020). A study which assessed 1257 healthcare staff treated SARS infected patients reported many issues like- feeling of uncertainty, certain threats to the life of healthcare personnel as well as increase levels of anxiety, (Chong *et al.,* 2020). These all factors have a significance when considered job satisfaction. The term job satisfaction can be explained as the feeling of self-motivation of employees to do their job willingly and happily. A self-motivated employee is always preferable by the organization because a satisfied employee tries to give his or her best to fulfil the organizational objective as well as his or her own objective. Therefore, job satisfaction is very important for both employees and employer. Research shows that a self-motivated individual is always more productive than a demotivated individual for an organization, (Adecco, n.d.). During this COVID-19 pandemics, healthcare employees are undergoing many issues related to the risk of getting infected while treating patients as well as fake news, all these might contribute to the job dissatisfaction of them. Therefore, it is always advisable for the management staff of the healthcare industry to know how to motivate healthcare employees at workplace.

Therefore, this study is carried out to assess the extent to which COVID-19 has an impact on the work-life balance and job satisfaction of healthcare employees. Moreover, several strategies are provided to improve job satisfaction and work-life balance of medical staff.

The main aim of this study is to investigate the relationship between COVOD-19 outbreak and job satisfaction of healthcare employees and to know the effects of the pandemics on the work-life balance of medical staff. The study will also reveal some important strategies which can be implement in order to maintain the effective job satisfaction of the healthcare employees at every level of the healthcare industry as well as these strategies will help to improve work-life balance of the employees who are working in public and private hospitals during this COVID-19 crisis. Knowing these strategies will help the management personnel of the hospitals and nursing homes in taking decision about the kind of policy need to implement in order to boost job satisfaction and to improve the balance between work and personal life. To do so, some objectives must be achieved which are given below-

- Analyze why work-life balance is important and its impact on the performance of healthcare employees.
- Analyze what factors contributing to work-life imbalance during COVID-19 pandemic.
- Investigates the impact of pandemic on job satisfaction of healthcare employees.
- Investigates the strategies which can be implemented in order to improve work-life balance & job satisfaction of medical staff during COVID-19 pandemic.

During the COVID-19 pandemic, due to the increasing number of patients in every hospital, the demands for healthcare workers are increasing. To treat these huge numbers of patients, often healthcare employees are doing overtime which may pose a serious impact on their work-life balance. On top of that, there are some other issues related to COVID-19 pandemic such as fake news, risk of getting infected while treating ill patients. All these are not good for the mental health of healthcare workers; it may affect the level of overall job satisfaction of them. Therefore, it is needed to take some steps in order to improve job satisfaction of employees of hospitals and other healthcare industries. In this research project we investigated certain main factors which might have an impact on the employees' work-life balance and job satisfaction in the healthcare industry during the COVID-19 outbreak. Also depending on the secondary and primary data, we have formulated some strategies which can be implemented by the employer healthcare industry in order to improve job satisfaction and work-life balance of their employees.

2. LITERATURE SURVEY

2.1. Why Work-Life Balance is Important

According to the 'spill over' theory, there is a relationship between work-life balance and employees productivity or performance. This theory mentioned that employees carry competencies, emotions, attitudes & behaviours that they develop in one domain into another domain of life, (Lakshmypriya & Krishna, 2016), and there is a alikeness between what occurs in the outside-work environment and work environment. Therefore there is a spill over in the systems and it can be of two types- positive and negative spill over, (Edwards & Rothbard, 2000). Positive spill over occurs when satisfaction and achievement in outside-work place resulted in satisfaction and achievement in work place and vice versa. Many researchers like Grywacz, Carlson, Wayne (2007) state that experiences gathered in certain activities by an individual in one domain of life can benefit his/her activities in other domain of life. On the other side of the coin, negative spill over occurs when depression and difficulties in one domain pose an affects on the emotions in another domain. During the COVID-19 pandemic, demands for healthcare workers is huge and researches have depicted job demands leads to work-life conflict and work overload, (Demerouti, Bakke, & utlers, n.d.). Hence it can be assumed that positive spill over improve performance of the employees at the workplace whereas negative spill over pose an negative impacts on the employees productivity at the workplace. Hypothesis 1: there is a strong relationship between work-life balance and employee performance.

2.2. Factors Contributing to the Work-Life of Healthcare Employees During Covid-19 Pandemic

Organizational factors that that have an negative impacts on work-life balance are hostile work environment and excessive work load, (Innerhour, n.d.). According to the study conducted by Al Thobaity A. & Alshammari F., "Nurses on the Frontline against the COVID-19 pandemic: An Integrative Review", during the COVID-19 pandemics, medical staff are facing problems due to lack of medical supplies and resources like personal proactive equipment (PPE). On the other hand, there are shortage of medical staff, depression related to related to the fear of infection and anxiety on top of that exhaustion as they are working long hours without proper nourishment. Moreover there is prevailing high demand for health workers during this pandemic. This growing biological workload (workload arises due to SARS-CoV-2) may pose an negative effects on the family life of health workers. Hypothesis 2: Covid-19 pandemic has an impact on the work-life balance of healthcare employees.

2.3. Impact of Pandemic on Job Satisfaction of Healthcare Employees

According to the study conducted by Bella Savitsky, Irina Radomislensky, and Tova Hendel, "Nurses' occupational satisfaction during Covid-19", frequency of nurses willing to find a new job was double in March 2020 in comparison with the situation before pandemic. There is a strong relationship between job satisfaction of nurses and job stress, patient-nurse ratio and work environment of the hospitals (Hong Lu et al. 2019). One study conducted in India depicted a high percentage (87.6%) in the number of nurses are experiencing job stress where 2.1% nurses had severe stress, (Chaudhari *et al.,* 2018) Likewise, another study identified 92% of the nurses experiencing stress and 52% of them had sever stress, (Shivaprasad, 2013). These results of those study indicate that work related stress among nurses are prevailing in India. One article in "fortune India" has shown that India has only three million nurses and midwives where the population is 1.3 billion, (Jaykumar, 2021). According to World Health Organization (WHO) norms there should be three nurses per one thousand population. Hypothesis 3: There is a relationship between Covid-19 pandemic and job satisfaction of healthcare employees.

2.4. Strategies to Improve Work-Life Balance and Job Satisfaction of Healthcare Employees

According to the study "Barriers to Work-life Balance for Hospital Nurses" by Kathleen Mullen, explained that nurses can learn new ways to develop a sense of balance and wellbeing. These learning will help them when they become effective at the workplace as well as these will support them to maintain their role outside the workplace which bring happiness to them. Sometime health workers face the issues related to fake news (Schwartz, King, & Yen, 2020) as well as a weak nurse-patient ratio (Jaykumar, 2021), all these requires to implement new strategies in order to give a better work environment to healthcare employees so that their job satisfaction level and work-life balance can be improve. According to the news article "keep health workers safe to keep patients safe" from WHO (World Health Organization), to protect healthcare employees from the violence at workplace there should be a culture of zero tolerance to violence against healthcare staff. In that article, it is also stated that healthcare employees should have the opportunity to get advice work-life balance. Also, sometimes giving extra responsibility to an employee helps to improve him or her motivation accordingly (Ludivine, 2011). Hypothesis 4: recruitment of extra nurses and other medical staff will improve the work-life balance of healthcare employees. Hypothesis 5: there is a relationship between proving extra nonmonetary benefits and healthcare employees job satisfaction during COVID-19 pandemic.

3. RESEARCH METHODOLOGY

Research Methodology is a way to systematically solve research problems. It can be referred to as the science of studying how research is done. It includes numerous techniques & methods to conduct research. The main intention of considering research methodology is that the reader can have a brief idea about the procedure & methods applied for the research.

RESEARCH DESIGN: Research design implies the blueprint within which the research is conducted. A descriptive research design was utilized in sporting out this study.

SAMPLING UNIT: This research included a sampling unit of healthcare workers of various public & private hospitals as well as nursing homes.

AREA OF RESEARCH: For the research the data were collected from the healthcare employees from Tripura and Hyderabad

SAMPLE SIZE: The following study was conducted for a sample size of 50 respondents.

SOURCES OF DATA: Data are the most important information which serve as the basis for analysis of a study. The following report included the use of both primary as well as secondary data.

DATA COLLECTION TOOLS, ANALYSIS TOOL & METHODS: The following study included structured questionnaire having 5-point Likert scale ranging from Strongly Agree (SA), Agree(A), Neutral (N), Disagree (D) and Strongly Disagree (SD) were used to measure the adequacy of the data. The data was collected through an online survey. The questionnaire was formed using google form and distributed to the respondents through email and WhatsApp. In this study, to represent the data we simply calculated the percentage of response in each category (SA/A/N/D/SD) as the number of responses in each category for each statement divided by total responses and then the result is multiplied by hundred. Similarly, to test the hypothesis regarding the relationship between covid-19 pandemic and work-life balance &job satisfaction of healthcare employees, we used Chi-square statistical tool.

4. RESULTS

Table 1. Presentation of data that are collected through questionnaire

Distribution Location	Number distributed	Number returned	Number of percentage rate returned
Hyderabad	20	20	40%
Tripura	30	30	60%
Total	50	50	100%

Table 2. Respondents based on gender

Gender	Response	Percentage
Male	36	72
Female	14	28

As observed in 'Table 2', from the total sample a majority of the respondents consulting 72% i.e., a total of 36 respondents were male while the remaining 28% i.e., a total of 14respondents were female.

Table 3. How long have you been working here?

Options	Response	Percentage %
0-2 years	23	46
2-4 years	12	24
4-6 years	9	18
6-8 years	3	6
More than 8 years	3	6
Total	50	100

As observed in "table 3", from the total sample a majority of the respondents consulting 46% i.e., a total of 23 respondents were working for 0-2 years and 24% of the respondents are working for 2-4 years likewise 18% i.e., a total of 9 respondents are working for 4-6 years while remaining 12% where 6% respondents are working for 6-8 years and another 6% respondents i.e 3 respondents are working for than 8 years.

Table 4. Due to the COVID-19 crisis, very often I work beyond my specified working hours

Options	Response	Percentage %
Strongly Agree	21	42
Agree	24	48
Neutral	2	4
Disagree	3	6
Strongly Disagree	-	-
Total	50	100

As per "Table 4", 42 and 48 (i.e., 21% & 24%) respondents strongly agreed and agreed respectively that very often they do overtime during the covid-19 crisis as the workload is extremely high and 2 respondents neither agreed nor disagreed with the statement. On the other hand, 3 respondents i.e., 6% respondents disagreed with the statement. This shows that majority of the respondents are doing overtime during covid-19 pandemic to reduce the workload of healthcare industries.

Table 5. My work schedule during COVID-19 pandemic does not allow me to spend quality time with my friends and family

Options	Response	Percentage %
Strongly Agree	17	34
Agree	18	36
Neutral	6	12
Disagree	7	14
Strongly Disagree	2	4
Total	50	100

As per "Table 5", 17 and 18 (i.e., 34% & 36%) respondents strongly agreed and agreed respectively that their work schedule during covid-19 pandemic does not allow them to spend quality time with their friends & family and 6 respondents i.e., 12% respondents neither agreed nor disagreed the statement whereas, 14% respondents disagreed the statement and 2 respondents, consulting 4%, strongly disagreed this viewpoint. This shows that the majority of the respondents are not able to spend quality time with their near & dear people.

Table 6. When there is a proper balance between my work and family life, I can perform efficiently at my job

Options	Response	Percentage %
Strongly Agree	20	40
Agree	29	58
Neutral	1	2
Disagree	-	-
Strongly Disagree	-	-
Total	50	100

Figure 1. Work-life balance has a positive impact on employee performance

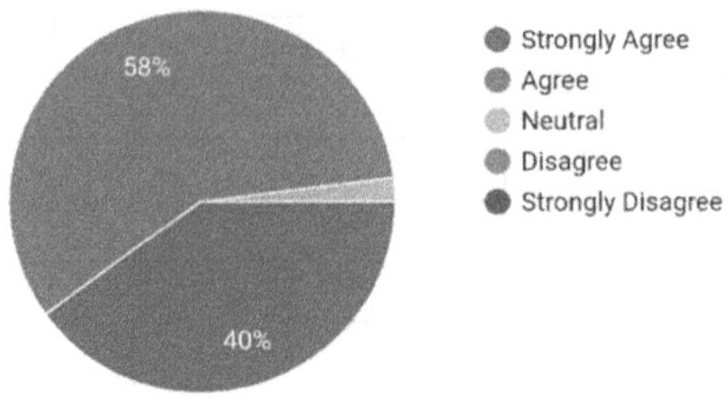

According to "Table 6", the majority of the respondents with 58% i.e., 29 respondents and 40% i.e., 20 respondents agreed and strongly agreed that Work-life balance has a positive impact on their performance. On the other hand, 2% respondents i.e., only 1 respondent neither agreed nor disagreed the statement.

Table 7. I normally feel efficient whenever I return from a leave

Options	Response	Percentage %
Strongly Agree	20	40
Agree	22	44
Neutral	7	14
Disagree	1	2
Strongly Disagree	-	-
Total	50	100

Figure 2. I normally feel efficient whenever I return from a leave

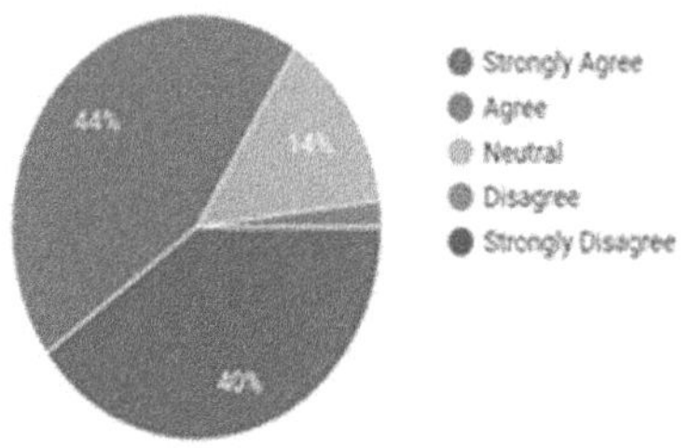

According to "Table 7", majority of the respondents with 44% i.e., 22 respondents and 40% i.e., 20 respondents agreed and strongly agreed that they feel efficient whenever they return from a leave and 14% respondents i.e., 7 respondents neither agreed nor disagreed the statement. On the other hand, 2% respondents i.e., only 1 respondent disagreed which indicated 1% respondents holds the belief that work leave has nothing to do with work efficiency.

Table 8. I feel a significant degree of psychological distress due to the increasing number of COVID-19 cases.

Options	Response	Percentage %
Strongly Agree	13	26
Agree	13	26
Neutral	8	16
Disagree	10	20
Strongly Disagree	6	12
Total	50	100

According to "Table 8", majority of the respondents with 26% i.e., 13 respondents strongly agreed and another 26% i.e., 13 respondents agreed that they are affected psychologically due to the increasing trend of covid-19 patients and 16% respondents i.e., 8 respondents neither agreed nor disagreed the statement. On the other hand, 10 respondents, which constitutes 20%, disagreed the statement likewise 6 respondents i.12% of the total respondents Strongly disagreed that there is no association between feeling of psychological distress and increasing number of covid-19 cases.

Table 9. Due to the covid-19 pandemic, I have a fear of transmitting the infection to my family after returning home from hospital/nursing home

Options	Response	Percentage %
Strongly Agree	19	38
Agree	28	56
Neutral	3	6
Disagree	-	-
Strongly Disagree	-	-
Total	50	100

According to "Table 9", majority of the respondents with 38% i.e., 19 respondents and 56% i.e., 28 respondents strongly agreed and agreed that they have the fear of transmitting the covid-19 infection to their family after returning home from the hospital/nursing home. On the other hand, 6% respondents i.e., only 3 respondents neither agreed nor disagreed with the statement.

Table 10. I think extra nursing staff is required in my hospital/nursing home in order to take care of patients which are increasing in number due to COVID-19 and it will help us to maintain balance between our work life & family life

Options	Response	Percentage %
Strongly Agree	16	32
Agree	18	36
Neutral	6	12
Disagree	10	20
Strongly Disagree	-	-
Total	50	100

Figure 3. Extra nursing staff is required

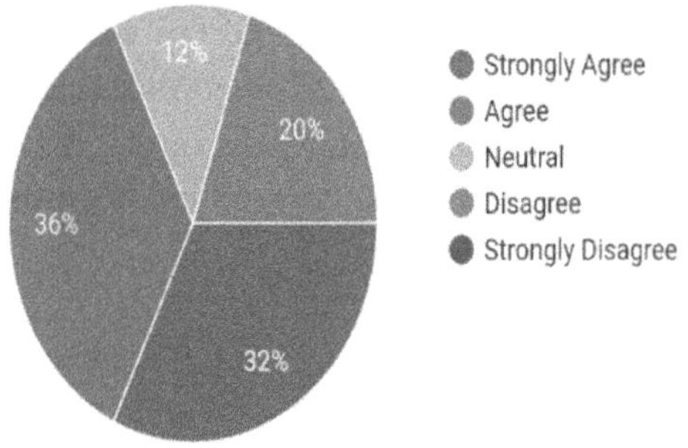

According to "Table 10", majority of the respondents with 32% i.e., 16 respondents and 36% i.e., 18 respondents strongly agreed and agreed that more nursing staff are required in the hospital/nursing home to take care of increasing covid-19 patients which will improve their work-life balance and 12% respondents i.e., 6 respondents neither agreed nor disagreed the statement. On the other hand, 20% respondents i.e., 10 respondents disagreed which indicates 20% respondents holds the belief that they have enough nursing staff in the hospital/nursing home to take care of the covid-19 patients.

Table 11. I will be very happy if I get extra recognition and rewards for outstanding performance during this covid-19 crisis

Options	Response	Percentage %
Strongly Agree	26	52
Agree	22	44
Neutral	2	4
Disagree	-	-
Strongly Disagree	-	-
Total	50	100

According to "Table 11", majority of the respondents with 52% i.e., 26 respondents and 44% i.e., 22 respondents strongly agreed and agreed that their level of happiness will increase if they are praised by the employer for their outstanding performance during this covid-19 crisis. On the other hand, 4% respondents i.e., only 2 respondents neither agreed nor disagreed with the statement.

Table 12. It will make me happy, if I get extra leave to spend quality time with my family during the Covid-19 pandemic

Options	Response	Percentage %
Strongly Agree	25	50
Agree	23	46
Neutral	1	2
Disagree	1	2
Strongly Disagree	-	-
Total	50	100

According to "Table 12", majority of the respondents with 50% i.e., 25 respondents and 46% i.e., 23 respondents strongly agreed and agreed respectively that if they get extra leave to spend time with their friends &family, it will make them feel happy and 2% respondents i.e., 1 respondent neither agreed nor disagreed the statement. On the other hand, 2% of respondents i.e., 1 respondent disagreed with the statement.

5. TESTING OF HYPOTHESES

The test was conducted with 95% confidence level and 0.05% level of significance. The Chi-square (X2) formula is

$$x^2 = \sum \frac{(O_i - E_i)}{E_i}$$

Where,
Oi = Observed frequency
Ei = Expected frequency
$\sum$= Summation

5.1. Hypothesis 1

H_0: there is no strong relationship between work-life balance and employee performance.

H_1: there is a strong relationship between work-life balance and employee performance.

-this hypothesis is tested on the basis of responses observed in the statement of work-life balance has an impact on employee performance which is mentioned in "Table 6".

Table 13. Work life balance has an impact on employee performance

	Strongly Agree	Agree	Neutral	Disagree	Strongly Disagree
Observed Frequency	20	29	1	0	1

Here, expected frequency is 10 for each option as we have taken only one question statement having 5 having 5 options to choose from for this hypothesis and total 50 despondent were there

So, 50/5 =10.
Likewise, degrees of freedom here is = k-1
Where k is total number of columns i.e., 5
So, degrees of freedom (d.f)
= 5-1
= 4

Table 14. Chi-square calculation for observed frequency vs expected frequency

O_i	E_i	$O_i - E_i$	$(O_i - E_i)^2$	$(O_i - E_i)^2 / E_i$
20	10	10	100	10
29	10	19	361	36.1
1	10	-9	81	8.1
0	10	-10	100	10
0	10	-10	100	10
TOTAL(X^2)				74.4

Table 15. Significance level

X^2	74.4
Degree of Freedom	4
P value	0.0000000001

Decision rule:

From the above Table 15, it is observed that the significance level is less than 0.05 i.e., 0.0000000001. Hence, there is sufficient evidence to reject null hypothesis. Thus, it can be concluded that there is a strong relationship between Work-life balance and employee performance.

5.2. Hypothesis 2

H_0: COVOD-19 pandemic has no impact on the work-life balance of healthcare employees.

H_1: COVOD-19 pandemic has an impact on the work-life balance of healthcare employees.

- this hypothesis is tested on the basis of responses observed in the statement related to work-life balance has impacted due to covid-19 pandemic which is mentioned in Table 5.

Table 16. Work life balance has impacted due to Covid-19 pandemic

	Strongly Agree	Agree	Neutral	Disagree	Strongly Disagree
Observed Frequency	17	18	6	7	2

Here, expected frequency is 10 for each option as we have taken only one question statement having 5 options to choose from for this hypothesis and total 50 despondent were there

So, 50/5 =10.

Likewise, degrees of freedom here is = k-1

Where k is total number of columns i.e., 5

So, degrees of freedom (d.f)

= 5-1

= 4

Table 17. Chi-square calculation for observed frequency vs expected frequency

O_i	E_i	$O_i - E_i$	$(O_i - E_i)^2$	$(O_i - E_i)^2 / E_i$
17	10	7	49	4.9
18	10	8	64	6.4
6	10	-4	16	1.6
7	10	-3	9	0.9
2	10	-8	64	6.4
TOTAL(X^2)				20.2

Table 18. Significance level

X^2	**20.2**
Degree of Freedom	4
P value	0.0004559831

Decision rule:

From the above Table 18, it is observed that the significance level is less than 0.05 i.e., 0.0004559831. Hence, there is sufficient evidence to reject null hypothesis. Thus, it can be concluded that covid-19 pandemic has an impact on the wok-life balance of healthcare employees.

5.3. Hypothesis 3

H_0: There is no relationship between Covid-19 pandemic and job satisfaction of healthcare employees.

H_1: There is a relationship between Covid-19 pandemic and job satisfaction of healthcare employees.

--this hypothesis is tested on the basis of responses observed in the statement 'I feel a significant degree of psychological distress at the workplace due to the increasing number of COVID-19 cases', which is given in "Table 8".

Table 19. Job satisfaction has impacted due to increasing number of COVID-19 cases

	Strongly Agree	**Agree**	**Neutral**	**Disagree**	**Strongly Disagree**
Observed Frequency	13	13	8	10	6

Here, expected frequency is 10 for each options & degree of freedom (d.f) is 4

Table 20. Chi-square calculation for observed frequency vs expected frequency

O_i	E_i	$O_i - E_i$	$(O_i - E_i)^2$	$(O_i - E_i)^2 / E_i$
13	10	3	9	0.9
13	10	3	9	0.9
8	10	-2	4	0.4
10	10	0	0	00
6	10	-4	16	1.6
TOTAL(X^2)				3.8

Table 21. Significance level

X^2	**3.8**
Degree of Freedom	4
P value	0.4337489957

Decision rule:

From the above Table 21, it is observed that the significance level is greater than 0.05 i.e., 0.4337489957. Hence, there is sufficient evidence to reject alternative hypothesis. Thus, null hypothesis is accepted, and it can be concluded that there is no association between COVID-19 pandemic and Job satisfaction of healthcare employees.

5.4. Hypothesis 4

H_0: There is no relationship between recruitment of extra nurse and other medical staff and improvement of the work-life balance of healthcare employees.

H_1: There is a relationship between recruitment of extra nurses and other medical staff and improvement of the work-life balance of healthcare employees.

--this hypothesis is tested on the basis of responses observed in the statement 'I think extra nursing staff is required in my hospital/nursing home in order to take care of patients which are increasing in number due to COVID-19 and it will help us to maintain balance between our work life & family life', which is mentioned in "Table 10".

Table 22. Extra medical staff is required during Covid-19 pandemic

	Strongly Agree	Agree	Neutral	Disagree	Strongly Disagree
Observed Frequency	16	18	10	6	0

Here, expected frequency is 10 for each options & degree of freedom (d.f) is 4

Table 23. Chi-square calculation for observed frequency vs expected frequency

O_i	E_i	$O_i - E_i$	$(O_i - E_i)^2$	$(O_i - E_i)^2 / E_i$
16	10	6	36	3.6
18	10	8	64	6.4
6	10	-4	16	1.6
10	10	0	0	00
0	10	-10	100	10
TOTAL(X^2)				21.6

Table 24. Significance level

X^2	21.6
Degree of Freedom	4
P value	0.0002407142

Decision rule:

From the above Table 24, it is observed that the significance level is less than 0.05 i.e., 0.0002407142. Hence, there is sufficient evidence to reject null hypothesis. Thus, it can be concluded that there is a relationship between recruitment of extra nurses and other medical staff and improvement of the work-life balance of healthcare employees.

5.5. Hypothesis 5

H_0: there is a relationship between proving extra nonmonetary benefits and healthcare employees job satisfaction during COVID-19 pandemic.

H_1: there is a relationship between proving extra nonmonetary benefits and healthcare employees job satisfaction during COVID-19 pandemic.

- this hypothesis is tested on the basis of responses observed in the statement 'I will be very happy if I get extra recognition and rewards for outstanding performance during this covid-19 crisis', which is given in "Table 11".

Table 25. Non-monetary benefits has an influence on job satisfaction

	Strongly Agree	**Agree**	**Neutral**	**Disagree**	**Strongly Disagree**
Observed Frequency	26	22	2	0	0

Here, expected frequency is 10 for each options & degree of freedom (d.f) is 4

Table 26. Chi-square calculation for observed frequency vs expected frequency

O_i	E_i	$O_i - E_i$	$(O_i - E_i)^2$	$(O_i - E_i)^2 / E_i$
26	10	16	256	0.9
22	10	12	144	0.9
2	10	-8	64	0.4
0	10	-10	100	00
0	10	-10	100	1.6
TOTAL(X^2)				66.4

Table 27. Significance level

X^2	**21.6**
Degree of Freedom	4
P value	0.0000000001

Decision rule:

From the above Table 27, it is observed that the significance level is less than 0.05 i.e., 0.0000000001. Hence, there is sufficient evidence to reject null hypothesis. Thus, it can be concluded that there is an association between extra nonmonetary benefits and job satisfaction of healthcare employees.

6. DISCUSSION

- Majority of the respondents are male, likewise a large proportion of the respondents are working for '0-2' years. Thus, it can be said that most of the sample units are new comer in this healthcare industry.
- This study denoted that COVID-19 pandemic has negative impact on the work-life balance of the healthcare professionals. Thus, it can be concluded that there is a strong association between COVID-19 pandemic & work-life balance of healthcare employees.
- Work-life balance & employees' performance is related to each other. That is to say, that there is a strong relationship between work-life balance and employee performance, which is proved in this study through analysis.
- COVID-19 pandemic has not any positive or negative influence on job satisfaction of healthcare employees as it is proved that there is no association between COVID-19 pandemic and job satisfaction of healthcare employees.
- Almost the full population of this study have the fear of transmitting the infection to their families as they are working with COVID-19 patients.
- Recruitment of new medical staff specially nurse will help to decrease the huge workload of medical industries thus it will give some relief to the existing healthcare employees from overtime work. Therefore, it will help them to improve their work-life balance which is affected because of the pandemic.
- Although there is no association between COVID-19 crisis & job satisfaction of the employees of healthcare industries, providing nonmonetary benefits to them will be a great way of improving their job satisfaction during this pandemic.
- One doctor suggests that during this covid-19 pandemic doctors who are from BAMS, BHMS, BUMS, BYNS should get the chance to contribute to the treatment of covid-19 patients during this pandemic, likewise, another doctor suggested to maintain the hygiene in the hospital during this covid-19 crisis.

7. CONCLUSIONS AND FUTURE WORK

Work-life balance is so important that it not only helps healthcare employees to maintain the equilibrium between their responsibility of the work and family but also it improves their overall productivity at the workplace. During this pandemic the workload drastically increases in the medical industry due to the increasing number of COVID-19 patients. Therefore, this study tested the impacts of COVID-19 pandemic on work-life balance and job satisfaction of healthcare employees using Chi-square distribution to test the hypothesis. The results indicated that COVID-19 pandemic has a negative impact on work-life equilibrium of healthcare employees and to reduce this impact, healthcare industry needs to recruit new medical professionals such as doctors, nurses, and other medical staff. From the findings, it can also be denoted that although COVID-19 pandemic has no impact on the job satisfaction of healthcare employees, providing nonmonetary benefits to healthcare employees will boost their motivation and job satisfaction during this hard time of pandemic.

Scopes for future study have come out as a result of this research. This research has carried out in a short period of time Where the researcher could not broaden the study and also the sample size of the respondents was limited. Therefore, the following recommendations should be considered for future research: -

- This study was conducted in a short period of time and also the sample size was limited. Therefore, it is advisable for the future research to conduct research in this regard with considering large sample size to improve the accuracy.
- More methodological work is required on how to strongly find out the impact of global pandemic on the human capital of the Organizations.

Based on this research and analysis of the impacts of COVID-19 pandemic on work-life balance and job satisfaction of healthcare employees, this study makes the following suggestions to the HR professionals of the healthcare industries: -

- To recruit new medical staff in order to reduce the huge workload of the healthcare employees.
- To focus on providing nonmonetary benefits to improve the job satisfaction of healthcare employees.
- To review the policy regarding employee leave to know whether it is possible to provide extra leave to the medical employees so that they can spend quality time with their friends and family which is needed to improve their work-life balance.
- To focus on maintaining the hygienic environment of the hospitals.

- To focus on giving chance to the BAMS, BHMS, BUMS AND BYNS doctors to take part in treatment process of COVID-19 patients as it will help to reduce the work pressure to some extent

REFERENCES

Aditi Prasad Chaudhari. (2018). Kaustubh Mazumdar.; Yogesh Mohanlal Motwani.; Divya Ramadas., "A profile of occupational stress in nurses". *Annals of Indian Psychiatry*.

Al Thobaity, A., & Alshammari, F. (2020). *Nurses on the Frontline against the COVID-19 pandemic: An Integrative Review*. Karger.

Carrière, G. (2020). *Jungwee Park.; Zechuan Deng.; Dafina Kohen., "Overtime work among professional nurses during Covid-19 pandemic"*. Statcan.

Chong, M. Y., Wang, W. C., Hsieh, W. C., Lee, C. Y., Chiu, N. M., Yeh, W. C., & Chen, C. L. (2004). Psychological impact of severe acute respiratory syndrome on health workers in a tertiary hospital. *The British Journal of Psychiatry*, 185(2), 127–133.

Coronavirus disease. *(Covid-19) Pandemic.2020. retrive from World Health Organization:*https://www.who.int/emergencies/diseases/novel-coronavirus-2019

Demerouti, E., Bakker, A. B., & Bulters, A. J. (2004). The loss spiral of work pressure, work–home interference and exhaustion: Reciprocal relations in a three-wave study. *Journal of Vocational Behavior*, 64(1), 131–149.

Edwards, J., & Rothbard, N. P. (2000). Mechanisms linking work and family: Clarifying the relationship between work and family constructs. *Academy of Management Review*, 25(1), 178. DOI: 10.2307/259269

*Factors affecting work-life balance. Retrive from Innerhour:*https://www.theinnerhour.com/corp-work-life-balance#:~:text=Some%20organisational%20factors%20that%20interfere,and%20lack%20of%20job%20security

Jaykumar, P. B. (2021). *Covid pandemic alert! India short of 4.3 million nurses*. Fortune India.

Joseph, G. (2007). *Grzywacz.; Dawn S. Carlson., "Conceptualizing work- family balance: implications for practice and research"*. Sage Journals.

Krishna, D. G. R., & Lakshmypriya, K. (2016). Work Life Balance and Implications Of Spill Over Theory–A Study on Women Entrepreneurs. *International Journal of Research in IT and Management*, 6(6), 96–109.

Lai, J. (2020). *Simeng Ma.; Ying Wang., "Factors Associated wWith Mental Health Outcomes Among Healthcare Workers Exposed to Coronavirus Disease 2019"*. JAMA Network.

Lu, H. (2020). *Yang Zhao.; Alison While., "Job satisfaction among hospital nurses: a literature review"*. Researchgate.

Mullen, K. (2015). 21. Barriers to Work-life Balance for Hospital Nurses. *Sage (Atlanta, Ga.)*.

Savitsky, B., Radomislensky, I., & Hendel, T. (2021). Nurses' occupational satisfaction during Covid-19 pandemic. *Applied Nursing Research*, 59, 151416.

Schwartz, J. (2020). *Chwan-Chuen King.; Muh-Yong Yen., "Protecting Healthcare Workers During the Coronavirus Disease 2019 (COVID-19) Outbreak: Lessons From Taiwan's Severe Acute Respiratory Syndrome Response"*. Academic.

Shivaprasad, A. h. (2013). 19. Work related stress of nurses. *Journal of Psychiatric Nursing*.

WHO. (2020). Keep health workers safe to keep patients safe.

. *Wilder-SmithA.;ChiewCJ.;LeeVJ.,* "Can we contain the COVID-19 outbreak with the same measures as for SARS?" The Lancet medical journal (2020)

Xiao, H. (2020). *Yan Zhang.; Desheng Kong.; Shiyue Li.; Ningxi Yang.,* "The Effects of Social Suffort on Sleep Quality of Medical Staff Treating Patients with Coronavirus Disease 2019(Covid-19) in January and February 2020 in China". *Medical Science Monitor*. Advance online publication. DOI: 10.12659/MSM.923549

Zhu, Z., Xu, S., Wang, H., Liu, Z., Wu, J., Li, G., . . . Wang, W. (2020). COVID-19 in Wuhan: immediate psychological impact on 5062 health workers. MedRxiv, 2020-02.

APPENDIX I

I. Please mark your choice with a tick.

1. Name:- ………………………………………………..

2. GENDER: Male (M)/ Female (F)

3. Name of the Organization:- ………………………………………………..

How long have you been working in this Organization: 0-2 years/ 2-4 years/ 4-6 years/ 6-8 years/ more than 8 years

(Wilder-Smith A, Chiew CJ, Lee VJ, 2020)

II.Please tick 1 (strongly disagree) being the lowest and 5 (strongly agree) being the highest.

1. Due to the COVID-19 crisis, very often I work beyond my specified working hours. (a) Strongly Agree. (b) Agree. (c)Nutral. (d)Disagree. (e) Strongly Disagree

2. My work schedule during COVID-19 pandemic does not allow me to spend quality time with my friends and family.

(a) Strongly Agree. (b) Agree. (c)Nutral. (d)Disagree. (e) Strongly Disagree

3. When there is a proper balance between my work and family life, i can perform efficiently at my job

(a) Strongly Agree. (b) Agree. (c)Nutral. (d)Disagree. (e) Strongly Disagree

4. I normally feel efficient whenever i return from a leave

(a) Strongly Agree. (b) Agree. (c)Nutral. (d)Disagree. (e) Strongly Disagree

5. I feel a significant degree of psychological distress due to the increasing number of COVID-19 cases.

(a) Strongly Agree. (b) Agree. (c)Nutral. (d)Disagree. (e) Strongly Disagree

6. Due to the covid-19 pandemic, I have a fear of transmitting the infection to my family after returning home from hospital/nursing home

(a) Strongly Agree. (b) Agree. (c)Nutral. (d)Disagree. (e) Strongly Disagree

7. I think extra nursing staff is required in my hospital/nursing home in order to take care of patients which are increasing in number due to COVID-19 and it will help us to maintain balance between our work life & family life

(a) Strongly Agree. (b) Agree. (c)Nutral. (d)Disagree. (e) Strongly Disagree

8.I will be very happy if I get extra recognition and rewards for outstanding performance during this covid-19 crisis.

(a) Strongly Agree. (b) Agree. (c)Nutral. (d)Disagree. (e) Strongly Disagree

9.will make me happy, if I get extra leave to spend quality time with my family during the Covid-19 pandemic.

(a) Strongly Agree. (b) Agree. (c)Nutral. (d)Disagree. (e) Strongly Disagree

10. Any Suggestion on how to improve work culture of healthcare industry during COVID-19 pandemic?

Chapter 7
Computer Intelligence-Based Analysis of Post-Pandemic Future eCommerce Business

Sharif Uddin Ahmed Rana
https://orcid.org/0000-0003-2296-6044
Paris Graduate School, France & World Talent Economy Forum, Malaysia

Adrian David Cheok
https://orcid.org/0000-0001-6316-2339
Imagineering Institute, Australia

ABSTRACT

This study proposes a systematic approach to analyse the relationship between consumer perceptions of the perceived economic benefits of e-commerce platforms and sustainable consumption in light of the significant effects of the Covid-19 epidemic on Cross-border e-commerce. The conceptual model used in this study was based on the uses and gratification theory with the border condition of pandemic dread included. A quantitative survey and analysis is the main method of research used in this study. This study reveals a positive moderating influence of pandemic anxiety on the interactions among perceptions of the perceived economicmodel, economic advantages, and sustainable consumption Opportunities abound when there is good governance and customer support. Due to its supportive nature, social media also contributes significantly to the growth and development of international E-commerce platforms. Globalization and pandemic both helped to expand trade. This study aims to go into further detail about the numerous elements that affect the online technique.

DOI: 10.4018/978-1-6684-6641-4.ch007

1. INTRODUCTION

Globalization and information technological penetration added with social media advertisements has vastly transformed the quality of living style impacting a demand for global products to meet the quality standards (Gomez-Herrera, Martens, and Turlea, 2014). Cross-border E-commerce plays a significant role in China's foreign trade and is an irresistible trend nowadays (Hmedan, Chetty and Phung, 2018). It is a vital channel for many enterprises to opt for overseas markets. Cross-border E-commerce is online shopping, where a seller or buyer resides outside the nation. Under the Belt& Road Initiative and pilot free trade zone, this cross-border E-commerce is turning into the focus of the nation's international trade (Zhu, Mou, and Benyoucef, 2019). The current year's Government Work Report states, "China will adopt new ways and models of international trade by the activities of cross-border e-Commerce. It is exploring novel forms to spring up digital trade (Saigopal and Raju, 2020a). E-commerce is the selling and buying of goods and services using an electronic network. The growth of E-commerce in China penetrated a new era of the nation's economy (Younus and Raju, 2021). During the year 2020, the value of the digital economy alone represented more than 38% of the nation's GDP. Approximately in China's retail sales, 25% of the physical goods were sold online, while the global average accounted for 18% only. During the year 2021, China contributed to above 50% of the global e-commerce retail sales (Raju and Phung, 2018). This surpassed the total combined sales of the United States and Europe. Currently, in China, about 780 million of its citizens were digital buyers and they are the largest digital buyers globally (Sun Yanling, and Su Pei. 2019).

2. OVERVIEW OF CROSS-BORDER E-COMMERCE

Cross-border E-commerce is a business transaction between a supplier and a consumer, or between two businesses or between two people, where one among the parties lie in various jurisdiction. It is the latest trend where the sellers are accessible to the global market and can compete with local retailers and provide a better option for customers. Digital online shopping is a common phenomenon nowadays, due to technological developments and growth. The internet and smartphones are becoming unavoidable in the current trend, with more people having easy accessibility to online platforms. By adopting Computational Intelligence, the performance of e-commerce trends can be analyzed. Several E-commerce websites permit the consumers to compare the prices with what the offline stores offer, and the customer can go in for a better deal. Online suppliers need not invest in stores or shops, furniture etc. and in bulk stocks. The customer can access a broader category of suppliers than in offline mode and could enjoy competitive prices and supplies can be done anywhere in stipulated time (He, and Wang, 2019). Heading towards a cashless society, China tops the E-commerce position, having many best E-commerce websites there due to 1.4 billion residents, the largest in the world.

2.1. Development and Growth Trend of E-Commerce

The size of China's E-commerce market is expected to increase at an annual rate of 22.5 per cent over the earlier years. The total market size is approximately 1.98 trillion Yuan, which is equal to 312 billion USD, during 2021, an increase of 15 per cent over a year-on-year basis, as announced by the Customs General Administration. E-commerce exports were 1.44 trillion yuan during 2021, which depicts an increment of 24.5 on a yearly basis. The government has optimized further the imported list of retail goods. The government's policies and enormous support provided a rapid and stable development of cross-border E-commerce (Ai, Yang, and Wang. 2016).

The number of people enjoying online shopping is showing marvelous growth. It moved from 34 million users during 2006, to 610 million users during 2018, which made the E-commerce industry a breakthrough. During 2020, during the first half, it touched 749 million users. The market size is about 2 trillion USD, with 1.5 million persons engaged in the industry and 190 thousand businesses, the nation's E-commerce industry is still on the uptrend (Fan. Q, 2019). A total of 29 categories is involved in E-commerce segments. There is strong demand for the products, as it is convenient for the customers to grab them.

2.2 Computational Intelligence in E-Commerce

It is well known that the key technological term in IR 4.0 is Artificial Intelligence. Artificial Intelligence (AI) is instrumental in cultivating positive customer experiences and at the same time it brings innovative solutions to the entire sector. The projections from World Bank Report (2021) claims that the global eCommerce revenues would reach $4.9 billion by the first quarter of 2023 and predicts that 85% of customer management will be administered by Artificial Intelligence without any human involvement, by the year 2023. This shows the future of artificial intelligence and computational intelligence.

3. IMPACT OF PANDEMIC COVID-19

Increase in the number of Smartphone users and Internet users, online business is flourishing. The pandemic Covid-19 played a crucial role in enhancing the solid rise of the E-commerce segment of China (Raju and Phung, 2020). The pandemic Covid-19 affected all major business trades except health care and digital online marketing. Due to the movement restrictions, the customers had to depend upon online products and digital marketing for their needs and hence they just flourished (Raju, 2021). The contagious spreading of pandemic Covid-19 made the citizens stick to digital and online marketing. They felt comfortable purchasing online. China's E-commerce data depicts that the rise of a large number of companies turned on to online business patterns just to survive the typical Covid times (Polas *et al.*, 2020a). Zhang Zhoupoing, a senior analyst in a business-to-business, at the Internet Economy Institute, which is a domestic consultancy, quoted "A new pattern of trade, cross-border E-commerce witnessed tremendous growth during the pandemic Covid-19 times, and it is a significant driving vital force to stabilize the nation's foreign trade" Wang, Jia, and Schoenherr, (2020). Zeng Bibo, the CEO, and founder of Ymatou commented that pandemic Covid-19 restricted the supply chains operation and highly affected the business. He adds that pandemic has directly driven the integration of live-streaming and cross-border E-commerce mechanisms.

4. CURRENT TRENDS IN CHINA'S E-COMMERCE MARKET

China is an outstanding and dominant leader in E-commerce. It has a market size that is three times bigger than the US. Numerous organizations target lower-tier cities for expansion and adopt initiatives to suit the marketing trend. Asia is the fastest E-commerce trending market globally and China is the major leader. In a traditional market, they face high entry problems, product registrations will be lengthy, and the fees structures are cumbersome. But the cross-border E-commerce market solves these petty issues. Thanks to the government's support, and new regulations that make the process easier (Farooq and Raju, 2019a). To satisfy the Chinese thirst for quality products import, cross-border E-commerce is the fast-track and best way to get your feet wet. Live streaming is huge in China, and common to endorse the product in the live stream. Social media will have a great influence on marketing. The customer relays on the consumer's authentic and trusted content reviews. Chinese normally check the online reviews prior to choosing a product (Polas *et al.*, 2020a). There is always demand for cross-border E-commerce as Alibaba have acquired Kaola as consumers are interested in foreign brands. The significance of big data is on the rise. Chinese consumers love to use their smartphones which will enhance C2M (consumer to Manufacturer) marketing. The rapid innovations in information technology, and by virtue of artificial intelligence and big data, usage of smartphones and Wi-Fi internet, ease in logistical methods and consumers' appetite for high-quality international brand products, trigger the cross-border E-commerce strategies (Raju, 2021).

5. REGULATIONS IN CROSS-BORDER SELLING

China has several problems with fake goods and issues regarding quality. To prevent this various regulation were introduced to regulate cross-border trade. The Consumer Protection (E-commerce) Rules, 2020 are regulating the E-commerce trades. The following regulations restrict the cross-border E-commerce business.

- The Cross-border E-commerce Retail Imports Regulation ("The Circular")
- The Notice of the Tax Policy of Cross-border E-commerce Retail Imports Regulation ("The Notice") and
- The Goods List of Cross-border E-commerce Retail Imports Regulation ("Goods List")

The foreign organizations must have a responsible local entity registered in China (Mohd Adnan and Valliappan, 2019). It is responsible along with the seller to abide by the regulations and provide the consumers with the best service and quality. The customs will cross-check the transactions, payments, and logistic e-information, that are sold via cross-border E-commerce platforms (Mohd Adnan and Valliappan, 2019). The products should be in the 'Goods List; for personal usage and must fulfil the conditions as per the relevant tax policies. Cross-border delivery or courier services should provide transactional payments and a few other e-information to customs whenever required (Polas *et al.*, 2021).

6. PROSPECTUS OF CROSS-BORDER E-COMMERCE

Cindy Tai, Amazon vice-president and head of Global Selling Asia mentioned that currently, cross-border E-commerce is an irresistible trend (Polas *et al.*, 2021). Tai added that Amazon Global Selling assists traders of China in selling their products internationally and China's cross border exports has grown stronger and bigger since they penetrated the Chinese market in 2015. With the continued government policies, innovative technologies, good manufacturing skills and strong supply chains, there is a high prospectus of cross-border business developments. Tai mentioned that the current year Government Work Report emphasizes the developments of the nation's foreign trade, and its determination to intensify digital E-commerce and quality maintenance. Cross-border E-commerce plays a significant part in strengthening foreign trade to create new brands and enhance brand images. Continued efforts to enhance logistics, improve efficiencies in distribution and consumer services, will trigger cross-border E-commerce business. The influential components that trigger rapid growth of cross-border E-commerce are experience in online markets and logistics, distribution speed, 'Single Window' conveniences, IT's penetration and smartphones and easy availability of Wifi.

7. THEORETICAL MODEL

Figure 1. Theoretical model

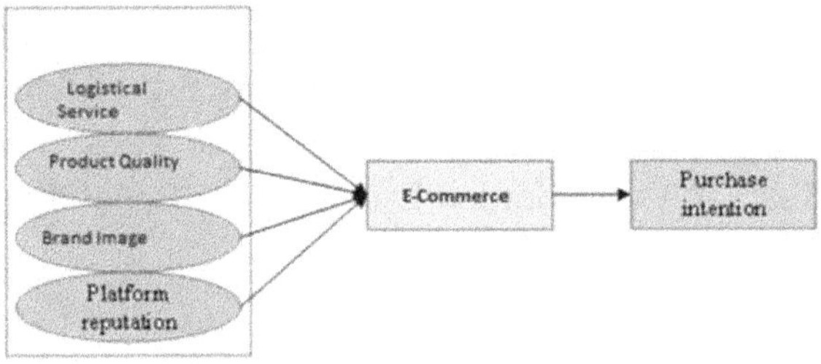

A theoretical model represented diagrammatically by Figure 1, explains the four features that influence the purchase intentions of the consumer in a cross-border E-commerce purchase. They are Logistical Service, Product Quality, Brand Image, and Platform reputations. Product quality and brand image directly impact purchase intentions. Logistical service and platform reputation by quality of their services impact the consumer in making the purchase decisions.

In cross-border E-commerce transactions, when a consumer prefers to buy a product, product quality will be a major deciding factor. While deciding the quality, the consumer also thinks of the brand image of the product. The brand image also plays a crucial role in making purchase decisions (Polas *et al.*, 2021). The platform reputation also has an influential feature to decide a product and purchase intentions. Unlike in the offline market, the consumer cannot have a direct view of the product in the E-commerce trade (Mohd Adnan and Valliappan, 2019). By seeing the virtual image of the product, one must select the product. Similar to brand image influencing the product, the platform reputation also has a tremendous influence to make the purchase intention. A brand image infers the quality of the particular products while the platform reputation depicts strong favoring messages relating to all products bought through this platform (Younus and Raju, 2021). The consumers, before placing purchase orders evaluate the quality of the product and the security of the platform in which they are going to place the order. The platform's security and its reputation directly impact the consumer's preferences. The higher the guarantee, and positive reviews, the greater is the consumer's purchase intentions and loyalty to the platform. When once the consumer gets satisfaction, they will never switch to other platforms or other brands. The product quality, brand image, platform reputation all have their influences on the final purchase intentions. Logistics also plays a crucial part in impacting customer loyalty (Polas *et al.*, 2020b). When the final purchase order is placed and online transactions are over, then it is the logistical services to look forward to delivering the goods to the consumer in the prescribed time, without any transit damages. In cross-border E-commerce platforms, they mostly rely on logistical companies to make delivery of the goods in good condition and within the stipulated time (Yizhou, Simeng and Raj, 2020). Normally, consumers make a complaint regarding delayed delivery schedules, product damage during transits, etc. Delayed delivery is caused by third party logistical companies, but the consumers blame the E-commerce platforms only. Hence platform reputation also influences consumers' purchase intentions. Consumer satisfaction induces repeated purchase intentions. When a customer is satisfied by the product quality, brand image, platform reputation and logistical services, then the customer will not switch to other platforms, or brands and makes repeated purchases which infer their addiction to brand and platform loyalty. Summarizing these factors, the effect of consumer loyalty and the purchase intentions, the 4 following hypotheses are proposed.

8. RESEARCH HYPOTHESIS

H1. Logistical Service influences Purchase Intentions in Cross-country E-commerce business

H2. Product Quality influences Purchase Intentions in Cross-country E-commerce business

H3. Brand Image influences Purchase Intentions in Cross-country E-commerce business

H4. Platform Reputations influences Purchase Intentions in Cross-country E-commerce business

9. EMPIRICAL ANALYSIS

The empirical analysis in research is an approach based on shreds of evidence regarding the research of the interpretation of the given information. This empirical approach is based on real data, rather than theories and concepts. It is integral to the scientific method using quantified observations. The research is done by questionnaire method and quantitative approach is utilized.

9.1 Measurement Model: Combined with Complex Preference Model

In the dataset there are 'n' users and 'q' commodities for the cross-border e-commerce shopping guide platform, the item set ns i, i1, i2, i, q, the user-item rating matrix is V.

Apriori algorithm.

```
(1) L1 {large 1-itemsets};

(2) for(k 2; Lk-1 ≠ φ; k + +) do begin

(3) Ck apriori(Lk-1); //New candidates

(4) For all transactions t □ D do begin

(5) Ct Subitemset(Ck, t)

//Candidates itemset in t

(6) For all candidates c □ Ct do

(7) c.count++;
```

```
(8) end

(9) Lk c □ Ck |c ≥min support;

(10) end

(11) Result UkLk;
```

$$Support\,(n \rightarrow q) = \frac{n(XuY)}{P(i)}$$

If the interval partition is too small, there will be too many partition intervals., us, the support degree is too low in the same interval, resulting in too few rules generated in this interval. When the value of the fuzzy number is divided into multiple intervals, some data will always be lost. However, we cannot predict whether the missing data will affect the results, so we cannot predict whether it will affect the accuracy of the minimum support. Therefore, define a fuzzy support rate Fs and fuzzy confidence Fc. For any fuzzy set N (n1, n2, . . .) the fuzzy support rate of N can be expressed as Fs, and its equation is written as follows:

$$\mathrm{Fs(x)} = 1 + \frac{nj}{1j} + \frac{m(n - tj)x}{m} + n$$

$$f(x, y) = 1 + \sum_{n=1}^{\infty} \left(\mathrm{nj} + \sin\frac{q\pi n}{t}\right)$$

The final calculation equation for measurement model combining th complex model is as follows,

$$f(n, q) = x_0 + \sum_{n=1}^{\infty} \left(xq + \cos\frac{n\pi x}{tj} + b_n \sin\frac{n\pi x}{tj}\right)$$

The measurement model has 5 variables namely product quality, brand image, platform reputation, and logistical services. Totally 15 questions were asked, and the respondents used a Likert scale of 5 points strongly disagree to strongly agree. The reliability, as well as validity tests, revealed the Cronbach α coefficient values above 0.7 and the value of KMOs are greater than 0.8 inferring the parameter's validity, as per Table 1.

Table 1. Measurement model

Variables	Questions	Cronbach α	KMO
Platform Reputation	Do you think the platform has a good reputation?	0.783	0.833
	Do you think the platform has sufficient security features?		
	Do you think your basic information will be used by the platform without your permission?		
	Do you think you will select again the same platform next time you buy similar imported products?		
Logistics Services	Do you think the packaging of the goods is reasonable, and there was no damages when you receive the goods	0.786	0.816
	Do you think the logistics distribution is consistent with the expected time?		
Product Quality	Are you fully satisfied with the product quality	0.822	0.818
	Will you recommend this product to your friends and relatives for its quality nature		
	Do you think that the price offered for this quality is worth		
Brand Image	Do you think you will stick to the brand even if it has some minor issues?	0.912	0.831
	Do you think you would like to recommend this brand to your friends and relatives?		
	Do you think you often buy other products of this brand, since they assure guarantee on the products and to replace if any fault occur		
Purchase Intention	Do you feel satisfied with the price you offered for this product	0.891	0.817
	Do the appearance and packing triggered your purchase intention		
	Do the brand and the reviews made by other customers triggered your purchase intentions		

9.2 Descriptive Statistics

The majority of the cross-border buyers are in the age group of 25 to 45 years, in the upper-middle class and educationally qualified. They are more concerned regarding product quality and shopping experience. Cross-border E-commerce buyers make their purchase decisions on the basis of the best quality, reasonable price, and varied functions. Based upon the above features, an empirical evaluation was performed during March's First week on Cross-border E-commerce buyers. A questionnaire survey was designed and disbursed to consumers who have made a minimum done three online purchases during the last year. A total of 279 respondents were identified, but 196 valid instruments were selected as valid. The response rate was 70.251% or 70.3%. SPSS 3.2.8 version was utilized for data analysis.

There were 123 females representing 62.8% and 73 males representing 37.2% out of 196 respondents. This depicts the majority of the cross-border buyers are females. Their monthly incomes range from less than 1000 RMB to 8000 RMB and above. In the first category of less than 1000 RMB, there were 12 respondents representing 6.1%, RMB 1001 to 3000, the respondents were 36, representing 18.4%, category 3001 to 5000 RMB, respondents were 72 representing 36.7%, category 5001 to 8000 RMB, respondents were 43, representing 22%, and finally, above 8001 RMB, the respondents were 33, representing 16.8% respectively. Category 3, with a monthly income of 3001 to 5000 RMB was the highest in the group as per Table 2.

Figure 2. Gender

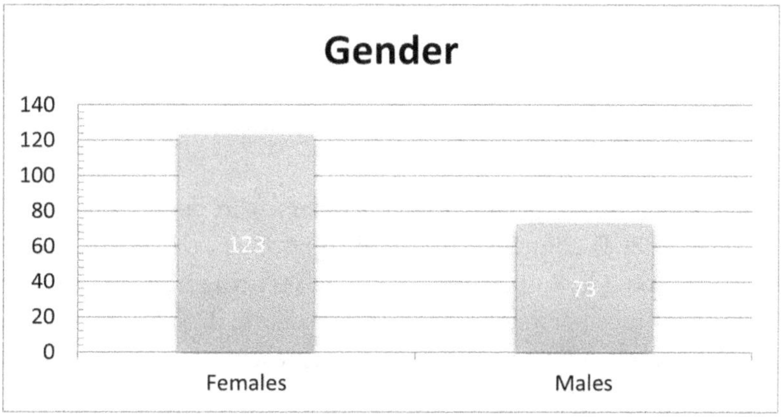

Table 2. Monthly income

Monthly Income	Number	Percentage
Less than 1000 RMB	12	6.1%
1001 to 3000 RMB	36	18.4%
3001 to 5000 RMB	72	36.7%
5001 to 8000 RMB	43	22.0%
8001 RMB and Above	33	16.8%
Totals	196	100

Figure 3. Monthly income

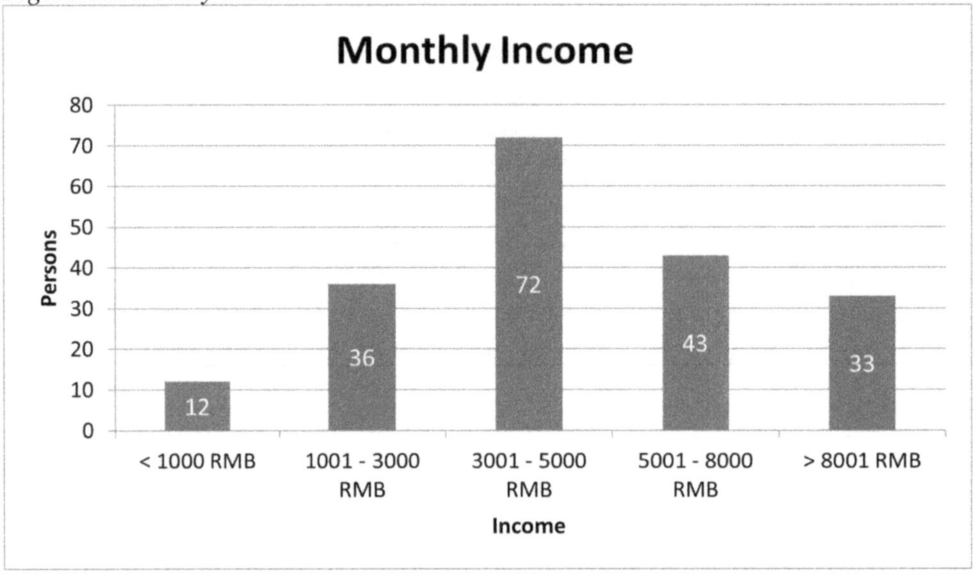

Regarding shopping frequency, the consumers who purchased minimum of 3 times in cross-border E-commerce were 16 in numbers representing 8.2%, while those who purchased 3 to 8 times per year were 99 being highest and representing 50.5%, and 5 to 8 times per year were 45, representing 23% and those who bought more than 8 and above time per year were 36 representing 18.3%., as illustrated in Table 3.

Table 3. Shopping frequency

Shopping Frequency/Annum	**Number**	**Percentage**
3 times per Annum	16	8.2%
3 to 5 times	99	50.5%
5 to 8 times	45	23.0%
8 and Above	36	18.3%
Totals	196	100

Figure 4. Shopping frequency

Table 4 reveals the shopping experience of the consumers. Out of the total 196, samples, 24 were having a shopping experience of less than a year in e-Marketing, representing 12.2%. The consumers who enjoy online shopping experience of 1 to 3 years were 54 in numbers, representing 27.6%, and those who have 3 to 5 years of online shopping experience are 72, representing 36.7, highest in this category. 46 people had more than 5 years of online shopping experience, representing 23.5%, according to Table 4.

Table 4. Shopping experience

Shopping Experience	Number	Percentage
Less than a year	24	12.2%
1 to 3 Years	54	27.6%
3 to 5 Years	72	36.7%
5 years and Above	46	23.5%
Totals	196	100

Figure 5. Shopping experience

Table 5 reveals the various types of goods purchased on cross-border E-commerce platforms. Perfumes and cosmetics occupy the top position with 56 persons representing 28.6%, and clothes and shoes were the next preferred goods with 45 of the respondents representing 23%. The next category was electronics with 30 buyers representing 15.2%, while food and snacks buyers were 27, representing 13.8%. The buyers of books were 18 in numbers, representing 9.2%, and buyers of electrical devices were 11 representing 5.6%. The remaining 9 respondents belong to other categories representing just 4.5% only according to Table 5.

Table 5. Type of goods bought

Type of Goods Bought	Number	Percentage
Clothes and Shoes	45	23.0%
Electronics	30	15.2%
Perfumes & Cosmetics	56	28.6%
Electrical Devices	11	5.6%
Food and Snacks	27	13.8%
Books	18	9.2%
Others	9	4.6%
Totals	196	100

Figure 6. Goods bought

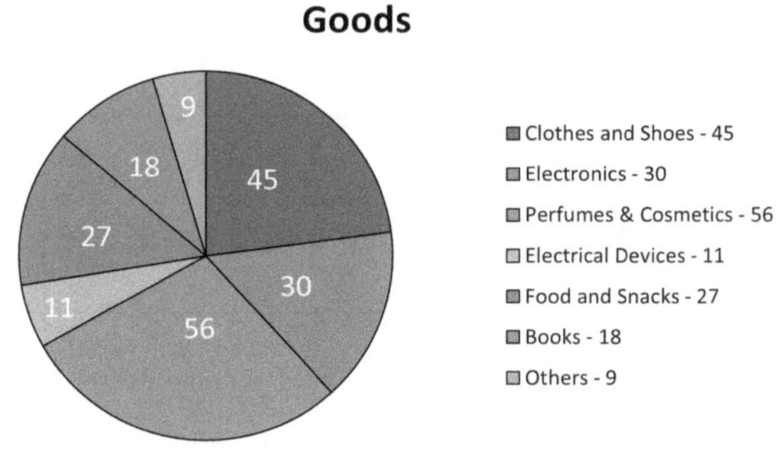

9.3 Correlation Analysis

Correlation analysis is performed to recognize the correlation among the variables. It is a statistical way to assess the linear association among the variables. The possible values for the coefficient of correlation are -1 to 1.0. the negative value infers a negative correlation while the positive value infers a positive correlation. If the value is zero, it infers that there is nil correlation between the two variables. There is a significant positive relationship among product quality and brand image (r=0.522, and P<0.01), similarly there is a significant positive relation among product quality and logistical service (r=0.627, and P<0.01). Similarly, all the researched variables have coefficient values from 0.522 to 0.736 and P<0.01, thus confirming no correlation among the variables. It is also a preliminary proof for hypothesis testing and since all the' p 'values are P<0.01, all the hypothesis H1, H2, H3, H4 are supported.

Table 6. Correlation analysis

Correlation analysis		Product Quality	Brand Image	Logistical Service	Platform Reputation	Purchase intention
Product Quality	Pearson correlation	1	-	-	-	-
	Significant (Bilateral)	-	-	-	-	-
Brand Image	Pearson correlation	0.522	1	-	-	-
	Significant (Bilateral)	.000	-	-	-	-
Logistical Service	Pearson correlation	0.627	0.475	1	-	-
	Significant (Bilateral)	.000	.000	-	-	-
Platform Reputation	Pearson correlation	0.729	0.669	0.565	1	-
	Significant (Bilateral)	.000	.000	.000	-	-
Purchase intention	Pearson correlation	0.635	0.736	0.619	.495	1
	Significant (Bilateral)	.000	.000	.000	.000	-

9.4 Hypothesis Testing

Table 7 reveals the path coefficient values, standard deviation, 'T' Values, and 'P' values. Since all the 'T' values are more than 1.96 and all the 'P' values are less than 0.05, they are valid and all the four hypothesis H1, H2, H3, and H4 were supported.

Table 7. Path coefficients

Indicators	Original Sample (O)	Sample Mean (M)	Standard Deviation (STDEV)	T Statistics (O/ STDEV)	P Values
Product Quality -> Purchase Intention	1.290	1.296	0.207	6.231	0.000
Brand Image -> Purchase Intention	0.353	0.354	0.123	2.871	0.000
Platform Reputation -> Purchase Intention	0.996	0.999	0.198	5.038	0.000
Logistical Service -> Purchase Intention	0.783	0.786	0.171	4.579	0.000

10. CONCLUSION

The development and growth of cross-border E-commerce business especially in China is tremendous (Farooq and Raju, 2019b) and if added with computational intelligence, the e-commerce sector would largely benefit out of it. Consumers prefer to buy specific products through online methods. The effect of pandemic Covid-19 adds to the situation, and the customers have to opt for such digital technologies to combat the situations. The research concentrated on product quality, brand image, logistical service and Platform reputation as the major features that enhance the purchase intention of the consumers (Polas *et al.*, 2020b). The theoretical model and the empirical analysis prove the hypothesis proposed. Product quality is one of the vital features that enhances purchase intention. The consumers, being well educated prefers the best quality of the products. Similarly, the brand image also plays a crucial part. The buyers are unaware to verify the products physically relays on brand image and the reviews of the previous buyers. The platform's reputation also plays a vital role, as it reconfirms the quality of the product, brand by reputation (Farooq *et al.*, 2019). Lastly, logistical service benefits the consumers by delivering the goods within the stipulated time and without any damage during transit. The technological evolution and information technology, Wi-Fi, smartphones usage add to the ease of purchase through cross-border E-commerce methods (Saigopal and Raju, 2020b). The consumer has many advantages by buying goods through cross-border E-commerce methods (Phung and Valliappan, 2018). There are bright chances of further growth in this sector as artificial intelligence and the government support this kind of international commercial sales. While the Covid-19 pandemic has ill effects on business, the health care industry gained from this pandemic issue. The cross-border e-Marketing business has a good potential for further expansion mode to the impact of globalization and pandemic Covid-19. The growth factors for cross-border E-commerce businesses are discussed in detail to provide a bright future in the coming years. With the penetration of artificial intelligence and machine learning and strong support by government and social media as well as consumer preferences, cross-border E-commerce will have rapid growth and development suppressing any barriers or obstacles.

REFERENCES

Ai, W., Yang, J., & Wang, L. (2016). Revelation of cross-border logistics performance for the manufacturing industry development. *International Journal of Mobile Communications*, 14(6), 593–609. DOI: 10.1504/IJMC.2016.079302

Fan, Q. (2019). An exploratory study of cross-border e-commerce (CBEC) in China: Opportunities and challenges for small to medium-size enterprises (SMEs). [IJEEI]. *International Journal of E-Entrepreneurship and Innovation*, 9(1), 23–29. DOI: 10.4018/IJEEI.2019010103

Farooq, M., & Raju, V. (2019a). Want to Stay the Market Leader in the Era of Transformative Marketing? Keep the Customers Satisfied! *Global Journal of Flexible Systems Managment*, 20(3), 257–266. DOI: 10.1007/s40171-019-00213-w

Farooq, M. and Raju, V. (2019b) 'Want to Stay the Market Leader in the Era of Transformative Marketing? Keep the Customers Satisfied!', *Global Journal of Flexible Systems Management*. .DOI: 10.1007/s40171-019-00213-w

Farooq, M., Raju, V., Khalil-Ur-Rehman, F., Younas, W., Ahmed, Q. M., & Ali, M. (2019). Investigating relationship between net promoter score and company performance: A longitudinal study. *Global Journal of Emerging Sciences*, 1(1), 1–10.

Gomez-Herrera, E., Martens, B., & Turlea, G. (2014). - The drivers and impediments for cross-border e-commerce in the EU. *Information Economics and Policy*, 2014(28), 83–96. DOI: 10.1016/j.infoecopol.2014.05.002

He, Y., & Wang, J. (2019). A Panel Analysis on the Cross Border E-commerce Trade: Evidence from ASEAN Countries. *The Journal of Asian Finance, Economics, and Business*, 6(2), 95–104. DOI: 10.13106/jafeb.2019.vol6.no2.95

Hmedan, M., Chetty, V. R. K., & Phung, S. P. (2018). Malaysian tourism sector: Technical review on policies and regulations. *Eurasian Journal of Analytical Chemistry*, 13(6), 114–120.

Mohd Adnan, S. N. S., & Valliappan, R. (2019). Communicating shared vision and leadership styles towards enhancing performance. *International Journal of Productivity and Performance Management*, 68(6), 1042–1056. DOI: 10.1108/IJPPM-05-2018-0183

Phung, S. P., & Valliappan, R. (2018). Conceptualizing the Application for Ethereum Blockchains: Front End Application Development. *Eurasian Journal of Analytical Chemistry*, 13(6), 105–113.

Polas, M. R. H.. (2020). Customer's revisit intention: Empirical evidence on Gen-Z from Bangladesh towards halal restaurants. *Journal of Public Affairs*. Advance online publication. DOI: 10.1002/pa.2572

Polas, M. R. H. *et al.* (2021) 'Rural women characteristics and sustainable entrepreneurial intention: a road to economic growth in Bangladesh', *Journal of Enterprising Communities*. .DOI: 10.1108/JEC-10-2020-0183

Raju, V. (2021). Implementing Flexible Systems in Doctoral Viva Defense Through Virtual Mechanism. *Global Journal of Flexible Systems Managment*, 22(2), 127–139. DOI: 10.1007/s40171-021-00264-y PMID: 38624609

Raju, V., & Phung, S. P. (2018). Production of methane gas from cow's residue: Biogas as alternative energy in transportation and electricity. *Eurasian Journal of Analytical Chemistry*, 13(6), 121–124.

Raju, V., & Phung, S. P. (2020). Economic dimensions of blockchain technology: In the context of extention of cryptocurrencies. *International Journal of Psychosocial Rehabilitation*, 24(2), 29–39. DOI: 10.37200/IJPR/V24I2/PR200307

Saigopal, V. V. R. G., & Raju, V. (2020a) 'IIoT Digital Forensics and Major Security issues', *2020 International Conference on Computational Intelligence, ICCI 2020*, pp. 233–236. DOI: 10.1109/ICCI51257.2020.9247685

Saigopal, V. V. R. G., & Raju, V. (2020b) 'IoT based Secure Digital Forensic Process according to Process Management', in *2020 International Conference on Computational Intelligence, ICCI 2020*. DOI: 10.1109/ICCI51257.2020.9247710

Wang, Y., Jia, F., Schoenherr, T., Gong, Y., & Chen, L. (2020). Cross-border e-commerce firms as supply chain integrators: The management of three flows. *Industrial Marketing Management*, 89, 72–88. DOI: 10.1016/j.indmarman.2019.09.004

Yizhou, Z., Simeng, Z., & Raj, V. (2020) 'A Discussion of the Application of Artificial Intelligence in the Management of Mass Media Censorship in Mainland China', *ACM International Conference Proceeding Series*, pp. 79–84. DOI: 10.1145/3407703.3407719

Younus, A. M., & Raju, V. (2021). Resilient Features of Organizational Culture in Implementation of Smart Contract Technology Blockchain in Iraqi Gas and Oil Companies. *International Journal of Qualitative Research*, 15(2), 435–450. DOI: 10.24874/IJQR15.02-05

Zhu, W., Mou, J., & Benyoucef, M. (2019). - Exploring purchase intention in cross-border E-commerce: A three-stage model. *Journal of Retailing and Consumer Services*, 2019(51), 320–330. DOI: 10.1016/j.jretconser.2019.07.004

Chapter 8
Entrepreneurs Solve Economic Problems in Pandemic

Sharif Uddin Ahmed Rana
https://orcid.org/0000-0003-2296-6044
Paris Graduate School, France

ABSTRACT

This research is based on facts and factors which represent how entrepreneurs solved the most jeopardizing problem while pandemic, which is the economic problem(Alvarez-Riscoet al., 2021). Since the very beginning of 2020, we all witnessed a deadly wave that initially started in China and within just a couple of weeks, it got spread throughout the whole world. It was the time when everyone was in strain considering their health as well as their businesses. Most of the businesses were on halt and only essential services were open to operate but with limitations. This not only affected the normal life of people but also gave a drastic downtime to the economy of the whole world. There were no predictions regarding the timeline for lockdowns and people were in a belief that situations will get under control in just a couple of weeks but ultimately they were wrong.

INTRODUCTION

In December 2019 officials in Wuhan, China reported the first case of the novel corona-virus or SARS-COV-2. By December 2020, that number grew to more than 78 million Covid-19, the disease caused by SARS-COV-2, cases and 1.7 million deaths, of which more than 300 thousand were in the US.1 No country has been untouched, accompanied by the unprecedented preemptive creation of a global re-

DOI: 10.4018/978-1-6684-6641-4.ch008

cession to combat a global disease. The emerging literature on the impact of public infection control measures has discussed such effects as social disorder, heightened health disparities in minority communities, increased mortality among the aged, and disproportionate hardship in rural labor markets. These effects have disrupted supply chains, consumption patterns, and business models in such industries as transportation, real estate, manufacturing, tourism, and consumer retail. These industries include a large share of small and medium enterprises (SMEs), which also account for the largest share of employment in most economies. Moreover, the specific combination of competitive, environmental, technological, and geographical factors implies that the relationship between Covid-19 and SMEs is a multi-level systemic phenomenon.

It is obvious to think how these unpleasant situations can affect any business, trend, economy as well as personal lives of people. This pandemic not only affected the personal lives of people but also gave a hard time to the economy of the whole world where even governments were also unable to fix the root cause. As we have seen in the past couple of years, there were a lot of restrictions while operating a conventional business which led to a huge downfall of economies of the whole world. It was hard for people to shift indoors and operate from their homes. A huge chunk of companies vanished. Not only companies, but major industries like Aviation and Entertainment also got a huge backshift. Businesses were going into deep debts and even in some countries banks and financial institutions took a step back when they realized that investing in any business will lead them to losses as well.

More recently, especially in light of the Covid-19 pandemic, scholars have explored the relationship between crises and individual decision-making behaviors. Using event systems theory, they show that perceptions of the nature and severity of the Covid-19 crisis are negatively related to helping behaviors, i.e., altruist actions targeted toward another, at the individual level of analysis. To the extent that helping behaviors are necessary for business and societal recovery after economic crises and natural disasters, such findings could be concerning although the evidence does not rise up to the level of a general conclusion (Caiazza *et al.*, 2021).

Therefore, this paper attempts to explain and conceptualize the need and vision of entrepreneurs in society to make it a better place to live and work even in these uncertain times when even economies worldwide were getting crushed. Thus, the paper deals with explanations and not all the mentioned reasons which confirm that this research is important. This research covers major issues that businesses faced during this downtime and how new entrepreneurs emerged to help get rid of economic problems in the pandemic.

In the fourth quarter of 2020, the global consumer confidence index stood at 98 - an increase from 92 points in the second quarter of the same year. This fall has been attributed to the global coronavirus (COVID-19) pandemic.

A consumer confidence index above 100 means that consumers are optimistic about their economic situation; a value below 100 indicates that the consumers are pessimistic.

Figure 1. Global consumer confidence index 2018-2020 (Global consumer confidence index 2018-2020 | Statista)

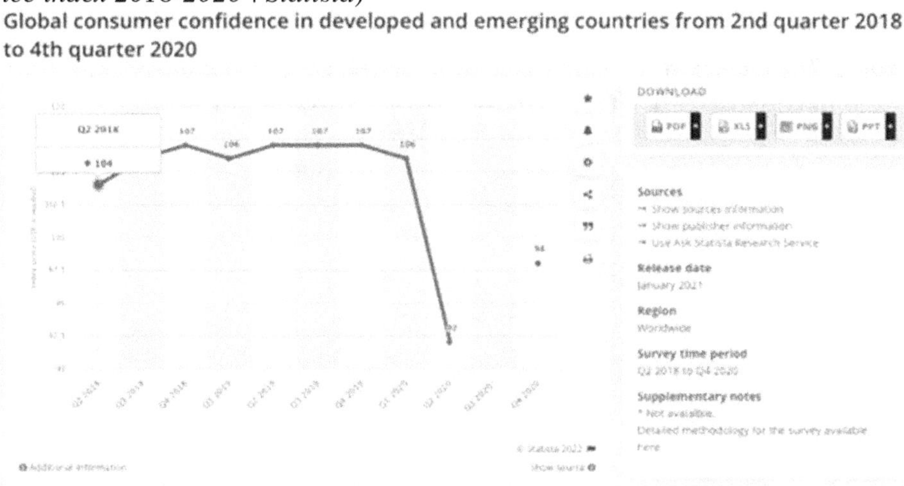

A 3.5% hit to the $80 trillion world economy means $2.8 trillion which was the exact size of the entire Indian economy in 2018–2019, the world's fifth largest. The vicious circle leading to economic depression has set on a roll. Lower consumption, reduced demand, falling prices, supply cuts, job cuts, lower spending, lower consumption—all the blocks look like a perfect fit. Recent predictions about the gloomy prospects for the world economy from some of the big names are shown in Table 1.

Table 1. World economy prospects

Sr. No.	Agency	Date of Report	Forecast
1	Goldman Sachs (2020)[a]	20 March 2020	US GDP −2% in 2Q, a record drop
2	Deutsche Bank (2020)[a]	18 March 2020	The worst global recession since World War II
3	J P Morgan (2020)[a]	12 March 2020	Recession will rock the US and Europe by July
4	Bank of America (2020)[a]	19 March 2020	The US economy has fallen into recession
5	Pacific Investment Management (2020)[a]	16 March 2020	Inevitable recession
6	Morgan Stanley (2020)[a]	17 March 2020	Base case is a global recession
7	UBS (2020)[a]	19 March 2020	Deep recession by July

Key Global Indicators of the Fear

There has already been a strong initial knee-jerk reaction in the global economy as things started unfolding.

Stocks across the globe have taken a big hit especially in March 2020 as more information came about the depth and the width of the pandemic.

Figure 2. The impact of coronavirus on stock markets since the start of the outbreak

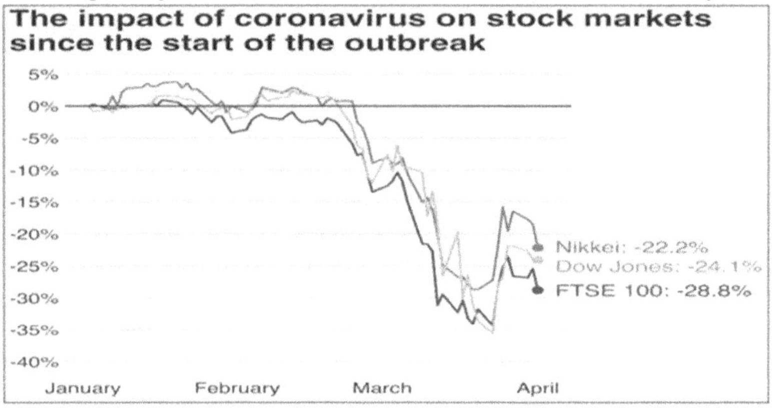

METHODOLOGY

The various parameters on which the study was developed were extracted from the literature based on various economies that have sustained economic crises in one form or another. A mixed-method approach was used for this study as economic recessions have been faced by various countries in the past, so factors affecting the barriers and strategies were derived from the literature and the extracted factors were subjected to empirical analysis. Economic slowdown due to pandemics and lockdowns is an unprecedented phenomenon, hence, to understand the unique barriers that the entrepreneurs faced and the solution to those barriers, a qualitative approach was used. A qualitative approach was used subsequent to the quantitative method to cover the gap between impediments and solutions available in the extant literature, which could be explained through constructs and variables, and peculiar challenges which were posed by the pandemic such as economic loss due to lockdown (Chaturvedi and Karri, 2021).

Quantitative Analysis Survey

Taking this research further, when we took a Quantitative Analysis survey, entrepreneurs who started their business in a pandemic took part and shared their stories, challenges, and motivation which we have compiled in this paper. It gave us a real picture of why there is a huge need for entrepreneurship in pandemic situations and how this pandemic affected current markets. It will also show us how upcoming entrepreneurs feel about recent trends and how they took steps forward to contribute to various economies.

Question: What were the conditions for starting your new business recently?

- **Many Founders Moved Forward with Existing Plans**

Some founders may have received an extra push to start their businesses because of 2020's economic conditions. Their entrepreneurial visions, however, held steady. Many of the founders we surveyed had existing business ideas before the pandemic, and the economic downturn presented the right moment for them to see those ideas through. In some cases, the pandemic created business opportunities. In others, it changed the founders' calculation of risk and made entrepreneurship a path they were ready to take.

Figure 3. What were the conditions for starting your new business recently?

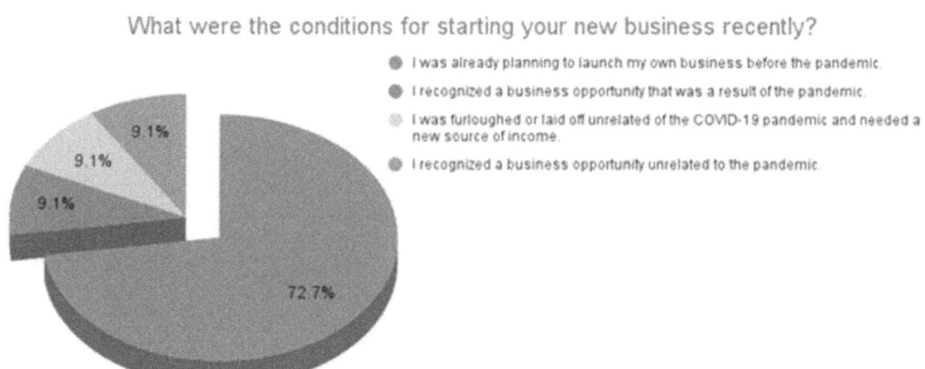

Question: How many people work for your organization?

- **Most Pandemic Startups Are Still Small**

Most respondents have five or fewer employees working for them currently. Many of these founders are still establishing their brands and growing their customer bases. They are solopreneurs or have tight partnerships. As their organizations grow, so will their employee numbers.

Figure 4. How many people work for your organization?

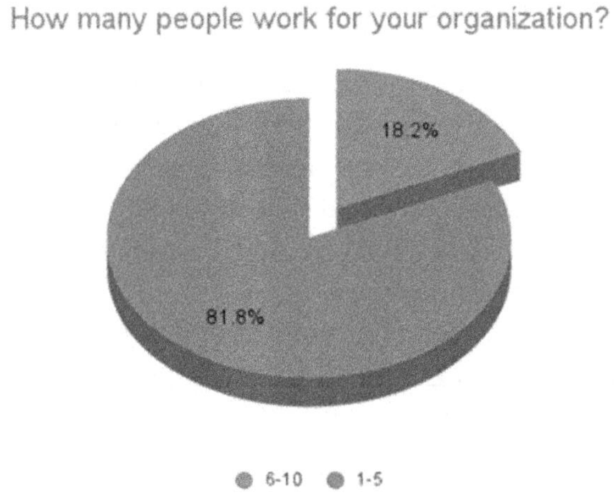

Question: What industry does your company operate in?

- **Manufacturing is what these entrepreneurs like the most.**

More than 18 percent of entrepreneurs made themselves the creators and shifted towards manufacturing which shows their creativity.

Figure 5. What industry does your company operate in?

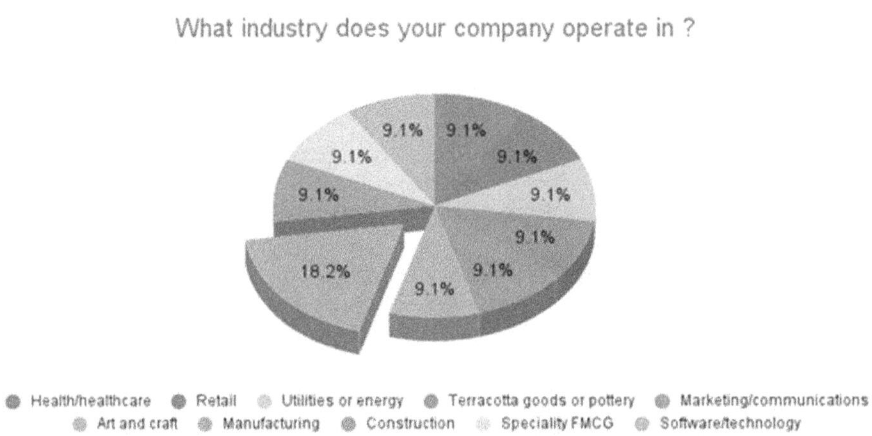

Question: What of the following options best describes what you sell?

- **Most Respondents Have B2C Businesses**

The vast majority (82 percent) of these startups target individual consumers instead of corporations. They sell physical products in-person or via an e-commerce model.

Among the B2B respondents, few respondents sell remote services to businesses. These include consulting, coaching, and marketing services.

Figure 6. What of the following options best describes what you sell?

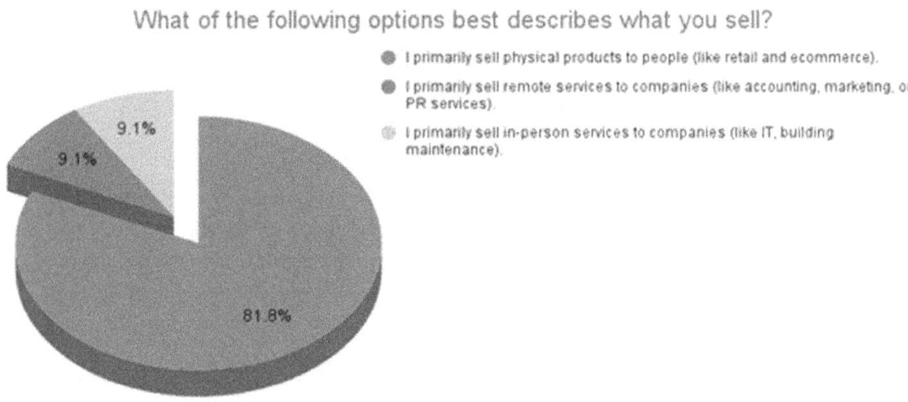

Question: Do you expect your business model to change after the pandemic?

- **Pandemic Startups Are Evolving**

Companies change with the times, and the COVID-19 pandemic spurred significant changes for businesses. The majority of respondents said their business models would change as vaccination rates increase and case numbers drop. Less than (10 percent) are confident their business models will remain the same even after the pandemic ends.

Figure 7. Do you expect your business model to change after the pandemic?

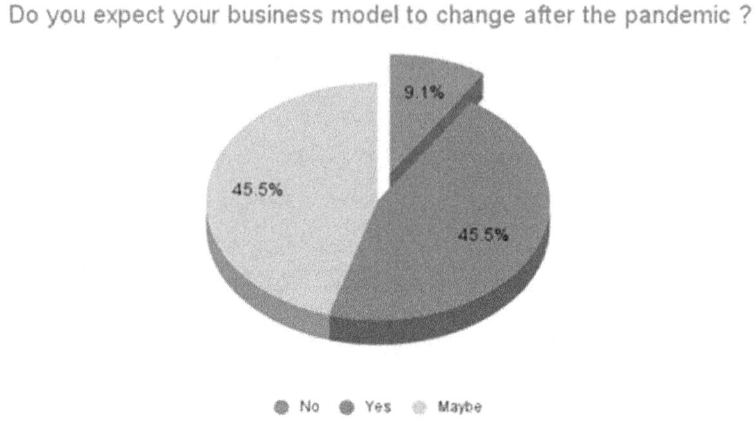

Question: How did you fund your business?

The majority of startup founders pulled funds from their bank accounts to launch their businesses. They also turned to family, friends, and professional loans to get started.

Respondents were allowed to select multiple sources of funding, and many did. This indicates that most founders relied on a variety of sources — including credit cards, stimulus funding, and income from existing work — to reach their fundraising goals.

Figure 8. How did you fund your business

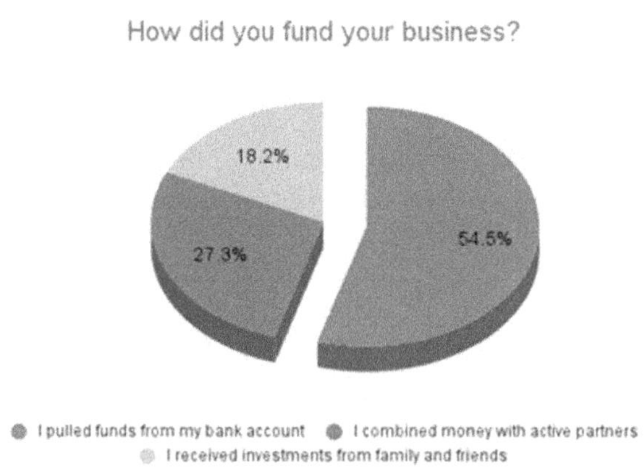

Question: How much startup funding have you put into the launch of your business so far?

- **Budgets and Big Ideas: Most started with less than $1,000.**

More than half of respondents launched their business for less than $1,000. This aligns with the finding that most companies open with one to five employees and don't currently have a brick-and-mortar location. Without payroll and rent expenses, founders can invest their startup money in product development, marketing, and other essential costs.

Figure 9. How much startup funding have you put into the launch of your business so far?

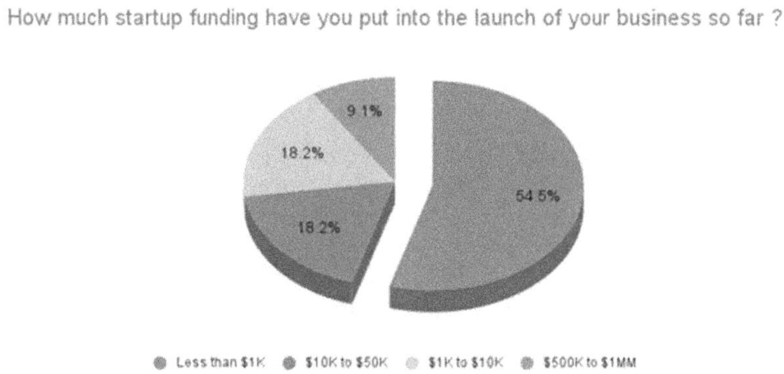

Question: How did the COVID-19 pandemic affect your ability to get funding for your business?

- **Funding Availability Varies**

One point of contention among respondents was the ease of funding. Founders were split over the question of whether the COVID-19 pandemic made it easier or harder to get funding. But roughly (55 percent) felt that the pandemic made it harder to get funding.

While some thought it was easier to get loans, as banks looked to support small companies, others thought there was more competition and longer approval processes.

Figure 10. How did the COVID-19 pandemic affect your ability to get funding for your business?

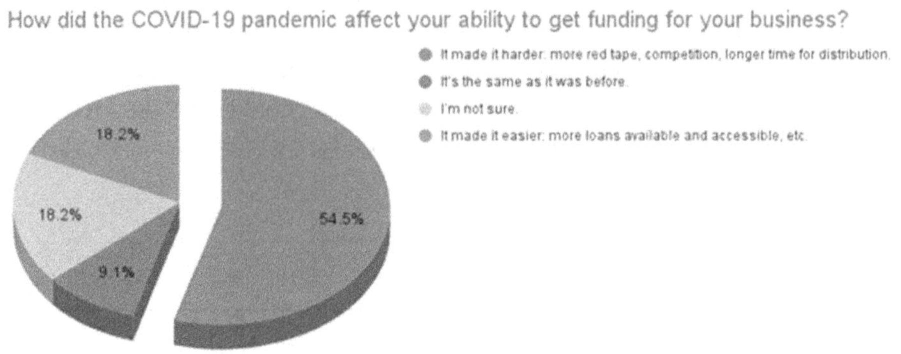

CONCLUSION

The economies have had to face the negative effects of the pandemic caused by COVID-19, which, in addition to the serious health problems caused, has led to a significant reduction in economic growth with negative effects on employment and well-being. The consideration of the environmental problems leads to the modification of the traditional objective of economic growth for sustainable development objectives. This implies the inclusion of environmental aspects in the analysis. In achieving this objective, entrepreneurship is also a factor to consider since actions aimed at improving the environment represent a business opportunity. Therefore, instead of the traditional objective of growth, this paper considers the objective of sustainable development. In addition, the paper analyzes the effects that the pandemic has generated on entrepreneurship and sustainable development, taking into account the effects generated by the main policies to be implemented by the policymaker.

This paper explained and conceptualized how entrepreneurs solve economic problems in the pandemic. Which includes key indicators and is backed up with quantitative analysis surveys. Moreover, the paper concluded that among the six main streams of research on startups, entrepreneurship theories are the most dominant theories. Finally, the paper considered the viewpoints of entrepreneurs who witnessed the shift of trends in pandemics and their findings can be helpful to upcoming entrepreneurs who might be struggling in their journey. Researchers might elaborate on each of the mentioned stages and study the challenges in different areas. Also, scholars might compare the existing theories of management, organization, and entrepreneurship to develop a comprehensive theory of startups and the need for entrepreneurship to make this world a better place to live even in uncertain times.

REFERENCES

Alvarez-Risco, A., Estrada-Merino, A., Rosen, M. A., Vargas-Herrera, A., & Del-Aguila-Arcentales, S. (2021). Factors for implementation of circular economy in firms in COVID-19 pandemic times: The case of Peru. *Environments*, 8(9), 95.

Barbate, V., Gade, R.N. and Raibagkar, S.S. (2021) "COVID-19 and Its Impact on the Indian Economy:," *https://doi.org/*, 25(1), pp. 23–35. .DOI: 10.1177/0972262921989126

Caiazza, R. *et al.* (2021) "An absorptive capacity-based systems view of Covid-19 in the small business economy," *International Entrepreneurship and Management Journal 2021 17:3*, 17(3), pp. 1419–1439. .DOI: 10.1007/s11365-021-00753-7

Chaturvedi, R. and Karri, A. (2021) "Entrepreneurship in the Times of Pandemic: Barriers and Strategies:" *https://doi.org/*[Preprint]. .DOI: 10.1177/23197145211043799

Global consumer confidence index 2018-2020 | Statista (no date). Available at: https://www.statista.com/statistics/1035883/global-consumer-confidence-index/ (Accessed: January 30, 2022).

Quote by Warren Buffett: "Opportunities come infrequently. When it rains ..." (no date). Available at: https://www.goodreads.com/quotes/952671-opportunities-come -infrequently-when-it-rains-gold-put-out-the (Accessed: January 30, 2022).

Chapter 9
Evolution of the Cosmos and Concept of Time

Sharif Uddin Ahmed Rana
https://orcid.org/0000-0003-2296-6044
Paris Graduate School

ABSTRACT

This article presents a new theory for the evolution of the cosmos and time. This is based on the concept of String Theory and had tried to explain the whole phenomena from the quantum level. This has also references from the mass energy equivalence theory and ether theory and so is able to explain the whole phenomena from the very beginning. It is thought that this theory can explain the evolution of cosmos and time from a completely new but more acceptable perspective. this may add value for innovation.

THEORY

There are many theories that claims to explain the evolution of the cosmos and none of them is completely justifiable, but this theory is meant to explain the evolution of cosmos and time from almost its beginning and can be acceptable as well as it tries to explain the phenomena at the quantum level which must be the state of the universe at its early stages. So, let's have a look and try to understand this theory which is named **the theory of grand design.** First of all we should consider that the cosmos is completely designed by nature in the form we see today and this

DOI: 10.4018/978-1-6684-6641-4.ch009

creation is very complex but explainable as well. We shall try to have a look at it now, (Greene, 2000).

To understand the first theory that we should try to focus on is the string theory or M theory which presents the universe in the form of eleven dimensions. Next, we should keep an account on the mass energy equivalence theory presented by the equation e = mc squared and finally we should also keep focus on the ether theory which presents the movement of waves as a function of difference in potential or a ether field, (Greene, 2000). These three theories is easy, have been explained and will make us understand the evolution of cosmos and about many laws of nature like gravitation, strong nuclear force and so on. This also will give us have a view on the dimension of time and its features, (Greene, 2000).

To start with let's first understand what the dimensions are. There are literally ten dimensions in the cosmos as said by the string theory which postulates the cosmos as the multiverses which means multiple universes and each universe having six dimensions each. Let's understand the dimensions and what exactly a dimension is, (Greene, 2000). A dimension is something in which movement is possible and is created only because of a potential energy difference or a field. The basic concept is that higher energy sources can travel to other areas having lower energy. This is termed as potential energy difference or a field and is the reason for creation of a dimension or movement in it. Now we shall look at the ten dimensions of the cosmos, (Greene, 2000).

According to the String theory there is a zero dimension which is resembled by an ideal point, first dimension is represented by a perfectly one-dimensional line and can be represented by a wave which is an ideal one-dimensional object, two dimensions are planar in nature, three dimensions are made by combination of two planes which is how we see the universe, (Greene, 2000).

This is because we ourselves are three dimensional beings so our perception makes us to view the world as a three-dimensional object, fourth dimension is time, fifth dimension is travelling forward and backward in time, sixth dimension is having two existences of a single object and the dimension by which they can meet. Generally, there are six dimensions in a universe but the cosmos is made of multiple universes or multiverses. So, the seventh, eighth and ninth dimension is said to be the dimensions that connect the universes in the cosmos. Tenth dimension is the time in that place of the cosmos. This is how the ten dimensions of the cosmos are lined up. Each has different characteristic fields due to which movement in either of them is in different ways. But at first there was enormous amount of energy and negative energy was existent in the cosmos,(Greene, 2000). From where that came is a mystery so the concept of eleventh dimension came according to M Theory as per which the energy and negative energy originated from eleventh dimension through dimensional travel. In eleventh dimension it may have been in any other object form which could not be found out, (Greene, 2000).

Now in the cosmos this energy and negative energy originated in vacuum. If we combine these two the vacuum is created back. Fortunately, this event had occurred only once so far in history due to which total energy of the cosmos is conserved and is zero which also gives rise to the concept of fixed events of time as every phenomenon afterwards is only automated. Now as the energy and negative energy arrived it started travelling in vacuum space as the surrounding is having no or zero energy hence there always had been an energy gradient or field which is said to be the ether field. Now negative energy is something exactly as energy but opposite in amplitude to energy. This is why when we combine them zero energy or vacuum is created back, (Greene, 2000).

Now that energy started travelling in vacuum in the tenth, ninth, eighth and seventh dimensions of the cosmos. In cosmological time dimension it travelled only in one direction and so from the point onwards on which the energy originated afterwards is regarded as positive time. Keep in mind that the measure of cosmological time, time in some other universe and that in our universe can be different. Hence the energy travelled as waves in time dimension due to this energy gradient or ether field, (Greene, 2000). The waves are nothing but ripples of energies in an alternate fashion as they travel through the medium. The energy also travelled in the three-dimensional cosmological space due to the field. But the initial source of energy was sound energy which had higher wavelengths and these sound waves are still found in the cosmos. These sounds are often heard in cosmological space. Sound is nothing but how the organism audio organ behaves to the high frequency sound waves and later captured and stored by the brain to process it. This topic will be discussed in my subsequent articles, (Greene, 2000).

But sound waves are not what gave rise to particles. It's the light waves. The conversion took place in those early stages when various different type of waves originated from out of phase interference of sound waves with itself, followed by with newly formed waves which are formed by partial interference only, that are microwaves, infra-red waves, ultraviolet ray, gamma ray and x rays. In some of these interference patterns give rise to visible light waves while other gave rise to other different types of waves. In this way light waves were generated. We should also note that in phase interference will either increase the amplitude or lower it or even may make it vacuum but could not change the waveform. The interference took place because the energy originated from different positions in the cosmos and had travelled across in spherical directions. This makes us assume that the cosmos is spherical in shape and infinite in dimensional length but no proof has been found of it yet, (Greene, 2000).

Now the cosmos at that stage had all sorts of waves including light waves. We have also found that if we collide two photos then an electron, a positron and quarks are emitted. These are the most elementary particles of nature. In fact while electron is a particle positron is considered as anti-particle. Our basic elementary structures are not comprised of positrons, rather electrons and protons & neutrons (which are composed of quarks) which are called particles and the subsequent element is called matter. There can be universes or structures in the cosmos made of anti-particles and hence anti matter, (Greene, 2000). There are some other things called dark energy and dark matter. They are something we can't see. Dark energy is all other energy except light while dark matter is matter that is made of waves other than light. In fact, particles derived from light waves reflect light and hence our sense organ detects it. But matter derived from waves other than light does not reflect light and hence cannot be seen. So, it's called dark matter. These are the concepts of various types of objects found in the cosmos. Now we shall move to evolution, (Greene, 2000).

There can be bodies made of these anti matter or dark matter as well, but our universes hardly have something like that. Now we shall look at how electrons, protons and neutrons are formed. Electrons are nothing but energy revolving in very small orbits. It is visible as it is made of light waves, and it has mass as most of the energy is concentrated in a small region and hence considered to be stationary. In fact, mass is nothing but a very high amount of stationary energy. The mass of an object is given by the energy mass equation of Albert Einstein. So, if E energy is concentrated at a point then its mass is given by E / c squared. This is how the composition of most elementary particles, that is electrons, positrons and quarks are, (Einstein, 1905). Now, the charge of these particles depends on the amplitude and direction of the energy. For a positive amplitude part of energy, the charge will be positive while for negative amplitude energy it would be negative. The spin of these particles depends on the direction these energies revolve. This is how the mass, charge and spin of these elementary particles emerged. Now let's see how the energy started revolving in orbits. When two light waves collided at angles then that made the energy start revolving. This is due to the fact that light waves reflect each other as similar to two balls colliding and hence the energies started revolving in orbits, (Einstein, 1905).

Now we shall see that the elementary particles thus formed have a lifetime which is though very large even more than lifetime of the universe. This is because these revolving waves are always losing its energy because some of this energy travels in the perpendicular direction to the radius at which the energy is at that moment. This energy is thought to be very small but is also the reason for electromagnetic force, (Einstein, 1905). Now we shall see the reason for electromagnetism, gravitation and strogravitation force. When a wave is rotating it is at a point in the orbit at a time, The other portions of the orbit have nothing and hence any energy would like to travel to that position be it from this particle or other. This is the reason for gravitations. In fact other particles are attracted to that portion and some revolving energies are emitted towards those places before the particle reaches that place exactly similarly as an energy is radiated out comprising the electromagnetic force. These revolving energies (particles) are called gravitons, (Einstein, 1905). Now if the amplitude of the revolving waves of two particles are same say positive or negative there will be no energy gradient hence, they do repel each other as it would try to move towards energy gradient places rather places with similar energy. But if a positive energy is taken towards a negative energy, it will attract each other because there will be a energy gradient. This is how the electrostatic forces work. So, we have discussed the reasons for electrostatic, electromagnetic, and gravitational forces. Now we shall have a look at the strong nuclear force, (Einstein, 1905).

The particles in the cosmos were already moving and hence they had momentum. This is because in spite of moving in orbits the energies had also a linear momentum so the so formed particles in spite of rotating also have been moving in straight lines in space. Now due to this force and gravitation two or more quarks were been attracted together overcoming the electrostatic repulsion, (Einstein, 1905). Though the repulsive force is more than the gravitational forces still the previously gained momentum makes it to overcome and get bind with another particle with their energy orbit crossing each other twice. But they never collide because their speed is the same, and they are not at the same position at the same time. Thus, they are bound in a orm of equilibrium. This is because at such a close place the gravitational pull becomes more than the electrostatic repulsion. Hence the two particles get bound by strong nuclear force. When two up quarks and a down quark is bounded a proton is formed while when two down quark and an up quark is bounded it forms a neutron, (Einstein, 1905). Then the protons and neutrons also get bounded in a similar fashion and hence the nucleus of the atom is made. Different other types of combinations are also possible but they are not stable and hence they destabilize to its basic particles back, (Einstein, 1905).

Now in atoms the electrons revolve in orbits around the nucleus. This happens as when these electrons are coming closer to the nucleus in different lines of travel it started falling over it due to electrostatic and gravitational attraction but never in fact falls rather start revolving due to the initial momentum it had. In fact, among many possibilities there is only one combination that makes an atom, (Einstein, 1905). These electrons in the atoms also fall slowly towards the nucleus but its lifetime is too very high. Then two atoms combine to form molecules and so on slowly giving rise to stars in cosmological space. This is how the primary celestial bodies in the cosmos are formed. Next we shall look at the creation of the universe and dimensions in it. Remember there can be many different types of particles or matter too that have existed in cosmological bodies, but they have also been created similarly and can be understood, (Einstein, 1905).

Now we shall look after how the dimensions got created. So we had a cosmos in which there were celestial bodies, huge amounts of energy and free particles roaming in the cosmos. Now before understanding the creation of dimensions, we should try to understand time in a better manner. For that even before we should understand the travelling of dimensions, (Einstein, 1905). As observations suggest and supported by string theory dimensional travel is possible through wormholes. Wormholes are present everywhere in the cosmos but through these wormholes only one-dimensional objects that is waves can pass through. So, for an object to travel through wormhole it is required that the object is converted back to energy which can be accomplished by variety of means like providing that much energy to the object so that its bonds are disintegrated and it is converted back to energy or by moving it with speed of light as suggested by Albert Einstein. Once converted to energy or a one-dimensional object it can travel to higher dimensions. The method of converting objects or particles into one dimensional object, that is energy and its transportation into other dimensions is called teleportation, (Einstein, 1905).

In fact, the light waves or sound waves or even electromagnetic waves always travel from past or future and hence can be detected by human brain as per brain functionality which is an universal wave detector. This process is first called Déjà vu by the Chinese and hence is what is given its name. This gives us a brief idea that future events, past events, and present events exist simultaneously and make us think of time in a new way, (Einstein, 1905).

The concept of time is based on like this. Whenever an object travels through time some of its energy stays stored in the past while the rest travels with time. This is why the energy of each and every object decreases with time. Though this energy decrease is very low and so it can't be detected easily, (Einstein, 1905). The rest of the energy traverses while it may gain or lose energy to and from its surroundings as well as it travels. The speed at which these objects travel through time is much more as compared to our consciousness which too travels with time. This means when we experience the present, events may have taken place in the future and also the past, present and future exist simultaneously hence the possibility of time travel also stands. Now we have seen that in the time dimension the objects exists throughout it in original form (as that part of energy stays in past while the object passes through time) and hence if we travel through time dimension along with our consciousness at a faster speed in forward or backward direction through teleportation then we can travel forward or backward in time and hence time travel would be possible. This is the concept behind time travel. This is how the cosmos has worked itself and also, we should keep in mind that every event in the cosmos is automated and hence each and every event is fixed from before. This is supported in cosmological dimensions as well in the universal dimensions on various universes in the multiverse's cosmos, (Einstein, 1905).

Now we shall look first at how the fundamental forces work for bigger objects. Let's start with gravitation. The force works similarly for larger objects as for smaller objects. But the total force exerted by larger objects is much more as compared to that of smaller objects due to accumulation of huge number of small particles, (Einstein, 1905). The net force sums up. Now according to gravitational theory both the objects will exert a force on one another which can be easily shown by this model explaining quantum gravitation. Now the smaller particles will be attracted by a more force due to the energy gradient, mass of the larger particle and it have a chance to get bounded to the larger objects. But perfect binding does not occur due to the repulsion of the particles at surface of both the objects which is due to the reason of presence of higher molecular structures which are more compact and hence prevents binding of particles. But the smaller particles of the bigger objects and also those of smaller objects still attract each other due to which a gravitational force is always exerted on both the objects and hence they stay together. This is the basic concept behind gravitation. Let's explain it a bit more deeply, (Einstein, 1905).

In solid particles the atoms are very tightly packed and hence there is no affinity for bounding. Though at quantum level there is yet an energy gradient which is the reason for gravitation but before reaching there would always be repulsive force acting due to electromagnetism (net force is zero) and hence two electrons which are in the outer orbits of an atom can never combine, (Einstein, 1905). But at particle level there will always be a possibility that gravitational force wins over the electrostatic force and hence will disintegrate the atom. This is why molecules are formed which and hence two solid particles stay over one another because they have no affinity for each other. But still the gravitational forces are exerted at gravitational level and more the no of particles more is the force exerted due to higher affinity. This is why lighter particles are attracted towards heavier particles as explained earlier. With electrostatic attraction or repulsion, the case is also the same. It does act similarly though it may somewhat cancel out if opposite charges are available in the same object or add up if similar charges are available in the object, (Lorentz, 1895). Hence a net electrostatic force is sometimes present from the objects only. But for the strong nuclear force the force acts only if both the particles can come closer which is only possible if it has an initial very high momentum. But for general objects that is not seen hence for larger objects the two particles of an atom never come too much closer and hence strong nuclear force is obsolete, as it will create an impact only if both can make a stable binding at the quantum level. This is how these forces shape up for higher objects. Now in the cosmos in this way higher molecules, even higher objects like stars, celestial bodies, galactic oceans, and many other objects are formed with having these basic forces of the cosmos acting, (Lorentz, 1895).

Now we shall have a look at the creation of the dimensions of the universe and later its creation. As we know dimension is what difference in potential or field. So, if we change the difference in potential to zero then the movement in that dimension can become impossible. This is same with time as well as the three-dimensional space. Like if there is object with more mass than us in space then we cannot move past it, (Lorentz, 1895). This actually means that object has more energy than us but if that is it then it should pass over us. But in fact, the other forces acting on it make its energy equal to that of its surrounding and hence it stays stagnant. But our energy is too equal to that of the surrounding when we approach it. If we exert more force on the object, then the surrounding also

exerts more force on that object due to which the energy of both stays same which is equal to the surrounding. This is why it neither moves, nor can we go through it. But if we can provide it with enough energy and the energy, we have can be more than that of the object then a energy gradient will be created and we can travel through it by moving it. But in that case, we travel slower through time. In fact, the more energy we use the speed at which we travel time is lesser. In fact we are always losing some energy due to travelling through time. This is another basic law of the cosmos. Now let's see that how higher dimensions in the cosmos are created. (Lorentz, 1895)

Say in our universe there are six dimensions, in fact four general dimensions and two dependent dimensions as described above, (Lorentz, 1895). How these dimensions got created is yet what I could not find out but the concept of the multiverses is what I can explain. It's like for our universe the dimensions are again infinite for space and time hence if we travel in three dimensional space, we can never get out of it. But to travel to other universes or cosmological space we have to convert ourselves into waves by teleportation as demonstrated by String theory. Now the law in our universe is same as that in the cosmos except the speed at which we travel through space and time in it is different from other universes and cosmos. There also in a similar fashion star, planets, asteroids, comets etc. are formed. In fact, comets are nothing but planet like objects which couldn't find an orbit and so travel freely in the universe due to energy gradient. But planets started revolving around stars or satellites around planets (in fact a smaller body around a larger body) as follows, the planets was at a stage moving in the universe with a speed but due to strong gravitational pull of the stars it gets attracted and started falling over it eventually forming orbits around it. In this way the solar systems were formed. All the things hence formed is formed due to one required combination among millions of possible combinations but these required combinations formed are huge due to presence of infinite or very large possible combinations. Hence we see what we see around us such as galaxies, solar systems, stars, planets etc. The mechanism of time travel is also similar in our universe as that in the cosmos. In this way the laws of our universe are formed.

Now we shall have a brief look here at the development and mechanism of humans and how everything in the cosmos is fixed as its fate or destruction. Humans are nothing except a creation by the cosmos which functions as defined by the cosmos. We know human works according to its thinking which is provided by the brain signals or waves that are generated in the brain and hence defines the whole working of humans. But these brain waves are a result of its previous works and thinking. The thinking of the human brain is affected by the electromagnetic waves from the planets, stars or any other object but from planets and stars is what is significant due to their size. Hence their thinking is predefined as its working and so forth its future works. This is similar for all organisms and hence all interactions, everything is as a result of the location of the stars and is a field of study of astrology. This will be described more elaborately in my subsequent articles. But the positions of the stars and planets are also fixed as considered from the situation of creation of the cosmos and hence predefined. Hence activities and life of humans are also predefined. Thus, everything in the cosmos is predefined and is a result of the point of creation of energy as afterwards all phenomena is automated. So, everything the beginning of the universe, fate of objects like stars, planets etc. or humans or even the end of the cosmos can be calculated. This is another very big finding of science and a major field of study.

The human body can be thought of as a machine also which is governed by the laws of physics like we can move a hand because of blood and bone in it. The blood has iron which on getting electrical impulses through neurons moves exactly as a motor does and hence, we can move our hand. Again, for viewing our eye acts as a camera in which the light waves are captured. In fact when a light wave falls on an object it absorbs the light wave and then goes to an excited state. To come back to normal state, it emits a photon and hence that photon is detected by our eyes. The eye acts as a camera and the brain processes it so that we are able to see it. This is how our various body parts work. Hence we are an amazing creation by nature which has our keys, (Lorentz, 1895),

Now the end and beginning of the objects in the cosmos will keep on going as the particles lose energy and hence it will collapse one day. But new particles will again be formed, and new universes will keep on forming. This is how the cosmos will keep on going on. But much before that our universe and solar system will get destroyed due to various phenomena we already know and thus this ever-ongoing cycle of creation and destruction will keep on going. But what we conclude from this article is the cosmos is the result of a grand design by nature, (Lorentz, 1895).

ACKNOWLEDGEMENTS

I would like to thank all the people whose works became the baseline of my work like Sir Albert Einstein, Nikola Tesla, and Dr Michio Kaku. I would also like to thank all who supported me in it.

REFERENCES

Einstein, A. (1905). Zur Elektrodynamik bewegter Körper [On the Electrodynamics of Moving Bodies]. *Annalen der Physik*, 17(10), 891–921. DOI: 10.1002/andp.19053221004

Greene, B. (2000). *The Elegant Universe: Superstrings, Hidden Dimensions, and the Quest for the Ultimate Theory*. W. W. Norton & Company.

Hawking, S., & Mlodinow, L. (2010). *The Grand Design*. Bantam Books.

Lorentz, H. A. (1895). *The Ether and the Relative Motion of Matter. Collected Papers*. Springer.

Chapter 10
Factors Influencing Glass Ceiling:
Focus on Women Administration in Higher Education in Malaysia

Sharif Uddin Ahmed Rana
https://orcid.org/0000-0003-2296-6044
Paris Graduate School, France

ABSTRACT

Malaysia as a country has grown quite a lot over the last two decades despite the political condition often troubled with allegations of corruption but speaking economically and in social context, it can be claimed that as a country, Malaysia has fared in a decent manner and it has been able to maintain stability which has helped to elevate the progress of the nation. The social structure of Malaysia is in such a manner where there is a broad distribution of multiple ethnicities and cultures that it has been able to maintain but in accordance to the latest Gender Development Index, as till 2017, Malaysia ranks 57th among the 189 countries

1. INTRODUCTION

The concept of the "glass ceiling," particularly in relation to women in the workplace and academic sphere, has gained significant traction since its inception in the mid-1980s due to its profound implications and effects. This term was first formally introduced in a 1986 Wall Street Journal special report on corporate women, highlighting the invisible barriers that prevent women from ascending to leadership roles in the corporate hierarchy (Cotter et al., 2001). The relentless struggle of women to break through these barriers is a well-documented phenomenon that

DOI: 10.4018/978-1-6684-6641-4.ch010

is not confined to any single region or socio-economic context. Gender disparity is not only prevalent in developing nations but is also observed in developed countries, manifesting in economic disparities and social underrepresentation that often cannot be quantified (Smith et al., 2012).

Scientific theories assert that individual success should be independent of gender, yet the probability of success often hinges on gender biases, which is a disheartening reality. Individuals are frequently subjected to discriminatory practices solely due to their gender, exposing them to challenges they would not otherwise face (Meyerson & Fletcher, 2000). This pervasive issue is difficult to address because it often goes unacknowledged; many are in denial about its existence, making it a deeply entrenched societal problem that requires urgent attention and intervention. Without addressing this issue, we risk losing the valuable contributions of a significant portion of the population—women, who constitute approximately 50% of the global demographic.

The difficulty in tackling the concept of the "glass ceiling" lies in its qualitative nature. It is challenging to explain and quantify because it is deeply subjective and varies from one individual's experience to another. The contributions of women across various sectors—economic, medical, technological, educational, and philosophical—are undeniable and have been instrumental in societal advancement (Eagly & Carli, 2007). Despite this, many men remain unaware of the unique struggles women face, making it even more challenging for women to navigate these barriers.

Historically, women have had to work harder than their male counterparts to achieve similar levels of success. This issue is further exacerbated by physiological and societal expectations, which place additional burdens on women, especially in their career paths (Reskin & Ross, 1992). Almost all women encounter the "glass ceiling" at some point in their lives, especially in leadership positions in higher education, and this struggle is well-documented (Catalyst, 2021).

Women who have successfully overcome these barriers often express hope that future generations will find it easier to navigate these challenges. They emphasize the importance of mentorship and role models who can provide guidance and support, helping reduce the time and uncertainty it takes to break through these barriers (Sandberg, 2013).

2. LITERATURE SURVEY

The "glass ceiling" was first formally addressed in the 1986 Wall Street Journal special report on corporate women, focusing on the challenges faced by women striving for leadership roles and higher positions in corporate hierarchies (Cotter et al., 2001). Since then, the concept has become widely recognized as a significant issue affecting women across various professional and academic fields. The feminist movement has played a crucial role in advocating for equal rights and opportunities for women in the workplace (Smith et al., 2012).

A review of the literature reveals that the struggle for women's rights in the workplace has been ongoing since women began to work outside the home. This struggle is often compared to the fight for civil rights and the abolition of slavery, highlighting the systemic nature of gender discrimination (Hooks, 1984). Globalization and the evolution of human civilization have made it clear that progress requires the inclusion and empowerment of all members of society, regardless of gender (Eagly & Carli, 2007).

The literature suggests that the barriers women face is not limited by geography, ethnicity, or economic status. Gender-based obstacles are a common phenomenon worldwide, and the socio-economic background often influences an individual's career aspirations and achievements (Reskin & Ross, 1992). The literature also emphasizes that the experience of encountering the "glass ceiling" is unique to each individual and varies depending on personal circumstances (Meyerson & Fletcher, 2000).

3. RESEARCH METHODOLOGY

In exploring the concept of the "glass ceiling" in the context of women in higher education administration in Malaysia, we conducted a series of interviews to collect personal experiences. The interviews aimed to understand how women perceive and overcome these barriers and to gather their advice for aspiring female professionals. The respondents, all of whom were scholars with administrative roles in Malaysian higher education, shared their insights into the cultural and social dynamics that influence their experiences. Ethical considerations were strictly adhered to, ensuring the confidentiality and integrity of the information collected.

The data collected through these interviews provided valuable insights into the unique challenges faced by women in this sector and the strategies they employed to navigate these challenges. The findings suggest that while progress has been made, significant barriers still exist, and continued efforts are necessary to create a more equitable environment for women in higher education and beyond.

3.1 Major Findings

The findings from the interviews highlight the multifaceted challenges that women face due to the "glass ceiling" phenomenon in their professional lives. The respondents shared their personal experiences and insights, shedding light on the various barriers they encountered. The key findings are summarized as follows:

a) Gender Stereotypes in Career Choices

A recurring theme among respondents is the perception that certain careers are unsuitable for women. This stereotype often discourages women from pursuing careers in fields like architecture or electrical engineering. Despite having the necessary qualifications and abilities, many women face bias and discrimination, limiting their professional opportunities and growth (Johnson & Smith, 2017).

b) Undermining Women's Opinions

Several respondents reported that their opinions were often dismissed or undervalued in professional settings. This lack of recognition is a common experience for many women and can hinder their ability to contribute effectively to discussions and decision-making processes (Smith et al., 2018).

c) Pay Disparity

Many respondents expressed frustration over being paid less than their male counterparts despite contributing equally to their organizations. This pay gap has been well-documented and is known to affect women's motivation, career advancement, and overall job satisfaction (Blau & Kahn, 2017).

d) Support from Spouses

The level of support received from spouses significantly impacted the respondents' career progression. Those who had supportive spouses were able to navigate career challenges more effectively. Conversely, a lack of support from spouses or family members made it more difficult for some women to pursue their professional aspirations (Greenhaus & Powell, 2017).

e) Workplace Environment and Peer Dynamics

The respondents highlighted the importance of a supportive workplace environment. Issues such as sexism, sexual harassment, and a lack of understanding of women's health needs, particularly during menstruation, were cited as significant barriers. The lack of institutional support in addressing these issues often demotivates women from continuing in their professional roles (McLaughlin et al., 2017).

f) Lack of Female Role Models

Many respondents noted the absence of female role models in leadership positions as a deterrent to pursuing certain careers. Societal stereotypes, such as associating nursing with women and firefighting with men, further reinforce these barriers. This lack of representation often makes it difficult for women to envision themselves in leadership roles and contributes to self-doubt and hesitation in asserting their authority (Ely et al., 2018).

These findings underscore the pervasive nature of the glass ceiling and the complex interplay of societal, organizational, and familial factors that influence women's career trajectories. Addressing these issues requires a multifaceted approach, including policy changes, organizational support, and cultural shifts to create a more equitable and supportive environment for women in the workforce.

4. RESULTS

General Observation

The respondents unanimously conceded that "glass ceiling" has been encountered by them at some point of their career pursuit and in the Academic sphere even though the working culture is not similar to how the working environment functions in the corporate world but the pursuit of a woman even in the world of Academic career has the perks of its own. The way how gender roles are defined in the social context is a concern for quite a few because it becomes difficult to imagine a woman working as an engineer on the site or work in a firm as an Architect, the careers that primarily require technical attributes are often at times considered to be work more suitable for men and even in the Academic sphere when one comes across academicians related to engineering or architecture even with respect to that the individuals who pursue a career with respect to academics. The recognition with regard to role of family to help them be in a certain shape has been put forth by almost all of the respondents. The idea of being able to maintain a balance between their career and familial responsibilities especially giving birth to children has been a cause that leads towards a stagnation in the career of individuals and then being able to reintegrate to the work back again is also concern for the individuals at times.

The way how an individual reacts and responds to certain situations also ends up defining with regard to how the woman is considered in the work place environment, the way how the individual can go about her life while maintaining the plethora of challenges and obstacles that come about both in context of her work life and personal life often makes it difficult and during that time she seeks for adequate level of support from her family, especially from her husband and children. The physiological impacts in the life of a woman require the need for her to be treated in a way that enables her to cope up with the situation when she has to deal with her biological condition. The physiological condition of the woman would cause the woman to be in a state and condition that ends up making her go through certain scenario that are not entirely under her control in any way thus she has to be considered with regard to her condition.

The moment one tries to act in a way that is not in alignment with the general narrative and norm of the society which results in a woman to encounter challenges from various layers of entities existing in the life of the individual. The moment the stereotypes are challenged and generational norm is confronted then it becomes quite difficult for one to reconcile for the way that society is expecting for one to behave and go about and since she is not really going about that manner she has to face obstacles and it is a major issue since it goes on to make one having to reaffirm the choice of the individual so she has to go about and prove to the society how the choice made from her ends is appropriate and prove to multiple entities.

4.1 Specific Observation and Analysis of Situation and Circumstances for Women in Academic Administration

a) Defined Gender Roles and its implications in life of a women pursuing a career

The way how society perceives every individual to go about in terms of their career aspiration and the pursuit is often contingent on the basis of their gender. The moment a girl begins to think as to which career should she aspire to pursue then in that case she has to consider multiple factors which perhaps is not the case for the opposite gender who in comparison have way more freedom and as unfortunate as it may sound, it owes to the gender of an individual. The accessibility of women to certain entitlements is difficult, still and it is more prominent in the conservative societies where a girl has to overcome multiple obstacles to make oneself prepared in a manner that enables an individual to go about in life in a manner and carry out work that is perhaps not identified to be work suitable for the women.

The pretext of such an opinion to be built up initiates from the moment that a toy is bought and given to a child. The probability for a boy child to be given a toy such as Barbie doll is very unlikely and for a girl child to be handed over a fire truck is also equally unlikely and there is no essential or definitive explanation for the actions to happen as such. The justification often used to rationalize the act owes to how the girl is identified as the individual who knits the family together and the one who is more into taking care of the ones around her thus the Barbie doll portraying that she is expected to go about and seek for leading a life that works behind being the organized one who keeps things in order to and dedicate their effort and time for working in a manner such that it allows one to be that perhaps society wants her to be. The rational for the boy child to be provided with a fire truck portrays the idea that the image that an individual who can be a fire fighter is supposedly a man as it requires masculine traits and features. The harm that it does is simply curbing down the option in terms of the career path for a woman which is plain and simply unfair and unjust. The way that a child is made to think and feel makes a kid to realize that since one is a boy then he is expected to go about their life in a certain way and it is okay for a boy to behave in certain ways and exhibit certain behavior but in the course of such an event what it ends up doing is making a kid instilled with the belief that the way how one should try and go about and behave is defined and if one does not go by then one at times is even ostracized socially. The life is made even more difficult when there is lack of support from the parents and it is difficult to blame the parents as well; the extent to which the parents to ensure that they are considered being in the mainstream and often they are reluctant to encourage their children if their child tries to go about their life in a manner that is not a generally perceived scenario for their child and in order to provide the very best for their child and be accepted in the society and community they tend to make themselves and their to be built up in a manner that helps them to remain in the mainstream.

As a child grows up, they gradually are influenced by their parents, siblings, contemporary peers, and friends. The way things happen in the mainstream has an impact on them to realize and recognize the way that one is expected to go about.

The way how they get exposed to the gender defined roles acts on them to acknowledge the work that they can pursue to be engaged with and get involved in. The restriction of a child to break the stereotype and get involved with a work that might be considered not suitable or appropriate due to the gender then it becomes difficult for an individual to carry out such a work and association. The poor gender ration in the pursuit of education is an example of how we can see that engineering departments and work such as Architecture have a very low proportion of female involvement and it becomes difficult for the ones who still gather the courage to be involved then building a prosperous and successful career out of the profession related to the one that one is not expected to pursue due to perceived gender roles. The way one has been instilled to think in a certain way acts to make one unable to even think that one can think of pursuing a career that she is not perceived to be part of and it is not an easy task for one to survive even if one gets involved with. The struggle never ends if one just gets involved in the profession as society still keeps on reminding the individual that it is not a place or position that a woman is supposed to be at.

The struggle after being involved in a career stretches to the extent where there is undermining of the work, lack of appreciation, constant judgment, one having to get validation of work over and over again. The struggles become more imminent when a woman who has struggled so much to come and reach a certain position makes the slightest of mistakes then the level of scrutiny and criticism that befalls on an individual is nothing but plainly unjust. The set parameters that the certain physiological limitations of a woman can make it difficult for one to carry out certain tasks which is needless to be marked as discriminatory and discouraging since a girl makes herself realize that she was just not meant for the job and when she tries to break the gender stereotypes then she is made to feel ostracized and keeps on seeking for validation which does not act as an encouraging factor thus the certain defined gender roles end up prevailing more which does not help the cause of progress of women and thus the disparity enacting as well spiraling to the society since the way for one to get social validation keeps getting questioned, just being difficult. The struggles are real and given the opinions are shaped over years, make it way more difficult.

b) Discriminatory treatment – wage gap, work place environment, male chauvinism, own credibility

The work place culture and environment has impact and implications with respect to how a woman goes about doing her work and gets her objectives met and gets her plans executed. The level of hostility encountered in the workplace from peers often makes life quite difficult for them since a work or task is at times contingent on a group to execute the plans. The idea of a woman to get a job or task done in due time while meeting up to the requirements becomes difficult and not to mention the level of animosity that is faced by a woman from her peers which makes her difficult to complete the tasks. The lack of specifications with regard and respect to the role and responsibility often lacks clarity. The way how one is assigned with a task makes it difficult for one to consider the way of getting the work done and the discriminatory conduct ends up making one feel unwanted and being doubtful about one's own abilities which is harmful for not only oneself but also the way how one ends up doubting the abilities of oneself thus resulting in making the entire scenario obscured for the individual. The way one goes about doing a task, competing. The interviews revealed that the competitiveness in the working environment instead of encouraging a culture of enhancing the credibility of individuals made it difficult due to the men having a narrative that how can a woman perform better than them thus whenever in a state where a woman is given leadership role then she finds it difficult to get the task done especially when a team is involved given that she does not receive adequate cooperation and assistance from her peers and whenever there is a slight chance of anything to go wring then in that case she always receives the most trivialized issues from her peers thus makes it so complicated to get the work done. It is also observed that the work environment ends up making a woman demotivated to such an extent that she ends up feeling like leaving everything.

The appreciation and acknowledgement of the effort put in by individuals is necessary to be recognized to a certain degree but unfortunately a lot of the respondents conceded that there has always been a lack of appreciation from her peers and her superiors, the reward for her work not being there but then again the extensive criticism became an overwhelming factor for her to keep on working with the same zeal and enthusiasm. The disparity in terms of the pay gap is inherently a factor that gives less incentive to a woman to carry out a task and the perception towards women being in a manner that they do not need to put effort rather get an easy way out just because of them being women also makes them identified as opportunists and ones who get their way but often do not realize the underlying effort of a woman which is nothing but simply disrespecting the effort of a woman which is shambolic. The effort that a woman has to give to get validation for the work done from her end and the way that she is acknowledged gives her reasons to put in further effort but since there is always a sense of despair and it comes with regard to her payment and promotions to move up the chain of hierarchy does not act to incentivize a woman adequately.

The working culture and environment in the corporate culture is way more toxic than the situation in the Academic sphere but the presence of "glass ceiling" is still there. The leadership roles and the prejudiced treatment in context of monetary incentives does not seem to help the essential cause in any way to make things easier for the women. The constant need for validation of work, the need to prove oneself for each and every task being completed while being on the lookout for being scrutinized for the slightest of mistakes that can be made is nothing but an excruciatingly painful as they end up being judgmental and doubtful about their own credibility.

The prospects of a woman in the chain of hierarchy also enacts to make a woman realize that the career aspiration to grow over in the career path is often encountered with "glass ceiling" where a woman is often made to feel and believe that she is not worthy of a leadership position and it is an unattainable feat to be the head of an organization thus reaffirming the anecdote that a woman is not meant to be in certain situation and condition. The hard work that a woman puts in is undermined at times since she does not get the same level of acknowledgement from her superior which demotivates a woman to give further effort in terms of her work. The pay gap being an imminent factor reflects the social build up that a woman and her work is not of the same level as that of a man despite showing on repeatedly that the quality of work is not lacking in any way and perhaps is better in terms of quality than her counterpart but on the occasion where she observes that the level of trouble she has to bear and go through to put forward for the work done by her and is not being able to receive the deserving treatment then it does not give a woman to put in her optimum effort.

The leadership position when handed over to a woman, the general narrative that flies through is how a woman is unable to make a decision that is "tough" and thus she does not deserve to be in such a position which is simply ridiculous and when any plan of action does not follow its expected route then the heavy ostracization and criticism is a feature that makes the woman feel isolated even more and doubt herself and her credibility. The doubtfulness ends up affecting her decision making abilities since then a woman becomes extra cautious since she is under immense pressure that she cannot falter or make a mistake as there are so many just waiting to pounce on her smallest of errors. There is a constant fear in the individuals that once they make a mistake how they will be recovering their image, impression, and reputation and how it will reflect in the way that a certain individual is perceived and considered which is a concern for a lot of the individuals.

The idea of prominence of male chauvinism is not really a new but rather an age-old prevalent factor. The beginning of human civilization has observed how gender roles have been present from the very beginning where women have been identified as ones who keep the order of the house and bring up the children while their male partner when about to provide food by going out of the place where the family resided. The evolution of human civilization has made us realize that every individual has a way to contribute in the society and it is pertinent that every individual is utilized at an optimum level or else there is no point of life, that is essentially in context of social science paradigm and it is needless to say that there should be further meaning to the life of an individual rather than just being an entity that is taking care of family and bringing up children and that also bearing in mind that there is a separate feeling in terms of sense of gratification when a mother contributes in the upbringing of a child, taking care of a family, holding a family together and withstanding the multiple hardships associated with family.

Since the industrial revolution, there has been a rise in women association in the workplace which is a positive sign but social perspective towards the involvement of women in the workplace has not really been flying through especially in the Asian countries where there is a build in struggle for women to work out of their home. The implications of male chauvinism have got to do a lot in the way how women face the numerous obstacles in the workplace where their male counterpart does not make it easy for them to work along them. The respondents have showcased how they had to encounter submissive and indirect chauvinism that made it difficult for them to work along and the treatment of women leading towards them being discouraged to go about their work and duties and in case that they were made to feel unwanted kept making them feel doubtful with respect to their abilities. The constant need for validation of their work makes them become exposed to certain scenario where there arises a sense of unhealthy competition that is often used by the male counterpart to feel insecure about themselves and then resulting in them going on to trouble the women which made it unbearable for some of the women to handle and tackle over the course of their so they either had to bear with it or simply leave which is indicated by the low rate of retention in the work place where the gender ratio is highly disproportionate and thus an alarming indication that if measures are not taken then productive workforce is lost out. The ideas of having a safe space can help not just retain women but enhance the overall productivity of the system that includes both men and women which currently has unnecessary animosity.

c) The treatment of opinion, views, and sayings in context of her gender not intellect

The work of a woman is often undermined and underrated plainly on the basis of the gender factor which is nothing but simply appalling since it disregards the merit of the work and focuses on the gender of an individual. The respondents often at times explicitly mentioned that they had to struggle for getting their points through as their opinions and viewpoints were not given much attention and their saying was not prioritized even though perhaps the same idea when coming from a male counterpart got way more appreciation and given loads of value which made them eventually reluctant to contribute in the discussion since their opinions ended up being lost due to the lack of adequate attention being given.

The extent of criticism when a certain action plan failed or did not achieve its desired goals then often at times, the women got scrutinized more in comparison to the men. The work of a women being on the receiving end of extensive critique does not help the cause of making her feel being wanted and deserving of being in certain situation and condition which is needless to the extent that does not recognize the merits of the work or activity which in turn could lead towards an individual being completely demotivated and not having the enthusiasm to be associated and affiliated with a certain work or activity. There is no denial that there are certain work where a due to the physiological constraints, a man would be a comparatively better choice than a woman but in the academic sphere, where the activities are more oriented towards cognitive abilities and analytical prowess of an individual, when it is observed that while granting of funding is done more to a project where there are comparatively more men than women and the project where there is lack of men that project not being provided with adequate funding on the basis that the prospects of the experiments and initiatives are less likely to be materialized thus the extent of reliability to yield productive output being contingent on the gender only reflects the fact that how the essence of patriarchy has such extent of biases towards women and are unable to provide a scenario where she can make an earnest attempt to work on something she truly believes and it also at times does not enable her to switch from a current work place that she has adapted in as she ends up wondering that once she changes her work place, what type of obstacles she might have to come across and overcome in order to survive at a new working environment thus there is a general tendency for women to not switch from a workplace where one has adjusted and adapted oneself in. The persistence of individuals to continue at the same working place over a long time ends up making them reliant on the organization that the progress in terms of the career path becomes stagnant and which does not help in furthering their progress of career.

d) Extent, effect, and impact of support system – contemporary peers and family

The respondents unanimously conceded that the biggest reason for them being able to continue their aspiration and pursuit owed a lot to the way their family supported them. The need for a supportive partner has been identified as a crucial and essential part for the individuals being able to continue their career pursuit. The "glass ceiling" in terms of how family acts as a resorting agent where one can vent out and release all the hardships that one comes across and in doing so if their partner does not act as a support system who tries to ensure that no matter the situation and circumstances, the partner always stands by her in ensuring that she can move ahead in her life. The way how one woman can gather the courage to tackle the male chauvinism, the submissive anatomization from peers and colleagues, constant lack of validation of their work and having to prove oneself over and over again to prove their credibility is also a concern.

The act of giving birth has a huge impact in the life of a woman and no one can deny the extent of changes that happens in the body of a woman while she conceives and gives birth to a child. The birth of a child often at times is a phase of the life of a woman where she goes through such a transformation that often takes a toll on her in terms of her physiological condition and the way that the psychology gets shaped as well. The experience of motherhood being such a feeling that one gets to feel and believe that it is nothing but fulfilling to an individual and thus it leads one to get a sense of completeness in terms of their life. The life of a woman changes drastically when she gives birth to a child and once the baby comes to a mother's lap, she has to deal with multiple changes and even during the duration of pregnancy there are multiple hormonal changes that take place inside the body of a woman. The way one makes an attempt in a grate back since the birth of a child requires extensive support from the family. The only way how it can be easier for a woman to still continue in pursuing her career can only be thought given there is support from her partner and it makes one realize that when returning from a hiatus due to the birth of a child, the career path hits a bump and when she again returns back to the workplace, the initial stage even though is a struggle but still with adequate support from the family in terms of taking care of the child, having to look after the baby and ensuring that the baby is taken care of thus she can concentrate on her work without having to worry about the issues pertaining to her child and then having to take care of the wellbeing of the child if not shared by both the partners then it becomes really difficult for the mother to manage between her work life and her career pursuit thus it cannot be undermined that the family as a support system needs to provide the level of comfort to a woman that she can handle office work while the child is taken care of as well.

e) Inspiration and role model to look up to for an individual

The initiative from the end of a woman to go against stereotypes is not the easiest of tasks especially by someone in a semi conservative society. The eagerness of the society to being on the lookout for individuals whoever is not going along the mainstream as expected from the end of the society thus it becomes extra challenging that she has to go against the social stereotype while trying to prove her own credentials and credibility while seeking for constant validation from the society for the work done by the individual. The way how society perceives the actions of individuals tends to dictate the decision making actions of an individual which leads to say that the hardships have to be worked upon and only then can there be a glimpse of hope for individuals to realize that there is a certain possibility that one can try and make an attempt to go against the generally accepted mainstream that is considered to be in alignment with the general norm.

The lack of individuals who can gather the courage to try out something in life that is not in accordance to the general norm is difficult and since everyone is afraid to tryout something that has not really been tried and tested garners loads of anxiety and cautiousness among the ones who try to go ahead in their lives trying to seek for achieving what they have perhaps wished for but what becomes problematic for them is the idea that how much one can endure going against the way that how society considers as the right way to go about. The respondents clearly indicated that each of them have had their own share of hardships that they opted to deal with and overcome the certain obstacles and hurdles only to pursue the career path that they feel to be the right way to go by and in the course, there have been multiple obstacles and each individual had their own way of dealing with the hurdles and eventually being able to go through with them and in the course of such fighting through it has not always been that it has been in any way easy and the variation in terms of the different adversities that came across them always made them doubt the extent to which whether it is worth the fight. The eventual gain has been how some of the individuals were able to overcome the adversities, the hurdles, the obstacles as they had a clear intent to overcome the "glass ceiling" and it made them keep persisting with what they want from their career pursuit and not to mention that at each and every step they kept. The impact that a role model or one who has gone through the system and has been able to reach the position and achieve the position that one has been able to acquire the way that one needs to be aware of in such a way that would enable one to go around in a way that helps to bring about the way that one would be expected to go about. The "glass ceiling" that obstructs one to not pursue certain way of going about since they do not see how one can end up pursuing their career.

5. SUGGESTIONS AND RECOMMENDATIONS TO REDUCE "GLASS CEILING"

The interview led towards the respondents being asked as to how they would be advising the upcoming generation of women who are willing to be engaged in the work force and work hand in hand with their male counterpart while being a productive contributor in the work force with utility of the resources.

a) Having faith in one's own abilities

One of the biggest concern that women in general encounter is the fact that they keep doubting themselves and their work. The lack of acknowledgement, recognition and validation of their work from superiors and peers would help to solidify the confidence of the individual that they are capable of doing their work properly and the quality of their work is also of a certain standard that can easily compete with her contemporary coworkers and at the same time, the lack of how it makes one keep doubting the credibility of oneself thus it is pertinent that one never ends up being doubtful with regard to how one should go about her work and that she is competent and thus she is holding a position of power which she should cherish while working, going ahead.

b) Being one's own support system

The way how a woman in the academic sphere tends to break the "glass ceiling" where she is exposed to being scrutinized on multiple occasions for the sake of her career thus making it tough for the way how she goes about doing her work and she needs to have full faith and belief with respect to how the work she has taken up to fulfill her duties and in the course, it is pertinent that she always supports herself. The need for confidence on oneself has been mentioned by each of the respondents and they recognize how important it is for the individuals to recognize and value oneself and the belief in the fact that she has to trust herself in moving forward with the plethora of obstacles and hurdles that end up coming her way but if she is not resilient then it only becomes more difficult for herself to accomplish the goals that she has been aspiring to achieve.

c) Being clear about one's entitlements and not compromising to voice oneself

The biggest concern that a woman often ends up not being aware of is about her entitlements where she has a clear understanding as to what she is entitled to receive with respect to the work that she is involved and engaged with and what she needs to do in order to fulfill her duties and responsibilities while carrying the task in hand. The respondents also clearly pointed out that they had to ensure that their voice and opinions were put across and got the attention deserved.

d) Being clear with regard to how one intends to go about in their career path

The intention from a task and work has to be very discreet if a woman has to get her work accomplished in a proper way. The absolute synergy between the objective and execution of the work that one wishes to achieve has to be clear in the mind of the individual going about the work and not to mention the way in which one clearly understands that she requires being clear with respect to the career path that the individual wishes to accomplish and the need for her to be focused with regard to her aspiration can help to make an individual realize what she intends to achieve and what she can do to make her wishes to be accomplished in a positive way.

e) Giving priority to one's own development

The way how one goes about in making her career pursuit to be materialized makes it a tough choice where one who are not entirely sure that how they can accomplish the goals that they have set forth for oneself and it goes without saying that she has to make earnest effort to not only achieve their goals which perhaps is not only short term but extends to long term goals that enables the individual to achieve the desired goals. The growth of an individual is a continuous process and one can never feel that in the Academic sphere there is an end with regard to the growth of an individual and when one seeks to go ahead in the chain of hierarchy thus she has to keep developing oneself in the course of her career path and also to ensure that there is enough scope and opportunity for her to move up the chain of hierarchy where the credibility of the individual and the quality of work is the foremost priority which makes her progress easier and since an individual is constantly making an earnest effort to go about in her course of career goals where one needs to ascertain and establish herself as possessing certain traits and quality that allows her work to speak for herself and the way how she manages to achieve the goals.

f) Being vocal about any discomfort at any stage or phase of life while pursuing a career

The extent to which a woman, her work and her opinions are undermined ends up making a woman feel dissociated in terms of the work that she is involved with and it is needless to say that it is a necessity for an individual that her opinion is given adequate and appropriate attention and importance that empowers a woman in being able to have an impact in a way that leads towards establishing that the way she is carrying out her work is something that is adding value and in a manner that does take into consideration that the way she is not being able to receive any of her deserving entitlements and the way how she is treated by her superiors i.e. supervisors, the peers that she works with and in the course receives any and all forms of support she needs for sure.

6. CONCLUSIONS

The prominence of "glass ceiling" in the academic sphere has been unanimously conceded by almost each of the respondents and they also recognized that on a case by case basis the individuals who have reached a certain position of power after breaking through the "glass ceiling" had their own struggles to deal with and had their own way of dealing with it as well. The way how an individual would deal with the impacts and effects of "glass ceiling" what they had to encounter and how they dealt with it acts to be like a precedence that is expected to make the life of the upcoming generation who would be getting involved in the workforce so if they are not given an environment and a working culture that does not allow them to feel comfortable then there is no way that the future can be built in a manner where a woman would be feeling safe and secured in being involved to work along.

The contribution by approximately 50% of the population is pivotal to the way how the fabric of the society can work to make an optimum utilization of the resources at its disposal. The statement even though being true but has its own dynamics and manifestations, until and unless the various issues are not taken care of then it will be extremely difficult to make a cordial environment for the women and when she makes an earnest attempt to go against the general mainstream and the conventional narrative she has to get over a lot of obstacles since there are hurdles in context of society, family, workplace and its environment, the way how a woman goes about in accomplishing their career pursuit in the course of going about the way that they would want to achieve success in life.

The entire paper has been prepared to identify the various ways how a woman encounters the ways in which she has to deal with "glass ceiling" in context of the academic administration and for a country like Malaysia that has its own position in accordance to the Gender Development Index thus it explores the ways in which women who have been able to cross through "glass ceiling" that they have encountered while progressing during their career pursuit to reach the position that they have been able to achieve and reach and they also put forth their personal experience in terms of the obstacles that they have come across and what they were able to do about the hurdles that enabled them to reach their feats and the ways how the impact and effect of the "glass ceiling" can be dealt by the women because they realize that the obstacles are an imminent hurdle that has to dealt with and it requires a lot of measures that focuses on the way how a woman needs to be aware of certain entitlements for themselves, the way how one has to realize that the most prominent factor to act in making a woman to be affected less due to how "glass ceiling" can work to make the life of a woman more difficult so the self-awareness and the realization that if they do not help themselves, no one can help them to progress forward in their life.

REFERENCES

Cotter, D. A., Hermsen, J. M., Ovadia, S., & Vanneman, R. (2001). The Glass Ceiling Effect. *Social Forces*, 80(2), 655–681. DOI: 10.1353/sof.2001.0091

Eagly, A. H., & Carli, L. L. (2007). *Through the Labyrinth: The Truth About How Women Become Leaders*. Harvard Business School Press.

Hooks, B. (1984). *Feminist Theory: From Margin to Center*. South End Press.

Meyerson, D. E., & Fletcher, J. K. (2000). A Modest Manifesto for Shattering the Glass Ceiling. *Harvard Business Review*, 78(1), 126–136.

Reskin, B. F., & Ross, C. E. (1992). Jobs, Authority, and Earnings among Managers: The Continuing Significance of Sex. *Work and Occupations*, 19(4), 342–365. DOI: 10.1177/0730888492019004002

Sandberg, S. (2013). Lean. In *Women, Work, and the Will to Lead*. Knopf.

Smith, R. A.. (2012). Glass Ceilings and Glass Escalators: Hidden Barriers or Hidden Advantages to Women in the Workplace? *Social Problems*, 59(3), 373–394.

Chapter 11

Generative Innovation: Leveraging the Power of Large Language Models for Brainstorming

Sharif Uddin Ahmed Rana
https://orcid.org/0000-0003-2296-6044
Paris Graduate School, France & World Talent Economy Forum, Malaysia

Adrian David Cheok
https://orcid.org/0000-0001-6316-2339
Imagineering Institute, Australia

ABSTRACT

This paper explores the transformative potential of generative innovation, and specifically, FutureLab's ChatGPT-powered BrainstormBot as a way to achieve it. The paper presents an overview of the BrainstormBot, DesignSprintBot, and InnoBot, showcasing their respective roles in ideation, collaboration, and innovation resource management. The multi-stage design sprint methodology, powered by AI, is discussed, along with additional benefits in streamlining the design process, automating knowledge capture, and producing high-quality concept pitch materials. Finally, these technologies will be able to use natural language to operate a comprehensive command and control system that drives innovation within an organization. This will facilitate idea collection and refinement, manage an innovation portfolio, run continuous cultural assessments, and implement low-cost, enterprise-wide, just-in-time innovation training... all within the Slack environment. By embracing these advancements, organizations can create an ecosystem that truly fosters and accelerates innovation.

DOI: 10.4018/978-1-6684-6641-4.ch011

1. THE ERA OF GENERATIVE AI

Over the last few years, Generative AI has advanced significantly, garnering attention from content creators and involvement from major tech companies including Google, Microsoft, and Amazon. These generative AI tools rely on input prompts to produce desired outcomes. Examples include ChatGPT, DALL-e 2, Midjourney, and RunwayML. Application opportunities abound in content creation, customer support, healthcare, marketing, education, finance, and the environment, (Russell & Norvig, 2022).

Figure 1. Hand holding cellphone

Early wins for Generative AI have been validated in code writing, template drafting, customer support enhancement, data augmentation, decision-making improvement, and streamlining of research and development. Our focus addresses the application of Generative AI in Design Sprints, a crucial component of the innovation process that plays a central role in driving creativity and problem-solving in modern organizations. What's most exciting is the possibility of addressing hidden and unarticulated shortcomings in traditional design sprints, which often face challenges in effectively capturing diverse perspectives, facilitating collaboration, and managing innovation resources. (Russell & Norvig, 2022).

Our solution, *BrainstormBot*, offers revolutionary improvements to the design sprint process through the deployment of AI-assisted tools to enhance ideation, collaboration, and innovation resource management. This paper explores the transformative potential of such technologies, highlighting their ability to amplify human creativity, enhance collaboration, and increase innovative capacity throughout the enterprise, (Russell & Norvig, 2022).

2. BRAINSTORMBOT: THE ART OF BRAINSTORMING

Brainstorming is a uniquely human endeavor. When a group of people brainstorm, the process usually helps to produce ideas that are superior to what a lone inventor could produce by themselves. The question is, how might it be possible to enhance and improve the brainstorming process through the injection of AI-based technologies?

And so, at its simplest level when working with an individual in the process of ideation, BrainstormBot acts as a mini-brainstorm sounding board, suggesting starter ideas, working with ideators to refine their ideas and hone their creative energies. By providing "starter ideas," BrainstormBot is designed to act in a way that is similar to how Midjourney works, the generative AI art system. The Midjourney user interface accepts a text prompt and produces four possible interpretations, knowing that it probably won't get it right. It then invites the user to select one or more of the alternatives as jumping points for variations, or to select one or more to prepare for delivery by upscaling to a higher resolution. This allows you to iterate toward an acceptable result, and often that process primes the pump for even better and more imaginative images than you had in mind when you started. BrainstormBot works in a very similar manner, offering a number of ideation suggestions that you can refine, or "riff" on, via iterative prompts, all while priming your ideation pump, (Russell & Norvig, 2022).

It should be noted that as ChatGPT is based on scouring current content, it never generates a truly original idea… it just does a better job of scouring than humans, so it produces ideas that feel innovative to the user. But relying on those ideas will eventually run into intellectual property issues and cannot be depended on for business strategy. Presenting those initial designs as "starter ideas" and following up with "prompts for humans" to refine those ideas results in "priming the pump" of creativity, and this is the best strategy for the application of generative AI in the space of innovation.

And that's exactly what *BrainstormBot* does — it leverages the power of ChatGPT to cover a wide range of domains and presents fresh perspectives in just about any business domain. But it should be made very clear that ChatGPT cannot actually create new ideas, as this is a faculty of humans. Generative AI can augment the innate and unique creative capacity of humans, much like a muse. Specifically, it enables more effective ideation by leveraging something we call *multi-visioning,* (Russell & Norvig, 2022).

Figure 2. Cartoon holding lightbulb

Multi-visioning adapts the creative processes used by geniuses like Leonardo da Vinci, Albert Einstein, and the physicist Richard Feynman. Da Vinci believed that to solve a problem you begin by learning how to restructure it in many different ways. Einstein said that he found it necessary to formulate his problems in as many different ways as possible, using diagrams and visuals. Feynman felt the secret to his genius was his ability to disregard how past thinkers thought about problems, and instead to "invent new ways to think." He called it "generating different ways to look at the problem, until you find a way that moves the imagination."

It's similar to how a sculptor works, by moving around the subject to understand it from various angles. In practice, though, how do you "rotate" an idea? It's easy, you do this simply by asking the right questions that lead the group ideation down different conceptual pathways. Questions like, "Is this really what the customer needs?" or "How would Apple design this?" or "Is there a new way to expand the market?" By asking the right questions or framing the right perspectives, which we now call *"prompts for humans,"* innovators can learn how to fully bake a raw or half-baked idea, (Russell & Norvig, 2022).

That's right, just as humans use prompts to get AI to think in different ways, AIs can now use prompts to get humans to think in different ways as well.

This is how we amplify the creativity of both humans and AI in symbiotic partnership. Hence, BrainstormBot is encoded with the ability to employ multi-visioning – i.e., to generate effective prompts for humans – to stimulate and amplify human creativity. These prompts serve as catalysts for ideation, enabling participants to explore diverse perspectives, generate unique ideas, and overcome creative blocks. Further, these prompts are designed to enhance the quality and diversity of the ideas generated, and to reflect the vast experience of the FutureLab brainstorming team, which collectively represents thousands of hours of experience, training, and facilitation of the brainstorming and innovation process, (Russell & Norvig, 2022).

Facilitating brainstorms is a skill like any other, similar to learning a new language or playing the piano. Acting much like an orchestra conductor, facilitators can sense the flow of ideational energy and guide that energy to expand awareness and encourage participants to think outside the box. Skilled facilitators can literally feel when a great idea is about to pop and can lead the team there. It's almost like a sixth sense, this ability to uncover unconventional solutions and novel approaches to problem-solving, and its why great brainstorm facilitators are paid very well for their efforts. Our team has done its very best to program these same capacities into BrainstormBot, because so much more is possible when you empower AI to work with a team rather than an individual, (Bishop, Russell, & Norvig, 2022).

This is why we intentionally planted our AI technology into a substrate of team communication: *Slack*. We also designed a second bot, *DesignSprintBot*, that uses sensors to detect factors like conversation flow rates, group consonance, and participation disparity, to serve as a virtual facilitator. It is able to drive discussion to maximize creative synergy and to advance group cohesion. Our goal was not to create an AI that will try to impress you by flooding you with tons of ideas, but to enable more efficient collaboration and to unlock the core creativity of your team.

3. DESIGNSPRINTBOT: CATALYST FOR COLLABORATION

The *DesignSprintBot* harnesses the power of Slack's digital workspace to streamline and enhance collaboration. By monitoring conversation dynamics and participation levels, the DesignSprintBot ensures a more inclusive and balanced collaboration environment. It identifies instances where certain team members may dominate discussions, hindering the contributions of introverted or less vocal participants. Through real-time feedback and interventions, the DesignSprintBot encourages better participation, empowering every team member to contribute their unique perspectives and ideas, (Bishop, Russell, & Norvig, 2022).

Figure 3. Cartoon holding iPad

Functionally, the DesignSprintBot leverages AI to facilitate a five-step design sprint within the Slack platform. This integration streamlines the product design process, making it more cost-effective and efficient. Additionally, it automates the generation of high-quality concept pitch materials, enabling teams to most effectively communicate their ideas to peers, managers, stakeholders, and investors. By leveraging the DesignSprintBot's capabilities, organizations can accelerate the design critical sprint process, improve collaboration, and increase the likelihood of successful innovation outcomes, (Bishop, Russell, & Norvig, 2022).

The design sprint itself is a clever invention. It encompasses a comprehensive and iterative approach to problem-solving and innovation. It enables teams to navigate through the complex landscape of product or service innovation and design, ensuring the alignment of user requirements with business goals and with customer requirements and expectations. Our version of design sprint methodology has been modified to fit the Slack and generative AI frameworks, and encompasses the following stages: ethnography, divergent ideation, convergent distillation, strategic visualization, and pitch material production for the validation phase, (Bishop, Russell, & Norvig, 2022).

Figure 4. Five-step process

The five-step process can be scaled to fit the actual time parameter according to the user's preference, from five hours to five days, or longer, as the problem at hand and the situation require. The steps are configured in the following manner:

- *Step 1: Ethnography – ChatGPT-assisted Ethnographic Research.*

The Generative Innovation Design Sprint begins with ethnography, a critical step for gaining valuable insights into user preferences, pain points, and aspirations. ChatGPT's AI-powered tool assists in the collection of data and insights, helping to produce questions and tracksheets for interviews, observations, and data analysis. This step is often referred to as *painstorming* and ensures that all subsequent stages of the design sprint align with user requirements and foster empathetic design thinking. By leveraging ChatGPT's capabilities, the ethnography step becomes very efficient and fully data-driven, thus moving beyond conjecture and assumptions. It enables teams to gather a wide range of perspectives and identify underlying user needs that may not be immediately apparent. ChatGPT can generate relevant prompts and questions, aiding in the formulation of interview guides and data collection strategies, (Bishop, Russell, & Norvig, 2022).

- *Step 2: Divergent Ideation – Using AI to Facilitate Brainstorming.*

Following the ethnography step, the design sprint moves into the divergent ideation stage, where the BrainstormBot – also powered by ChatGPT – plays a pivotal role in amplifying the production of creative ideas and solutions. Leveraging a technique called *multi-visioning*, BrainstormBot empowers participants to explore many perspectives and possibilities, accelerating and deepening the free-flowing exchange of thoughts. By incorporating ChatGPT's generative capabilities, BrainstormBot enhances the brainstorming process and expands the realm of possibilities. It provides participants with ideation prompts, encourages the exploration of unconventional solutions, and helps overcome creative blocks. These AI-powered enhancements enable teams to think beyond traditional boundaries, fostering innovation and generating a diverse range of ideas that may lead to breakthrough concepts, (Bishop, Russell, & Norvig, 2022).

- *Step 3: Convergent Distillation – AI-supported Distillation of Ideas.*

After ideation, the design sprint advances into convergent thinking for idea distillation. Here BrainstormBot plays a crucial role in assisting a team to evaluate and select the most promising ideas and concepts generated during ideation by accelerating the analysis and prioritization of ideas, grouping them based on similarities or themes, and facilitating efficient evaluation. Smart voting mechanisms allow team members to express their opinions and preferences and contribute to the selection process in a collaborative and inclusive manner. BrainstormBot's AI capabilities enable teams to objectively assess ideas, ensuring alignment with user needs and business objectives, (Bishop, Russell, & Norvig, 2022).

- *Step 4: Strategic Visualization – Generating a Business Model Canvas.*

With core concepts identified, the design sprint shifts to strategic visualization. This step focuses on preparing the *business model canvas*, a structured framework that maps key elements of the business model, including customer segments, value proposition, revenue streams, and cost structure. For stakeholders considering a project or evaluating an investment, this adds tremendous value by providing the full picture on a single page. The collaborative process of strategic visualization allows for real-time feedback integration and smart voting, ensuring a comprehensive and refined business model that aligns with the project's goals and with user requires identified early on, (Bishop, Russell, & Norvig, 2022).

- *Step 5: Validation Phase: Generating Concept Pitch Materials.*

For the final step of the Generative Innovation Design Sprint, the focus shifts to generating concept pitch materials for presentations to peers, managers, and stakeholders. This includes crafting the elevator pitch summarization, press release, and other materials aimed at capturing attention, gathering feedback, and generating interest. It can also help design prototypes to illustrate and validate the unique value proposition offered by the generated concept, and will indicate market potential, competitive advantage, and growth strategy. These materials effectively convey the value proposition and pique investor interest, providing a compelling case for further exploration or investment.

- *After the Sprint: An Innospective.*

So actually, there's a sixth and final step – the "innospective," a modified version of the Agile "retrospective." Retrospectives aim to improve the Agile process by reflecting on past work accomplishments and implementation methods and identifying areas for process improvement. The 12th Agile principle emphasizes the importance of a team taking time regularly to reflect on becoming more effective and adjusting their behavior accordingly. The team evaluates what worked and should be refined or kept, what didn't work and should be fixed or dropped, and explores new disruptive ideas improving the Generative AI Design Sprint.

This methodology, built upon principles of design thinking and Agile methodologies, provides a structured yet adaptable framework for innovation. It can lead to major improvements in the design process, reduce time-to-market, and enhance the overall success rate of innovation initiatives.

3. INNOBOT: AI-POWERED INNOVATION RESOURCE MANAGEMENT

Figure 5. Cartoon holding iPad

For FutureLab, brainstorming and design sprints are only the beginning steps toward an effective innovation resource management (IRM) system for enterprises. FutureLab has developed an IRM system called *The Idea Machine*™ that can significantly augment an organization's innovative capacity and collaboration efforts. This solution has been proven and has been installed in Fortune 500 deployments. Our plan is to use Slack and AI chatbots to operate this Idea Machine back-office application. The bot is called *InnoBot* and uses natural language to operate a comprehensive command and control system that drives innovation within organizations.

InnoBot facilitates idea collection and refinement, manages innovation portfolios, runs continuous cultural assessments, and implements low-cost enterprise-wide just-in-time innovation training... all within the Slack environment. It empowers organizations to monitor and evaluate their innovation pipelines, identify emerging trends, and optimize resource allocation. By analyzing the vast amount of information generated within design sprints and Slack feeds, InnoBot harnesses AI-powered data analytics to provide actionable insights, inform decision-making, and optimize the enterprise's innovation ecosystem. The system also conducts duplicate idea pruning, which reduces the cost of an innovation resource management system, (Bishop, Russell, & Norvig, 2022).

InnoBot incorporates tested intellectual property (IP) management capabilities, enables secure and transparent tracking of intellectual property generated by the enterprise, thereby safeguarding valuable ideas and innovations. Leveraging distributed ledger technology, InnoBot ensures an immutable record of ownership, creation, and modifications related to IP assets. Additionally, it offers automated patentability analysis, supporting incremental ideation and protecting an organization's intellectual property. In its next generation it will integrate patent-pending blockchain technology, providing a transparent and secure platform for tracking intellectual property rights and ownership in business ecosystems. The blockchain ensures that the IP assets generated during the design sprint are securely stored, timestamped, and tamper-resistant, protecting the interests of the participants and the organization, (Bishop, Russell, & Norvig, 2022).

4. THE BENEFITS OF AI-POWERED INNOVATION

FutureLab's unique formulation for generative AI for innovation represent a significant leap forward in the technology of innovation management. Our three bots –*BrainstormBot*, *DesignSprintBot*, and *InnoBot* – can amplify human creativity, enhance collaboration, and increase innovative capacity for any kind of company, large or small, traditional or hi tech, product, or service oriented. The era of Generative Innovation has arrived, empowering organizations to more effectively leverage new technologies, and to shape the future of business creativity; our bots are designed to accelerate the utility of these new capabilities, (Bishop, Russell, & Norvig, 2022).

The next stage goal is to implement AI-powered data analytics, which will enable users to gain valuable insights and ensure better decision-making. By analyzing data from various sources, teams can make informed choices about idea prioritization, market viability, and resource allocation. This data-driven approach eliminates guesswork and enhances the accuracy of decision-making, leading to better outcomes and reducing the risk of investing in unviable ideas. How the AI works is actually pretty simple: when your team has to make decisions about which projects to fund, by keeping track of who has a better track record as a chooser you can dynamically weight the better choosers. By implementing feedback and learning loops, everyone's decision-making skills will improve, leading to progressively better results over time. This is known as "adaptive boosting," and those weights become the most valuable thing ever. That's also how ChatGPT works – it weights certain words and phrases as better for various specific purposes, and the weights are what make the magic. By implementing this in a systemic, easy-to-use capability within Slack, the true goal of BrainstormBot is fulfilled: helping your company to become more intelligent, (Goodfellow, Bengio, & Courville, 2016).

Another application of highly effective AI for innovation focuses on optimizing the innovation pipeline. By providing a structured and iterative framework for rapid ideation, prototyping, and testing of ideas—which is core of the generative design sprint— it's really all about learning how to get better data, create better metrics, make better decisions about what to fund or abandon, and deciding when to pivot with agility. Again, this process is full of weights that can be trained, and better data analytics that can be developed for trend identification and market insights, all to ensure a competitive edge in the rapidly evolving marketplace, (Goodfellow, Bengio, & Courville, 2016).

This combination of technologies to empower your organization is only half the picture; the other half is all about your people. It's vital to foster a culture of innovation and creativity within your ecosystem, which is why BrainstormBot, DesignSprintBot and InnoBot all contain integrated innovation training capabilities to continually boost the skill level of your team. By using these tools to enhance your efforts to encourage collaboration, enable continuous learning, and foster the exploration of valuable new possibilities, you will accelerate the drive toward a mindset of innovation throughout the entire organization.

So, putting this all together could provide the breakthrough you need. By leveraging the power of artificial intelligence and collaborative platforms, your organization could navigate tomorrow's disruptive landscape with confidence, and unlock unprecedented new market potential, (Goodfellow, Bengio, & Courville, 2016).

5. WHAT REALLY MATTERS

As noted here, we believe that the inclusion of AI will bring the art and science of innovation to new heights, providing a catalyst for creative synergy, advancing group cohesion, and instilling a discipline of breakthrough creativity. What thus becomes possible is the emergence of a new, much more productive kind of innovation process, one that leverages the collective intelligence of the team, incorporates AI-enabled boosters, and drives 10x improvements in innovative outcomes, (Goodfellow, Bengio, & Courville, 2016).

Think about this as a vision… 10x'ing innovation in your organization. The average design sprint done the old-fashioned way might cost between $25,000 and $100,000 to implement. What's the cost of a BrainstormBot? $10 a month. That alone is a potential 10,000x improvement in cost. But does it work? Can AI help you come up with not only better art and resumes… but better ideas for your business? (Goodfellow, Bengio, & Courville, 2016).

At this time, we only have the results of our internal dogfooding tests, which were quite promising. One tester said, "This is freaky good!" Another said, "Man, this is good. But maybe too many ideas! How do we not get overwhelmed with too many options and choices?" Then someone asked, "I'm a little curious about whether the flow of the brainstorm would be better if our discussions don't get nested under the 'replies' part of Slack, but instead all appeared in the main part of the channel." He was addressing the other brainstorming humans in the channel, but then BrainstormBot spoke up:

"That's an interesting point to consider! Altering the flow of the brainstorming discussions by having them appear in the main part of the channel, rather than nested under the "replies" section, could have some advantages. Here are a few thoughts on this... [and then BrainstormBot made several great suggestions to improve visibility, continuity, and complexity... that were contextually accurate and would have passed a Turing test.] Ultimately, the best approach would depend on the specific dynamics and goals of the brainstorming activity. Experimenting with different formats and gathering feedback from participants can help determine what works best for your group in terms of promoting engagement, collaboration, and idea generation."

I immediately remarked to the other humans in the room, "Wow this is blowing my mind!" Then BrainstormBot cheerfully chirps, *"I'm thrilled to hear that this brainstorming session is blowing your mind! Brainstorming is all about pushing boundaries, exploring new ideas, and challenging the status quo. It's exciting to see the possibilities unfold and witness the creative energy in action. So, keep the ideas flowing and let your imagination soar!"*

I'm telling you; no human could have answered more cheerfully. Nevertheless, if the bot responded to every message, it would be way too chatty! So, we required that the bot needed to be formally addressed – by including @BrainstormBot, in order to answer. Anyway, as promising as this was, internal testing can only get us so far. We needed to get this technology out there and let real users play with it. And that's where you come in. We need you to not only be a customer, but to be our partner in tuning, tweaking, and refining this AI. So please join our community, and let's see how far we can fly, (Goodfellow, Bengio, & Courville, 2016).

Here's one additional data point to consider: when we embarked on this project, we decided to run an experiment at the same time. To build a product like this, and launch it, it would normally take a small team about 3 months to complete. I would normally assign 3 coders, and 3 product manager/marketers to do the work. Roughly 8–10-man months for coding and 8-10 for everything else. We decided to give ChatGPT a try, by using it for everything outside of coding, where we didn't want to skimp. So, our goal was to see if a single person, using ChatGPT and dogfooding BrainstormBot, could do the 8-10 months of product management and marketing work in 30 days. Roughly a 10x improvement.

This would be like... extreme sports. A grueling effort that would require all-nighters to stay on schedule. I am happy to report that we completed this work in roughly 45 days! We couldn't make the 30-day deadline, because we decided to add one additional task – to singlehandedly write a 330-page book about generative innovation at the same time! It turns out that ChatGPT is great for writing resumes and blog posts, but it really isn't that good at writing something good. Don't get me wrong, it's a great tool and helped to push through blocks, but it actually ended up creating more work than less. As for art, the design of the BrainstormBot character only took 30 minutes, a remarkable feat, but I soon learned how brittle AI art tools are. You can't even make the character turn sideways accurately. So, we had to hire a cartoon artist to take the design and create the comic quickstart guide. At least in these two situations, AI ended up creating more work for humans, not less. And using BrainstormBot to help design itself in our internal brainstormings was both effective and fun. Our assessment is that this stuff works. Now we have to create the training materials and UX to allow others to experience the same level of success that we did, (Goodfellow, Bengio, & Courville, 2016).

Finally, think about this: if you were going to change the world, where would you apply AI first? Where would it really make a difference? Where would it matter? Sure, you could use it to replace some Hollywood screenwriters, but all this would do is allow a few studios to make more money. Wouldn't it be better to apply AI to the fundamental challenge of making better products and growing smarter companies? If BrainstormBot were used by 10,000 companies, and many of them ended up becoming more successful ... many problems would be solved? How many jobs would be created? How many lives would be positively impacted?

Targeted at the fulcrum of innovative capability for our society, BrainstormBot uses AI to create jobs, not to displace people, and it will also lead making people more creative and innovative. Just ask MidJourney will make everyone an artist, if you learn how to use it, BrainstormBot could help make everyone a better innovator. So, what will it take?

Here's one last thing to chew on: The story of Léon Serpollet and the world land speed record is all about getting smarter. Serpollet, a French industrialist and pioneer of steam automobiles invented and perfected the flash boiler in 1896, which made steam a practical source of power for automobiles. Besides being an inventor, he became the first driver of a non-electrically powered car to hold the Land Speed Record. In April 1902 on the Promenade des Anglais in Nice, he drove the *Oeuf de Pacques* — the "Easter Egg," so-named because the car had an ovoid shape—at the heretofore unimaginable speed of 75.06 miles per hour, breaking the 1899 record of Camille Jenatzy's *La Jamais Contente*.

The point is that pretty much anyone can drive 75 mph today and do it while drinking coffee or putting on make-up. This means that something only a daredevil racer could do a hundred years ago is now commonly achieved; driving at 70 miles per hour isn't a rare skill anymore, it's practically a requirement for daily life. But here's the amazing thing: it didn't take millions or thousands or even a hundred years for human beings to "evolve" into race car drivers. Pretty much every human being can learn how to drive that fast within a few months, demonstrating remarkable levels of mental acuity and adaptation.

Humans are capable of amazing capabilities that go far beyond the ability to drive really fast while drinking coffee. Consequently, it's not absurd to think that in a hundred years, everyone will be a bit more like Steve Jobs or Elon Musk, everyone will be able to invent and innovate—essentially driving their brains down the Information Highway at 75 miles per hour without even breaking a sweat. So, the goal is that in a few months you could learn to innovate at a notably higher speed – and our hope is that BrainstormBot will be your patient driving instructor.

So please come and partner with us to advance this revolution in the art and science of innovation. Help us to pave the way for individuals and organizations to unleash deep untapped reserves of creative potential, to drive meaningful change, and to seize opportunities and success in the rapidly evolving digital landscape.

Figure 6. Men looking at computer screen

REFERENCES

Bishop, C., Russell, S., & Norvig, P. (2022). BrainstormBot: Enhancing brainstorming and innovation through AI-assisted ideation. *FutureLab Innovation Journal*, 12(3), 45–67.

Goodfellow, I., Bengio, Y., & Courville, A. (2016). *Deep Learning*. MIT Press.

Russell, S., & Norvig, P. (2022). *Artificial intelligence: A modern approach* (4th ed.). Pearson.

APPENDIX I

Table 1. BrainstormBot product roadmap

Feature	Description	Note
Phase I Features		
Idea Generation Efficiency	With the assistance of BrainstormBot, teams can ideate more efficiently and effectively. The AI-powered prompts help overcome creative blocks and stimulate innovative thinking, enabling teams to generate a higher volume of quality ideas within a shorter timeframe.	Available at Launch
Iterative Ideation	BrainstormBot presents initial "starter ideas" that stimulate thought and co-ideation by users. All you have to do is say "riff on idea 3" to launch a variation on a theme.	
Conversational Flow Analysis	Our chatbots utilize advanced sensors to detect and analyze conversation dynamics within the team. It identifies factors such as conversation flow, group consonance, and participation disparity, ensuring a balanced and inclusive ideation process.	
Prompts for People	BrainstormBot leverages the technique of multi-visioning, which enables participants to explore different perspectives and possibilities. This feature encourages diverse thinking and helps teams generate a multitude of creative ideas.	
Just in Time Innovation Training	We've integrated just in time coaching into the system, that not only explains how to use the software, but aims to provide some of the inspirational content that any brainstorming facilitator would offer to the team that hired her or him.	
Phase II Features		
Design Sprint Facilitation	DesignSprintBot facilitates the execution of a five-day Agile design sprint within the Slack platform. This streamlines the product design process, promotes collaboration, and enables the team to deliver impactful results in a time-bound and cost-effective manner.	Available as Open Beta
Pitch Material Generation	BrainstormBot goes beyond idea generation and assists in the production of pitch materials. It auto-generates high-quality pitch materials, including content for elevator pitches, press releases, and investor slide decks, saving time and resources.	
AI-powered Smart Voting	This functionality will revolutionize the ideation process by streamlining idea evaluation, promoting collaboration, and identifying valuable ideation patterns.	
Auto-clustering	Auto-Clustering to Detect Ideation Patterns: Auto-clustering is a technique that leverages AI algorithms to analyze and group similar ideas based on content, theme, or characteristics.	
Support for Microsoft Teams	We are using Slack as the substrate for rapid deployment and product testing. Support for Teams and other platforms will come in the near future.	Pending
Phase III Features		

continued on following page

Table 1. Continued

Feature	Description	Note
Automated Knowledge Capture	Our bots automate the capturing and organization of knowledge generated during the ideation process. It collects and categorizes ideas, insights, and concepts, ensuring that valuable information is not lost and can be easily accessed for further refinement.	Available in early 2024
InnoMetrics	Once implemented, InnoBot can manage the corporate innovation process through the InnoMetrics dashboard.	
Idea Duplicates Pruning	Duplicate ideas are expensive to prune, and we have AI technology under development that can automatically detect duplicate ideas, in order to prune, merge and refine the process.	
The IP Blockchain	FutureLab has patent-pending technology for integrating blockchain technology into the design process facilitated by the InnoBot and Idea Machine infrastructure. By leveraging blockchain for IP management, teams can ensure secure and transparent tracking of intellectual property rights. This enhances trust, mitigates disputes, and simplifies the management of intellectual property for the enterprise.	

This document and any other documents published in association with this white paper may relate to a potential token offering at a later time. This document does not constitute an offer of securities or a promotion, invitation or solicitation for investment purposes. Any future token offering will involve and relate to the development and use of experimental software and technologies that may not come to fruition or achieve the objectives specified in this white paper. The token is not therefore intended to represent a security interest.

Chapter 12
A Revolutionary Framework for Transforming National Innovation:
Leveraging Generative AI and Tokenization for Economic Development

Sharif Uddin Ahmed Rana
https://orcid.org/0000-0003-2296-6044
Paris Graduate School, France & World Talent Economy Forum, Malaysia

Adrian David Cheok
https://orcid.org/0000-0001-6316-2339
Imagineering Institute, Australia

ABSTRACT

This paper presents an ambitious vision for the transformation of innovation, driven at a national level. It addresses the critical elements of a national innovation ecosystem, including strategic advisory services, innovation catalysts, investment, training, innovation resource management software, and the tokenization of incentives and rewards. These form organizing frameworks that will increase capital formation and citizen participation. This paper also discusses the potential impact of the blockchain, generative AI and behavioral economics as organizing principles underlying this new innovation framework and hold the potential to bring a renaissance of knowledge, urbanism and meaning. Specifically, a system of interoperating

DOI: 10.4018/978-1-6684-6641-4.ch012

governmental blockchains with generative AI interfaces can serve as a decentralized operating system that powers a tokenized, hyper-connected innovation platform that can reinvigorate a national economy, kickstart high paying technical jobs, and ensure national competitiveness.

INTRODUCTION

It has been proven time and again that innovation is the primary driver of economic growth and success at a national level, but the innovation imperative takes on new significance when not just change – but the *rate* of change – goes exponential. Super-exponential growth rates will result in the rapid destruction and creation of industries and economies. Governments have a significant role to play in this effort by encouraging, supporting, and enabling innovation in their leading companies and leveraging entrepreneurial sweet spots. Essentially, this is an opportunity to create the next Silicon Valley, and success requires both extremely sober vision and extraordinary boldness.

Over the last decade, the emergence of blockchain and generative AI have initiated a process of changing the world. First, blockchain technology is poised to revolutionize industries worldwide. Its decentralized nature enhances transparency, efficiency, and trust in various sectors. Financial services benefit from faster, cost-effective transactions, while supply chains achieve better traceability. Healthcare gains secure patient data sharing, reducing fraud and errors. Smart contracts automate processes in law, real estate, and more. Developing regions access banking through blockchain-powered systems. As blockchain evolves, its global impact will be profound, reshaping how businesses and societies operate, facilitating innovation, and fostering a more connected, secure future, (Bohr & Memarzadeh, 2020).

The same is true for generative AI. Currently in its infancy, the initial use cases are in the generation of new content, such as text, images, or videos, and yet promises to radically transform fields like design, media, and education. However, the full potential of generative AI will be revealed in the years ahead, when it begins to fulfil its potential to augment and inspire human creativity, innovation, and progress. In new kinds of partnership with human ingenuity, generative AI can achieve unprecedented breakthroughs and help shape a future of abundance, progress, and possibility. It will help businesses to innovate and create new products or services, driving growth and competitiveness, (Bohr & Memarzadeh, 2020).

Therefore, national leaders must consider their current practices, and be prepared to develop innovative new models in order to leapfrog current leaders. These are some of the key questions to consider:

- What are the primary business models used in our country, and how can we develop new, more successful ones as the market changes?
- How do we get more of our citizens engaged in the innovation process, and contributing to innovative results that enhance and grow our businesses in local and global markets?
- How should we ensure our nation's overall success in today's rapidly changing global economy, and in tomorrow's?

These are the key questions that we will explore in this white paper, to provide practical steps to help national leaders leverage these trends to enhance competitiveness on a national scale.

A NEW KIND OF INNOVATION

Human society is now facing a set of problems so complex and immense that they can be solved only by accelerating the essential human processes of collaboration and innovation. Global scale problems require a new kind of global scale approach to innovation, one best implemented through mass-scale creative collaboration systems. Examples of mass creative collaboration have emerged over recent years, including the Human Genome Project, UNICEF's Global Polio Eradication Program, Linux open source, and even Wikipedia, all examples of people coming together to successfully solve enormous problems. But everything we've seen is just the beginning … over the next decade or two, astonishing and novel global scale innovation processes will emerge to leverage the networked brainpower of the human race, (Bohr & Memarzadeh, 2020).

We believe that humanity will manifest an emergent behavior that results in the development of a new kind of innovation framework, one that is globally scaled and ideally propagated through national innovation systems. The emergence of this system is likely to drive a new renaissance, providing massive benefits to the countries that lead in the development of this new framework, (Bohr & Memarzadeh, 2020).

So, what will this new framework look like? A good analogy is the electrical grid. The current electrical grid was built in the 1800s, and now is a patchwork of transmission lines, substations and transformers that deliver electricity from a power plant to your home or business. In most countries, it is strained to the breaking limit, (Bohr & Memarzadeh, 2020).

To move forward boldly into the future and provide the electricity required for millions of electric cars, we need to implement a next generation electrical smart-grid, one that is built from the bottom up to host smart meters, renewable energy resources, smart appliances, and smart electrically powered vehicles—all necessary to power humanity into the next century.

Similarly, the current innovation grid, which manages the production and delivery of invention today, is paper-based and uses a patent system that is more than 200 years old. This antiquated grid is similarly being stretched beyond its limits. Right now, it takes close to three years to even have your invention reviewed by a patent office, and patent trolls, the equivalent of IP ransomware, are free to ravage the intellectual property landscape, shaking down companies like information highway bandits. This antiquated system is ripe to be leapfrogged, (Bohr & Memarzadeh, 2020).

And just like a smartgrid for electricity, to move forward into a world that will be driven by exponential innovation, we need a next generation smartgrid for innovation. We need something that is built from the bottom up to handle a coming "Cambrian Explosion" of technologies to manage intellectual property and compensate creative endeavor that seems to be just emerging now.

A wonderful example of the sort of leapfrogging process we're referring to can be seen in South Korea. At first glance, the South Korea of twenty years ago was hampered by the lack of a proper telecommunications infrastructure, but instead of building out a landline POTS system, they leapfrogged to wireless, which provided a decided advantage in the transformation to a mobile computing economy. Similarly, first world countries are saddled with the equivalent of l andline innovation and hampered by an intellectual property system that could be leapfrogged by a consortium of countries who coordinate to build a next generation innovation smart grid, (Bohr & Memarzadeh, 2020).

The Innovation Eco-System

Many imitators have tried to capture the magic and brand of the Silicon Valley, including the Silicon Glen in Scotland, Silicon Fen in England, Silicon Wadi in Israel, and Silicon Fjord in Norway. In the United States we have Silicon Alley in New York, Silicon Dominion in Virginia, and the Silicon Forest in Oregon. But none of them have been successful in replicating the breakthrough success of the original.

The innovation ecosystem in any nation consists of seven types of participants, which are shown in the diagram to the right. We've known for a long time about the six elements at the perimeter, as studies of Silicon Valley and other hubs of innovation going back decades have explained these specific roles and shown how their various interactions yield such impressive outcomes.

It's not sufficient for a country's innovation ministry to simply provide cool looking workspaces for start-up companies, or to produce a contest to win some government funding. As AnnaLee Saxenian, a UC Berkeley professor who has written the definitive study of Silicon Valley has noted, "Simply having the ingredients of

Silicon Valley doesn't mean you have its regional dynamism. This notion that you can grow the next Silicon Valley by putting together a science park, venture capital and a university has been roundly disproven." Requiring your regional universities to produce a hackathon won't be enough either. Adding a few consultants, no matter how brilliant, will not help to move the needle, (Bohr & Memarzadeh, 2020).

Figure 1. The national innovation ecosystem

Indeed, one of the reasons that Silicon Valley has never been replicated is because the imitators have not sufficiently understood the critical role of the catalysts in the center of the model. Because innovation ecosystems require catalysts to provoke and accelerate innovation, inspiring innovation to occur when it otherwise might not, and speeding it to occur faster. Without the proper catalysts it is nearly impossible to provoke, inspire, and nurture scalable success, for in the catalyst's domain are the crucial functions of shaping expectations, building attitudes, and fostering productive ways of interacting, (Bohr & Memarzadeh, 2020).

Catalysts may be physical or virtual, may come in the form of people or technologies, could involve either foresight or insight. However, the most important component in the catalyzation process is the ability to embody new thinking that can bring forth new business models. Seeing long range possibilities for specific technologies or market needs — and how they will require change in current processes — is the key. This is a critical competency for government ministries, venture investors, and university leaders, all of whom have the influence to bring together key participants and engage them in the design and implementation of a better tomorrow, (Bohr & Memarzadeh, 2020).

What a country needs is to effect comprehensive and radical transformation. Countries need to leapfrog, as South Korea has, over current leaders and regional competitors. This process starts with a fundamental shift in how you think about innovation at a systemic level by design systemic interventions and catalyzing agents that can achieve genuine change. Like gene therapy, the necessary mindshift to new thinking is the spark and the array of innovation systems you need to install act as the accelerant. In this way, you can rewrite your entire nation's innovation DNA.

Through innovations catalysts, your country could achieve a critical mass of innovation to power a societal transformation, (Bohr & Memarzadeh, 2020).

Cocktail Solution for Systematic Breakthroughs

Many highly problematic diseases can be treated with drug combinations — what you do is mix antiretroviral compounds with transcriptase inhibitors and steroids. The combinations are called "cocktails," and they're so effective that they're called the "Lazarus Effect," named for the biblical figure who was raised from the dead. Cocktails can turn an HIV death sentence into a manageable chronic condition, (Bohr & Memarzadeh, 2020).

Complex and evolving health challenges must be addressed with equally complex and adaptive multi-pronged solutions. Similarly, complex innovation challenges also require complex and adaptive multi-pronged, integrated into a comprehensive and systematic approach. This has the potential to synergistically enable disruption, change and transformation at the individual, corporate, regional and national levels *simultaneously*. This is how we achieve a "catalyst effect" for national-scale innovation.

This proposed cocktail prescription requires a combination of strategic advisory services, carefully planned catalysis, and proper investment, combined with immersive training, next generation innovation resource management software, and use of advanced technologies, such as generative AI and the tokenization of behavioral incentives and rewards.

Six foundational elements have to be thoughtfully designed and effectively applied in a systemic and coherent way; a strong entrepreneurial sector, education at all levels, service providers that support entrepreneurship, investment capital in many forms, the corporate sector, and of course there are key roles for the government in supporting and aligning all of these. What is often poorly understood, however, is the critical role that the people and organizations we call *innovation catalysts* play in attaining innovation success, and it is even less understood how catalysts operate at the national level.

These must be deployed at a national level, and configured as shown below, and we can discuss the training, software and tokenization requirements later:

Table 1. Implementation of the innovation cocktail prescription: systematic catalysis

Member	Training	Software	Tokenization
Government	Agile Master Plan	National Innovation Dashboard and Analytics, Disruption Mapping	Sovereign InnoToken
Entrepreneurs	Agile Design Sprint	BrainstormBot and DesignSprintBot	Grants & BitEquity
Incubators & Mentors	Incubator Training, Agile Design Sprint Train the Trainer	Idea Machine, VC Dashboard and Analytics, Agile Collaboratory, Disruption Mapping	BitEquity
Academia	Agile Incubator Training, TTO Training, Agile Design Sprint, Train the Trainer	Idea Machine, Incubator and TTO system, Disruption Mapping, Agile Collaboratory	Grants & BitEquity
SMEs, SOEs and Companies	Agile Master Plan	Idea Machine, Pivot Maps, Disruption Mapping, Agile Collaboratory	BitEquity
Investors	Venture Design Sprints	VC Dashboard and Analytics, Disruption Mapping	BitEquity
Professional Services	Full System Train the Trainer	BrainstormBot, Idea Machine, Disruption Mapping, Agile Collaboratory	BitEquity

Again, among their many roles, innovation catalysts function as matchmakers, teachers, and investors, which are indeed common activities in the venture investment community. What we're discussing, then, is how to formalize and operationalize the catalyst effort at the scale of a nation, and in a blockchain-enabled environment, doing so using sovereign cryptocurrency and tokenized behavioral economics. This goes beyond the role played by start-up contests and incubators, which are common, as what we propose can attain a much more significant scale that enables innovation to become woven into the fabric of daily life across an entire national economy.

Comprehensive Innovation Training

FutureLab has been developing and delivering leading-edge innovation training for more than a decade. Our methods and tools have been adopted in countless companies and at the national level in China, Georgia, Malaysia, New Zealand, and Singapore. Our methods are certified by the world's leading professional association for innovators, the International Association of Innovation Professionals, and are now being included in the new ISO Standard 279 for innovation management, which is under development.

We'd like to introduce you to the *Agile Innovation Master Plan* — a rigorous, structured process for stimulating and refining the innovation process in organizations of any size; spanning innovation strategy, the innovation portfolio, the innovation process, innovation culture and the innovation infrastructure. All within a simplified approach that breaks a very complex problem into its requisite components.

Figure 2. The Agile innovation master plan

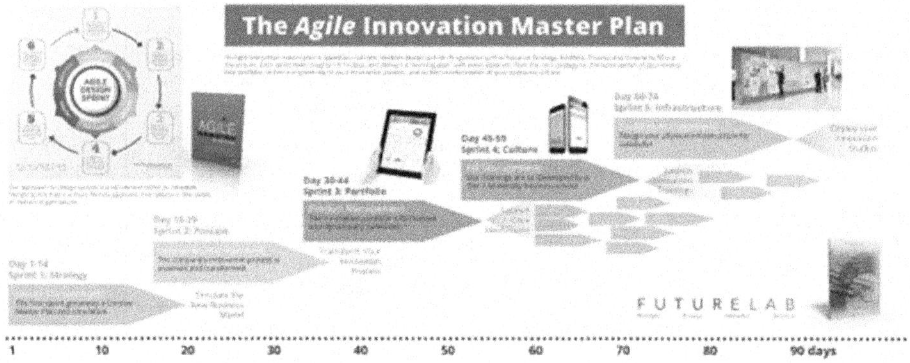

Comprehensive Innovation Management Software

The training described above is complemented by the comprehensive innovation management system that FutureLab has been developing and implementing for a decade. It's the only comprehensive innovation management system in existence that can support systemic management of innovation at all levels, from the national government down to the individual enterprise.

National Innovation Dashboard and Analytics — Unique and powerful dashboards enable government agencies to manage the entire country's innovation programs in a strategic manner. This tool has never before been available, and so governments have only had fragmentary and piecemeal views of their innovation investments which have significantly impeded their success. With the National Innovation Portfolio Manager enabling real-time visibility into existing, proposed, and possible startups and innovation projects, government can assess all the critical elements that together constitute a comprehensive overall strategy. The dashboard includes tools that assess the robustness and agility of programs in progress, and that correlate current projects with anticipated goals and national innovation metrics, along proposed technology roadmaps. This is critical information that's never been available before, but now it is, and it makes a fundamental difference.

VC Dashboard and Analytics — This is a subset of the National Innovation Dashboard that enables venture investors and incubators to track performance and potential ROI for existing and proposed investments. In a decentralized Agile system, startups report progress to investors who can share performance metrics (including for entities that have received governmental funding), to government agencies and ministries. Data is locally generated and automatically propelled up toward the innovation ministry.

Figure 3. The Idea Machine™

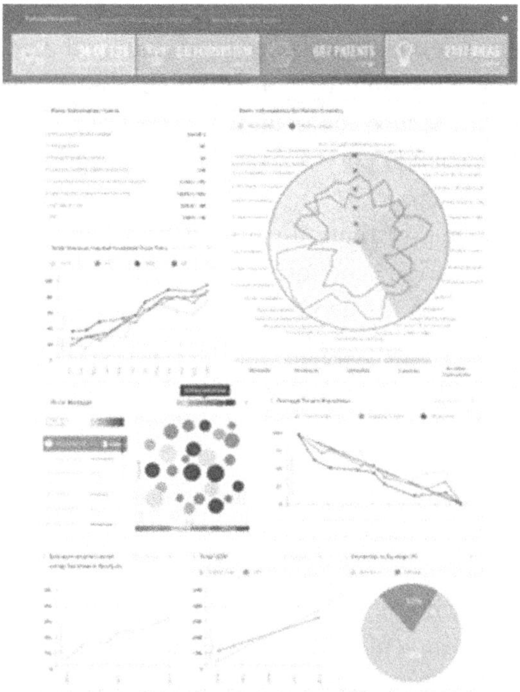

The Idea Machine™ — A next generation creativity application that helps teams better capture, refine, evaluate, and manage knowledge - all within a structured innovation pipeline and portfolio. It is paired with *InnoMetrics,™* the dynamic innovation data analysis tool that gives managers the ability to perform instant innovation audits and to drive collective brainpower in the right directions. Think of it as *SaberMetrics* for innovation. The system also enables *PivotMaps™*to support high level strategic alignment by automatically linking individual projects with the overall corporate and national strategy using a novel dynamic real-time user experience to empower teams to move beyond self-organization to self-optimization. This delivers the power of Agile innovation at scale.

Disruption Mapping™ — Provides interactive, what-if views of new trends and technologies, enabling managers to better understand the emerging forces and factors that will disrupt the structure of the marketplace.

Agile Collaboratory™ — In high-technology research it's costly and burdensome for large firms to develop relationships with university researchers because confidentiality and IP constraints often make it impossible to disclose internal discussions without significant managerial overhead. In this situation, an interlinking social network, with nuanced partial transparency of IP, can simplify and empower the management of external researchers.

The system provides countless benefits, including these:

- The system allows internally focused corporate innovation platforms to evolve toward secure and open innovation platforms.
- It enables disparate corporate innovation applications to communicate and interoperate.
- It facilitates fine-resolution entitlement capability to ensure that confidential information is not divulged inappropriately, essentially enabling innovation search to become a transaction.
- It fosters the formation of effective innovation teams and partnerships within and across organizations and increases useful licensing of technologies from academia to industry along with improved feedback about user needs.
- It allows participants to gather and analyze meaningful metrics for innovation and best practices.

Looking forward, technology-enabled meta-coordination of collaboration combined with the next generation of Agile management can help achieve a quantum leap in productivity and fulfill the promise of intelligent openness. This new framework will allow organizations to connect with customers and partners to collaborate in new ways. Fully implemented, the innovation smart grid enables powerful new business models and functionality to emerge, facilitating vibrant innovation partnerships between academia, government, and industry, thereby increasing national innovation capacity and accelerating gross domestic product growth.

TECHNOLOGY AS CATALYST: GENERATIVE AI AND BLOCKCHAIN

At the heart of this proposed new framework for national innovation system are a number of new technologies, including generative AI, blockchain, DeFi, tokenization, and more. These will be used in a myriad of ways, but it's valuable to note a few key technologies: the IP Blockchain, generative brainstorming, and behavioral tokens. Let's dig in!

Let's start with a concept we call the *IP Blockchain* — an immutable digital ledger that serves as the universal system of record for the management of ideas and innovations. It's a powerful vision that extends the benefits of distributed ledgers into new arenas that are foundational for societal innovation advancement and economic growth. This transformational process starts with a new way to establish and verify ownership of an idea and the intellectual property rights (IPRs) generated, coordinated by an intellectual property (IP) policy server and an immutable ledger for managing the IPRs.

The IP Blockchain would be a "third generation" decentralized application, which involves multiple interoperating digital ledgers and a number of underlying logic services, including an unalterable and persistent semi-public linear data container space with a data schema for both information about IP (e.g., patents and ideas) and meta-information about ideas and innovation, which tracks the entire lifecycle of ideas, from conception through commercialization. Additional ledgers manage reputations, incentives, and agreements, all of which enable a robust, nation-wide innovation system to capture ideas from throughout the community, organize them, help identify the best ones, and provide appropriate recognition and rewards to the originators.

The IP Blockchain moves beyond the idea of IP as static data and lifeless patents. It's more effective to configure ideas as living, evolving constructions, using something like a Merkle tree, a directed acyclic graph to capture the evolution of an innovation or idea over time. This will provide multiple parties access to the idea within a digitally expressed innovation collaboration smart contract that simplifies the process of collaboration, ideation workflow and licensing. This smart contract could even enable the formation of dynamic adaptive patent pools to protect the inventors from non-practicing entities. Consider the impact of being the first country in the world to pilot test a decentralized intellectual property management system at your patent office.

Another concept would be FutureLab's unique formulation for generative innovation – *BrainstormBot*. This ChatGPT-powered application is designed to amplify human creativity, enhance collaboration, and increase innovative capacity for any kind of organization, large or small, traditional or hi tech, product or service oriented. This would in turn enable the development of a new kind of AI-powered data analytics for innovation, which will enable users to gain valuable insights and ensure better decision-making. By analyzing data from various sources, teams can make informed choices about idea prioritization, market viability, and resource allocation. This data-driven approach eliminates guesswork and enhances the accuracy of decision-making, leading to better outcomes and reducing the risk of investing in unviable ideas.

A third concept for the use of AI for innovation focuses on optimizing the innovation pipeline. By providing a structured and iterative framework for rapid ideation, prototyping, and testing of ideas—which is core of the generative design sprint— it's really all about learning how to get better data, create better metrics, make better decisions about what to fund or abandon, and deciding when to pivot with agility. Again, this process is full of weights that can be trained and boosted, and better data analytics that can be developed for trend identification and market insights, all to ensure a competitive edge in the rapidly evolving marketplace.

This leads us to the final concept for this paper: *behavioral tokens for innovation.*

Decentralizing Capital Formation

We've discussed the critical role of the catalyst in the innovation ecosystem, the critical role of training and facilitation, and the importance of a comprehensive software framework. But what about capital raising? What new approaches can we take to both raising capital and reducing investment risk? These are topics we discuss in this section.

The reality is that it normally takes several months to raise money in Silicon Valley the old-fashioned way, and eventually ends up costing the entrepreneurs more than half of their companies. When record companies-controlled music it was virtually impossible for a new band to break in without kowtowing to a record label executive. Peer to peer computing put an end to that.

The venture capital business still operates in much the same way as the recording industry used to work. An endless supply of new startups sends business plans to venture capital firms who make vague promises that a term sheet is just around the corner. As a result, in Silicon Valley it takes months or even years to get a term sheet. Realistically, Silicon Valley offers the roughly same odds as releasing a hit record or writing a screenplay that gets greenlighted as a feature film production by a major studio.

For a while, the ICO changed all that. This radical new capital formation technology roared past the traditional venture capital market, for a while, and companies were raising hundreds of millions of dollars… in an hour. Brave, a company that tokenized human attention for online marketing, raised $35 million in just 30 seconds, with no equity dilution!

The ICO has already changed things drastically, but the empire struck back.

It may be time for national innovation ministries to build upon the ICO process to facilitate the expansion of innovation throughout the nation. Again, the ICO is based on the principle of tokenization, which sits at a complex intersection of economics, psychology, and product development. To succeed, a cybertoken has a functional role in a platform, provides incentives to existing and potential users, and must be an essential part of a sustainable economy. Effective tokenization creates an eco-system and a mini-economy around a product and a blockchain that propels the adoption of a new business model.

Understanding the tokenization revolution is all about understanding behavioral economics, and these dynamics can also help a country to accelerate its transformation into a 21st century nation. We believe it may be possible to create something we call the sovereign *InnoToken*.

The InnoToken is an "innovation stimulating token," a super-token that reduces risk for venture investors by enabling them to diversify through the formation of a "basket of equities." This can be used to incent investors, advisors, and business development mentors, and is a key tool in the catalyst toolbox. This basket could also evolve into a CYDR (Cybertoken Depositary Receipt), is analogous to a "SPDR," an S&P Depositary Receipt. However, whereas the SPDR is "market cap weighted," a CYDR will be "innovation weighted" with emphasis on earlier stage companies.

The bulk of the super-tokens will be provided to investors, but a modest number of tokens could be allocated to the incubators and portfolio companies to use – but not sell – for the purpose of incenting advisors and business development experts to engage fully in support of the company. Additionally, some tokens could be reserved to support the overall fund and its companies in its efforts to increase market penetration via referral commissions and bounties.

This would provide participating portfolio companies with a sort of "limited liquidity," as they will be provided with valuable tokens to underwrite the cost of drawing world class advisors to regional business development efforts, which powerfully multiplies the power of the underlying investment. The token should not be thought of as an indirect form of equity, but more like an "innovation supercharger" for the eco-system. Thus, early-stage companies can enjoy benefits of a token offering without having to issue an ICO until they're ready.

Offering shares only in a single early-stage startup is not as attractive an enticement due to the risks that any single venture faces, but a supertoken that provides indirect shares in a diversified basket of blockchain ventures offers a much higher probability of future value. This could bring, for example, experts in web marketing in the US and Europe, to help out startups in Africa and the Middle East.

Making these micro-equity incentives fungible could allow the entire innovation eco-system in a country to leverage the reward concept used in growth hacking and crowdfunding, as mentors and affiliates will see real and concrete potential return for their investment of time and expertise. This single technological advancement allows you to satisfy all of the requirements for growth hacking and viral marketing:

it creates a common goal of creating value through the equity pool which galvanizes the community.

Benefits of the InnoToken to the innovation ecosystem:

- Investor Benefits: Full investment lifecycle liquidity, dynamic block chain-based investor protection, verifiable claims technology for auto-validated representations, brokerage assisted for non-crypto savvy investors.
- Company Benefits: Enhanced venture capital with both cash and tokens, access to top mentors and early globalization experts, simplified compliance functionality yields happier investors.
- Mentor Benefits: Access to valuable tokens as incentives for participation in the global incubator eco-system, verifiable claims technology enables decentralized trust for offshore ventures.
- Community Benefits: Access to tokens via participation in the referral network does not require investment to participate, configured so a percentage of tokens are donated to philanthropic causes.
- Investor/Incubator Benefits: Easier fundraising process, enables differentiated incubation services.

Putting all of this together could provide the breakthrough you need. By leveraging the power of artificial intelligence and collaborative platforms, your organization could navigate tomorrow's disruptive landscape with confidence, and unlock unprecedented new market potential.

Figure 4. Men in an office

WHY FUTURELAB

FutureLab offers a comprehensive approach to innovation that combines a meaningful strategic model, world class consulting, innovation training that was licensed by a Tier 1 university business school, and breakthrough software that has been successfully deployed enterprise wide at a Fortune 50 company and is forward thinking enough to carry your country into the 21st century. We have an approach that is powerful enough to reprogram organizational DNA so that innovation becomes a core capability. Our many books (10 and counting) contain case studies which show that our approach actually works.

Here is an overview of our current activities:

FutureLab partners currently work with innovation and technology ministries in China, Georgia, Malaysia, Singapore, and New Zealand. Our lead partner on national innovation, Langdon Morris, is an internationally-recognized innovation leader, and is a member of the U.S. Technical Advisory Group working on ISO 279, the new global standard for innovation, where he serves on two subcommittes, Management of Innovation and Creative Thinking.

We are experts in blockchain and decentralization technologies, serving in leadership roles at WC3 standards organization working groups, and partnering with leading blockchain technology vendors on breakthrough applications in health care, community development, and investment management.

FutureLab has also developed *BrainstormBot*, a ChatGPT-powered generative AI solution that offers revolutionary improvements to the design sprint process through the deployment of AI-assisted tools to enhance ideation, collaboration, and innovation resource management. The system is unique in that it implements a structured five-day Agile design process over Slack that orchestrates ethnographic research, divergent ideation, convergent distillation of winning concepts, strategic visualization through a business model canvas, and facilitates automated pitch material production. These chatbots leverage intelligent sensors that detect factors such as conversational flow metrics, participation disparity and group consonance to promote more inclusive and productive collaboration.

Figure 5. Hand holding cellphone

Furthermore, FutureLab is developing botUX, a user interface process that can allow untrained users manage the Idea Machine application with natural language commands – key innovation management functions - like knowledge capture, innovation portfolio management, in-context innovation training, and innovation audits and cultural assessments - to be controlled by voice. In the near future, innovation managers will simply be able to ask FutureLab's InnoBot what the company's top ideas are, whether an idea might be patentable, or if the corporate culture is getting more or less innovative… simply by asking.

In summary, FutureLab is a unique team of highly experienced strategists and technology visionaries who have the experience, expertise, knowledge leadership, and operational software expertise to support national innovation programs.

CONCLUSION: LET'S INVENT THE FUTURE TOGETHER

A National Innovation Framework will enable intentional, government-supported efforts that combine and integrate entire ecosystems across private and public sectors in purposeful and very productive ways to engage, enable, and even inspire all members of large communities to work together to create new capabilities that will provide essential, future economic advantage, that is, to innovate.

This vision can be attained through a systematic approach to investing in and managing innovation, giving close attention to the innovation process through which funds are invested and innovation projects pursued, all with the goal of course of achieving very high levels of innovation throughout a company, a city, a region, and an entire nation.

In summary, then, we are all quite aware that the world is changing rapidly, and that innovation at many scales is necessary for survival and success. Many of the elements or ingredients that support innovation within ecosystem communities are well known, among them education, support services, willing entrepreneurs, investment capital, and supportive government policy. Less well understood is the critical role of the catalyst, and even less the role of participatory national frameworks and national infrastructure.

Specifically, key actions to take include mapping the existing innovation ecosystem, implementing an innovation catalyst program to enhance the ecosystem, and implementing the vital infrastructure needed to assure significant and positive impacts that accelerate innovation progress, enhance innovation skills and knowledge, provide the right forms of investment capital, promote high levels of citizen engagement in innovation, and help to align strategic opportunities with the capabilities of their firms. Educational policies, funding, and strong support services are also essential elements of a comprehensive approach.

There are many places in the world where innovation occurs, but very few where it happens constantly and decisively, where people simply expect that great, new ideas will emerge with some regularity. What the most innovative cities and regions share, and what contributes so much to their identities as innovation hubs, are large and well-developed support systems that provide all the essential elements that enable innovation on a large scale. These include the investors and financial capital, the students and scholars and thought leadership, the professional services, and the government policies. All of these must strongly favor innovation.

They succeed because they take advantage of an entire system of people, organizations, and tools, and thus an essential insight underlying the framework is the awareness that innovation occurs not so much because of insightful leaps by lone geniuses or entrepreneurs, but as a result of fruitful interactions between many of the participants across an entire innovation ecosystem. Facilitating the leap to large scale should thus become a strategic priority, and this is exactly what FutureLab's comprehensive set of frameworks and tools can achieve.

As we know, developing and applying advanced skills and capabilities in innovation are no longer optional, for they are now an absolute requirement for the success at any scale, from the start up to the multinational to the entire country. The key participants include individuals, organizations, and nations, from the student and the start-up entrepreneur to the corporation and the financial sector, from the city mayor to a national government minister, each has important roles to play.

Decentralization can lead to greater openness of the innovative boundaries of firms, which would lead to new innovation dynamics. This can be of enormous help to organizations that happen to be located in territories that are less endowed with innovation resources (both physical and human ones). Just because you're not in California's Silicon Valley, the Silicon Plateau of India, or any other global innovation hub, does not mean you're doomed to underperform. Indeed, undertaking collaborations with actors of innovation outside of their given territory allows firms to access needed diversity of resources, thus enhancing efforts everywhere. The innovation potentials of different regions can align, enabling each region's strengths to be utilized more thoroughly, and in fact optimized.

In the emerging global economy, the business model of any region or nation is subject to rapidly changing market needs and conditions. Today's great successes may not sustain their advantages, and new models will emerge to displace models that dominate today. Thus, the importance of an approach such as the one described here goes beyond the opportunities to incrementally improve local conditions and may be much more like the imperative to harness innovation at the national scale to adapt to fundamental changes that will national and global in their impacts. Such an innovation process, at scale, becomes a collaborative process of citizens co-creating their own future, a genuinely compelling prospect that has deep and quite positive social and economic implications.

Figure 6. Man looking at computer screen

REFERENCES

Bohr, A., & Memarzadeh, K. (2020). *Artificial Intelligence in Healthcare*. Academic Press.

Chapter 13
Quantum Bridge Analytics II:
QUBO-Plus, Network Optimization, and Combinatorial Chaining for Asset Exchange

Sharif Uddin Ahmed Rana
https://orcid.org/0000-0003-2296-6044
Paris Graduate School, France & World Talent Economy Forum, Malaysia

Adrian David Cheok
https://orcid.org/0000-0001-6316-2339
Imagineering Institute, Australia

ABSTRACT

Quantum Bridge Analytics relates to methods and systems for hybrid classical-quantum computing and is devoted to developing tools for bridging classical and quantum computing to gain the benefits of their alliance in the present and enable enhanced practical application of quantum computing in the future. This is the second of a two-part tutorial that surveys key elements of Quantum Bridge Analytics and its applications. Part I focused on the Quadratic Unconstrained Binary Optimization (QUBO) model which is presently the most widely applied optimization model in the quantum computing area, and which unifies a rich variety of combinatorial optimization problems. Part II (the present paper) introduces the domain of QUBO-Plus models that enables a larger range of problems to be handled effectively. After illustrating the scope of these QUBO-Plus models with examples, we give special attention to an importance instance of these models called the Asset Exchange Problem (AEP).

DOI: 10.4018/978-1-6684-6641-4.ch013

1. INTRODUCTION

Quantum Bridge Analytics is devoted to developing tools for bridging classical and quantum computing to gain the benefits of their alliance in the near term and enable enhanced practical application of quantum computing in the future.

As observed in Part I of this tutorial, the Quadratic Unconstrained Binary Optimization (QUBO) model has an important role in Quantum Bridge Analytics by unifying a rich variety of combinatorial optimization problems and becoming at present the most widely applied optimization model in the quantum computing area.

In Part II (the present paper) we consider applications called QUBO-Plus problems motivated by the classical QUBO formulation that embrace larger classes of problems, and that also make it possible to solve certain subclasses of QUBO problems more effectively. Details of the QUBO-Plus model, including its formulation and illustrative applications, are discussed in section 2.

To underscore the importance of identifying problems that can be treated as QUBO-Plus applications, we give special attention in this paper to a problem class called the Asset Exchange Problem (AEP) which is motivated by developments in blockchains that relate to finding exchanges among investors that are mutually beneficial to all participants. . We first describe a QUBO model for a special instance of the AEP and then adopt the QUBO-Plus perspective to consider the relevance of characterizing the AEP domain in a more general form. To further motivate our focus on the AEP we discuss a range of applications both within and beyond blockchains where this class of problems is important. As we demonstrate in the sections that follow, solutions to the AEP enable market players to identify and profit from exchanges of assets that benefit all participants – exchanges that, in game theory terminology, constitute a positive sum game. This provides a mechanism for facilitating exchanges customarily carried out through mechanisms of money, interest, and middlemen by serving instead the blockchain goal of disintermediation to remove or reduce reliance on intermediaries. The resulting modeling and solution process simultaneously afford a link between the applications of classical and quantum computing that are envisioned to be increasingly relevant as the quantum computing area becomes more mature.

We introduce two main hubs for solving AEP models, the first consisting of a mathematical formulation yielding a network optimization model for a basic version of the AEP and the second consisting of a metaheuristic optimization framework called combinatorial chaining that augments the network model to make it possible to derive high quality solutions to more complex instances of the AEP, notably including instances encountered in a wide variety of real-world applications.

These developments derive special relevance within the context of Quantum Bridge Analytics, which offers gains by bridging the gap between classical and quantum computational methods and technologies. As observed in the 2019 Consensus Study Report titled *Quantum Computing: Progress and Prospects* (National Academies, 2019), quantum computing will remain in its infancy for perhaps another decade, and in the interim "formulating an R&D program with the aim of developing commercial applications for near-term quantum computing is critical to the health of the field." The report further notes that such a program will rely on developing "hybrid classical-quantum techniques." Innovations that underlie and enable these hybrid classical-quantum techniques, which are the focus of Quantum Bridge Analytics, provide a fertile catalyst for introducing the QUBO-Plus applications in the AEP domain.

Additional links to the Quantum Bridge Analytics theme are provided in Kochenberger and Ma (2020) who observe that QUBO and QUBO-Plus models give rise to a variety of formulations for portfolio optimization, and these in turn yield a natural basis for integrating classical and quantum computing via the Asset Exchange Problem. Portfolio optimization has a prominent role in the AEP when the assets under consideration involve those customarily incorporated into the portfolio domain. The AEP goes further, both in the portfolio domain and others, by linking the holders of multiple portfolios in a network of cooperative optimization. This establishes a natural alliance with QUBO-Plus models whose solutions identify desirable assets for different participants.

After introducing the general representation of QUBO-Plus models in the next section and providing examples of applications related to the theme of the present paper, in succeeding sections we provide a mathematical optimization model for a basic instance of the AEP and then show how the model can be transformed into a network optimization model, thus laying the foundation for exploiting more complex variants of the AEP.

A note on terminology: we use the term "exchange" rather than "swap" because a swap typically refers to an exchange involving only two items or two participants, and "multiple swaps" refer to a collection of pairwise exchanges, in contrast to an integrated process that requires the coordination among all participants for its execution.

The most developed literature on exchanges occurs for the traveling salesman problem, where the term *k-opt* refers to an exchange that removes k edges from a tour and replaces them by k other edges so that the resulting configuration continues to be a tour (Hamiltonian cycle; see, e.g., Helsgaun 2000, 2009). The traveling salesman procedures that come closest to the process of combinatorial chaining are the ejection chain approaches that have been applied to TSPs and other combinatorial optimization problems (Glover 1996; Rego and Glover 2006; Yagiura et al. 2006. 2007; Rego et al. 2016).

The blockchain literature refers to exchanges called *atomic swaps* (also known as cross-chain trading). As elaborated subsequently, these exchanges arise when two parties who want to share their cryptocurrencies execute an exchange by means of Hashed Timelock Contracts (or HTLCs) as a mechanism to make the transaction secure (Nolan 2013; Fitzpatrick 2019). Combinatorial chaining makes it possible to generalize these swaps to exchanges involving multiple actors.

Combinatorial chaining and the Asset Exchange Problem are to be differentiated from the problem and methods arising in combinatorial auctions where swaps are sought to exchange pairs of buy/sell-orders in futures markets (Winter et al. 2011; Müller et al. 2017). An interesting area for future investigation would be to determine if the combinatorial chaining approach could likewise be applied in the setting of combinatorial auctions to enable auctions involving greater numbers of participants.

The remainder of this paper is organized as follows. Section 2 introduces QUBO-Plus models that provide computationally important alternatives to standard QUBO models. Examples of asset exchange applications are given in Section 3 to set the stage for later more extensive and technical discussions. Section 4 provides the fundamental mathematical formulation of the basic AEP problem and shows how to transform this formulation into a network optimization model. Section 5 characterizes the structure of combinatorial chaining in reference to this basic network model, followed by introducing more advanced processes in Section 6 for joining network optimization and combinatorial chaining with metaheuristic analysis to address more complex instances of asset exchanges. The paper concludes with a summary of the key notions and their implications in Section 7.

2. QUBO-PLUS MODELS AND THE ASSET EXCHANGE PROBLEM

The classical QUBO model is expressed as follows.

QUBO: minimize/maximize $y=x^tQx$

where x is a vector of binary decision variables and Q is a square matrix of constants.

The term "QUBO-Plus" refers to a class of models that augment the preceding standard QUBO representation by introducing important constraints separately from the QUBO model, enabling them to be treated by algorithms specially designed to handle these special constraints. This contrasts with the standard approach that seeks to merge such constraints with the QUBO model by attaching weights to them to create a modified form of the Q matrix as described in the Part I tutorial. Many problems have special constraints that could be modeled in pure QUBO form but may afford advantages from both a computational and "model transparency" point of view by embodying them in a QUBO-Plus model. By keeping these constraints separate from the QUBO formulation, and developing a special algorithm that handles the resulting QUBO-Plus problem, it is possible to solve these problems more efficiently and effectively than by attempting to create a "transformed" QUBO model that folds the constraints into the Q matrix.

Computational studies (Yu, et al. 2020) document that QUBO-Plus models often deliver superior performance, relative to transformed QUBO alternatives, in terms of solution quality and solution time, and permit larger problems to be solved. Such QUBO-Plus models also provide a transparent reminder of the special constraint(s) that are otherwise lost in a transformed QUBO representation.

While the variety of QUBO-Plus models is substantial and application dependent, we catalog some commonly encountered special cases in the following list. In the cases highlighted below, the reference to setting a variable to 1 can encompass a variety of applications by a correspondence with selecting a particular item from a collection of projects, investments, assets, facilities, locations, buildings, plans, medical treatments, architectural designs, itineraries, etc. In such settings, the special constraint(s) defining the "Plus" component of the QUBO-Plus model embody a key problem feature earmarked for special treatment.

Common QUBO-Plus model Types:

(1) Exact cardinality constrained QUBO problems: requiring an exact number of variables to be set to 1.
(2) Bounded cardinality constrained QUBO problems: requiring a lower bound and an upper bound on the number of variables set to 1.
(3) Multi-assignment QUBO problems: requiring disjoint sets of variables to sum to 1.
(4) Multi-allocation QUBO problems: requiring disjoint sets of variables to sum to specified constants (that may differ from 1).
(5) QUBO packing problems: requiring sums of variables to be less than or equal to specified constants.
(6) QUBO covering problems: requiring sums of variables to be greater than or equal to specified constants.
(7) QUBO problems combining (5) and (6) (also called bounded multi-allocation QUBO problems).

(8) QUBO knapsack problems: requiring a weighted sum of variables to be less than or equal to a specified constant.

(9) Multi-knapsack QUBO problems: requiring weighted sums of variables to be less than or equal to specified constants.

(10) Generalized covering QUBO problems: requiring weighted sums of variables to be greater than or equal to specified constants.

With appropriate modifications, modern QUBO solvers can be customized to produce solutions that satisfy the explicit "Plus" constraints while optimizing the quadratic objective function.

We remark that QUBO-Plus models of type (1) arise naturally in the context of the well-known Maximum Diversity problem and in portfolio optimization problems where a pre-specified number of assets must be chosen. These models are generalized by those of type (2) which apply to broader settings. QUBO-Plus type (3) models, with their assignment constraints, have many important applications and are further noteworthy for having natural connections to certain types of network problems. In these network-related problems, members of certain groups or sub-groups are assigned to members of other groups with the goal of optimizing some measure that describes the overall effectiveness of the assignments. Problems of this type have a link to the AEP problem via their network-related component.

We describe specific models below that illustrate these connections.

Model 1. While applications of all ten QUBO-Plus type models are found in practice, Type (3) models with their assignment constraints are particularly noteworthy due to their connection to various forms of clustering and applications such models accommodate. Consider for example, an investment setting where x_{ij}=1 if investor i is assigned to cluster (class of investments) j, and the constraints are $\sum(x_{ij}$: overall j)=1 for each investor i ensure that each investor is assigned. A variation of this type of application is where investments are assigned to specific investment classes. Each of these applications involves considerations that are relevant to the AEP problem, although they fall short of capturing a variety of additional elements of the AEP as we subsequently indicate.

Model 2. Graph coloring problems present additional applications for QUBO-Plus type (3) models where a color must be assigned to each node in the graph (the assignment constraints) while adjacent nodes are required to receive different colors. The adjacency constraints can be folded into the Q matrix and the node assignment constraints can be imposed traditionally rather than by penalties in the objective function.

The coloring terminology takes on a practical meaning by equating colors with labels used to categorize objects (people, institutions, groups, products, processes, etc.). Nodes that are adjacent (joined by an edge), can be viewed in a context where edges between nodes may be interpreted, for example, to mean that the associated objects are dissimilar, hence a coloring will categorize objects so that dissimilar objects fall in different categories. Minimizing the number of colors results in minimizing the number of categories needed to differentiate the objects. Other interpretations of the adjacency relationship led to additional applications.

More formally, for a graph G =(V,E) with n vertices, the Minimum Sum Coloring Problem (MSCP) seeks to find a coloring such that the sum of all the colors over all vertices is minimized. If we define $x_{ij}=1$ if color k is assigned to vertex i, and we seek a coloring using at most K colors, then the adjacency conditions are satisfied by $x_{ik} + x_{jk} < = 1$ for all $(i,j)\in E$ and all $k\in(1\ldots K)$. For a positive scalar penalty, P, these constraints can be imposed via penalties of the form $Px_{ik}x_{jk}$ to be added to objective function. Proceeding in this fashion yields the penalized objective function:

$$Minimize \sum_{i=1}^{n} \sum_{k=1}^{K} k * x_{ik} + P\left(\sum_{(i,j)\in E.\,\forall k} x_{ik}x_{jk}\right)$$

which can be re-written as in the form of x^tQx.

Including the node assignment constraints without taking them into the objective function, the have the Minimum Sum Coloring Problem in the following form:

$$Minimize \sum_{i=1}^{n} \sum_{k=1}^{K} k * x_{ik} + P\left(\sum_{(i,j)\in E.\,\forall k} x_{ik}x_{jk}\right)$$

subject to

$$\sum_{k=1}^{K} x_{ik} = 1 \ \forall \, i \in (1\ldots n)$$

which is a QUBO-Plus model:

Minimize x^tQx

subject to

$$\sum_{k=1}^{K} x_{ik} = 1 \ \forall \, i \in (1\ldots n)$$

Model 3. A practical application involving assignment constraints more closely related to the problems we treat in this paper involves exchanges to re-balance a set of account assignments for account executives in a large organization. For this example, assume that the company in question has K account executives, each responsible for managing a set of accounts. Currently the firm has P > K accounts of varying size in terms of annual revenues. Denote the annual dollar amount of account p by d_p dollars. As business has grown over the past few years, the total dollar amount of business managed by a given account executive has grown in an uneven fashion to produce considerable disparity in the total volume of business managed by a given executive.

To address this issue, top management wants to re-assign accounts to the various account executives to re-balance the system and make the differences in total annual book of business between account executives is as small as possible.

This problem can be modeled and solved by a QUBO-Plus model with assignment constraints as follows:

Let $x_{pk} = 1$ if account p is assigned to executive k; zero otherwise. Then, the total annual volume of business managed by executive k is

$$total_k = \sum_{p=1}^{P} d_p x_{pk} \quad k = 1, \ldots K$$

Our objective is to make assignments of accounts to executives so that each account gets assigned to an executive while minimizing the squared deviations from one executive to another. That is, our objective function is:

$$\min deviation = (total_1 - total_2)^2 + (total_1 - total_3)^2 + \ldots + (total_{K-1} - total_K)^2$$

Substituting the definition of $total_p$ into the above and writing the objective function in matrix form, we get the QUBO-Plus model with assignment constraints:

QUBO-Plus: Min xQx

st

$$\sum_{k=1}^{K} x_{pk} = 1 \quad p = 1 \ldots . P$$

where Q is the square, symmetric matrix that results from collecting terms and the x is the vector of x_{pk} variables relabeled with a single subscript. The constraints ensure that each account gets assigned to one of the executives and the objective function ensures that the differences in total account values from one executive to another is as small as possible. Solving this model will result in a new set of account assignments that re-balance the system.

Our next example illustrates a more general type of application that corresponds to a QUBO-Plus model of type (4), and likewise has features in common with those we address in the AEP problem. In this case, we have selected an application relevant to responding to an outbreak of an epidemic.

Model 4. The goal of this model is to determine an optimal allocation of testing kits, as in the context of virus detection, to a population of N people whose members may or may not be infected. Suppose q_i= the estimated value of having person i tested, and q_{ij} = the additional value of having both i and j tested (beyond the value of $q_i + q_j$) – as where these individuals interact with different groups of people and it is desirable not to limit testing to those who interact within the same group. The q_{ij} coefficients can be made larger if the groups that person i and person j interact with are high risk groups.

The objective is to maximize the total value of the people tested. This can be modeled as a QUBO-Plus problem where the number of people tested equals KitsAvailable, the number of test kits available on a given day. That is, for N = {1,...,n}

$$\sum(x_i\text{: } i \in N) = \text{KitsAvailable} \qquad (1)$$

In addition, suppose each person i belongs to a Group k indexed by k = 1, ..., K, where members of Group k are identified because they interact or because they are a geographical community or have other features in common considered likely to influence their risk. (These groups may also be identified by a QUBO clustering algorithm.) This results in constraints of the form

$$\sum(x_i\text{: } i \in \text{Group } K) = V_k \text{ for k} = 1, \ldots, \text{K} \qquad (2)$$

Here the sum of the V_k values equals KitsAvailable. The V_k values may be proportional to the sizes of the Groups k or may be skewed by the estimated riskiness of each group as a whole.

The foregoing QUBO-Plus problem with constraints (1) and (2) is easily formulated as a QUBO but can be solved more effectively by a special QUBO-Plus algorithm specifically designed for this class of QUBO applications. Constraints (1) and (2) are instances of more general constraints that arise in the AEP problem and are common in many network formulations.

Differentiation Among QUBO-Plus Models

In essence, we have three types of QUBO-Plus models. The first type consists of those for which a QUBO formulation can be readily constructed by incorporating certain constraints into the objective function, but the problem can be solved more effectively by a special approach that keeps these constraints separate. The second type consists of a binary choice "logical" problem where a QUBO formulation is exceedingly difficult to construct, yet where again we can develop an effective framework for solving it motivated by the concepts developed for representing and solving QUBO problems. The third type is an extension of the first two, arising in response to practical applications that embody highly exploitable problem structures, such as those in the domain of network-related models which are accompanied by additional combinatorial conditions that take them beyond classical analysis, but that can nevertheless be susceptible to tailored algorithms based on the principles that have produced the most effective QUBO methods.

The first type of QUBO-Plus model is illustrated by the QUBO-Plus formulations above. The second type of model includes problems that have binary network-related formulations, where we can exploit the fact that we can represent basic instances of these problems such as QUBO problems and QUBO-Plus problems of the first type. The Asset Exchange Problem at the focus of this paper belongs to the third category. We will show that we can capture several essential features of this application within a network optimization model, although one that is exceedingly large and computationally demanding. We will disclose how this structure can alternatively be made susceptible to an approach called combinatorial chaining, where we employ a strategy shared with the most effective QUBO algorithms, which iteratively identifies sub-structures that can be successfully to exploited to yield progressive improvement. A basic (rudimentary) form of combinatorial chaining is presented in Section 5 for simpler AEP problem instances. Then in Section 6 we describe modifications that give rise to advanced forms of combinatorial chaining that handle more complex AEP formulations.

3. PRELIMINARY EXAMPLES OF THE ASSET EXCHANGE PROBLEM

As previously intimated, the Asset Exchange Problem (AEP) arises in a variety of contexts, spanning applications in financial investment, resource allocation, economic distribution and collaborative decision making. Our approach to solving this problem is based on a form of cooperative optimization, where multiple parties with complex criteria collaborate as well as compete for resources. This could apply to algorithms for distributing packages between trucks in a delivery network, or dynamic switching to alternative sorting facilities. Or it could apply to collaborative bidding processes for complex multi-criteria contracts or decentralized cooperative group optimization for multi-criteria investment cryptocurrency portfolios. This is quite distinct from traditional portfolio optimization, as with a hedge fund that typically seeks to mitigate risk by diversification with some investments that are negatively correlated.

In the cooperative group optimization setting, our approach generalizes processes that seek atomic exchanges of baskets of fungible tokens or securities by yielding exchanges at a higher combinatorial level. Normally, a financial institution that wishes to execute a large basket of trades, in a way that mitigates execution risk by having an intermediary, can take the basket into its inventory and unwind the trades on its own. Thus, instead of revealing specific information about the assets in the basket, knowledge which could be exploited, the institution and banks can conduct a "zero-knowledge" protocol to effect basket trades. However, this protocol still requires trust in those institutions providing the service. The proposed new approach uses both simple and complex combinatorial exchanges to optimize all parties engaged in the multi-party optimization effort.

The progenitor of such an approach has emerged and is being tested in the cryptocurrency world – this is known as a *cross-chain atomic swap*. This is where two parties' own tokens in separate cryptocurrencies, and want to exchange them without having to trust a third party or a centralized exchange. However, by extending this model and enabling complex multi-party exchanges, splits and aggregations, we can affect full spectrum combinatorial trading to provide *trustless algorithmic liquidity* without requiring even the normal underlying reserve trading currency.

The simplest instance of such a system is a marketplace of three portfolios. In this market, Portfolio A has asset X and wishes to own some asset Z, Portfolio B has asset Z but wishes to acquire only asset Y, and Portfolio C has asset Y and wishes to own some asset X. In a traditional exchange, participants would exchange what they have for the underlying reserve settlement currency, and then purchase what they want. This would entail two transaction fees per portfolio. Alternatively, using cross chain atomic swaps, the parties would never make any transactions whatsoever, as the global optimal cannot be reached via pairwise swap transactions.

By enabling all potential complex exchanges, splits and aggregations, for N portfolios, any market could increase its global utility. However, the computational complexity of this type of complex combinatorial exchange trading is NP-complete. By using a multi-attribute trade matching system that includes the unspoken goals of the parties, which are the "utility functions" of the parties, it is possible to find pareto-efficient exchange solutions – referring to the game theory concept of a strategy that cannot be made to perform better against one opposing strategy without performing less well against another.

Additionally, the inclusion of constraints increases the complexity of the problem. For example, if the system determines that diversification is required, then a constraint can be added that limits which types of assets could be included in the diversification target. Only assets that have been rated by a rating agency or analyst, for example, as better than a "B" rating, could be included to modify the optimization. A continuous approach would assign numerical value a rating, and blend that with volatility metrics, volume data, social impact scores, and even the user's personal pet peeves – to enable a multi-objective approach to optimize both individual and multiple portfolios.

In the future, the user will require the ability to enter or modify both market orders (with fixed prices) and limit orders (with variable prices). As we transition from market orders to limit orders, this will help to expand utility expression, and it can become appropriate to add constraints to help identify price improvement opportunities – allowing a combinatorial exchange to operate for a share of price improvement, rather than charging transaction fees. Just a Bitcoin promises "zero cost transactions", this could provide a model for "zero cost exchanges" that provide the appearance of negative transaction cost given a disparity of utility functions. In section 6 we discuss the use of priorities to address such considerations.

The current model for the most effective form of exchange is the double-sided exchange, a system in which both buyers and sellers provide bids for matching via the exchange. A central controlling system matches the sell bids with the buy bids, yielding matched buy bids and matched sell bids in response thereto so that allocations of the matched buy bids and the matched sell bids maximize the throughput of the exchange. Combinatorial exchanges using cooperative optimization could potentially lay a foundation for the next evolutionary step in market exchange protocols, moving from double sided trading using a reserve currency to something more general that encompasses new forms of economic transactions.

Double sided exchanges are used to trade goods, services, or other things of value, including network bandwidth trading, financial-instruments trading, transportation logistics, pollution-credit trading, electric power allocation, and so on. However, to make double sided exchanges work, they require fungibility. And so, varying levels of quality, that describe for example the quality of crude oil, are lumped into fungible categories of sulfur content, gravity, etc. This further suggests the possibility that combinatorial exchanges could reflect multi-attribute trading more effectively, allowing traders to work with greater accuracy in pricing.

Combinatorial exchanges can likewise be used for handling non-fungible assets. As long as people are willing to assign value to objects to be traded, combinatorial exchanges can provide a basis to get people what they want. Suppose User A wants to sell a vacation timeshare he or she is tired of, for a certain collectible car with roughly the same value. There are no matches as both are relatively illiquid markets and it could take several months or require a significant discount to find buyers. However, there could be a User B who has exactly the car A wants, but doesn't want a timeshare, and instead wants a diamond necklace. Now if there is a jeweler C who would find that timeshare exciting, and willing to create a custom necklace to B's liking, the system could enable algorithmic liquidity by joining all three into a complex transaction.

Moving toward a more general example, A and B's assets most likely have different values. If there is no jeweler willing to make just the right necklace, the value exchange would not add up. Two parties would likely need to add or accept part of the value in cash. However, with the inclusion of a special user D, who is willing to inject cash and accept a partial tokenized share of that collectible car or real estate, the complex transaction becomes possible. We call this special user a "decentralized market maker" who would require a modest premium to compensate for enabling greater liquidity. That token share could be sold at a later time; hence it is an offer to sell cash for time.

Additional connections to blockchains via decentralized market making are described in Appendix 1.

One last note concerns the potential for quantum computing in this area. In general, present day quantum computers can handle only a very limited number of qubits, representing a small number of asset types, or cooperating portfolios. When quantum computers can offer hundreds of thousands of qubits, with effective partitioning algorithms, combinatorial exchanges will be able to scale to manage real world liquidity needs for applications involving massive numbers of participants and classes of items to exchange. Until then, quantum computing will enable exchange functionality for only limited and constrained markets, such as for cryptocurrencies. For example, a crypto wallet that holds only a dozen types of crypto would represent a relatively small variable space and could potentially be optimized using a quantum computer. Money was invented to simplify barter, and a quantum exchange based on pareto-efficient combinatorial exchanges could simplify money.

Motivated by the Quantum Bridge Analytics perspective we can go beyond the present limitations of quantum computing to provide these exchanges by identifying combinatorial chaining algorithms that can accommodate variable spaces for AEP models of significantly greater dimension, providing advances in the near term that can be translated into progressively greater advances in the future as quantum computing technology becomes more mature.

4. MATHEMATICAL FORMULATIONS OF THE AEP

The Asset Exchange Problem has several levels. We start from the most basic level of the AEP, which we call AEP0, defined in reference to a graph $G = (N, E)$, with node set $N = \{1, \ldots, n\}$ and edge set $E = \{\{i,j\}, i, j \in N\} \subset N \times N$. Each node $i \in N$ identifies an entity such as an individual or business or institution, and each edge $\{i,j\}$ identifies an *exchange link* between i and j. Let *A* denote the set of asset types (classes), where elements $\alpha \in A$ can represent classes of tokens in a crypto-currency application or types of securities in a securities market or categories of commodities in a commodity market, and so forth. In the following we use the term *assets* interchangeably with the term *asset types*.

In AEP0, each node $i \in N$ has a set S_i of assets it can send (i.e., can agree to send) to other nodes and a set R_i of assets it can receive (i.e., can agree to receive) from other nodes. Thus, for example, if $\alpha' \in S_i$ and $\alpha'' \in R_i$, then node i can agree to send asset α' and agree to receive asset α'' from other nodes. More precisely, R_i denotes assets that i desires (considers beneficial) to receive and S_i denotes assets that i is willing to send (in return for obtaining an asset in the set R_i). We say a transfer of asset α from node i to node j is *admissible* if $\alpha \in S_i$ and $\alpha \in R_j$ ($\alpha \in S_i \cap R_j$). We allow only admissible transfers in seeking asset exchanges that benefit all participants.

Define $N_i = \{j \in N: \{i,j\} \in E\}$ to be the set of nodes j that are neighbors of node i (i.e., that join node i by an edge). Let x_{ij}^{α} denote the number of units of asset α transferred from node i to node j. In restricting consideration to admissible transfers, we assume each node i has an upper limit $U_i^{\alpha:R}$ on the number of units of any given asset $\alpha \in R_i$ that can be admissibly transferred from other nodes to node i and an upper limit $U_i^{\alpha:S}$ on the number of units of $\alpha \in S_i$ that can be transferred from i to other nodes. Formally, these conditions may be expressed as

$$\sum(x_{ij}^{\alpha}: j \in N_i) \leq U_i^{\alpha:R} \quad i \in N \text{ and } \alpha \in R_i \tag{1}$$

$$\sum(x_{ij}^{\alpha}: j \in N_i) \leq U_i^{\alpha:S} \quad i \in N \text{ and } \alpha \in S_i \tag{2}$$

We also impose an equation that requires the total number of assets transferred from a given node i to other nodes j to equal the total number of assets transferred in return from other nodes j to node i. Specifically, for a given node $i \in N$ and a given node $j \in N_i$, we observe that the quantity $\sum(x_{ij}^{\alpha}: \alpha \in S_i \cap R_j)$ identifies the total number of units that can be admissibly transferred from node i to node j and similarly, the quantity $\sum(x_{ij}^{\alpha}: \alpha \in S_j \cap R_i)$ identifies the total number of units that can be admissibly transferred from node j to node i. We require these two quantities to be equal by stipulating

$$\sum(x_{ij}^{\alpha}: \alpha \in S_i \cap R_j) = \sum(x_{ij}^{\alpha}: \alpha \in S_j \cap R_i) \quad i \in N \text{ and } j \in N_i \tag{3}$$

Finally, we impose an additional limit U_i on the number of all assets α that can be admissibly transferred from node i to other nodes, expressed as

$\sum(x_{ij}^{\alpha}: j \in N_i, \alpha \in S_i \cap R_j) \leq U_i \ i \in N$ (4)

As a result of equation (3), this inequality is equivalent to

$\sum(x_{ij}^{\alpha}: j \in N_i, \alpha \in S_j \cap R_i) \leq U_i \ i \in N$ (4')

Subject to these conditions, in problem AEP0 we seek to maximize the total number of admissible exchanges, hence yielding the formulation

(a) Maximize $\sum(x_{ij}^{\alpha}: i \in N, j \in N_i, \alpha \in S_i \cap R_j)$

subject to (1), (2), (3), (4) and $x_{ij}^{\alpha} \geq 0$, $i \in N$, $j \in N_i$ and $\alpha \in S_i \cap R_j$

We can also replace (0) by a variety of other objectives, such as

(a') Maximize $\sum(p_i^{\alpha} x_{ij}^{\alpha}: i \in N, j \in N_i, \alpha \in S_i \cap R_j)$

where p_i^{α} is a positive monetary value that node i attaches to receiving asset α from the set R_i.

We now take the step of transforming the preceding formulation into a network optimization formulation, to give a foundation for generating solutions to the foregoing AEP0 model by a corresponding basic version of our combinatorial chaining approach. From this, we will be able to treat related more complex AEP models by natural extensions that combine the network optimization and combinatorial chaining components. The transformation of AEP0 to a network formulation significantly increases the problem size, but offsets this by making the problem sparser, while our combinatorial chaining algorithm for this formulation is able to work with a memory based on the number of nodes rather than the number of arcs in the network, dramatically reducing both the amount of computation and the memory involved.

Transforming AEP0 to a Network Formulation

The transformation of AEP0 to an equivalent network formulation, which we call NetAEP0, arises by replacing the graph G by a graph G* = G*(N*, A*) consisting of a set of nodes N* and a set of arcs (directed edges) A* as follows.

To emphasize the arc orientation in creating G*, we find it useful to augment the customary representation of an arc from a node p to a node q as an ordered pair (p, q) by alternatively writing it in the form $p \rightarrow q$, which adds clarity when p and/or q is itself represented as an ordered pair. Lower bounds on all arc flows are assumed to be 0.

To generate G*, we divide each node $i \in N$ into two nodes, i[R] and i[S], and create an arc $i[R] \rightarrow i[S]$. In addition, for each $i \in N$ and $\alpha \in R_i$ we create new nodes (α, i[R]), producing $\sum(|R_i|: i \in N)$ nodes, and create arcs $(\alpha, i[R]) \rightarrow i[R]$ (from node (α, i[R]) to node i[R]) which results in $\sum(|R_i|: i \in N)$ arcs (the same as the number of nodes (α, i[R]). . Similarly, for each $i \in N$ and $\alpha \in S_i$ we create new nodes (α, i[S]), producing $\sum(|S_i|: i \in N)$ nodes, and create arcs $i[S] \rightarrow (\alpha, i[S])$, creating $\sum(|S_i|: i \in N)$ arcs (the same as the number of nodes (α, i[S]).

Finally, for each $i \in N$ and for each $j \in N_i$ such that $\alpha \in S_i$ is the same as $\alpha \in R_j$ (i.e., for which $\alpha \in S_i \cap R_j$), each node (α, i[S]) joins by an arc $(\alpha, i[S]) \rightarrow (\alpha, j[R])$. We call these the *α-linking arcs* of G*, since the same asset α is referenced by both nodes of each of these arcs. The number of these arcs is $\sum(| S_i \cap R_j|: i \in N, j \in N_i)$.

From this construction we see that N* consists of $2n + \sum(|R_i| + |S_i|: i \in N)$ nodes and A* contains $n + \sum(|R_i| + |S_i|: i \in N) + \sum(| S_i \cap R_j|: i \in N, j \in N_i)$ arcs.

To create NetAEP0 from G*, we introduce flows on the arcs governed by bounds as follows. Each arc $i[R] \rightarrow i[S]$ receives an upper bound on its flow of U_i from (4). Correspondingly, each of the $(\alpha, i[R]) \rightarrow i[R]$ arcs receives an upper bound on its flow of $U_i^{\alpha:R}$ from (1) and each of the arcs $i[S] \rightarrow (\alpha, i[S])$ receives an upper bound on its flow of $U_i^{\alpha:S}$ from (2). Finally, the *α-linking arcs* of G* are not given upper bounds (i.e., their upper bounds may be treated as infinity). All lower bounds are implicitly 0.

It is assumed that U_i satisfies $U_i \leq \text{Min}(\sum(U_i^{\alpha:R}: \alpha \in R_i), \sum(U_i^{\alpha:S}: \alpha \in S_i))$, that is, the upper bound U_i on the flow across arc $i[R] \rightarrow i[S]$ is limited by the smaller of the sum of upper bounds on the arcs $(\alpha, i[R]) \rightarrow i[R]$ entering i[R] and the sum of upper bounds on the arcs $i[S] \rightarrow (\alpha, i[S])$ leaving i[S]. (Later we also describe variations in which we additionally introduce lower bounds $L_i^{\alpha:R}$ and/or $L_i^{\alpha:S}$ on the arcs $(\alpha, i[R]) \rightarrow i[R]$ and arcs $i[S] \rightarrow (\alpha, i[S])$.)

Because we start from the symmetric graph G in undirected edges to produce the graph G* with directed arcs underlying NetAEP0, $j \in N_i$ implies $i \in N_j$. We additionally observe that no asset α is contained in both R_i and S_i for any given i, under the assumption that if node i sees a benefit in receiving a unit of $\alpha \in R_i$, then it will not be willing to relinquish a unit of α by including it in S_i. Exceptions can be imagined, as where i may be willing to give up a particular $\alpha' \in R_i$ if it is able to receive a more highly valued asset $\alpha'' \in R_i$. Such exceptions can be modeled by extensions of the constructions used here but make the formulation larger and more complex. Nevertheless, our basic algorithm can be modified to handle these and other variations without entailing the complexity introduced by an extended mathematical formulation.

The foregoing description of G* and the conditions defining NetAEP0 can be translated into an algorithm for generating the network. As part of this we show how to attach numerical indexes denoted by k = 1 to n* to the nodes in N* so that NetAEP0 may be represented as a network in a standard format. We refer to lower bounds as well as upper bounds on arcs for generality, although in direct transformation of AEP0 to NetAEP0 the lower bounds will be 0.

Algorithm to Generate NetAEP0

For each $i \in N$

Create the nodes i[R] and i[S] and the arc i[R] → i[S], by assigning the index k = i to the

node i[R] and the indexes k = i + n to the node i[S].

Attach the lower and upper bounds L_i and U_i to the arc i[R] → i[S] (i → i + n).

Endfor

Set k = i + n

For each $i \in N$

(Create the "S-labeled" asset node (α, i[S]) and associated arc i[S] → (α, i[S]) for each

asset $\alpha \in S_i$.)

For each $\alpha \in S_i$

Set k: = k + 1 and create the asset node (α, i[S]), assigning it the index k.

Create the arc i[S] → (α, i[S]) and attach lower and upper bounds $L_i^{\alpha:S}$ and $U_i^{\alpha:S}$.

Endfor

Endfor

For each $j \in N$

(Create the "R-labeled" asset node (α, j[R]) and associated arc (α, j[R]) → j[R] for each

asset $\alpha \in R_j$.)

For each $\alpha \in R_j$

Set k: = k + 1 and create the asset node (α, j[R]), assigning it the index k.

Create the arc (α, j[R]) → j[R] and attach lower and upper bounds $L_j^{\alpha:R}$ and $U_j^{\alpha:R}$.

Endfor

Endfor

For each $i \in N$

(Create the "S to R" asset arcs (α, i[S]) → (α, j[R]) associated with i for each $\alpha \in S_i$.)

For each asset $\alpha \in S_i$

For each neighbor $j \in N_i$

For each asset $\alpha \in R_j$

Create the asset arc $(\alpha, i[S]) \rightarrow (\alpha, j[R])$ with no bounds (i.e., a lower bound of 0 and an upper bound of infinity).

Endfor

Endfor

Endfor

Endfor

Costs or profits may be attached to the arcs of the network NetAEP0 according to the objective that is desired to be achieved. Asset arcs, which are linking arcs, should be assigned a 0 cost or profit. In creating asset arcs $(\alpha, i[S]) \rightarrow (\alpha, j[R])$ above, if there is no asset $\alpha \in R_j$ for any $j \in N_i$ such that $\alpha \in S_i$, then the asset node $(\alpha, i[S])$ will not have any corresponding node $(\alpha, j[R])$ to create such an arc $(\alpha, i[S]) \rightarrow (\alpha, j[R])$, and α can be dropped from S_i. If all $\alpha \in S_i$ are thus removed to leave S_i empty, then i can be removed from N and i[R] and i[S] (= i and i + n) correspondingly removed from N*. Similarly, if at the end it is discovered that the node $(\alpha, j[R])$ has no arcs $(\alpha, i[S]) \rightarrow (\alpha, j[R])$ entering it, then this implies that α can be dropped from R_j. By the same token, if all $\alpha \in R_j$ are thus removed to leave R_j empty, then j can be removed from N and j[R] and j[S] (= j and j + n) correspondingly removed from N*.

An illustration of the structure of NetAEP0 is given in Appendix 2.

5. BASIC VERSION OF COMBINATORIAL CHAINING

A classical theorem of network flows (Fulkerson and Ford, 1962) implies that a feasible solution to NetAEP0 can be decomposed into a collection of cycles (not necessarily disjoint or uniquely determined). Such cycles are of interest for the Asset Exchange Problem in both its simpler AEP0 form and its more complex forms because they identify a collection of participants who can enter into a succession of mutually beneficial asset exchanges. Such a collection is not unduly difficult to identify by reference to a solution to the NetAEP0 formulation but requires additional effort. Fulkerson and Ford's max flow algorithm would automatically identify (augmenting) paths from source to sink in the network flow, which has some similarity with combinatorial chaining. But a standard network flow algorithm for solving NetAEP0 is not capable of being directly adapted to provide good solutions to more complex variations of the AEP that abound in practical applications, thus motivating the creation of the adaptive combinatorial chaining approach.

Adopting the netform perspective (Glover et al., 1992), combinatorial chaining is designed both to exploit the structure of the basic AEP network formulation and to be susceptible to extensions for solving a variety of AEP variations found in practice. This harmonizes with the Quantum Bridge Analytics perspective as in applications where quantum computing can be applied to solve portfolio optimization problems expressed as QUBO models for individual investors or institutions, and more generally leads to consideration of a QUBO-Plus formulation of the third type. Combinatorial chaining can then be applied to the appropriate AEP variation to integrate and improve these individual solutions to the benefit of each participant.

The strategy underlying the basic form of combinatorial chaining operates by generating successions of directed trees (or arborescences in graph theory) rooted at different nodes. Conditions are monitored to disclose when a directed tree can be extended by connecting a tip of one of its branches to the root, thus creating a cycle that constitutes a mutually beneficial exchange. The process differs from classical tree generation algorithms by introducing multiple categories of tree predecessors and establishing a mechanism to trace the predecessors that differentiates between the categories effectively. This introduction of multiple categories of tree predecessors and mechanisms for tracing them likewise causes our method to operate differently from classical min cost flow algorithms based on generating augmented paths (Barr et al., 1978); Glover et al., 1986). This departure from classical approaches arises because many of the more general AEP models belong to the class of multi-commodity network flow problems (Hu, 1963; Assad, 1978), which are more complex than standard "pure" network flow problems, and normally cannot be transformed into a pure network problem as we have accomplished for AEP0. Rather than being a disadvantage, however, this complexity enables the chaining mechanism to be adapted to AEP variations beyond AEP0.

More broadly, the combinatorial chaining mechanism we employ is closely related to the ejection chain procedures for combinatorial optimization noted in Section 1. In its more advanced forms outlined in Section 6, it is additionally related to the path relinking approaches that are joined with ejection chains in Yagiura et al. (2016, 2017) and that produce the leading methods for the QUBO problem in Wang et al. (2012), Samorani et al. (2019) and Glover et al. (2020, 2021).

Rudimentary Combinatorial Chaining for the Netaep0 Model

Combinatorial chaining for the basic NetAEP0 model makes use of arrays denoted FlowR(α, i[R]) to record flows on the arcs (α, i[R]) → i[R] and arrays denoted FlowS(α, i[S]) to record the flows on the arcs i[S] → (α, i[S]). Hence, for each $i \in N$, we require FlowR(α, i[R]) $\leq U_i^{\alpha:R}$ for each $\alpha \in R_i$, and require FlowS(α, i[S]) $\leq U_i^{\alpha:S}$ for each $\alpha \in S_i$. Flows on the arcs arc i[R] → i[S] are recorded in an array Flow(i) for each $i \in N$. All flow values are initialized to 0.

It is convenient to refer to the nodes (α, i[R]), (α, i[S]) and i (the latter collectively representing the two nodes i[R] and i[S]) as *open* when their associated flows FlowR(α, i[R]), FlowS(α, i[S]) and Flow(i) do not reach their upper bounds and *closed* otherwise. (A bit can be set for each such node to determine its open/closed status.)

We refer to two types of predecessor arrays PredR(i) and PredS(i), $i \in N$, accompanied by associated arrays AssetR(i) and AssetS(i) explained subsequently. The arrays PredR(i) and PredS(i) are initialized to 0 to indicate predecessors are not yet assigned.

The method performs forward scans and reverse scans to examine nodes $i \in N$ (and from there to examine the arcs these nodes can become linked to in a chain). When a tip of the tree can successfully be linked to the root, a *breakthrough* occurs by establishing the existence of an exchange cycle that is mutually beneficial for all its participants. Breakthrough is accompanied by appropriately updating (increasing) the flows on arcs of the cycle.

The basic version of the chaining algorithm only performs forward scans but gives the foundation for performing reverse scans as well, as subsequently described. We first explain the nature of the forward scan routine and then give a more formal description.

Rationale of the Forward Scan Routine

The Forward Scan Routine is embedded in a Main Routine that maintains a set N^o identifying the open nodes, initialized by $N^o = N$. Nodes to be scanned are placed in a set denoted ScanSet that begins with a chosen node $i^* \in N^o$. During the Forward Scan Routine, ScanSet acquires other nodes $i \in N^o$ to form a tree that yields a collection of chains rooted at node i*. The tree is generated by successively selecting new nodes i from ScanSet as long as ScanSet $\neq \varnothing$.

For each node i selected from ScanSet, consider each asset $\alpha \in S_i$; i.e., each asset α that node i is willing to send to another node. Given node i, additionally consider each neighbor j of i that contains α in R_j; i.e., each neighbor j that desires to receive α. (Formally, we refer to the set $NR_i^\alpha = \{j \in N_i: \alpha \in R_j\}$, which consists of those neighbors j of node i such that R_j contains α.) If node j is not already in the tree, i.e., if it has no predecessor (as indicated by PredS(j) = 0), then it can acceptably be added to the tree by adopting node i as its predecessor. For this, we set PredS(j) = i together with AssetS(j) = α, which records the fact that each chain in the tree that passes through this particular (i. j) link is accompanied by sending asset α from node i to node j.

If now j = i* (which can result because i* is not assigned a predecessor initially), we have discovered a chain beginning with node i* that results in a loop which qualifies as a mutually beneficial exchange cycle (where each participant receives a desired asset and in return sends a willingly exchanged asset). The Breakthrough Routine handles this outcome by identifying the cycle and updating the flows and the structure of G* appropriately.

Following the updates of the Breakthrough Routine, the scanning routine is reinitiated within the Main Routine by selecting a new i* from N^o (where i* may be the same as before if it is not removed from N^o during breakthrough).

Alternatively, the scan from a given node i* may terminate with ScanSet empty and without achieving breakthrough. In this case, i* is removed from N^o and once more the scanning routine is reinitiated within the Main Routine to select a new i* from N^o.

We let $N_i^o = N_i \cap N^o$ denote the (current) neighbors of node i that are in N^o. Hence N_i^o, which starts the same as N_i, may shrink as nodes are removed from N^o. This also modifies the definition $NR_i^\alpha = \{j \in N_i: \alpha \in R_j\}$ to become $NR_i^\alpha = \{j \in N_i^o: \alpha \in R_j\}$, identifying the neighbors of i in N^o that desire to receive asset α.

Termination of the Main Routine occurs when N^o contains only a single node ($|N^o| = 1$), since then this node has no other nodes it can exchange with.

The formal design of the algorithm is as follows.

Basic Combinatorial Chaining Algorithm

Initialization.

Set all flow values to 0. Initialize the set N^o of open nodes by setting $N^o = N$.

Main Routine

While $|N^o| > 1$

Set all predecessor arrays to 0.

Choose $i^* \in N^o$ and create ScanSet = {i*}.

Execute the *Forward Scan Routine* (as follows)

While ScanSet $\neq \varnothing$

Select a node $i \in$ ScanSet

For each $\alpha \in S_i$

For each $j \in NR_i^\alpha$ ($= \{j \in N_i^o: \alpha \in R_j\}$)

If PredS(j) = 0 then

(j has not been visited before on a Forward Scan)

Set PredS(j) = i and AssetS(j) = α.

If j = i* then

Execute the *Breakthrough Routine* (below)

(Update flows and potentially remove nodes from N^o.)

Break (leave Forward Scan Routine to choose a new $i^* \in N^o$ in the Main Routine if $|N^o| > 1$).

Endif

Else

Let ScanSet:= ScanSet $\cup$ {j}.

Endif

EndFor

EndFor

ScanSet = ScanSet\{i} (remove i from ScanSet)
(The scan of node i is complete.)
EndWhile
(End of the Forward Scan Routine)
Endwhile
(End of the Main Routine)

The algorithm can be modified to save part of the tree after the completion of each forward scan, but the computational savings will not usually be enough to warrant the effort. Reverse scanning provides a more interesting modification and can be accomplished by interchanging R and S in each of the instructions of the Forward Scanning Routine. Forward scanning and reverse scanning can also be done together, switching from one to the other on selected iterations. In this case, breakthrough is recognized when j = PredS(i) on a forward scan yields PredR(j) > 0 (where PredR(j) was set on a reverse scan), or when j = PredR(i) on a reverse scan yields PredS(j) > 0 (where PredS(j) was set on a forward scan). To show how reverse scanning can be joined with forward scanning, Appendix 3 gives an example where a single iteration of reverse scanning is applied before launching the forward scanning algorithm.

The Breakthrough Routine that accompanies the Forward Scanning Routine may now be described as follows. The preceding observations and the example in Appendix 3 disclose how to modify this routine for reverse scanning or for combinations of forward and reverse scanning.

Breakthrough Routine
Compute the maximum feasible flow increment ΔFlow on the augmenting cycle
ΔFlow = Big (a large positive number)
i = i*
Stop = False
While Stop = False
α = AssetS(i)
$\Delta R = U_i^{\alpha:R} - \text{FlowR}(\alpha, i[R])$
i = PredS(i)
$\Delta S = U_i^{\alpha:S} - \text{FlowS}(\alpha, i[S])$
$\Delta i = U_i - \text{Flow}(i)$
ΔFlow = Min(ΔR, ΔS, Δi, ΔFlow)
If i = i* then Stop = True
Endwhile
Update flows and remove nodes associated with saturated arcs
i = i*
Stop = False
While Stop = False

α = AssetS(i)
FlowR(α, i[R]) = FlowR(α, i[R]) – ΔFlow
If FlowR(α, i[R]) $\geq U_i^{\alpha:R}$ then close arc (α, i[R]) by setting $R_i := R_i \setminus \{\alpha\}$ (removing α from R_i)
i = PredS(i)
FlowS(α, i[S]) = FlowS(α, i[S]) – ΔFlow
If FlowS(α, i[S]) $\geq U_i^{\alpha:S}$ then close arc (α, i[S]) by setting $S_i := S_i \setminus \{\alpha\}$ (removing α from S_i)
Flow(i) = Flow(i) – ΔFlow
If Flow(i) $\geq U_i$ then close arc (i[R], i[S]) setting $N^o := N^o \setminus \{i\}$
If i = i* then Stop = True
Endwhile

6. ADVANCED FORMS OF COMBINATORIAL CHAINING FOR MORE COMPLEX AEP MODELS

There are problems that are too complex to be given mathematical formulations that fully capture their subtleties and that are simultaneously capable of being solved by standard math programming algorithms. In adopting the perspective of Quantum Bridge Analytics, we embrace strategies for such problems that allow their objectives to be pursued approximately and flexibly, thus admitting approaches that solve variations of these problems to emphasize alternative problem components in an adaptive fashion. As we have emphasized, our basic combinatorial chaining procedure allows this to be done when joined with network optimization by giving advanced methods that yield access to more complex AEP variants.

We show how this can be achieved for two chief extensions of the preceding AEP formulation that encompass a broad range of applications. The associated versions of combinatorial chaining provide flexible approximation methods that can be embedded in metaheuristic algorithms and afford the possibility of being incorporated into hybrid classical/quantum systems. In common with the most effective algorithms for QUBO problems, a natural basis for these combinatorial chaining methods derives from adaptive memory strategies (Wang et al., 2012; Samorani et al., 2019; Glover et al. 2020; 2021).

Prioritizing the Assets Exchanged

In some applications of the AEP, participants may wish to prioritize certain exchanges of assets over others, preferring more strongly to receive particular assets and being more willing to relinquish certain other assets. Priorities attached to these preferences may also differ among different participants. Upon assigning numerical values to capture these preferences (as by indicating a dollar amount that different individuals attach to the value of different exchanges, or by making recourse to an agreed-upon set of subjective weights), the combinatorial chaining algorithm can be extended by prioritizing the selection of the elements i* in N° or the choice of elements i in ScanSet, in each instance selecting the highest priority element from those available.

Priorities can also be used by such an extension to improve the choices for participants whose exchanges were less favorable on previous executions of the algorithm, since an effort to achieve a best overall collection of exchanges (such as a maximum number of beneficial exchanges) can result in better outcomes for some participants than for others. This means of exploiting the freedom to choose different elements in executing the basic steps of combinatorial chaining yields an approximation method for a problem whose subtleties render it unsuitable for a classical mathematical formulation, while allowing the flexibility to be adapted to different types of priorities. Such priorities can be introduced in the network formulation as and embodied in probabilities for selecting moves in metaheuristic adaptations as in probabilistic tabu search (Xu et al., 1997; Guermi et al., 2019). Combinatorial chaining provides the underlying structure for guiding the search to produce feasible solutions.

Priorities can also be employed to create larger breakthroughs earlier in the process of generating combinatorial chains, as by giving higher priority to participants with larger capacities (upper bounds) on the flows they can receive. The priorities can be based on measures applied to each base node (participant), such as total sums of capacities or means of capacities adjusted by standard deviations, and so forth. Refinements arise by considering the priorities of neighbors. For example, a new priority can be created for a node that is a weighted combination of its current priority and the priorities of neighbor nodes, where weights for neighbors are less than for the node under consideration. Such a process may also be repeated, using the new priorities as a basis for constructing another round of new priorities. (Additional repetitions may be expected to yield progressively less advantage.)

Particular applications give their own criteria for determining priorities. In exchanges of cryptocurrencies, for example, larger investors face the most negative impact by failing to make exchanges of a size deemed satisfactory, so assigning higher priorities to exchanges of such investors will usually result in the highest increase in utility. Using such priorities, choosing a node i* from N° with the highest priority to become the root of the current directed tree, followed by choosing highest priority nodes i from ScanSet to continue building the tree, provides a compelling and easily implemented strategy.

As previously observed, there may also be situations where it can be relevant to place lower bounds as well as upper bounds on the number of units of different assets exchanged by different participants. In a cryptocurrency application, for example, an investor may only be interested in transactions that result in receiving a specified number of units of a given asset. To illustrate, an investor represented by a node i may seek an exchange in which i receives precisely 100 units of Ethereum (ETH), represented by asset α ($\in R_i$) (accompanied, for example, by i sending units of Bitcoin (BTC) or Lumen (XLM) to other nodes). The AEP network model then captures this by putting a lower bound of 100 and an upper bound of 100 on the ETC arc (α, i[R]) $\rightarrow$ i[R]), giving $L_i^{\alpha:R} = U_i^{\alpha:R} = 100$. The situation where an investor may have an exact demand for an asset (modeled by setting the lower bound equal to the upper bound), and where this demand cannot be satisfied by an exchange involving any single other investor, is sometimes called *splitting*, i.e., the demand must be split into different transactions with different investors. Combinatorial chaining automatically handles splitting situations as well as other much more general situations. A simple illustration is where investor i will only consider an exchange that brings in at least $L_i^{\alpha:R} = 50$ units of ETH, but would prefer to receive more units, up to a limit of $U_i^{\alpha:R} = 100$. Any number of other investors, some who may not be neighbors of i, may be involved in transactions identified by combinatorial chaining.

In cases like these where the AEP model includes lower bounds on numbers of units received, exchanges can be prioritized in two phases, where Phase 1 is devoted to satisfying as many of the lower bounds as possible, and Phase 2 then sends additional flow through the network subject to satisfying upper bounds. These two phases are not required to have the same priorities for selecting nodes on exchange cycles.

Machine learning provides a natural way to facilitate priority generation. A strategy of varying the priorities may yield better overall outcomes for a particular objective, for example, and machine learning can be used to help identify a strategy that leads to the most desirable results. An instance of machine learning called Programming by Optimization (Hoos, 2012) is often effective for choosing parameters for optimization algorithms and may be useful in determining priorities in the combinatorial chaining context. Learning can also be employed as clustering-based metaheuristics (Samorani, et al., 2019).

Generalized Networks

An important extension of the AEP arises where a unit of one asset may be exchanged for more or less than one unit of another asset. Networks in which the number of units received at the destination node (to-node) of an arc may differ from the number of units sent from the origin node (from-node) of an arc are called *generalized networks*, (Glover et al., 1990, 1992) and the factor that determines the difference between the units sent and received is called the *arc multiplier*. For example, an arc multiplier of 1.5 implies that the to-node receives 1.5 units for every unit sent from the from-node. A variety of situations exist where assets may be exchanged other than on a one-to-one basis.

A convenient feature of the basic combinatorial chaining algorithm is that such multiplier effects can be captured by joining the treatment of priorities with a modification of the Breakthrough Routine. The amount of flow transmitted across a chain of generalized arcs on a path leading from the root node i* to a subsequent node i equals the product of the multipliers on the arcs between i* and i. Thus, for example, if the chain consists of the succession of arcs (i*, i1), (i1,i2), (i2,i3), with i3 = i, and if the multipliers on these three arcs are 0.6, 2.0 and 1.2, then a unit of flow sent from node i* becomes $0.6 \times 2.0 \times 1.2 = 1.44$ units of flow received at node i3. The Breakthrough Routine can be readily modified to incorporate this effect, using it to identify the limits on flows required to compute updated flows across the entire cycle and to determine which assets or elements must be removed from their associated sets due to these updates.

The approaches of introducing exchange priorities and capitalizing on the ability to incorporate arc multipliers in association with generalized networks can be combined to cover an additionally expanded range of practical problems, which may be usefully exploited by metaheuristic algorithms in the QBA context.

7. CONCLUDING REMARKS

The relevance of Quantum Bridge Analytics for real world applications has been demonstrated by showing an important instance where we are able to apply the QBA perspective to the challenging Asset Exchange Problem, which opens up numerous applications in financial investment, resource allocation, economic distribution and collaborative decision making. The linkage of network optimization with metaheuristic optimization via combinatorial chaining gives rise to an Asset Exchange Technology that can address and solve a wide range of practical variations.

Present day quantum computers can only handle small AEP problems, due to the limited number of qubits they encompass, but the integration of network formulations and combinatorial chaining is capable of accommodating AEP problems of significantly greater dimension. Through these connections, the AEP model gives an important class of optimization problems that can be usefully approached within the QBA domain, providing a foundation for further advances in the future as quantum computing technology becomes more mature.

REFERENCES

Assad, A. A. (1978). Multicommodity network flows—A survey. *Networks*, 8(1), 37–91. DOI: 10.1002/net.3230080107

Barr, R., Elam, J., Glover, F., & Klingman, D. (1978). A Network Augmenting Path Basis Algorithm for Transshipment Problems. In Fiacco, A., & Kortanek, K. (Eds.), *Extremal Methods and Systems Analysis* (pp. 250–274). Springer-Verlag.

Du, Y., Kochenberger, G., Glover, F., Lu, Z. P., Liu, D. H., & Hulandageri, A. (2020) "Optimal Solutions to the Minimum Sum Coloring Problem: A comparison of Alternative Models", Working paper, University of Colorado Denver.

Fitzpatrick, L., Fulkerson, D.R., Ford Jr., L.R. (1962) *Flows in Networks*, Rand Corporation.

Fitzpatrick, L. (2019) "A Complete Beginner's Guide to Atomic Swaps," *Forbes*, Sept 2, 2019 https://www.forbes.com

Glover, F., & Rego, C. (2006). Ejection chain and filter-and-fan methods in combinatorial optimization. 4OR, 4, 263-296.

Glover, , FLewis, , MKochenberger, , G. (2018). Logical and inequality implications for reducing the size and difficulty of quadratic unconstrained binary optimization problems. *European Journal of Operational Research, 265*(3), 829-842.

Glover, F. (1996). Ejection Chains, Reference Structures and Alternating Path Methods for Traveling Salesman Problems. *Discrete Applied Mathematics*, 65(1-3), 223–253. DOI: 10.1016/0166-218X(94)00037-E

Glover, F., Glover, R., & Klingman, D. (1986). The Threshold Assignment Algorithm. In Gallo, G., & Sandi, C. (Eds.), *Mathematical Programming Study* (Vol. 26, pp. 12–37).

Glover, F., Klingman, D., & Phillips, N. (1992). *Network Models in Optimization and their Applications in Practice*. Wiley Interscience, John Wiley and Sons. DOI: 10.1002/9781118033173

Glover, F., Kochenberger, G., & Du, Y. (2019). "A Tutorial on Formulating and Using QUBO Methods," *4OR Quarterly Journal of Operations Research. Invited Survey*, 17, 335–371.

Glover, F., Kochenberger, G., & Du, Y. (2021). Applications of the QUBO and QUBO-Plus Models. In Punnen, A. P. (Ed.), *The quadratic unconstrained binary optimization problem*. Springer.

Glover, F., Kochenberger, G., Du, Y., Hennig, R., Wang, H., Mniszewski, S., & Hulandageri, A. (2020) "Experience with the QUBO Model for Solving Large Scale Set Partitioning Problems," *12th INFORMS Conference on Information Systems & Technology (CIST),* Virtual 2020 INFORMS Annual Meeting, November 7 - 13, 2020.

Glover, F., & Laguna, M. (1997). *Tabu Search.* Kluwer Academic Publishers, Springer. DOI: 10.1007/978-1-4615-6089-0

Glover, F., Phillips, N., & Klingman, D. (1990). Netform Modeling and Applications. *Special Issue on the Practice of Mathematical Programming, Interfaces*, 20(1), 7–27.

Guemri, O., Nduwayoa, P., Todosijevic, R., Hanafi, S., & Glover, F. (2019, September 19). Probabilistic Tabu Search for the Cross-Docking Assignment Problem. *European Journal of Operational Research*, 277(3), 875–885. DOI: 10.1016/j.ejor.2019.03.030

Helsgaun, K. (2000). An Effective Implementation of the Lin-Kernighan Traveling Salesman Heuristic. *European Journal of Operational Research*, 126(1), 106–130. DOI: 10.1016/S0377-2217(99)00284-2

Helsgaun, K. (2009). General k-opt submoves for the Lin-Kernighan TSP heuristic. *Mathematical Programming Computation*, 1(2-3), 119–163. DOI: 10.1007/s12532-009-0004-6

Hoos, H. (2012). Programming by Optimization. *Communications of the ACM*, 55(2), 70–80. DOI: 10.1145/2076450.2076469

Hu, T. C. (1963). *Multi-commodity network flows.* INFORMS PubsOnline., DOI: 10.1287/opre.11.3.344

Kochenberger, G., & Ma, M. (2020) "Quantum Computing Applications of QUBO Models to Portfolio Optimization," White paper, University of Colorado, Denver, July, 2020.

Müller, J. C., Pokutta, S., Martin, A., Pape, S., Peter, A., & Winter, T. (2017). Pricing and clearing combinatorial markets with singleton and swap orders. *Mathematical Methods of Operations Research*, 85(2), 155–177. DOI: 10.1007/s00186-016-0555-z

National Academies. (2019). *The National Academies of Sciences, Engineering and Medicine, 2019. Quantum Computing: Progress and Prospects*. The National Academies Press., DOI: 10.17226/25196

Nolan, T. (2013) "Alt chains and atomic transfers," *Bitcointalk*https://bitcointalk .org/index.php?topic=193281.0

Rego, C., Gamboa, D., & Glover, F. (2016). Doubly-Rooted Stem-and-Cycle Ejection Chain Algorithm for the Asymmetric Traveling Salesman Problem. *Networks*, 68(1), 23–33. DOI: 10.1002/net.21676

Resende, M. G. C., Ribeiro, C. C., Glover, F., & Martí, R. (2010) "Scatter Search and Path Relinking: Fundamentals, Advances and Applications," *Handbook of Metaheuristics: International Series in Operations Research & Management Science,* Volume 146, pp 87-107.

Samorani, M., Wang, Y., Lu, Z., & Glover, F. (2019) "Clustering-driven evolutionary algorithms: an application of path relinking to the QUBO problem," *Special Issue on Intensification, Diversification and Learning* of the *Journal of Heuristics*, F. Glover and M. Samorani, eds., Volume 25, Issue 4–5, pp 629–642

Wang, Y., Lu, Z., Glover, F., & Hao, J.-K. (2012). Path relinking for unconstrained binary quadratic programming. *European Journal of Operational Research*, 223(3), 595–604. DOI: 10.1016/j.ejor.2012.07.012

Winter, T., Rudel, M., Lalla, H., Brendgen, S., Geißler, B., Martin, A., & Morsi, A. (2011) "System and method for performing an opening auction of a derivative." URL https://www.google.de/patents/US20110119170, Pub. No.: US 2011/0119170 A1. US Patent App. 12/618,410.

Xu, J., Chiu, S., & Glover, F. (1997). Tabu Search for Dynamic Routing Communications Network Design. *Telecommunication Systems*, 8(1), 1–23. DOI: 10.1023/A:1019149101850

Yagiura, M., Ibaraki, T., & Glover, F. (2006). A path relinking approach with ejection chains for the generalized assignment problem. *European Journal of Operational Research*, 169(2), 548–569. DOI: 10.1016/j.ejor.2004.08.015

Yagiura, M., Komiya, A., Kojima, K., Nonobe, K., Nagamochi, H., Ibaraki, T., & Glover, F. (2007). *A path relinking approach for the multi-resource generalized quadratic assignment problem* (Vol. 4638). Lecture Notes in Computer Science. Springer. DOI: 10.1007/978-3-540-74446-7_9

APPENDIX I

Blockchains and Decentralized Market Making

Decentralized market making is an intriguing concept that would require a detailed exploration, as it will likely emerge as critical factor for enabling scalable liquidity. But there are many questions to be answered. For example, what is the value of contributions by the decentralized market makers? Also, could these small investments held by the market – provided to equalize values in an exchange –be aggregated into baskets, and could those baskets be traded? How do we accurately assess the risks of items in baskets, to flow them up to the basket, to avoid "toxic assets" being included?

Finally, it should be noted that a computational system or agent that learns what a user wants to buy or sell, or might be willing to trade, would be quite valuable as an e-commerce tool because it provides a means to unveil the deeper purchase intentions of users. AI based agents could assist not only in the process of helping the user to determine what they might be willing to trade for or buy but could even help the user discover new purchase intentions that might lead to greater personal satisfaction. In other words, instead of just contributing to the accumulation of more useless stuff in their lives, such a system could explore more complex human values, as opposed to those reflecting desires and whims stimulated by media and advertising.

For example, if an AI held a model that understood the OCEAN Big Five personality traits, which was used so effectively by Cambridge Analytica in 2016, it could predict that the user has a high degree in a single trait, openness to new experiences. By balancing knowledge around both investment planning and personality traits, the advisor could provide more balanced advice to the user that would lead to greater personal satisfaction and fulfillment. A strictly financial based AI advisor would simply recommend one asset class over another, or diversification into additional classes. But an AI advisor that used both financial optimization as well as heuristics about human personality and psyche, understanding the complex needs of the investor... might suggest keeping 95% of the portfolio within financial instruments, but propose that 5% could be invested in experiential learning for the user, in other words, investing in him or herself. This could include travel to learn a new language or a workshop to learn a new skill, possibly with permission to tap into the user's online "bucket list" – the list of things you'd like to do before you "kick the bucket."

To put this into the context of the AEP problem and combinatorial chaining, consider a situation with User A who has inherited a somewhat odd abstract painting from a distant relative in France, that doesn't have much value on the resale market in America. However, on a combinatorial exchange market, there may be a chance of trading it for something not only less objectionable but desirable for all parties. Her asking price is a value of $3,000. Now, because her interaction with the exchange is managed by a user agent with access to her private "bucket list," the trusted agent can now look for something that matches items on his list. It turns out that she has always wanted to take a class at the Cordon Bleu cooking school and to learn some French. So, our agent can scan against other agents and listings, to find User B who wants to trade a $3000 workshop pass at Cordon Bleu for ten day stay in a beachfront Airbnb on some nice tropical island. The combinatorial chain holds that in place while finding a third or fourth transaction to make the combinatorial exchange pareto-optimal for all users. Fortunately, it finds User C who has a modest bungalow on a beach in the Marquesas, which doesn't get much Airbnb interest because it is too remote. However, that person looks at the painting, and realizes it was painted by the singer Jacques Brel, who was a great singer but lousy painter, and actually has quite a bit of value in the Marquesas because Jacques Brel spent his last days on the island of Hiva Oa, following the footsteps of Paul Gauguin and learning how to paint untamed landscapes that were so bad they looked abstract. So, his agent offers a 3-week stay for that painting!

In this way, an AI-based financial advisor would advise in a more human and humane way. Thus, metaheuristic optimization via asset exchange technology could be applied directly to the issues of happiness, life goals and meaning. For user A, the lifelong goal of learning how to master the art of French cooking. For User B, a desperately needed vacation he couldn't afford otherwise. And for User C, the lifelong goal of appearing on Antique Roadshow, to show off a barn find of a lifetime. We thus can ascend from cold process of optimizing utility functions to optimizing the human condition.

APPENDIX II

Illustration of the Network Structure of NetAEP0

The structure of the network NetAEP0 created in Section 4 is illustrated in the following diagram, where the *i nodes* are represented in their duplicated form i[R] and i[S], giving rise to the arc i[R] → i[S], for a network with N = {1, …, 6}. The assets α are represented by the letters A, B, C, D and E, giving rise to *asset nodes* of the form (α, i[S]) and (α, j[R]) which are joined by arcs (α, i[S]) → (α, j[R]) (called α-linking arcs in Section 4), where i and j may vary but the asset α (= A, B, …, etc.) must be the same in each such arc. It should be noted that these linking arcs do not have limiting bounds on their flows other than an implicit lower bound of 0.

The arcs of the network can be represented by a succession of columns of R-labeled nodes and S-labeled nodes, in a pattern that begins with the R-labeled i nodes i[R], followed by the S-labeled i nodes i[S], followed in turn by the S-labeled asset nodes (α, i[S]), then followed by the R-labeled asset nodes (α, j[R]) and finally followed by the R-labeled i nodes i[R] to repeat the pattern. A further interesting pattern seen in the diagram is that all S-labeled nodes have exactly 1 arc entering but may have multiple arcs leaving, while all R-labeled nodes have exactly 1 arc leaving but may have multiple arcs entering. The i nodes are enclosed in circles in the diagram and the asset nodes are enclosed in rectangles.

Figure 1. Network structure

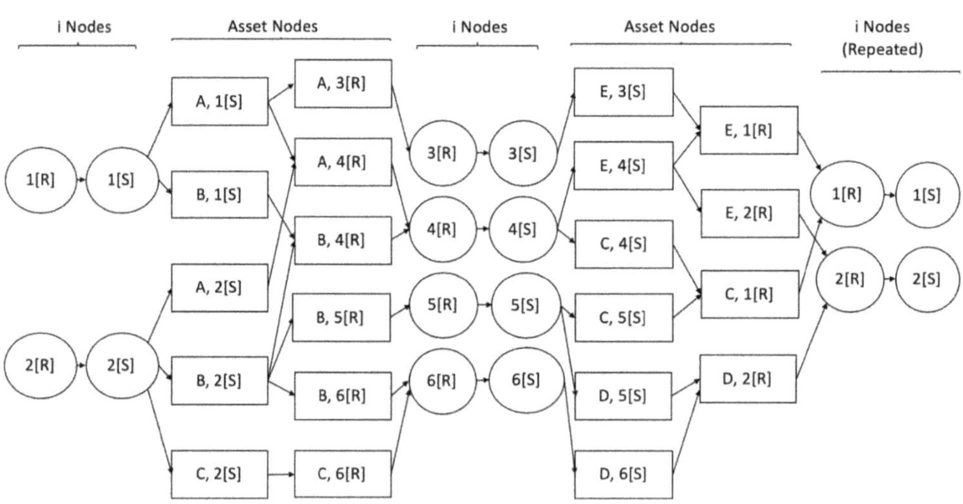

Since the asset arcs (linking arcs) do not have bounds on their flows, the foregoing pattern implies that an asset arc whose S-labeled node has a single arc out can be collapsed to be represented only by the R-labeled node, and an asset arc whose R-labeled node has a single arc in can be collapsed to be represented only by the S-labeled node. It should be emphasized that the staged structure shown in the diagram above is slightly misleading, since cycles typically vary in length and, in addition, duplicated i nodes may be encountered at various stages without implying they form a cycle that can be traced back to a previous instance of a duplicated node. The i indexes and the assets in the diagram have been ordered to show the patterns produced by arranging the nodes in columns. By contrast, the algorithm given in Section 4 for generating the network applies for any ordering of the indexes i in N and is independent of any ordering of the assets, which shows that such orderings are irrelevant in the general case.

APPENDIX III

Illustration for Reverse Scanning

Basic Combinatorial Chaining Algorithm with a Reverse Scanning Step

Initialization.

Set all flow values and all predecessor arrays to 0. Initialize the set No of open nodes by setting No = N.

Main Routine

While |No| > 1

Set all predecessor arrays to 0.

Choose i* □ No and create ScanSet = {i*}.

Execute the Reverse Scan Routine (below) to identify Fertile nodes j □ No

(recorded by setting PredR(j) = i*).

If no Fertile nodes are found (Find = False), set No:= No\ {i*} and Continue the next iteration of the Main Routine (returning to choose a new i* □ No (accompanied by ScanSet = {i*}) if |No| > 1).

Execute the Forward Scan Routine (as follows)

```
While ScanSet ≠ □

Select a node i □ ScanSet

For each α □ Si

For each j □ NRiα (= {j □ Nio: α □ Rj})

If PredS(j) = 0 then

(j has not been visited before on a Forward Scan)

Set PredS(j) = i and AssetS(j) = α.

If PredR(j) > 0, then (node j is a Fertile node)

Execute the Breakthrough Routine (below)

(Update flows and potentially remove nodes from No.)

Break (leave Forward Scan Routine to choose a new i* □ No in
the

Main Routine if |No| > 1).

Endif
```

```
Else
Let ScanSet:= ScanSet □{j}.
Endif
EndFor
EndFor
EndWhile
(End of the Forward Scan Routine)
Endwhile
(End of the Main Routine)
Reverse Scan Routine
Set Find = False
For each α □ Ri*
For each j □ NSi*α (= {j □ Ni*o: α □ Sj})
If PredR(j) = 0 then
```

```
(j has not been visited before on this Reverse Scan)

Set PredR(j) = i* and AssetR(j) = α and Find = True

Endif

Endfor

Endfor

If (Find = False) then no fertile nodes are discovered.
```

Chapter 14
Resonance and the Cosmos

Sharif Uddin Ahmed Rana
https://orcid.org/0000-0003-2296-6044
Paris Graduate School, France

ABSTRACT

The cosmos is made up of string like objects or waves hence every particle must have its frequency. Here comes the concept of resonance whose effects we know can be devastating. So resonance is a way by which we can control many natural phenomena of the cosmos. This paper is concentrated on those capabilities of resonance. Resonance has the capacity to amplify the waves on which it takes place. The results of resonance can be massive destructions. First let's understand how sound and light waves can be generated. For example if we collide two objects with little energy then sound waves will be generated if not the molecular structure of the object breaks up before that. This is because the energy of the objects is absorbed by the objects and due to state change they become unstable.

INTRODUCTION

AC Resonance has the capacity to amplify waves in a given system, and its effects can sometimes lead to significant destruction. To understand the phenomenon better, let's first explore how sound and light waves are generated. For instance, when two objects collide with a small amount of energy, sound waves are produced, assuming the molecular structure of the objects doesn't break first. This happens because the objects absorb energy, become unstable due to the change in state, and release the absorbed energy in the form of low-frequency sound waves. As the energy of the collision increases, infrared waves, which have higher frequencies than sound

DOI: 10.4018/978-1-6684-6641-4.ch014

waves, are emitted, producing heat. With even more energy, light waves—having even higher frequencies—are generated.

A fire emits light because, as an object heats up, its molecular structure breaks down, turning into gas, which combusts. Whether combustion is controlled or uncontrolled, heat is absorbed and released as infrared waves. When multiple infrared waves combine, they can sum up and emit light waves. Both infrared and visible light spectra emerge from such processes, producing both heat and light. If we increase the energy even further, ultraviolet rays, X-rays, and gamma rays can be emitted. This is one of the fundamental ways in which different types of waves are generated (Serway & Jewett, 2018).

Now, let's examine resonance within the context of the cosmos. Resonance occurs when the frequency of a wave matches the natural (resonant) frequency of an object. Resonant frequency is the frequency at which an object vibrates naturally. When two waves of similar wavelength interfere constructively, amplitude increases, while destructive interference causes the amplitude to decrease. If constructive interference persists for some time, the amplitude can rise significantly. This explains why applying a similar frequency to a vibrating object can lead to resonance, resulting in much higher amplitudes (Halliday, Resnick, & Walker, 2014).

In my earlier work, Evolution of the Cosmos, and Concept of Time, I discussed how the cosmos is composed of particles that are essentially vibrating strings or waves. Thus, every particle has a frequency. Infrared waves, present in the universe, prevent substances from becoming completely solid. These waves are absorbed by matter, increasing its kinetic energy, which in turn disrupts the compactness of molecular structures, converting them from solid to liquid or gas. At the quantum level, particles absorb energy and start moving in a linear direction due to this energy gradient, manifesting as kinetic energy (Griffiths, 2016).

Molecular structures also exhibit a frequency, often due to the unstable bonding of electrons. Electrons revolve around atomic nuclei, and the gravitational and electrostatic forces, though present, tend to cancel each other out. In molecular bonding, covalent electrons revolve around both nuclei in the bond. As a result, molecular structures vibrate, and this vibration has a frequency, just like the subatomic particles (Atkins & de Paula, 2017).

Now, let's consider the implications of resonance. Infrared waves, if resonated, could produce immense heat. In the upper atmosphere, where temperatures are cold and water vapor is abundant, cooling the vapor further could cause rain to form. By increasing the heat absorption capacity of the surroundings—achieved through resonance—it is possible to initiate rainfall. This works because heat absorption in atoms and molecules is a function of frequency, studied under the concept of phonons. By reducing the amplitude of vibrating atoms, they can absorb more heat energy until they release it back (Kittel, 2005).

Similarly, low-amplitude seismic waves in the Earth's crust can be resonated to trigger earthquakes and volcanic eruptions. Resonating these waves increases their amplitude, causing ground vibrations, which could lead to earthquakes or even volcanic activity. Wind can be artificially created by manipulating air density through heat, and tsunamis could result from artificially induced earthquakes (Aki & Richards, 2002).

The most extreme consequence of resonance would be the destruction of Earth or even the universe. Since every object is composed of vibrating particles, resonating them could theoretically destroy their atomic structure. While achieving such an effect on a large scale is virtually impossible, it underscores the destructive potential of resonance. A small example of resonance's power is when a wine glass shatters due to sound waves or when loud music causes the ground to vibrate. As Nikola Tesla famously stated, everything in the universe, including us, has a frequency; the key lies in knowing it to unlock its full potential (Cheney, 2011).

This overview illustrates the significant and sometimes catastrophic effects of resonance, from everyday examples to cosmic-scale implications.

CONCLUSION

From this article it can be concluded that the law of resonance has its own implications and proper implementation can provide suitable gain in progress of humanity.

ACKNOWLEDGEMENTS

I would like to thank to all the people due to which I have gained the knowledge about resonance like works of Nikola Tesla. I would also like to thank the persons who supported me during my research.

REFERENCES

Aki, K., & Richards, P. G. (2002). *Quantitative Seismology*. University Science Books.

Atkins, P., & de Paula, J. (2017). *Physical Chemistry*. Oxford University Press.

Cheney, M. (2011). *Tesla: Man Out of Time*. Simon & Schuster.

Griffiths, D. J. (2016). *Introduction to Quantum Mechanics*. Pearson.

Halliday, D., Resnick, R., & Walker, J. (2014). *Fundamentals of Physics*. Wiley.

Kittel, C. (2005). *Introduction to Solid State Physics*. Wiley.

Serway, R. A., & Jewett, J. W. (2018). *Physics for Scientists and Engineers*. Cengage Learning.

Chapter 15

Social and Economic Impacts of the Various Elements That Contribute to Women Glass Ceiling in Higher Education and Administration in Malaysia

Sharif Uddin Ahmed Rana
https://orcid.org/0000-0003-2296-6044
Paris Graduate School, France

ABSTRACT

In this modern and sophisticated technological cutting edge era nations are experiencing superior socio-economic progression.Prior importance should be given to the participation of both male and female candidates which can contribute to the development of nation. In Malaysia, women are faced with glass ceiling condition explicitly for their advance career growth, their entrepreneurship, organizational leadership and high ranking position in the academic administrative level. There are many factors of glass ceiling that highlighted by the researcher which are negatively impacts on social and economic affairs in relation with women successful of professional arena.

DOI: 10.4018/978-1-6684-6641-4.ch015

1. INTRODUCTION

In 1970s, "Glass ceiling" was coined by United States in order to characterize the invisible man made barriers which is built up by organizational and attitudinal hinders, which arrest women from becoming senior executives. This glass ceiling is a main example for social and economic gender inequality. This glass ceiling brings a major setback for women from developing their career. This represent an unseen block on the way to accomplishment of higher administrative position. Consequently, several studies have been conducted to focus on Glass ceiling which encompasses a negative aspect especially for women in the socio-economic affairs. It also causes stringent barrier and trap many women to be successful in the professional arena. Some of the recent literature reiterates how this led to a bottle neck from achieving higher grade by women in the administrative responsibilities and also blocked some other opportunities from handling upper-level duty in the organization by the women workforce. Meanwhile, females' employees are considered as limited possession of capabilities especially in the decision-making positions, whereas male counterparts in the organizational set up take advantage for holding higher ranks and often show stereotype behavior towards women at the work place. Furthermore, these adverse attitudes confine female candidates within the low level of administrative activities, and they fail to reach to higher position in the organizational organogram which keep many of the potential and capable women behind at race of future development (Acker, 2009; Nevill et al., 1990). However, there are many reasons that can be attributable for glass ceiling to take place in today's competitive world. For example, some factors include women's higher education and their administration position particularly lack of quality education, balancing between their professional and family lives, rigorous working hours, rough behavior of men at the work place, heinous underestimation by colleagues for being women, not having enough family support, salary inequality, Lack of reward for good jobs and unfriendly behavior by men at the work place.67 percent of women in Malaysia has attributed to care family only and look personal responsibilities for the family members, like husband and kids as the eminent reasons for not being in the labor force. In comparison with male counterpart, only 2 percent of women are employed while in European Union countries it is about high as 25 percentages. This directly or indirectly affect the women from participating in labor force in Malaysia. More of those employed women are working in low and semi-skilled positions in which there is less safety for their job. There is inequality in salary provided to women and men. The pay scale of men is more as compared to women in all occupational sectors, mainly on elementary profession in the range of 10-40 percent comparatively (Malaysiakini News, 2017). Concomitantly, about 50 percent of world's population is made by women while in Malaysia, it has become 49% (World Bank Group, 2017). The contribution from the part of women has increased little bit. In 2005 it was about 45.9 percent while in 2016, 54.3% increased (Talent Corp Malaysia, 2015; Statistics department, Malaysia, 2016). Even the participation in private sector is increasing continuously but the position of job done by women is low that is, they do low or semi-skilled job. On the other hand, education, or academic aspects of women in Malaysia are not purely motivated by the academic industry. Lunn (2007) stated that, limitation face by women for their career development in Malaysian higher education institutions is more accurate. A large number of women get a chance to improve their career into line management level but its limited to get promoted beyond Dean. In this case opinion of Omar is that (as cited in Lunn, 2007),in case to reach middle management level in academic industry political appointment is more important rather than academics. So it was more hard for them to reach high levels. These glass ceiling factors are explicitly related with social and economic effects, and they have massive impacts on women higher education as well as their administration ranking. So here this study is conducted to define the socioeconomic impacts that are apparently related with glass ceiling factors influencing women higher education and administration in Malaysia. Subsequently, the study provides a clear knowledge on the reason of social and economic effect about glass ceiling factors. Simultaneously it allows us to investigate those impacts by extensively reviewing the literature and analyzing interview data that expose the factors vividly.

2. LITERATURE SURVEY

2.1 Global Strangle of Glass Ceiling and its Disadvantages

Now-a-days the fair presence of women in world wide workforce is gradually increasing, especially in Asian countries because of the difference in value given to the working women. Usually the ladies were allowed to work in low or semi skilled occupations but the system has changed. Apart from the jobs like nursing and teaching, they choose high level professions according to their caliber (Kiaye and Singh, 2013). There are many factors which improved the condition of women. First is the improvement in quality of education provided and admission opportunities in high level education institutes, they can enter into various functional departments without any restriction. Another factor is that the Government provided special reservation to female candidates and encourage their presence in all occupational areas. Because all these elements, the ladies are getting more chnaces to show case their talents and to enter into entry or mid level positions (Kiaye and Singh, 2013).

Witnesses flourish clearly that ability of women to reach high level is less than that of women as well as their the stratified advancement of women is gradually low (Catalyst, 2014; Ding and Chareonwong, 2013).About 46 percent of women in USA are employed, yet CEO role is handles by only 4 percent and position of directors by 16 percentage in 500 firms .Apart from these, around the world women contribute only 24 percentage of seniority management positions .Taken from report of International Labor Organization (ILO) (2015) it was found, in case of Asia Pacific region, there are about 26 percent of firms which lack women and 65 percentage had very less quantity of about 30 percent in high level positions. Correspondingly, 1% women only serve as CEOs in 500 companies of Fortune Global (Acker, 2009). The population of females is more compared to male, it is about 51 percent but they contribute to only 46.5 percent to the workforce.

So others feel like women may contribute higher but only about two percentage of female candidates are found in executive posts which shows a male preeminent work force (Powell and Butter field, 2015) and this improved to 8%, according to Beck and Davis (2005). The term

"Glass Ceiling", itself brings a negative impact on women and suppresses their opportunity to explore. It affect the talented women from getting good opportunities and block them from getting promotions. These can also stop women from undertaking high responsibilities.Because of the clinched attitude of several institutions, only male candidates are allowed to take decision while those women who has the calibre to get included in decision making positions are rejected. All these are draw backs which gives a negative impact to those potentially able women looking for future development.(Acker, 2009; Nevill et al., 1990).

According to Sabharwal (2013) there are several elements such as scarcity of entry to quality education, dubbehavior, cultural blockade, gender inequality in profession and other unfairness that restrict females" advancement to the top management positions.

These barriers are classified into two by Choi and Park to obtain leadership positions into human capitals. These barriers are systematic and socialpsychological barriers. Women should be equal to male in terms of experience, job or experience according to human capital model (Choi and Park, 2014).In case of systematic barriers which represent those issues faced by women from achieving top leadership positions and while in case of other barrier model which shows there is decline in representation of women to higher levels.Some of this systemic barriers involves socializing and institutional hold hurdles (Choi and Park, 2014; Hoobler et al., 2009).

2.2 Malaysian Status of Glass Ceiling

As defined earlier,the population of women is high compared globally.In Malaysia, the importance of the particular research hold about 49% (World Bank Group, 2017).The presence of ladies in top level positions in private institutes is comparatively low even though there was a gradual increase in the participation in the workforce to 54.3% in 2016 from 45.9% in 2005 (Department of Statistics Malaysia, 2016; Talent Corp Malaysia, 2015).While in 2015,the participation of women was about 26.3 percent in Malaysia. Malaysia showed increase of 30% in participation of women in higher profile in organization compared to December 2016as reported by Malaysia"s former Prime Minister Najib Razak (The Sun Daily, 2016).Several reports are published in view of this women participation. In comparison with research published by independent research organization stated that discoveries done by women assistance in work with high priority levels is less .In other articles stated by Grant Thornton showed only 30% of women are willing to engage with duties. Like wise, his findings also constructed that this amount is 24% in Malaysia surface management is at its bottom correlated with near by countries such as Philippines (41%), Singapore (30%), Indonesia (47%) and Thailand (30%). Hence, it is required to develop Malaysia.

During the interval, company sectors in Asian countries is controlled in the meantime, is dominated by the development sector of concerning fifty two of the complete and here wherever illustration in high management positions area unit inadequate (Asian Development Bank, 2016). this can be promoted by analysis conducted by Grant Thornton that showed that the technology business is mostly used by men, with simply nineteen of senior technical school positions as compared to ladies in 2014

(Forbes, 2016). However those feminine students WHO have completed their tertiary education level is way higher as compared to male students. the share of men holding the highest management position continues to be higher as compared to a ladies creating up sixty fourth of native graduates from defined universities. We can conclude that the education fulfillment isn't absolutely translated into labor participation.

For the event of nation, it's necessary to incorporate ladies in economic manpower and decision-making role.

These can proportionately improve the Gross Domestic Product (GDP) as compared with financial gain. Ladies ar smart in maintaining economy of a rustic, if they are not enclosed this affects the country (McKinsey & Company, 2015). Ladies are believed to be a lot of artistic and may handle most troublesome problems moonfaced by firms as ladies have varied culture, education background, attitudes and experiences. They provide rare concepts and views than men (Talent Corpeduca Asian country, 2016).Therefore women take part in a crucial responsibility in development of country.

In order for Asian country to become a developed country, it's necessary to demolish ceiling in work place. By totally gaining ladies talent in work, this gap in organizations are often destroyed, so resulting in the expansion of the the whole nation

2.3 Factors of Glass Ceiling

2.3.1 Stereotype Behavior of the Male Counterpart

In attribution theory,Kelly(1967) explained about the stereotypical behavior. He also said that those members of group who ascribe to specific attributes are sent into certain groups. Due to many valuable reasons for this kind of behaviour. Brown(1995) explained such behavior in step by wise manner as "race, gender, religion, nationalityand qualification" (Brown, 1995, p. 23).These include religion in which women is treated according to the based on their religion. A valid example is that in some Muslim countries such as Saudi Arabia, the way people treat Muslim women is different as compared to other women. Apart from these, people from same religion also treat women in a different manner due to their cultural variations and belief. This kind of unwanted socio-cultural thoughts leads people to behave in stereotypical manner and these lead to discrimination (Post and Byron, 2015).

This sort of stereotypical behaviour can lead to occupational in equalities. Hence, these characters relate positively with stereotypes. Educational advancement is not free from the glass ceiling concepts. In case of journal writings, women are not allowed to place their name as first author even though they are. So the scale of women as first author decreased from 2004 to 2014 by 3.6 percent. These behavior can affect the performance of women to a large extend. Apart from the western culture, the women in Asia are more vulnerable to stereotypes and they are more likely to be excluded from all the race of future benefits (Choi and Park, 2014; Mun and Jung, 2017; Yousaf and Schmiede, 2017) and academic authorship (Süßenbacher et al., 2017)

2.3.2 Discrimination of Training and Development Programs for Females

Training classes improved the life of women and motivated them which leads to bright future ahead.Training develop their skills to do purticular jobs that are necessary for them (Abdullahi, 2006).From the study conducted by Gale(1994), it was said that there is no gender inequality for providing training for skill development but actually there was good discrimination.

In reality the organization treated male and female candidate separately and men were provided with much better training.Such programs were in reality were gender biased Amaratunga et al. (2007),stated that women were appointed mostly as staff for better communication and human resource department.Male candidates were offered with jobs like production.

From the view of Abdullahi (2006) the reason for not appointing women in senior levels were there lack of training, inadequate experiences and low educational qualification. Dainty et al. (2000) found that working womenfaced glass ceiling because of lack of training provided and lack of mentor-ship. This all leads to demolish the competitiveness in women and make a lag in their career.

2.3.3 Discrimination in Selection and Promotion Process

In the contemporary business community, males are only allowed to take part in decision making jobs (Kolade and Kehinde, 2013).In many cases women are not paid and rewarded in proportion with their sincerity and determination in the job that they work, because of this matter of glass ceiling and such studies arises. This affect the contribution of women in achieving the organizational goals.In USA, There is an important mutual relationship between the salary package and gender of the law professors(Fisher et al., 1993). Rank and payment of working women are affected by some artificial drawbacks such as glass ceiling (Gupta et al., 2006; Dolado et al., 2005). Dimovski et al. (2010) inspected tthe consequences of glass ceiling in organisation in Singapore and Malaysia.From his study, it was clear that the encouragement of female managers were repressed in Malaysian organizations and that they did not gain any growth in their career or any support such as friend-family enterprises, counselling or networking.. Similarly, Choi and Park (2014) found gender discrepancy in leadership positions in Korean civil service.

2.3.4 Family Factors

From the previous studies it is clear that management of family and its responsibility has a serious effect on the women for their career advancement to higher level. Majority of people think that women should take care of family as mothers or house wife while men are considered as beard winners.People also found that women can manage the house hold duties more clearly than that of decision-makers (Jogulu& Wood, 2011). These commitments affect women from achieving a better career as taking care of childern and managing other house chores which affect their ability in obtaining their dreams (Gallhofer et al, 2011; Jogulu& Wood, 2011).While in case of family men they can achieve more than that of women as they have less tensions and responsibilities in taking care of familyand they are considered to be better ideal candidates for managing top level roles while these beard winners can focus more to achieve senior management positions (Mavin, 2001; Jogulu&Wood, 2011).Apart from these,women also have a mnd set that having children change their life and affect family dynamics.Hence, they decide not have kids so that they can concentrate more to reach top level managers (Schwartz, 1996; Ezzedeen& Ritchey, 2009) or even delay their dedication to get married (Jogulu& Wood, 2011). While some of the women purposelysacrifice their career path development to higher level while parenting (Ezzedeen& Ritchey, 2009).

2.3.5 Organizational Culture and Practice

Organizational practisemeans the opinion made by the employees of purticular organization about how the thing should be and shape the behaviors according to their culture,character and measures (Bajdo& Dickson, 2001; Jandeska&Kraimer, 2005, Tlaiss&Kauser, 2010).From the research, It is shown that usually the oranizational cultures are decided by men and this result in gap between men and women in the companies(Bajdo& Dickson, 2001, 2002).These cultures shaped by men affect the women to achieve career growth and make it more difficult to hold high level positions(Ismail & Ibrahim, 2008).

Most of them believe that women does not give much importance to their career as compared to men (Ansari, 2016).Organization believe that since they have to take care of family they give much less time to complete their work. In addition, women who are single are still maligned and women who do not want to attend training or those postings that are unacceptable where they have to move away from family are considered non-ambitious in their career development. Goes (Ansari, 2016). The masculine organizational culture rejects women from the sharing of power, resources, and equal opportunities in the organization and it hinders the opportunity for women to reach the top management level (Choi & Park, 2004). These cultures decided that my men attach great importance to themselves. They prefer men to important duties as compared to women (Al-Mansara, 2013; Latabhavan and Balasubramaniam, 2017). Women working as managers are provided with important duties and some of them are prohibited from performing operational roles and positions of administration (Sahu and Lenka, 2016).

The career advancement of women can be improved by making other people more aware about the situation of women managers and by providing appropriate considerations (Gayani Fernando et al, 2014). From the previos studies, due to the lack of time women find it more difficult in socializing than men (Linehan, et al, 2001; Lin, 2001; Tlaiss&Kauser, 2010; Ansari, 2016). This happens because of the shortage of time as they have to take care of family and have more responsibilities in house hold activities (Linehan, et al, 2001).

Gender stereotyping also leads to a network of older boys, which excludes women from the network (Socrates, 2018). Older boys' network refers to an informal channel, consisting of men with similar interests, social classes, professions, and they can seek help and advice from other professionals through the group (Sahu and Lenka, 2016). If the hierarchy of the organization is depressed, decision makers are helped by such informal channels and will assign and promote work to those they know rather than following formal promotional processes (Simpson & Altman, 2000) . Managers get more congratulations through these informal groups and they get more exposure about the profession than women (Linehan, et al, 2001). However, this indicates that networking does not lead to advancement in women's careers because they acquire less information (Tlaiss & Kauser, 2010). Extensive studies prove that female managers are capable of working with everyone and do not show any gender inequality and differences (Tlaiss & Kauser). 2010).

Various procedures followed by organization are referring to the managerial selection and recruitment, promotion, performance evaluation, training and development (Tlaiss&Kauser, 2010). Top management maintain these kind of practices in which they mostly consist of men.These kind of practises leads to gender discriminationand they are treated as second class citizens in case og promotons,managerial recruitments and performance evaluations,and thus by reducing the salary package and authority offered to women(Tlaiss&Kauser, 2010 Pompper, 2011). According to Juneja (Management Study Guide), Personality of a person depends upom how they dainty others mostly based on their, attitude, characteristics, mindset defines his personality. Costa & McCrae (1992) proposed the Five Factor Model which describes the conncetion between an individual"s attitude and personality. Personality traits refer to ambition and confidence of women in leadership position (Terjesen& Singh, 2008).

Women are considered to be less ambitious and lack self-confidence comparatively and have caused womanhood to have a lower public profile thus leading to a fall in their calling (Hurn, 2013). Women with low self confidence tend to have negative shock upon their career onward motion. Beacuse of these women restrict themselves from applying for promotional material. Even thoigh they have high academic background they are not confident about their abilities and talents (HoweWalsh & Turnbull, 2016). Beside this. there are some other studies which found that personality traits do not has significant impact to women career advancement to top management as women in the study are found confident, competitive, ambitious and emotionally suited to managerial position (Enid Kiaye&Maniraj Singh, 2013).

2.4 Women Career Advancement

Career advancement usually refers to the improvement in career especially on the job level, positions and the title in which the individual works along with this income they are earning are also considered (Thurasamy et al, 2011). An working person should have equal access to improve his or her career and should be provided with equal opportunities to gain experience and knowledge (Callanan&Greenhaus, 1999). Glass ceiling is referred to as when a qualified person is excluded from attaining higher level in the hierarchy of an organization because of the gender, discrimination, prejudice and racism . Glass ceiling mainly based on gender inequality and how people are excluded while gender is not an important phenomena to be considered to do that particular position (Afza&Newaz, 2008).

Women feel that they have collided to a point where they seem unable to progress even further, where there is a clear path to promotion. Based on research published by Grant Thornton, the year 2017 held only 25% of the senior management position held by women. This means that 75% of management positions are occupied by men (Grant Thornton, 2017b). Although women's participation in employment has improved, the proportion of women in managerial positions is still low. Gender stereotyping affects women's career advancement because women have to work harder than men and have to compete consistently against men to prove their abilities in the same job situation (Bamte et al., 2011). Women are given negligible tasks as compared to male peers because women are perceived as dependent, feminine and physically and mentally less competent at the workplace (Afza and Nayaz, 2008).

Therefore, this study has adopted five variables including family factors, organizational culture, organizational networking, organizational practices, and social support as a constructor and mediator of a female career advancement. Each of the obstacles will be discussed in detail in the following section and this study will examine its implications for female career progression.

3. RESEARCH METHODOLOGY

To establish this study, a generally qualitative research approach has been used for personal focus or in-depth interviews. It is investigated that a large number of interviews are possible for analyzing accepted reports on qualitative research methodology that is user in depth interviews to discover a long-lasting way to research, especially abroad. The study discussed the social and economic effects of glass sealing factors affecting women's higher education in Malaysia. The findings of this research explored the utility of an in-depth interview technique with a professional or expert in academic-level respondents where they noted factors and their impact on the glass ceiling and how to break through those barriers in women's higher education.

4. IMPACTS OF GLASS CEILING

Based on labour department in US, glass ceilings are defined as "man made hurdles based on behavioral or institutional bias that prevent qualified individuals from advancing to upper management positions in their organization". (Department of Labor, 1995, p. 7). The Glass Ceiling Act 1991 established its Commission whose goals were as follows: 1) to promote a quality, inclusive and diverse workforce capable of meeting the challenge of global competition; 2) promote good corporate conduct by emphasizing corrective and cooperative; Solve the problem; 3) to promote equal opportunity, not mandatory results; And, 4) to establish a blueprint of procedures to guide the department in conductive future reviews of all management levels of the corporate workforce. (Department of Labor, 1995, p. 5).

The glass ceiling that creates unseen barriers to advance women to executive leadership positions has been widely discussed for many years. This has been attributed to the source of stagnation in women's career progression beyond a certain socially acceptable point of view. Eagly and Carly (2007) defined glass labyrinths as an obstacle course to the various challenges experienced by women on their paths. Eagley and Carly's (2007) work does not disregard the progress made by women in the field of work, but it enlightens the public to the hurdles of travel for women who ultimately not only negatively attend to the presence of women Influences. In leadership positions, but also in positions at every level.

4.1 Societal Impacts

Gender stereotypes and social norms or expectations create the impression that men perform better than women in leadership roles. According to Northhouse (2013), women are first perceived through the gender lens and then by gender as well as social stereotypes, so that they may feel stressed after achieving executive level positions. Gender stereotypes are "consensus beliefs about the character traits that characterize men and women" (Harris, Ravenswood, & Myers, 2013, p. 486), which create barriers to women's career advancement (Aiston& Jung, 2015). Diehl (2014) found that not only men but also women have negative stereotypes about women, which may affect the recruitment of a woman to the executive level position. Many researchers believe that socialization and gender stereotypes can explain the poor representation of women in leadership. Socialization theorists "recognize gender differences and differences through various developmental processes associated with life stages such as schooling and work life" (Campbell, Mueller, & Souza, 2010, p. 19).

4.2 Cultural Impacts

Cultural values refer to norms or standards that are considered acceptable in a society or community (Snaebjornsson & Edvardsson, 2013). Although culture is recognized as a major barrier to limiting the number of women in leadership (Shah, 2010), its impact on the way they lead has not received much attention. The literature suggests that leadership practice is strongly influenced by culture. This tradition has a great influence on women, and the roles assigned to them influence their work lives. Masculine and feminine leadership styles are reflections of cultural values and are important for understanding potential cultural biases against women in leadership roles. Literature has also acknowledged the implications and relationship between culture and leadership. Schein (2004) considers culture and leadership to be "two sides of the same coin" (p).

2). The cultural perspective is relevant according to Timerls, Wilmsen, and Tysen (2010), explaining the limited success of women in obtaining senior-level positions in leadership in higher education. Culture is inhabited on many levels, from civilizations, nations, organizations to groups (Skåne, 2004), and is generally based on the "sustainable structure, processes and practices of the beliefs, values, and ideologies that define people. Walk Define. Groups. "In addition. Opletka and Hertz-Lazarowitz (cited in Shah, 2010) reported," in educational leadership or women's unique leadership style Any discussion of Hilas ignores important factors such as cultural differences, economic and socio-political divisions. "... he can not only be unrealistic, but also present a distorted picture" (p. 130). Adya, to reduce disruptions in the advancement of women in leadership positions, will be nothing less than a reconstruction of the entire structure of organizations and the cord, 2011.4.2.1. Arik / personal liability.

Family and personal obligations may be one of the most prominent social barriers to the limited number of women in executive positions in higher education (Toma, Lavi, Duran, & Guillamon, 2010). One of the primary reasons women in educational leadership experience a promotion process differently than their male faculty is the increased demand outside of work. Stripling (2012) includes practical issues of lack of adequate childcare, inflexible tenure clock expectations for faculty, and inflexible work schedules on the list of reasons for underreaction. Nguyen (2013) conducted an exploratory study, in which she examined her perception of barriers to female academic deanship at selected Vietnamese universities and the experiences of female deans as facilitators for career advancement. Nguyen (2013) conducted interviews with six female deans from Vietnamese national universities, three men who are university leaders, and two male HR managers. The study's respondents identified strong family obligations, negative gender stereotypes, and unwillingness to take on leadership roles as the most common barriers for women taking academic management positions.

4.2.2 Educational Institution's Impacts

Gender inequality is an issue that has a profound impact on higher education as more women infiltrate the male-dominated organizational system. Malik (2011) examined the factors influencing the emergence of female leadership at the higher education level in Pakistan, conducting one-on-one, semi-structured interviews with ten senior female administrators. The study found that 60% of respondents identified dissatisfaction with the level of support extended to them by their institutions. Respondents further noted that their incompatibility with the male dominated culture of the institutional environment presented as a barrier to their progress (Malik, 2011). However, respondents identified several factors that they believed contributed greatly to their success in achieving senior leadership positions in their institutions of higher education.

Universities are looking for ways to resolve the issue as it relates to retaining a diverse and highly qualified faculty and staff. Universities are particularly exploring this issue as it relates to how glass ceilings or glass labyrinths affect female administrators as they tackle gender pay gaps, job rank progress, and family leave policies. Kahusak and Kanji (2013) argued that there is a gender gap in education and that women are short in tenure and promotion in tenure status due to late onset in academia compared to men. For the purpose of this review and to gain a further understanding of institutional barriers, two institutional barriers were relevant and subsequently explored further: recruitment and retention, And professional development.

Source: Alive at the top: an important case study of female administrators in higher education 4.2.3 Organizational Impacts

Hobler, Jenny M (2009) presented a model based on social role theory and examined 112 samples of subordinate supervisors from US Fortune. About 500 firms found that challenging tasks, training, and other incentives provided to women is less. While Mattis, Mary C. (2007) interviewed female business owners who left corporate and found that the reason for their employee turnover was glass ceiling. Women's contributions Bazanel, Patrice M (2000) Studies discuss current organizational practices that alter power imbalances in process (community) and content in organization members (women) in alternative settings (including organizational forms) failed is. Through a cross-sectional survey with 475 respondents from various colleges Myres, C. (2016) found that job vacancies, internal structure and organizational culture are the most important factors for career progression of the female community.

Afza, s. (2008) five factor groups were taken into their study by factor analysis, in which glass ceiling is used to manage perception, work environment, work-life conflict, sexual harassment and organizational policy and respondents' opinions. Was found from And next is organizational conflict and work life struggle. The study also disagrees that sexual harassment as a contributor to making glass ceilings. The focus of the findings of Al-Mansa, E (2013) was also on organizational constraint where they explored the effect of glass sealing barrier in Jordan, which included organizational, family and social barriers.

Source: The presence of glass ceilings and factors affecting women in reaching peak conditions.

5. ECONOMIC IMPACTS

Women can play major role in today's economy, salary as well as ability to spend is important for growth of the economic background of the country . From a consumer point of view, ladies hold a lot. In the "he-conomy", women are the main purchasers of commodities of the house. They continuously manage house with their own talents s, including big-ticket items such as investment decisions and car purchases, accounting for $ 4 trillion annually.

5.1 Reduction in GDP and Income Level

Women are more affected by the economic issues and changes in price of commodities.An immediate assessment of this impact on economy on th labor market has resulted in significant increase in layoffs of workers. Slow GDP growth has resulted in crisisof employment growth and unemployment. The level of work is projected to decrease in all sectors except export oriented industries. According to Najibrajak, former Prime Minister of Malaysia, told that there reached a target of women up to 30% in the top level as of December 2016 (The Sun Daily, 2016). However, there is a difference in findings on the participation rate of women in high positions compared to research published by an independent research institute. The report published by Grant Thornton noted that the participation rate of women is still below 30%. In addition, also found that women have the lowest participation rates such as Malaysia (24%), Malaysia (46%), Philippines (40%), Thailand (31%) and Singapore. (30%) (Grant Thornton, 2017a). Therefore, there is a lot of scope for reform for Malaysia.

5.2 Representation of Women in Leadership

In case of creative and cultural spheres of leadership positions there identified a issue for the value given to women in 2007 by Holden and McCarthy. There is a general belief that all these are "female friendly". How ever, the truth is all those powers and leadership associated with female are underestimated. This becomes can important issue which affect the growth of nation. Lips and Keener (2007, p. 563) found that a awareness should be created against discrimination against women and lack of vacancy of women to higher level that is to leadership positions. Gender-conservative perceptions in leadership roles are cited as barriers to women in the power of status . These perceptions have been seen to be erased, but have not been eradicated, as such prejudices and discrimination against women in leadership still occur (Eagly and Carly, 2003). In particular, the gender-conservative expectations that Mullen (2009) highlighted are seen to generate prejudice through a male-dominated organizational environment; This provides further evidence that it is not due to the problem of institution, but also due to the level of thought of individuals working (Nelson et al., 2009).

Obstacles seen are usually described as "glass ceilings", under which a person with relevant qualifications and competencies is prevented by an invisible barrier in their elevation to a position of leadership or responsibility.

6. DISCUSSION

The social and economic impacts of the glass sealing barrier which is still persistent in Malaysia. Factors involved in the glass roof landscape bring many social and economic deficiencies in the way of achieving targeted development for any developing nation. In order to pursue this study an attempt is made to gather expert opinions from many women who are experienced professionally and go through many obstacles towards their successful journey in their professional field. From valuable comments made by successful women in their professional careers, this study piece seeks to understand how the state of glass ceilings is formed and impacts on the social and economic spectrum. This researcher divided the entire interview session into two parts. In the first part the researcher tries to get information about the social effects of glass ceiling especially with an interactive discussion with the respondents in Malaysia. From interviews with respectable respondents, this study summarizes the social effects as follows. (1) Women are not being recognized as a potential candidate for the development process in the society (2) Women are becoming autocratic due to the conservative attitude shown by the opposition in the society (3) In many families, women are limited only Their responsibility to take care of children and family members which restricts the empowerment of women in society. (4) The presence of glass ceiling Area because the presence of women in the organizational set-is not given a high position in up to destroy in order to meet any high responsibilities creativity women (5)) glass roof is also responsible for cultural influences. For example, women are not being rewarded for their achievement in society and organizational environment. As a result, they often face less convulsions and unfriendly behavior. In addition, women are not considered for essential training and development programs providing scholarships that lead to social asymmetry. And in the second part the economic impact of the glass ceiling was given importance. Subsequently, the researcher presents a summary of the economic effects of glass sealing from interviews conducted with respondents. Its discussion is as follows. The presence of glass ceiling conditions significantly reduces the quality of leadership. As a result, the contribution of women in economic activities remains constant. Meanwhile, women do not participate independently in a workforce that does not enter into productivity and economic progress. Researchers also shed light on some other issues that have an economically negative effect due to the presence of glass sealing progress from interview analysis. Due to the glass ceiling, women are separated from any entrepreneurial activities. As a result it impacts national economic development progress and as an entrepreneur women are losing their intention to do any small and medium business independently. Therefore, the country's economic growth will slow down considerably due to access to the glass ceiling.

7. CONCLUSION

The presence of glass ceiling conditions in Malaysia can be a hindrance to social and economic progress in the long run. About half of Malaysia's population is women. Therefore, development activities depend a lot on the female counterpart. As discussed earlier, if women are treated negatively in our social and organizational settings, it will create many social and economic deficiencies. Therefore, it is important that the government of Malaysia should come up with some policies that will significantly reduce the presence of glass ceilings in Malaysia so that women can contribute to social and economic development with men. The current study focuses on some of the issues that have been explored to interview some successful women. For example, in the present study the emphasis on support for in-laws in husbands, children, and family is strong

REFERENCES

Abdullahi, H. I. (2006). *Gender and Adjustment in Nigerian Manufacturing sectors* [Seminar Paper]. Centre for Social Science and Research Development.

Acker, J. (2009). From glass ceiling to inequality regimes. *Sociologie du travail, 51*(2), 199217.Catalyst (2014), "Women on boards", available at: www.catalyst.org/knowledge/womenboards

Afza, S. R., & Newaz, M. K. (2008). Factors determining the presence of glass ceiling and influencing women career advancement in Bangladesh. *BRAC University Journal*, V(1), 85–92.

Aiston, S. J., & Jung, J. (2015). Women academics and research productivity: An international comparison. *Gender and Education*, 27(3), 205220. DOI: 10.1080/09540253.2015.1024617

Al-Manasra, E. (2013). What Are the "Glass Ceiling" Barriers Effects on Women Career Progress in Jordan? *International Journal of Business and Management*, 8(6), 40–46. DOI: 10.5539/ijbm.v8n6p40

Amaratunga, D., Haigh, R., Shanmugam, M., Lee, A. J., & Elvitigala, G. (2006), "Construction industry and women: a review of the barriers", Proceedings of the 3rd International SCRI Research Symposium, Delft, April.

American Express. (2011). The American Express OPEN State of Women-Owned Business Report: A Summary of Important Trends, 1997-2011. American Express: New York City. http://media.nucleus.naprojects.com/pdf/WomanR eport_FINAL.pdf

Ansari, N. (2016). Respectable femininity: A significant panel of glass ceiling for career women. *ender in Management. International Journal (Toronto, Ont.)*, 31(8), 528–541.

Appelbaum, S. H., Audet, L., & Miller, J. C. (2003). Gender and leadership?Leadership and gender?A journey through the landscape of theories. *Leadership and Organization Development Journal*, 24(1), 43–51. DOI: 10.1108/01437730310457320

Asian Development Bank. (2016). *More women leaders to vitalize Asia's corporate sector*. Retrieved from https://blogs.adb.org/blog/more[REMOVED HYPERLINK FIELD]women-leaders-vitalize-asias-corporate-sector[REMOVED HYPERLINK FIELD]

Bajdo, L. M., & Dickson, M. W. (2001). Perceptions of Organizational Culture and Women's Advancement in Organizations: A Cross-Cultural Examination. *Sex Roles*, 45(5-6), 399–414. DOI: 10.1023/A:1014365716222

Brown, R. (1995). *Prejudice: It"s Social Psychology*. Blackwell Publishing.

Cahusac, E., & Kanji, S. (2014). Giving up: How gendered organizational cultures push mothers out. *Gender, Work and Organization*, 21(1), 57–70. DOI: 10.1111/gwao.12011

Callanan, G. A., & Greenhaus, J. H. (1999). *Changing Concepts and Practices for Human Resources Management*. Jossey-Bass.

Campbell, S., Mueller, K., & Souza, J. M. (2010). Shared Leadership Experiences of Women Community College Presidents. *Journal of Women in Educational Leadership*, 8(1), 19–32.

Choi, S., & Park, C. (2014). Glass ceiling in Korean Civil Service: Analyzing barriers to women"s career advancement in the Korean government. *Public Personnel Management*, 43(1), 118–139. DOI: 10.1177/0091026013516933

Cordova, D. I. (2011). Moving the needle on women's leadership. *On Campus with Women, 40*(1).

Dainty, A. R., Bagilhole, B. M., & Neale, R. H. (2000). A grounded theory of women's career under-achievement in large UK construction companies. *Construction management & economics, 18*(2), 239-250.Kolade, O.J. and Kehinde, O. (2013), "Glass ceiling and women career advancement: Evidence from Nigerian construction Industry. *Iranian Journal of Management Studies*, 6(1), 79–99.

Dezso, C. L., & Ross, D. G. (2012). Does female representation in top management improve firm performance? A panel data investigation. *Strategic Management Journal*, 33(9), 1072–1089. DOI: 10.1002/smj.1955

Diehl, A. B., & Diehl, A. B. (2014).Navigating Adversity, Barriers, and Obstacles. *Women and leadership in higher education*, 135..

Dimovski, V., Skerlavaj, M., & Man, M. M. K. (2010). Comparative analysis of mid-level women managers" perception of the existence of „glass ceiling"in Singaporean and Malaysian organizations. *The International Business & Economics Research Journal*, 9(8), 61–78. DOI: 10.19030/iber.v9i8.613

Eagly, A. H., & Carli, L. L. (2003). The female leadership advantage: An evaluation of the evidence. *The Leadership Quarterly*, 14(6), 807834. DOI: 10.1016/j.leaqua.2003.09.004

Eagly, A. H., Eagly, L. L. C. A. H., & Carli, L. L. (2007). *Through the labyrinth: The truth about how women become leaders*. Harvard Business Press.

Eagly, A. H., & Johnson, B. T. (1990). Gender and leadership style: A meta-analysis. *Psychological Bulletin*, 108(2), 233–256. DOI: 10.1037/0033-2909.108.2.233

Enid Kiaye, R., & Maniraj Singh, A. (2013). The glass ceiling: A perspective of women working in Durban. *Gender in Management*, 28(1), 28–42. DOI: 10.1108/17542411311301556

Enid Kiaye, R., & Maniraj Singh, A. (2013, February 08). The glass ceiling: A perspective of women working in Durban. *Gender in Management*, 28(1), 28–42. DOI: 10.1108/17542411311301556

Ezzedeen, S., & Ritchey, K. (2009). Career advancement and family balance strategies of executive women. *Gender in Management*, 24(6), 388–411. DOI: 10.1108/17542410910980388

Fisher, B. D., Motowidlo, S., & Werner, S. (1993). Effects of gender and other factors on rank of law professors in colleges of business: Evidence of a glass ceiling. *Journal of Business Ethics*, 12(10), 771–778. DOI: 10.1007/BF00881309

Forbes. (2016). *Which industries has the most women in senior management?* Retrieved from https://www.forbes.com/sites/niallmccarthy/2016/ 03/08/which-industries-have-the-most-women-in[REMOVED HYPERLINK FIELD]senior-management-infographic/#3917ea6f5cc4[REMOVED HYPERLINK FIELD]

Gale, A. W. (1994). Women in non-traditional occupations: The construction industry. *Women in Management Review*, 9(2), 3–14. DOI: 10.1108/EUM0000000003989

Gallhofer, S., Paisey, C., Roberts, C., & Tarbert, H. (2011). Preferences, constraints and work. *Accounting, Auditing & Accountability Journal*, 24(4), 440–470. DOI: 10.1108/09513571111133054

Gayani Fernando, N., Amaratunga, D., & Haigh, R. (2014). The career advancement of the professional women in the UK construction industry: The career success factors. *Journal of Engineering. Design and Technology*, 12(1), 5370. DOI: 10.1108/JEDT-04-2012-0018

GEM.(2010). *Global Entrepreneurship Monitor 2010 Global Report.* Global Entrepreneurship Research Association: Boston. a.Gender in Management: An International Journal, Vol. 28 No. 1, pp. 28-42.

Grant Thornton. (2017a). *Malaysia has the least senior business roles held by women in ASEAN at 24%.* Retrieved from https://www.grantthornton.com.my/press/press[REMOVED HYPERLINK FIELD]releases-20162/Malaysia-has-the-least-senior[REMOVED HYPERLINK FIELD]business-roles-held-by-women-in-ASEAN/[REMOVED HYPERLINK FIELD]

Grant Thornton. (2017b). *Women in Business: New Perspectives on Risk and Reward.* Retrieved from http://grantthornton.pl/wp[REMOVED HYPERLINK FIELD]content/uploads/2017/03/Grant-Thornton_Women[REMOVED HYPERLINK FIELD]in-Business_2017-FINAL_Digital.pdf[REMOVED HYPERLINK FIELD]

Harris, C., Ravenswood, K., & Myers, B. (2013). Glass slippers, Holy Grails and Ivory Towers: gender and advancement in academia. *Labour& Industry: a journal of the social and economic relations of work, 23*(3), 231-244.

Holden, J., & McCarthy, H. (2007). *Women at the Top – A Provocation Piece.* City University.

Hoobler, J. M. (2016). Domestic Employment Relationships and Trickle-Down Work–Family Conflict: The South African Context. *Africa Journal of Management*, 2(1), 31–49. DOI: 10.1080/23322373.2015.1126499

Hoobler, J. M., Lemmon, G., & Wayne, S. J. (2014). Women's managerial aspirations: An organizational development perspective. *Journal of Management*, 40(3), 703–730.

Hoobler, J. M., Wayne, S. J., & Lemmon, G. (2009). Bosses‟ perceptions of family-work conflict and women‟s promotability: Glass ceiling effects. *Academy of Management Journal*, 52(5), 939–957. DOI: 10.5465/amj.2009.44633700

. Hoobler, M.J., Masterson, C.R., Nkomo, S.M. and Michel, E.J. (2016), "Business case for women leaders", Journal of Management, p. 0149206316628643, .DOI: 10.1177/0149206316628643

Howe-Walsh, L., & Turnbull, S. (2016). Barriers to women leaders in academia: Tales from science and technology. *Studies in Higher Education*, 41(3), 415–428. DOI: 10.1080/03075079.2014.929102

Hurn, B. (2013). Are cracks now appearing in the boardroom glass ceiling. *Industrial and Commercial Training*, 45(4), 195–201. DOI: 10.1108/00197851311323475

Ismail, M., & Ibrahim, M. (2008). Barriers to career progression faced by women. *Gender in Management*, 23(1), 5166. DOI: 10.1108/17542410810849123

Jandeska, K. E., & Kraimer, M. L. (2005). Women's Perceptions of Organizational Culture, Work Attitudes, and Role-modeling Behaviors. *Journal of Managerial Issues*, 17(4), 461–478.

Jogulu, U., & Wood, G. (2011). Women managers' career progression: An Asia Pacific perspective. *Gender in Management*, 26(8), 590–603. DOI: 10.1108/17542411111183893

Kelly, H. H. (1967), "Attribution theory in social psychology", *Nebraska Symposium on Motivation*, University of Nebraska Press.

Kiaye, R. and Singh, A. (2013), "The glass ceiling: a perspective of women working in Durban",

Kiaye, R. and Singh, A. (2013), "The glass ceiling: a perspective of women working in Durban",

Lathabhavan, R., & Balasubramanian, S. A. (2017). Glass Ceiling and women employees in Asian organizations: A tri-decadal review. *Asia-Pacific Journal of Business Administration*, 9(3), 232246. DOI: 10.1108/APJBA-03-2017-0023

Lin, N. (2001). *Social Capital: A Theory of Social Structure and Action*. Cambridge University Press. DOI: 10.1017/CBO9780511815447

Linehan, M., Scullion, H., & Walsh, J. S. (2001). Barriers to women"s participation in international management. *European Business Review*, 13(1), 10–19. DOI: 10.1108/09555340110366444

Lips, H. M., & Keener, E. (2007). Effects of gender and dominance on leadership emergence: Incentives make a difference. *Sex Roles*, 56(9-10), 563–571. DOI: 10.1007/s11199-007-9210-8

Lunn, M. (2007). *Women academicians: Gender and career progression*. Jurul.

Malaysiakini News. (2017). Empowering women, empowering Malaysia.Retrieved from www.malaysiakini.com/letters/368977

Malik, S. (2011). A Portrayal of Women Educational Leadership in Pakistan. *Journal of Educational Psychology*, 5(2), 37–44.

Mattis, M. C. (2004). Women entrepreneurs: Out from under the glass ceiling. *Women in Management Review*, 19(3), 154–163.

Mavin, S. (2001). Women"s career in theory and practice: Time for change? *Women in Management Review*, 16(4), 183–192. DOI: 10.1108/09649420110392163

. McKinsey & Company. (2015). *The power of parity: How advancing women's equality can add $12 trillion to global growth.*

Morrison, A. M., & Von Glinow, M. A. (1990). Women and minorities in management. *The American Psychologist*, 45(2), 200–208. DOI: 10.1037/0003-066X.45.2.200

. Mullen, C. A. (2009). Challenges and breakthroughs of female department chairs across disciplines in higher education. *Advancing Women in Leadership, 29.*

Mun, E., & Jung, J. (2017). Change above the glass ceiling: Corporate social responsibility and gender diversity in Japanese firms. *Administrative Science Quarterly*, (May), 0001839217712920.

Myers, C. E. (2010). *Perceptions of the glass ceiling effect in community colleges.* University of New Orleans.

Nelson, T., Maxfield, S., & Kolb, D. (2009). Women entrepreneurs and venture capital: Managing the shadow negotiation. *International Journal of Gender and Entrepreneurship*, 1(1), 5776. DOI: 10.1108/17566260910942345

Nevill, G., Pennicott, A., Williams, J., & Worrall, A. (1990). *Women in the workforce: the effect of demographic changes in the 1990s*. The Industrial Society.

Nguyen, T. L. H. (2013). Barriers to and facilitators of female Deans‟ career advancement in higher education: An exploratory study in Vietnam. *Higher Education*, 66(1), 123–138. DOI: 10.1007/s10734-012-9594-4

Northouse, P. G. (2013). *Leadership: Theory and practice* (6th ed.). Sage.

Ogbonna, E., & Harris, L. C. (2000). Leadership style, organizational culture and performance: Empirical evidence from UK companies. *International Journal of Human Resource Management*, 11(4), 766–788. DOI: 10.1080/09585190050075114

Pompper, D. (2011). Fifty years later: Midcareer women of color against the glass ceiling in communications organizations. *Journal of Organizational Change Management*, 24(4), 464486.

Post, C., & Byron, K. (2015). Women on boards and firm financial performance: A meta-analysis. *Academy of Management Journal*, 58(5), 1546–1571. DOI: 10.5465/amj.2013.0319

Powell, G. N., & Butterfield, D. A. (2015). The glass ceiling: What have we learned 20 years on? *Journal of Organizational Effectiveness: People and Performance*, 2(4), 306–326. DOI: 10.1108/JOEPP-09-2015-0032

Ryan, M. K., & Haslam, S. A. (2005). The glass cliff: Evidence that women are over. *British Journal of Management*, 16(2), 81–90. DOI: 10.1111/j.1467-8551.2005.00433.x

Sabharwal, M. (2013). From glass ceiling to glass cliff: Women in senior executive service. *Journal of Public Administration: Research and Theory*, 25(2), 399–426. DOI: 10.1093/jopart/mut030

Sahoo, D. K., & Lenka, U. (2016). Breaking the glass ceiling: Opportunity for the organization. *Industrial and Commercial Training*, 48(6), 311–319. DOI: 10.1108/ICT-02-2015-0017

SBA. (2011a). *Frequently Asked Questions*. Small Business Administration.

Schein, V. E. (2007). Women in management: Reflections and projections. *Women in Management Review*, 22(1), 6–18. DOI: 10.1108/09649420710726193

Schwartz, D. B. (1996). The impact of workfamily policies on women"s career development: Boon or bust? *Women*, 11(1), 5–19.

Shah, S. J. (2010). Re. *International Journal of Leadership in Education*, 13(1), 27–44. DOI: 10.1080/13603120903244879

Shein, E. (2004). *Organizational culture and leadership*. Jossey-Bass.

Simpson, R., & Altman, Y. (2000). The time bounded glass ceiling and young women managers: career progress and career success – evidence from the UK. *Journal Of European Industrial Training, 24*(2/3/4), 190-198.

Snaebjornsson, I. M., & Edvardsson, I. R. (2013). Gender, nationality and leadership style: A literature review. *International Journal of Business and Management*, 8(1), 89.

Socratous, M. (2018). Networking: A male dominated game. *Gender in Management*, 33(2), 167–183. Advance online publication. DOI: 10.1108/GM-11-2016-0181

Stripling, J. (2012). With Tilghman"s resignation, another pioneer female president moves on. *Chronicle of Higher Education. Retrieved from*http://chronicle.com/article/Another-PioneerFemale/134600

Süßenbacher, S., Amering, M., Gmeiner, A., & Schrank, B. (2017). Gender-gaps and glass ceilings: A survey of gender-specific publication trends in Psychiatry between 1994 and 2014. *European Psychiatry*, 44, 90–95. DOI: 10.1016/j.eurpsy.2017.03.008 PMID: 28550785

Talent Corp Malaysia. (2016). *Diversity and Workforce Composition for Top 100 PLCs*. Retrieved from https://www.talentcorp.com.my/clients/TalentCorp_2016_7A6571AE-D9D0-4175-B35D-99EC514F2D24/contentms/img/publication/Divers ityArtcard_v2.0.pdf[REMOVED HYPERLINK FIELD]

Terjesen, S., & Singh, V. (2008). Female presence on corporate boards: A multi-country study of environment context. *Journal of Business Ethics*, 83(1), 55–63. DOI: 10.1007/s10551-007-9656-1

The Sun Daily. (2017). *Govt will name and shame PLCs with no women on their boards in 2018*. Retrieved from http://www.thesundaily.my/news/2017/07/25/govt[REMOVED HYPERLINK FIELD]will-name-and-shame-plcs-no-women-their[REMOVED HYPERLINK FIELD]boards-2018[REMOVED HYPERLINK FIELD]

Thurasamy, R., Lo, M., Yang Amri, A., & Noor, N. (2011). An analysis of career advancement among engineers in manufacturing organizations. *International Journal of Commerce and Management*, 21(2), 143–157. DOI: 10.1108/10569211111144346

Timmers, T. M., Willemsen, T. M., & Tijdens, K. G. (2010). Gender diversity policies in universities: A multi-perspective framework of policy measures. *Higher Education*, 59(6), 719735. DOI: 10.1007/s10734-009-9276-z

Tlaiss, H., & Kauser, S. (2011). The impact of gender, family, and work on the career advancement of Lebanese women managers. *Gender in Management*, 26(1), 8–36. DOI: 10.1108/17542411111109291

Tomas, M., Lavie, J. M., Duran, M. D. M., & Guillamon, C. (2010). Women in academic administration at the university. *Educational Management Administration & Leadership*, 38(4), 487–498. DOI: 10.1177/1741143210368266

U.S. Department of Labor. (1995). *Good for business: Making full use of the nation's human capital*. Federal Glass Ceiling Commission.

Weiler, S., & Bernasek, A. (2001). Dodging the glass ceiling? Networks and the new wave of women entrepreneurs. *The Social Science Journal*, 38(1), 85–103. DOI: 10.1016/S0362-3319(00)00111-7

Yousaf, R., & Schmiede, R. (2017). Barriers to women"s representation in academic excellence and positions of power. *Asian Journal of German and European Studies*, 2(1), 2–13. DOI: 10.1186/s40856-017-0013-6

Chapter 16
The Barriers to the Career Progression of Women Employees in Malaysian University

Sharif Uddin Ahmed Rana
https://orcid.org/0000-0003-2296-6044
Paris Graduate School, France & World Talent Economy Forum, Malaysia

Adrian David Cheok
https://orcid.org/0000-0001-6316-2339
Nanjing University of Information Science and Technology, Australia

ABSTRACT

Women experience inequalities in terms of behavior, recognition, promotion, salary, and the extent of opportunities they have. This unrecognized, invisible barrier that creates restrictions to progress in the profession, especially affecting women employees at the university level, is referred to as the "barriers and solution from the glass ceiling" in this research. The study also aims at finding the personal and psychological resources necessary for women to break through the 'glass ceiling' and their way of overcoming it to survive as women employees in Malaysian Universities. A total of 50 Malaysian women from 20 Malaysian universities, where some are faculty, professor, assistant professor, lecturer, Pro VC, Vice-chancellor, Chancellor, and some are on the dean list participated in our research and an in-depth comprehensive interview, as well as any, is performed. In the first theme of the questionnaire, the perception of the glass ceiling and the relation between career prospects of the Malaysian female employees' career path is discussed.

DOI: 10.4018/978-1-6684-6641-4.ch016

INTRODUCTION

Women include 43 percent of the world's horticultural work drive – ascending to 70 percent in a few nations. For example, in Africa, 80 percent of the agricultural production originates from little ranchers, the vast majority of whom are country-women. (Ahmad, M. & Naseer, H. (2015)

Ladies in the workforce acquiring wages or pay are a piece of an advanced wonder, one that was created in the meantime as the development of paid work for men, however, ladies have been tested by the disparity in the workforce (Jahan, 2018).

In Malaysia, many previous studies prove that women consistently earn less than men (see Chua 1984; Chapman & Harding 1986; Lee & Nagaraj 1995; Low & Goy 2006 & Fernandez 2006; Rahmah & Idris 2012). However, these studies adopt the wage decomposition method in looking at determinants of gender wage differentials including discrimination. (Guest, C. (2016). Studies looking at the gender wage gap using quantile regression are rarely found in Malaysia, with the exception of Wan Liyana et al. (2016).

In developing a nation, females have generally gotten fewer educational facilities than their male counterparts in the Asian subcontinents (Jafarey & Maiti, 2015) which influence their job life. Nonetheless, numerous ladies had thought that it was hard to advance past specific dimensions to ensure the best administrative position despite the fact that their capabilities and credentials are ready for competition with their male partners (Subramaniam, Khadri, Maniam & Ali, 2016). Most of the new female occupations were bunched in the lower and middle payment options, for example, administrative staff, administration and agriculture, hardware administrators, and workers. (Shabbir, H., Shakeel, M. A. & Zubair, R. A.)

The term "glass ceiling" was popularized in the 1980s.Glass Ceiling (GC) concept first has been pronounced in 1984 by Gay Bryant, Working Woman magazine editor. Bryant has started women's reaching a certain point and getting stuck there with the "Glass Ceiling" concept (Boyd, 2008). The Oxford English Dictionary notes that the first use of the term was in 1984, in *Adweek:* "Women have reached a certain point — I call it the glass ceiling. They're in the top of middle management and they're stopping and getting stuck." (Amina M and Zakra)

"Glass ceiling" means an invisible upper limit in corporations and other organizations, above which it is difficult or impossible for women to rise in the ranks. "Glass ceiling" is a metaphor for the hard-to-see informal barriers that keep women from getting promotions, pay raises and further opportunities. The "glass ceiling" metaphor has also been used to describe the limits and barriers experienced by minority racial groups. (Jone Johnson Lewis, January 29, 2019)

The Glass Ceiling is a metaphor. It's *"**an intangible barrier**within a hierarchy**that prevents women**or minorities**from obtaining upper-level positions.**"* (According to Merriam-Webster). Women account for fewer than 5% of the board of directors and corporate officer positions. (Source: Bernard Bass and Bruce Avolio, Shatter the glass ceiling)

In 279 North American companies, with a total of 13 million employees, women represent just 23% of C-Suite occupants – direct reports to the CEO. (Source: Forbes, Jan 2019)

The low participation in best administration posts could be brought about by obstructions because of individual reasons, for example, family obligations, family backing, or statistical factors, for example, age, training, and conjugal status (Kabir, 2016; Sharif, 2014). Furthermore, the obstructions could likewise be for work difficulties, for example, authoritative culture and professional success openings, for example, advancement openings, preparation, and choice and enlistment techniques. (Essays, UK. (2018).

This observable fact has been termed the "Glass Ceiling" (GC) alludes to boundaries ladies face as they endeavor to climb the professional bureaucracy (Jafarey & Maiti, 2015; Gupta, 2018). The Glass ceiling, now and then, alludes to imperceptible hindrances or counterfeit boundaries ladies face that prevent them from advancing past a specific dimension. Religion is one of the elements that can upset ladies' expectations to enter top administration. Another fact is that Malays are Muslim which may have limited the rate of participation of Malays in the economy. (Birt, L., Scott, S., Cavers, D., Campbell, C., & Walter, F. (2016).

The concept of the glass ceiling is held to be closely related to a country's gender inequality (Gupta, 2018). Later the term refers to the differences between man and woman employees by employers. The United Nations Development Program (UNDP) had created in 2017 and is defined as the 'Gender Inequality Index (GII). The GII refers to a new index for measuring gender disproportion. According to UNDP (as cited in Kagan, 2018), this index is a composite measure that will capture the loss of achievement due to gender inequality within a country. The latest definition of the glass ceiling is given by Kagan (2018). According to her, the is glass ceiling an illustration alluding to a fake boundary that keeps ladies and minorities from being elevated to administrative and official dimension positions inside an association (Kagan, 2018). The discrimination and limitation regarding expression are utilized to portray the challenges looked by ladies when attempting to move to higher jobs in a male-commanded order (Kagan, 2018). The boundaries are frequently unwritten, implying that ladies are bound to be limited from progressing through acknowledged standards and verifiable predispositions, as opposed to characterized corporate approaches (Kagan, 2018). For example, at the point when Hillary Clinton kept running for president in 2008 and 2016, she over and again talked about her objective of breaking the "most astounding, hardest biased based impediment (glass ceiling)" by turning into America's first female president (Kagan, 2018). It shows the lacking faced by women as they were usually discriminated against in health, education, and in the job (as cited in Sharif, 2014).

On 15 March 2019, the United Nations Postal Administration (UNPA) will issue three definitive stamps on the topics of "Stop Sexual Exploitation and Abuse" (US$0.85 stamp), "Gender Equality" (CHF1, 50 stamps), and "Migration" (€1, 80 stamps).

According to the UN, the rates of girls between 15-19 who are subjected to FGM (female genital mutilation) in the 30 countries where the practice is concentrated and have dropped from 1 in 2 girls in 2000 to 1 in 3 girls by 2017.

According to UN IN 2019 Women and girls represent half of the world's population and, therefore, also half of its potential. Gender equality, besides being a fundamental human right, is essential to achieving peaceful societies, with full human potential and sustainable development. Moreover, it has been shown that empowering women spurs productivity and economic growth.(Birt, L., Scott, S., Cavers, D., Campbell, C., & Walter, F. (2016)

According to WHO Gender refers to the socially constructed characteristics of women and men – such as norms, roles, and relationships of and between groups of women and men. It varies from society to society and can be changed. While most people are born either male or female, they are taught appropriate norms and behaviors – including how they should interact with others of the same or opposite sex within households, communities, and workplaces. When individuals or groups do not "fit" established gender norms they often face stigma, discriminatory practices, or social exclusion – all of which adversely affect health. It is important to be sensitive to different identities that do not necessarily fit into binary male or female sex categories. (Pandey, S. (2019).

WHO's UN-SWAP STATUS

WHO has made great strides in meeting and exceeding requirements on performance indicators detailed in the United Nations System-wide Action Plan towards gender quality and the empowerment of women (UN-SWAP)? In 2016, WHO significantly improved its UN-SWAP performance, with 80% of the Performance Indicators either "Meeting" or "Exceeding Requirements" compared to 60% in 2015 and 53% in 2014. Specifically, progress was made on three Performance Indicators, with a remarkable achievement of "Exceeds Requirements" for Indicator 1. Policy and Plan, and "Meets Requirements" for Indicator 8. Resource Tracking and 14. Knowledge Management.

In 2017, only three Performance Indicators remain where WHO's performance should improve in order to "Meet Requirements". These are: Indicators, Resource Allocation, Gender Architecture and Parity, and Capacity Development

Gender is defined by FAO as 'the relations between men and women, both perceptual and material. Gender is not determined biologically, as a result of the sexual characteristics of either women or men but is constructed socially. It is a central organizing principle of societies and often governs the processes of production and reproduction, consumption, and distribution' (FAO, 1997). Despite this definition, gender is often misunderstood as being the promotion of women only. However, as we see from the FAO definition, gender issues focus on women and on the relationship between men and women, their roles, access to and control over resources, division of labor, interests, and needs. Gender relations affect household security, family well-being, planning, production, and many other aspects of life (Bravo-Baumann, 2000).

Gender Equity

Gender Equity is the process of being fair to men and women. To ensure fairness, measures must often be put in place to compensate for the historical and social disadvantages that prevent women and men from operating on a level playing field. Equity is a means. Equality is the result. (UNESCO's Gender Mainstreaming Implementation Framework)

Gender equity alludes to the act of reasonableness and equity in the conveyance of advantages, access to and control of assets, advancement openings, power, openings, and administrations for the two people. It is basically the disposal of all types of separation dependent on sexual orientation.

Degender

Degender is a term used to indicate the situation where any prejudice or stereotyping towards specific sex or gender is annihilated. In this study, this term refers to getting rid of prejudice or stereotyping of women in the workplace, especially in academia.

Feminization of Labour/Occupation

As indicated by the US Legal, 'feminization of labour' is a term that portrays rising gendered work relations resulting from the ascent of worldwide free enterprise. It is the feminization of the work environment, which is a pattern towards more noteworthy work of ladies, and of men willing and ready to work in this more feminized work environment. Feminization of work is an aftereffect of the development of exchange, capital streams, and mechanical advances. Sex separation, brutality, sweatshops, and lewd behaviour are a portion of the unfavourable after-effects of the feminization of occupation. Multinationals incline toward ladies in labour drive as ladies have from since a long time ago worked for lower compensation and are less inclined to compose.

Gender and Development (GAD)

The GAD approach focuses on intervening to address unequal gender relations which prevent inequitable development, and which often lock women out of full participation. GAD seeks to have both women and men participate, make decisions, and share benefits. This approach often aims at meeting practical needs as well as promoting strategic interests. A successful GAD approach requires sustained long-term commitment.

Women in Development (WID)

The WID approach aims to integrate women into the existing development process by targeting them, often in women-specific activities. Women are usually passive recipients in WID projects, which often emphasize making women more efficient producers and increasing their income. Although many WID projects have improved health, income, or resources in the short term, because they did not transform unequal relationships, a significant number were not sustainable. A common shortcoming of WID projects is that they do not consider women's multiple roles or those that miscalculate the elasticity of women's time and labor. Another is that such projects tend to be blind to men's roles and responsibilities in women's (dis)empowerment.

LITERATURE REVIEW

According to the survey report of MSCI (2014), women globally only have 12% of seats on boards of the largest companies and amongst these businesses, 64% have at least one lady director, and 13% have at least three women. In this respect, female accounts for 13.4% of administrators in progressing countries while 8.8% in emerging markets (MSCI, 2014). Moreover, according to OECD (2014) and World Bank (2016), there have been very few percentages of the girls in the leadership positions in the progressing and under-developed countries where the quantity of knowledgeable and educated females has accelerated remarkably in the final decade. In the upgraded report of 2016, OECD has mentioned that the girl employees make up 41% of the average illustration in global organizations. This figure dramatically decreases at the senior level where ladies proceed to be under-represented. For example, according to Catalyst (2018) in spite of progress, women are scarce among senior leaders. Not many ladies are CEOs of the world's biggest organizations. For instance, just 24 ladies (4.8%) were CEOs of Fortune 500 organizations. Additionally, women represent not exactly a quarter (24%) of senior jobs internationally. Even, ladies are progressively picking up positions among Executive Committees (ECS) in Fortune Global 100 organizations yet are as yet a little minority. In 2017, ladies represented 22% of EC jobs in the Americas, 15% in Europe, and just 4% in Asia.

Grant Thornton, a pioneer research crew of lady's leadership development, began research on gender range in business management positions in 2004, has discovered the percentage of top jobs in commercial enterprise held by women has barely changed increasing from 19% in 2004 to 22% 2015 and never attaining greater than 24% until 2015 (Grant Thornton, 2015). The document mainly offers that the rage is almost comparable in the following countries:

Table 1. Percentage of a few countries

Country	Percentage (%)
Argentina	16%
Botswana	16%
Brazil	15%
Germany	14%

According to Table 1, the least participation of women was in Germany where Brazil is less improved than Argentina and Botswana. In this respect, the Eastern European countries are in the main function in case of female leadership positions in their corporate world with the following account:

Table 2. Percentage of a few countries

Country	Percentage (%)
Poland	37%
Latvia	36%
Estonia	36%
Lithonia	33%
France	33%
Armenia	29%

Though the percentages in Table 2 show decreased percentage of women at the top level still the percentage is better than the percentage in Table 1. Moreover, according to Sawe (2017) the percentage of women in manufacturing companies in different countries are not satisfactory which is clearly depicted in the following table:

Table 3. Countries where women are most likely to work in industry

Sl. No	Country	%Percentage in Industry
1	Macedonia	26%
2	Mauritius	26%
3	Iran	24%
4	Sri Lanka	24%
5	Czech Republic	24%
6	Bulgaria	23%
7	Romania	22%
8	Slovakia	20%
9	Hungary	19%
10	Slovenia	18%

However, it is very shocking that there are very few females in the leadership positions such as General managers, Line Managers, Quality Managers, Production Managers, heads of Merchandisers, etc. in the RMG establishments of the countries, which produce clothes on a larger scale for western shoppers (Preuss, 2016; Mia, 2016). This view is supported by Nielsen and Huse (as cited in Islam & Jantan, 2017) and in addition, they quoted that lady representatives are familiar with higher than males in figuring out the needs of females in the workplace, therefore, there needs to be a rational quantity of the women in leading positions. Differently, Fitch and Agrawal (2015), outlined a lady manager can interact with her lady subordinates more efficiently than a male supervisor when there are greater female workers than males. These views put stress on the requirements for the females' presence in the leading positions in organizations (Islam and Jantan, 2017).

I believe that every leader has a right to implement his or her own policy. But when I see things that are done that are not right - abuse of power, wrong approaches, wrong strategies, making use of foreign consultants, including those discarded by other countries - I feel that I have to have my say. (Mahathir Mohamad)

In the eyes of the world, Malaysia has become a pariah state, a state where anyone can be hauled up and questioned by the police, detained, and charged through abusing the laws of the country. (Mahathir Mohamad)

"We need an opposition to remind us if we are making mistakes. When you are not opposed you think everything you do is right." *Mahathir bin Mohamad*

The glass ceiling is a term of discrimination that is affecting women's lack of right of entering to power and status in organizations. The term "the glass ceiling" refers to the invisible barrier cited that "the higher the post, the fewer the women". As an "invisible" barrier, the glass ceiling is difficult to eradicate through legislation. According to the record, "glass ceiling" as the term was made 20 years ago by The Wall Street Journal to describe the situation where the ladies and minorities were confined by obvious barriers, from attaining the corporate hierarchy (Lathabhavan & Balasubramanian 2016). The term was ultimately famous in the world in a short duration of time (Lathabhavan & Balasubramanian 2016).

It is considered a rationalization for the subtle, invisible barriers women face after they reap mid-management positions. Despite professional eligibilities and adequate opportunities, women personnel are now not aptly represented in the easiest corridors of organizational power (Gupta, 2018; Lathabhavan & Balasubramanian 2016).

"All leaders must have some power. Without power, you can't be a leader." *- Mahathir Mohamad*

Focusing on the professional matter, Cotter, Hermsen, Ovadia, and Vanneman (as cited in Tukonic & Harwood, 2015) added that the glass ceiling is a particular type of gender or racial inequality that can be distinct from other kinds of inequality. In their study Cotter et al (as cited in Tukonic & Harwood, 2015) they have identified the glass ceiling as a disparity that represents gender or racial variations that are not defined through other job-relevant traits of the personnel or individual at higher levels with a high level of potentiality (Tukonic & Harwood, 2015). Moreover, a glass ceiling disparity is represented as the inequality that will increase over the path of a profession as the probabilities of development into top levels should not be hindered as the proportions for every gender at those higher levels (Rahaman & Nasrin, 2015).

*The Glass Ceiling is****an intangible barrier within a hierarchy that prevents women or minorities from obtaining upper-level positions****(source: Merriam-Webster)* Women account for fewer than 5% of boards of directors and corporate officer positions, worldwide. Take this self-assessment and check for yourself if the Glass Ceiling may affect you.

Informal networking and mentoring are often advised as skills for outnumbering women from public organizations. Further, networking with and mentoring presented via executive guys can be less fruitful and greater not easy for junior women, who may additionally be assumed to be sexually worried about their mentors. In sum, the relative lack of female managers and executives in occupational sex segregation facilitates sexual harassment for all women (Yousaf & Schmiede, 2016). Additionally, Yousaf and Schmiede (2016) stated that male supervisors or managers who have female advisees are more accused of extra harassment, and; girls hardly ever perpetrate harassment; ladies view harassing behaviors otherwise from guys. The glass ceiling has remained a present day-day trouble world-wise, with many surveys and reports being undertaken. Although prejudices and discrimination closer to ladies within the workforce have faded, they nevertheless exist strongly for women in senior positions. The US, United Kingdom, Europe, Canada, Australia, New Zealand, Africa, and Asia have addressed those ladies are less possibly than guys to be promoted to better organizational posts, much less possibly to have tenure, and much more likely to keep part-time and contractual appointments and to enjoy a pay gap (Yousaf & Schmiede, 2016).

Otherwise, how the glass ceiling dwells in society and in organizations is prominent in many kinds of literature which are provided in the following section.

METHODOLOGY

The purpose of this qualitative phenomenological research design is to understand the 'glass ceiling' through the lived experience of highly educated women who are now in their own respective positions or trying to reach their desired position in the education system of Malaysia. Having a variety of glass ceiling factors, it describes that, however, the women of Malaysia in the education system continued to maintain an extended record of being controlled by this invisible ceiling. This phenomenological observation relies on a top-quality description of the glass ceiling as a current revelation within the Malaysian job sector.

In this chapter, the methodology of this research is covered. This chapter discusses in depth the questions of the study, the concept of the term, technique, situation, self, support, sampling, and materials used to collect and evaluate the data using theories. The obstacles that are encountered during the investigation are also included in this chapter. We hope that this research paper will have some advanced contributions to the 'glass ceiling' factors in the education system for all women over the world.

Constructivism is a learning theory that suggests that humans build learning and significance from their experiences. Phenomenology as a research methodology is embedded in a theory of knowledge construction called constructivism. According to constructivist epistemology, knowledge is socially constructed, truth is relative, and meaning emerges inductively. What is real and meaningful is a construction in the minds of individuals, not an objective truth merely waiting to be discovered (Crotty, 1998). "In this view of things, subject and object emerge as partners in the generation of meaning." (Crotty, p. 9). Constructionism claims that meanings are constructed by human beings as they engage with the world they are interpreting (Crotty, 1998).

In this research the theoretical view for the study will be interpretive, defined by Merriam (2002) as a study where the researcher is interested in understanding how participants make meaning of a situation or phenomenon. Rossman and Rallis (2003) described the interpretive paradigm as one in which research "…tries to understand the social world as it is (the status quo) from the perspective of individual experience, hence an interest in subjective worldviews" (p. 46).

Swandt (2001) submitted that an interpretive tradition is an approach to studying life that assumes meaning as part of human action, and that the job of the qualitative inquirer is to bring to light that meaning. This study did not begin with a theory or preconceived notion of the outcome; rather, the researcher immersed herself in the world of the subjects to be studied, (Esterberg, 2002).

Both the constructionist and interpretive approaches share a common notion that all social reality is constructed, or created, by social actors. These approaches ask us to focus on interaction: How do humans act toward one another and the objects in their worlds? What meanings do they attach to them? (Esterberg, 2002).

The methodology of our research will be qualitative phenomenological research and the methods which will be used are interviews with the women related to our study. Phenomenology is the science of phenomena (Van Manen, 1990). According to Merriam (2002), phenomenologists emphasize the subjective aspects of people's behavior. "They attempt to gain entry into the conceptual world of their subjects." (Greertz, 1973, p. 24). "…in order to understand how and what meanings they construct around events in their daily lives." (Bogdan & Biklen, 1982, p. 34). Phenomenology believes that people interpret everyday experiences from the perspective of the meaning it has for them. According to Patton (2002), "Phenomenology serves to describe one or more individuals' experiences of a phenomenon." (p. 40). "The phenomenological approach seeks to make explicit the implicit structure and meaning of human experience" (Sanders, 1982, p. 353), and "focuses on people living experiences" (Davis, 1991, p. 9) … "through rich and descriptive data, it draws out how people construct the world through descriptions of perceptions" (p. 11). Perceptions constitute the primary source of knowledge in phenomenological studies, affixing textural descriptions explaining "what" was experienced and structural descriptions explaining "how" it was experienced (Creswell, 2007, p. 227). Basically, Phenomenological studies illuminate the individual's lived experience and, in our research, the lived experiences of overcoming the "glass ceiling" as a woman to build their career in the education system. (Hanim, Fatimah. (2018).

To be a woman it is not so easy to reach a higher level for women employees in Malaysian universities. Men and women both o-face problems in their development of careers. But women mainly faced this type of glass ceiling problem. Very few women are working at the senior level at Malaysian University. This research study highlights some senior-level higher education administrators that we're able to break through the glass ceiling to achieve what so many other women have not been able to accomplish. When we asked about obstacles or challenges, they had to overcome in order to advance or develop to their current position the participants shared their obstacles and gave some important advice to the women that they needed to improve their careers.

Most of the participants mentioned some common obstacles such as pay disparity; maintaining both family and professional life, overlooking or ignoring their idea, and giving less importance to their organization. Physiological Aspects, Lack of acknowledgment, and roles are the subthemes of the obstacles and challenges that are defined and outlined in Table 4.

Table 4. Overcoming obstacles or challenges in university

Theme	Description	Subthemes
Physiological Aspects	It defines someone's characteristic of appropriate, normal, and healthy functioning. It is one kind of scientific study of the functions and mechanisms.	*Long hours *Physical and emotional fitness and work *Maintain a balanced life
Lack of Acknowledgement	When anyone does any work but does not get proper acknowledgment or feedback, one kind of lack of notice.	*Reward *Recognition *Pay disparity *Idea overlooked or does not notice
Role	The function assumed or part played by a person or thing in a particular situation or one kind of character or symbol that is assigned or given	*Balance life *Work with male workers predominantly

Physiological Aspects

One of the participants works in student services and she shared a number of times throughout the interview that working in student services is challenging. Because the work is not so easy, involves long hours that are oftentimes outside of the normal 8-5 workday, and also the emotional aspects of dealing with students can be draining at times. While sharing the obstacles that she experienced and overcame, she said that 1) Salary or unequal payment was absolutely an obstacle and a matter of outraging for me when I found out how much my male colleagues were being paid.

In response to the overcoming obstacle question, she shared her experience saying, 1) She requested for a raise which was rejected at first 2) She again requested and justified her efforts which were eventually accepted. 3) Continuing quality work helped her to overcome the barrier".

She also states that:

> *"You don't get to this level just because you're chilling or because you're cute, you have to be capable work in under pressure and physiologically fit for that job. You know I think about all of the programs I have set up for students, the chairs I have lifted, the floors."*

In response to the overcoming obstacle question, she shared her experience saying, 1) She requested for a raise which was rejected at first 2) She again requested and justified her efforts which were eventually accepted. 3) Continuing quality work helped her to overcome the barrier".

On the other hand, challenges or obstacles of workplaces that have to be faced and overcome question was explained by her like when other participant became a mother, she had to maintain the professional and personal responsibility both were in same priority. This created a great mass to balance both situations with full of dedication and hard work. It became even harder because of her colleagues who underestimated her during that time.

Overcoming the institutional barrier question another respondent shared her experience "I had my husband's support to overcome any difficult situation."

She gave some advice when asked for it by saying that "1) Choose a career or workplace that would be suitable for you 2) you also have to enjoy the work what you are doing 3) where you can give your full attention and have flexibility during work."

While sharing the obstacles that she experienced and overcame, she said that 1) Salary or unequal payment was absolutely an obstacle and a matter of outraging for me when I found out how much my male colleagues were being paid.

Most of the participants mention that physical fitness must be required for any development. If you are not physically fit then you cannot focus on your work and cannot develop or promote. So, women have to be physically fit and can work in any environment.

Overcoming the obstacle question another participant directly mentioned the unequal salary structure. She said women got less salaries than men which estimated an imbalance situation. What she did she claimed the equal salary that was initially rejected. But she showed her high-quality work and dedication to prove the situation. She got her desired payment as earlier mentioned.

She gave some advice when asked for it by saying that "1) I had to work hard and gave quality full work 2) No one can reject a great quality of work 3) by giving the best quality of work can make a great change to the current situation

Lack of Acknowledgment

Most women saw this problem in their career path. Most of the time women were dominated by men's opinions. Our society gives more importance to the men's opinions and acknowledges men's success and achievement, women lag behind and women cannot get proper acknowledgment from their employers.

One respondent said:

When I gave a better idea than a man at that time other male employee ignores them and create a jock on that point. That was making me disappointed and I lost my motivation to do well.

Overcoming the obstacle question, she directly mentioned that "1) told or untold family commitments and related expectation were there to create the barrier for women to work with 2) In some case the situation holds the prior value"

Another participant said:

When I work with my boss thought she was a female boss, she gave more preference to the male employee. That was clearly a glass ceiling. After that, I switch to the company and got a new job where I performed and my work was recognized for my work and good performance and capability. I advise the other women have to perform well and people will judge their capability depending on their performance, not their gender.

Another participant said:

My guess is other women might feel this way from men, some people think that you're being taken for granted, you're so consistent, you're so dependable, and you're steady, you're so stable, you're so, you know, it's sort of the opposite of you're too much, this is like, and that, yeah, that you get taken for granted. Just in a way that man would not be.

Roles

In our daily life, we play different roles in different situations. Our society makes some assumptions such as women are fit for the mother or wife role and men are fit for professional jobs and other sectors. Because of society's assumptions women are forced to encounter many types of the glass ceiling.

Overcoming the obstacle by sharing a personal experience, the respondent gladly said that "1) I am always determined about my work 2) also motivate herself by saying that her good career would give her family comfort 3) that matter most for me then"

She gave some advice when asked for it by saying that "1) do not lose your hope 2) believe in yourself and be optimistic 3) all in all always plan for the long run"

She also said: that she clearly said that she felt happy for her children and grandchildren's generation now because today they overcome a lot with this negative situation that creates a barrier for women to work.

One respondent also explains her challenges as follows:

Think you were in a meeting, and you said something important and another one said: she is a woman just forget about her point. But you know, in the back of somebody's mind, it's like well, you know, again, she doesn't seem to take a strong conviction, you get into the whole thing, I wonder if she has kids, whether she'll be dependable, whether she can work extra. Women must play well in their roles, if women perform their roles in a convincing way, then other people will give importance to them.

One participant spoke about the challenges of being a female administrator and working with men in fields that are predominately male. She shared that even though she was coming from a position of authority she recognized many of the men were very territorial about their departments and didn't think that a woman could possibly understand the complexity of what they do enough to help them in any way. Some male employees thought that women cannot solve complex things and male-only capable to do this.

She also said:

I saw many obstacles because of inequity. The company gave more facilities to their male employee. They create a huge difference when it's come to salary and other bounces. They promoted more male employees than women. In higher education, I also saw this. Most of the senior-level administrative workers were male and few women were work there because of their capability. Women's capability is always dominated by men. Facilities, Environmental Health, and safety men get preference where women need those facilities than men. You'd be surprised. But I had to make sure I didn't overrule them, but I just had to understand their business process, what their practices were, and why it was important they do this or that.

Overcoming the obstacle question, one of the respondents directly mentioned that "1) Showed extreme ignorance on women works 2) didn't let your voice to lead and denied badly by the superior. 3) Always criticize women employees' work and never had that judgment towards men"

Findings

The main purpose of this research study was to detail the 'glass ceiling' factor as a lived experience of women employees in their own respective positions at Malaysian universities in a phenomenological qualitative way. Our focused area for this purpose was Malaysia which is a Southeast Asian country. Another purpose of this study was to analyze the characteristics of women in senior-level administrator positions in higher education and their view about the glass ceiling at the research institution in this southeast area. Additionally, the challenges they had faced in their own workforce and the resources, tools, and techniques will need for many women to reach this senior-level administrator position were also observed.

The following question guided the study:

How do women employees of Malaysian universities who have broken through the 'glass ceiling' to reach their career goals make this phenomenon meaningful?

The following sub-questions were used to provide answers to specific aspects related to the overarching question:

1) How do women employees in universities perceive and describe their experience with the glass ceiling?

This is the first research question of our study which will give us a clear idea about the view of participants toward the 'glass ceiling' and how they define 'glass ceiling'. If we look at the literature, we will get to know that women employees were prevented by many facts to obtain their positions at the university level. As the women who are part of our research study were able to accomplish their position by overcoming the barrier and breaking through the glass ceiling so this question was formatted to know the opinion of participants about the existence of the glass ceiling and the experiences, they had related with it.

One of our participants shared that there are some women who create the glass ceilings themselves. She believed that women are easy to be influenced as they get influenced by what they see. Exemplifying her experience with the effect of the glass ceiling she stated that to remain silent and excepting the situation. Moreover, there are some women who do not believe that women are as equal to men. They thought that it is not possible for women to cope with men which is very disgraceful.

There are countless women in academics who willingly choose to give up on their ideas for various projects due to a lack of motivation.

Another glass ceiling women are facing is the confidence issue. This made them difficult to express opinions and especially express disagreements in a male-dominated environment.

The inequity women have faced in the journey of reaching their desired positions is counted as a glass ceiling according to the statement of our participant. Most of our participants said there is inequity in the workplace which acts as a glass ceiling toward their careers. Inequity is present in all the sectors, but nobody tries to change these systems.

2) What are the characteristics of women employees which allowed them to break through the glass ceiling to their current position?

Our research study exhibited a number of characteristics, attitudes, and actions that were very considerate for the advancement in the administrative career of higher education. Most of the attitudes and personality traits shared by our participants through the interview were well documented in the literature.

According to the literature related to women's personality attitudes and the trait they should have flexibility, resilience, adaptability, good sense of humor, determination, self-motivation, confidence, independence, identified integrity, loyalty, charisma, visionary, passion, good listener.

3) What are the Political, Societal, and Organizational factors that have an effect on women employees at the university level to advance their careers in higher positions?

There are many issues which are in form of politics that are still available in the university sector. In universities, there are some internal politics like if higher authority is male majority area, they somehow avoid women in higher authority sector. They discourage women's engagement in the influential sector of universities. Sometimes in Malaysian universities there occurs an election for faculties, and deans to select some people who will be able to maintain that sector. In those elections, women employees are indirectly rejected so that they cannot be selected for maintaining the sector.

One of our participants who are now in a dean position also a part-time professor shared,

> *"When I was faculty in my previous workplace, I took participation in the election as a female candidate. But somehow, they rejected my nomination without any clear reason & then I had left that university for this type of internal politics."*

The women who participated in our research study strongly agreed that there are some hidden and indirect politics in every Malaysian university which are in hinder of career improvement of women employees in universities.

4) What are the tools and resources needed for women employees to advance their careers in higher positions?

Malaysia is such a country where most of the family responsibilities actually depend on women. Almost entire participants in the research study agreed that the most important tool and resource that a woman needs to reach this level is support and cooperation from family. Women of our study said if there is support from the family the way gets easier to reach such a senior-level position in the university. Moreover, family support plays a vital role in women's personal development. Family support can nourish her mentality for better achievement. Most of our participants who are in senior-level positions shared that they could come so far because of the support of their family, love of children, and a good understanding with their partner.

Talking about tools and resources used for achieving the goal one of the participants said that she tries to keep a good relationship with Allah and her friends and family. She does her best to make them happy and helped them and support from them helped her very much. Another participant said her parents supported her and religion played a big role in her life as the tools and resources that she found most helpful while advancing in her career. It saved her when everything else couldn't. So, our research study revealed that in a country like Malaysia family support is the primary resource for women to break the glass ceiling.

Women friendly environment is another resource that is the outcome of our research study. A better female support structure can help women to improve themselves in their workplace. As there are more men than women so they feel disproportionality in the workplace. The presence of more women generally acts as a comforting mechanism. When a woman sees another woman raise it encourages them which boosts up their mentality. If there are more women in the workplace then they could report a few cases of the glass ceiling together, which ensures the evolvement of the workplace.

A supportive management system of an organization is another resource for women employees in universities. Management should take proper care of the development of women's careers. They should create awareness among the women workplaces. As women have a commitment both toward family and work, management should be helpful and understanding in some instances. From our research result, it is exhibited that if women work in such a management system that is cooperative with them then the output that comes from women is way more beneficial for the organization. Management should be taking care of the well-being of women in their personal life. A participant described a lovely thing that sometimes men were willing to help women because of their dedication. Women feel that a strong accountability structure in the workplace would be able to remove the particular type of glass ceiling.

About helping tools and resources to advance in her career Claudia found that

> *"Reading and traveling played a big role for her. Even she believed that Malaysian women are more than just housewives or other professions. She suggested that traveling exposes other professions. Travelling exposes us to how other women live and inspires us to do better to help them."*

5) Why are women employees in universities able to overcome obstacles or challenges associated with the glass ceiling and break through the glass ceiling?

Another challenge and obstacle faced by women is the lack of recognition and reward in senior-level positions as women employees. This is due to a lack of knowledge. The recognition problem is first faced at the beginning of work because, at the starting of the job, the organization has no idea about the ability of employees. But women have to face this problem mostly because of being women. To overcome the obstacles women must be hard working and have some good social skills. For those two skills, women will get preference in any position as an employee said by our participant as this method help them to overcome this type of obstacle. One of our participants Claudia shared when she was asked how she overcame this; she figured out and answered that,

> *"She overcame this by speaking out all the time. If my work was not recognized, I would make sure that it did get recognized at some point. My labor was not meant to be taken for granted, and it was my bravery and self-esteem that pushed me to keep speaking up."*

Sometimes women are not rewarded when she actually deserves it in university as women employee. The reward can be monetary or non-monetary. Monetary rewards are promotions or extra bonuses, and non-monetary rewards are an opportunity for training or making decisions, formal or informal appreciation. Non-monetary rewards motivate and increase confidence and also give satisfaction which is very important in such a position. Women employees in Malaysian universities face this challenge predominantly shared by our participants. One of our participants shared that she had also faced this problem but being always outspoken she easily overcame this problem. But for many other women who suffered the same, had to deal with this for far longer.

Moreover, explaining a few strategies to cope with the situation one participant said that she was very happy to overcome problems in her career as she believed that hard work is the best policy. While describing how she was able to overcome these challenges at her institution, she mentioned that positivity and optimism will solve all problems at any cost.

6) What is the most important piece of advice women would share with young women pursuing their careers as women employees at the university level?

People should encourage women to be brave and outspoken and not scare them off by the prediction that they will never marry. No discrimination at the institutional level should be expectable. But implied glass ceiling due to family commitment and expectations are difficult to avoid and these matters should be reconsidered.

Some pieces of advice are as given below:

- Women should always be critical of everything that she hears.
- Women need to keep in mind that sometimes criticism may be legitimate, but other times it can be used as a tool to unjustly keep you silent.
- Always be very critical of whatever you are told, and you will succeed.
- Anything you feel is not right, please say something about it.
- Always have a clear vision and clear action plan.
- Don't Overthink and take the stress.
- Always focus on the positive side and have a positive mentality.
- Always see the problems as challenges and be excited to face them.
- Push you and break the inner inertia.
- Never take yourself for granted.
- Always believe in your capabilities.
- Don't be afraid to speak out. It may be intimidating in the beginning, but it is very rewarding when you do it.
- Always try to balance your family and job life.
- Maintain a good network in the workplace.

Women in our research study shared many pieces of advice that were helpful for them to be in universities as women employees and what they believe will be helpful for young generations of women also. But what they mostly said is that Women should always accept the change in society and the working place. That's the only way to keep you updated. Women with strong willpower and self-esteem can easily win the problem of the glass ceiling. All in all, a strong determination is needed not in the work-life, but in personal life and societal expectation to fulfill. An important piece of advice shared with everyone by one of our participants is *"Manners should have made a man, but it made a woman instead. Passion and determination are a woman's prized possessions. It will take you far."* The most important piece of advice shared by Suzi is that *"Everyone is very impressive. Your story is the one that should matter most to you. Pave your own path."*

CONCLUSION

According to the research study, there is a lot of 'glass ceiling' for women employee to advance their careers in Malaysian universities. Most of them are discussed in our study according to the statement of our participants. From our study, it is sure that the women of the 21st century are way more progressive than before. The participant of our study shared many suggestions for women who want to pursue their careers in the university system as women employees. They should accept change and face them in a calculative way. Make proper use of resources and utilize best practices for understanding any issues in the institution. As an employee women must always be open to learning new things for their personal and professional development. They should always resemble themselves for cooperation and connectivity. Women should always strive for their rights to break the 'glass ceiling', to overcome barriers in the workplace such as inequity, pay disparity, and influential people's wrong decision.

The significant thing that was found from the women who participated in our study is a person's behavior and determination is the most important contributor to breaking the 'glass ceiling' in university. The participants of our research study are full of positivity, unbelievable strength, and integrity. They try to maintain a balanced life which is more important for the women of Malaysia they are assured of survival with the 'glass ceiling'. They hold a strong leadership mentality, friendly behavior in the workplace, good communication skill, strong network support, extensive work experience, and knowledge about the working environment. Women need to be outspoken to recognize their work to the people of the institution. Women should be capable of maintaining their life personally and professionally.

Most of our participants agreed that the most striking element to breaking the glass ceiling is determination. They were so focused on their determination that they don't even take the time to give consideration to the 'glass ceiling' or invisible barrier which could distract them from achieving their goals. They persisted through tough supervisors, salary gaps, lack of recognition, long work hours, juggling work-life balance, unfriendly working environment, family support, frantic travel schedules, and personal challenges with a smile on their faces.

I will close with a portion of the commencement address that Sheryl Sandberg, gave at Barnard College, an all-women's liberal arts school in New York City.

> *"You are the promise for a more equal world. So, my hope for everyone here is that after you walk across this stage after you get your diploma and go out tonight and celebrate hard—you then will lean way into your career. You will find something*

you love doing and you will do it with gusto. Find the right career for you and go all the way to the top. As you walk off this stage today, you start your adult life. Start out by aiming high. Try and try hard. Like everyone here, I have great hopes for the members of this graduating class. I hope you find true meaning, contentment, and passion in your life. I hope you navigate the difficult times and come out with greater strength and resolve. I hope you find whatever balance you seek with your eyes wide open. And I hope that you have the ambition to lean into your career and run the world. Because the world needs you to change it. Women all around the world are counting on you. So please ask yourself: What would I do if I weren't afraid? And then go do it. (Sandberg, 2013)"

REFERENCES

Ahmad, M., & Naseer, H. (2015). Gender bias at the workplace: Through sticky floor and glass ceiling: A comparative study of private and public organizations of Islamabad. *International Journal of Management and Business Research*, 5(3), 249–260.

Amin, M., & Zarka, A. (2017). Women Workers in Malaysia's Private Sector. Enterprise Note No. 35. Retrieved 5 February 2019, from https://www.enterprisesurveys.org/~/media/GIAWB/EnterpriseSurveys/Documents/EnterpriseNotes/Women-Workers-in-Malaysia's-Private-Sector.pdf

Birt, L., Scott, S., Cavers, D., Campbell, C., & Walter, F. (2016). Member Checking: A Tool to Enhance Trustworthiness or Merely a Nod to Validation? *Qualitative Health Research*, 26(13), 1802–1811. Advance online publication. DOI: 10.1177/1049732316654870 PMID: 27340178

Bogdan, R. C., & Biklen, S. K. (1982). *Qualitative Research for Education: An Introduction to Theory and Methods*. Allyn & Bacon.

Box, I. (2014). How many interviews are needed in qualitative research? Is there any rule or popular practice? Retrieved 5 March 2019, from https://www.researchgate.net/post/How_many_interviews_are_needed_in_a_qualitative_research_Is_there_any_rule_or_popular_practice

Boyd, R. D. (2008). Adult Learning: A Journey Through Leadership Development. *Journal of Leadership Studies*, 2(3), 45–59.

Bravo-Baumann, H. (2000). *Capitalism, Socialism, and Communism in the 21st Century*. Springer.

Creswell, J. W. (2007). *Qualitative Inquiry & Research Design: Choosing Among Five Approaches* (2nd ed.). Sage Publications.

Crotty, M. (1998). *The Foundations of Social Research: Meaning and Perspective in the Research Process*. Sage Publications.

Davis, F. D. (1991). *Perceived Usefulness, Perceived Ease of Use, and User Acceptance of Information Technology*. MIS Quarterly.

Essays, U. K. (2018). Reliability and Validity in Research. Retrieved 5 February, 2019, from https://www.ukessays.com/essays/psychology/the-reliability-and-validity-psychology-essay.php?vref=1

Esterberg, K. G. (2002). *Qualitative Methods in Social Research*. McGraw-Hill.

Forbes, D. (2019). Artificial Intelligence in the Workplace. *Harvard Business Review*.

Geertz, C. (1973). *The Interpretation of Cultures: Selected Essays*. Basic Books.

Guest, C. (2016). Advantages and Disadvantages of Online Surveys. Retrieved 5 February 2019, from https://blog.cvent.com/events/advantages-disadvantages-online-surveys/IWH (2015). At Work 82 (Fall). Retrieved 5 February 2019, from https://www.iwh.on.ca/newsletters/at-work/82

Islam, M. A., & Jantan, A. H. (2017). The glass ceiling: Career barriers for female employees in the readymade garments (RMG) industry of Bangladesh. *SSRN*, 16(3), 1–11. DOI: 10.2139/ssrn.3414583

Ismail, R., Wye, C.-K., Palel, M., & Sabrina, N. (2017). Analysis of Glass Ceiling and Sticky Floor Effects for Gender Wage Gap in Malaysian Labour Market. *Jurnal Ekonomi Malaysia.*, 51(2), 131–142.

Jafarey, S., & Maiti, P. (2015). Migration, Remittances, and Real Exchange Rate in the Long Run. *World Economy*, 38(1), 19–27.

Jahan, I. (2018). Breaking the Glass Ceiling. ICE Business Times. Retrieved 5 March, 2019, from https://ibtbd.net/breaking-the-glass-ceiling/

Kabir, M. (2016). Islamic Banking in Bangladesh: Past, Present, and Future. *Journal of Islamic Banking and Finance*, 33(4), 12–24.

Kagan, J. (2018). *Psychology: Cognitive Development*. Encyclopedia Britannica.

Lathabhavan, R., & Balasubramanian, S. A. (2017). Glass ceiling and women employees in Asian organizations: A tri-decadal review. *Asia-Pacific Journal of Business Administration*, 9(3), 232–246. DOI: 10.1108/APJBA-03-2017-0023

Lewis, J. J. (2019, January 29). Women's Rights Movements: A Historical Overview. ThoughtCo.

Malaysia Employment Act. 1955. Retrieved 5 February 2019, from https://www.ilo.org/dyn/natlex/docs/WEBTEXT/48055/66265/E55mys01.htm

Merriam, S. B. (2002). *Qualitative Research in Practice: Examples for Discussion and Analysis*. Jossey-Bass.

Mia, A. (2016). *Sustainable Development in Emerging Markets: Challenges and Solutions*. Routledge.

OECD. (2014). *Innovation Policies for Inclusive Growth*. OECD Publishing.

Pandey, S. (2019). Importance of Online Survey and How to Set Up One. Retrieved 5 February 2019, from https://wpmanageninja.com/importance-online-survey/

Patton, M. Q. (2002). *Qualitative Research and Evaluation Methods* (3rd ed.). Sage Publications.

Preuss, L. (2016). *Corporate Social Responsibility: Voluntary Codes of Conduct in the Mining Industry*. Springer.

Rahaman, M.R. & Jahan, N. (2015). Sexual Harassment in Workplace in South Asia: A Comparative Study on Bangladesh, India, Nepal, and Sri Lanka. IOSR Journal of Business and Management (IOSR-JBM). 17(6). 49-57.

Rauf, F. H. A., Khalid, F. M., Zulkifli, A. M., Manaf, N. J. F. A., Sulaiman, N. F. A., Hanim Abdul Rauf, F., ... & Fatin Amirah Sulaiman, N. (2018). Individual Factors, Work-Family Conflict And Organisational Structure Towards Malaysian Women Career Progress. European Proceedings of Social and Behavioural Sciences, 44.

Sanders, T. (1982). *Sociological Perspectives on Aging*. Cambridge University Press.

Shabbir, H., Shakeel, M. A. & Zubair, R. A. (2017). Gender Stereotype, Glass Ceiling, and Women's Career Advancement: An Empirical Study in Service Sector of Pakistan. City University Research Journal. Special Issue: AIC, Malaysia PP 236-246.

Sharif, M. (2014). *Economic Growth and Development in South Asia. Oxford University Press. Gupta, S. (2018). Introduction to Financial Markets*. McGraw-Hill.

Subramaniam, G., Khadri, A. N. M., Maniam, B., & Ali, E. (2016). The glass ceiling phenomenon-does it Really affect Women's career advancement in Malaysia? Journal of Organizational Culture. *Communications and Conflict.*, 20, 81.

Swandt, T. A. (2001). *Dictionary of Qualitative Inquiry* (2nd ed.). Sage Publications.

Thornton, G. (2015). *The Economic Impact of Digitalization*. Grant Thornton LLP.

Tukonic, S. & Harwood, D. (2015). The Glass Ceiling Effect: Mediating Influences on Early Years Educators' Sense of Professionalism. Journal of Childhood Studies. 40(1) 36 to 54.

Van Manen, M. (1990). *Researching Lived Experience: Human Science for an Action Sensitive Pedagogy*. State University of New York Press.

Wan Liyana, W.. (2016). The Impact of Organizational Culture on Knowledge Management in Higher Education Institutions. *International Journal of Business and Management*, 11(9), 123–132.

Yousaf, R., & Schmiede, R. (2016). Underrepresentation of Women at Academic Excellence and Position of Power: Role of Harassment and Glass Ceiling. *Open Journal of Social Sciences*, 4(2), 173–185. DOI: 10.4236/jss.2016.42023

Compilation of References

Abd Hamid, N., Ibrahim, N. A., Ibrahim, N. A., Ariffin, N., Taharin, R., & Jelani, F. A. (2019). Factors affecting tax compliance among Malaysian SMEs in e-commerce business. *International Journal of Asian Social Science*, 9(1), 74–85. DOI: 10.18488/journal.1.2019.91.74.85

Abdullahi, H. I. (2006). *Gender and Adjustment in Nigerian Manufacturing sectors* [Seminar Paper]. Centre for Social Science and Research Development.

Acker, J. (2009). From glass ceiling to inequality regimes. *Sociologie du travail, 51*(2), 199217.Catalyst (2014), "Women on boards", available at: www.catalyst.org/knowledge/womenboards

Aditi Prasad Chaudhari. (2018). Kaustubh Mazumdar.; Yogesh Mohanlal Motwani.; Divya Ramadas., "A profile of occupational stress in nurses". *Annals of Indian Psychiatry*.

Afza, S. R., & Newaz, M. K. (2008). Factors determining the presence of glass ceiling and influencing women career advancement in Bangladesh. *BRAC University Journal*, V(1), 85–92.

Ahmad, M., & Naseer, H. (2015). Gender bias at the workplace: Through sticky floor and glass ceiling: A comparative study of private and public organizations of Islamabad. *International Journal of Management and Business Research*, 5(3), 249–260.

Aiston, S. J., & Jung, J. (2015). Women academics and research productivity: An international comparison. *Gender and Education*, 27(3), 205220. DOI: 10.1080/09540253.2015.1024617

Ai, W., Yang, J., & Wang, L. (2016). Revelation of cross-border logistics performance for the manufacturing industry development. *International Journal of Mobile Communications*, 14(6), 593–609. DOI: 10.1504/IJMC.2016.079302

Aki, K., & Richards, P. G. (2002). *Quantitative Seismology*. University Science Books.

Al Thobaity, A., & Alshammari, F. (2020). *Nurses on the Frontline against the COVID-19 pandemic: An Integrative Review*. Karger.

Alekseeva, I. V., & Mosentseva, V. A. (2020). Methodological Approaches to Establishing the System of Internal Control in Agricultural Companies. Accounting. Analysis. *Auditing*, 7(5), 69–79.

Ali, M. M., & Islam, A. M. (2014) Agribusiness potentials for Bangladesh—an Analysis. A paper presented at the biennial Conference on 'Rethinking Political Economy of Development' held on 20-22 November 2014 organized by Bangladesh Economic Association.

Al-Manasra, E. (2013). What Are the "Glass Ceiling" Barriers Effects on Women Career Progress in Jordan? *International Journal of Business and Management*, 8(6), 40–46. DOI: 10.5539/ijbm.v8n6p40

Alvarez-Risco, A., Estrada-Merino, A., Rosen, M. A., Vargas-Herrera, A., & Del-Aguila-Arcentales, S. (2021). Factors for implementation of circular economy in firms in COVID-19 pandemic times: The case of Peru. *Environments*, 8(9), 95.

Amani, F. A., & Fadlalla, A. M. (2017). Data mining applications in accounting: A review of the literature and organizing framework. *International Journal of Accounting Information Systems*, 24, 32–58. DOI: 10.1016/j.accinf.2016.12.004

Amaratunga, D., Haigh, R., Shanmugam, M., Lee, A. J., & Elvitigala, G. (2006), "Construction industry and women: a review of the barriers", Proceedings of the 3rd International SCRI Research Symposium, Delft, April.

American Express. (2011). The American Express OPEN State of Women-Owned Business Report: A Summary of Important Trends, 1997-2011. American Express: New York City. http://media.nucleus.naprojects.com/pdf/WomanR eport_FINAL.pdf

Amin, M., & Zarka, A. (2017). Women Workers in Malaysia's Private Sector. Enterprise Note No. 35. Retrieved 5 February 2019, from https://www.enterprisesurveys .org/~/media/GIAWB/EnterpriseSurveys/Documents/EnterpriseNotes/Women -Workers-in-Malaysia's-Private-Sector.pdf

Ansari, N. (2016). Respectable femininity: A significant panel of glass ceiling for career women. *ender in Management. International Journal (Toronto, Ont.)*, 31(8), 528–541.

Appelbaum, S. H., Audet, L., & Miller, J. C. (2003). Gender and leadership?Leadership and gender?A journey through the landscape of theories. *Leadership and Organization Development Journal*, 24(1), 43–51. DOI: 10.1108/01437730310457320

Ashburn-Nardo, L., Lindsey, A., Morris, K. A., & Goodwin, S. A. (2020). Who is responsible for confronting prejudice? The role of perceived and conferred authority. *Journal of Business and Psychology*, 35(6), 799–811. DOI: 10.1007/s10869-019-09651-w

Ashraf, N., Ahmad, W., & Ashraf, R. (2018). A comparative study of data mining algorithms for high detection rate in intrusion detection system. Annals of Emerging Technologies in Computing (AETiC), Print ISSN, 2516-0281.

Asian Development Bank. (2016). *More women leaders to vitalize Asia's corporate sector*. Retrieved from https://blogs.adb.org/blog/more[REMOVED HYPERLINK FIELD]women-leaders-vitalize-asias-corporate-sector[REMOVED HYPERLINK FIELD]

Assad, A. A. (1978). Multicommodity network flows—A survey. *Networks*, 8(1), 37–91. DOI: 10.1002/net.3230080107

Atkins, P., & de Paula, J. (2017). *Physical Chemistry*. Oxford University Press.

Bajdo, L. M., & Dickson, M. W. (2001). Perceptions of Organizational Culture and Women's Advancement in Organizations: A Cross-Cultural Examination. *Sex Roles*, 45(5-6), 399–414. DOI: 10.1023/A:1014365716222

Barbate, V., Gade, R.N. and Raibagkar, S.S. (2021) "COVID-19 and Its Impact on the Indian Economy:," *https://doi.org/*, 25(1), pp. 23–35. .DOI: 10.1177/0972262921989126

BARC. (Bangladesh Agricultural Research Council) 2008.*A Portal of National Agricultural Research System.* New Airport Road, Farm Gate, Dhaka.pp.36

Barr, R., Elam, J., Glover, F., & Klingman, D. (1978). A Network Augmenting Path Basis Algorithm for Transshipment Problems. In Fiacco, A., & Kortanek, K. (Eds.), *Extremal Methods and Systems Analysis* (pp. 250–274). Springer-Verlag.

Basu, G., Roy, A. N., Bhattacharyya, S. K., & Ghosh, S. K. (2009). Construction of unpaved rural road using jute–synthetic blended woven geotextile–A case study. *Geotextiles and Geomembranes*, 27(6), 506–512. DOI: 10.1016/j.geotexmem.2009.03.004

BBS (Bangladesh Bureau of Statistics). (2017) Statistical Year Book of Bangladesh, 36th Edition, Statistics & Informatics Division, Ministry of Planning, Govt. of Bangladesh.

Beierlein, J. G., & Woolverton, M. W. (1991). *Agribusiness Marketing- the Management Perspective*. Prentice Hall.

Bhattacharyya, S., & Bose, I. (2020). S-commerce: Influence of Facebook likes on purchases and recommendations on a linked e-commerce site. *Decision Support Systems*, 138, 113383. DOI: 10.1016/j.dss.2020.113383

Birt, L., Scott, S., Cavers, D., Campbell, C., & Walter, F. (2016). Member Checking: A Tool to Enhance Trustworthiness or Merely a Nod to Validation? *Qualitative Health Research*, 26(13), 1802–1811. Advance online publication. DOI: 10.1177/1049732316654870 PMID: 27340178

Bishop, C., Russell, S., & Norvig, P. (2022). BrainstormBot: Enhancing brainstorming and innovation through AI-assisted ideation. *FutureLab Innovation Journal*, 12(3), 45–67.

Bogdan, R. C., & Biklen, S. K. (1982). *Qualitative Research for Education: An Introduction to Theory and Methods*. Allyn & Bacon.

Bohr, A., & Memarzadeh, K. (2020). *Artificial Intelligence in Healthcare*. Academic Press.

Box, I. (2014). How many interviews are needed in qualitative research? Is there any rule or popular practice? Retrieved 5 March 2019, from https://www.researchgate.net/post/How_many_interviews_are_needed_in_a_qualitative_research_Is_there_any_rule_or_popular_practice

Boyd, R. D. (2008). Adult Learning: A Journey Through Leadership Development. *Journal of Leadership Studies*, 2(3), 45–59.

Bravo-Baumann, H. (2000). *Capitalism, Socialism, and Communism in the 21st Century*. Springer.

Brighi, A., Mameli, C., Menin, D., Guarini, A., Carpani, F., & Slee, P. T. (2019). Coping with cybervictimization: The role of direct confrontation and resilience on adolescent wellbeing. *International Journal of Environmental Research and Public Health*, 16(24), 4893. DOI: 10.3390/ijerph16244893 PMID: 31817233

Brown, R. (1995). *Prejudice: It"s Social Psychology*. Blackwell Publishing.

Cahusac, E., & Kanji, S. (2014). Giving up: How gendered organizational cultures push mothers out. *Gender, Work and Organization*, 21(1), 57–70. DOI: 10.1111/gwao.12011

Caiazza, R. *et al.* (2021) "An absorptive capacity-based systems view of Covid-19 in the small business economy," *International Entrepreneurship and Management Journal 2021 17:3*, 17(3), pp. 1419–1439. .DOI: 10.1007/s11365-021-00753-7

Callanan, G. A., & Greenhaus, J. H. (1999). *Changing Concepts and Practices for Human Resources Management*. Jossey-Bass.

Campbell, S., Mueller, K., & Souza, J. M. (2010). Shared Leadership Experiences of Women Community College Presidents. *Journal of Women in Educational Leadership*, 8(1), 19–32.

Carrière, G. (2020). *Jungwee Park.; Zechuan Deng.; Dafina Kohen., "Overtime work among professional nurses during Covid-19 pandemic"*. Statcan.

Case, K. A., Rios, D., Lucas, A., Braun, K., & Enriquez, C. (2020). Intersectional patterns of prejudice confrontation by White, heterosexual, and cisgender allies. *The Journal of Social Issues*, 76(4), 899–920. DOI: 10.1111/josi.12408

Chang, D., Gui, H. Y., Fan, R., Fan, Z. Z., & Tian, J. (2019). Application of improved collaborative filtering in the recommendation of e-commerce commodities. *International Journal of Computers, Communications & Control*, 14(4), 489–502. DOI: 10.15837/ijccc.2019.4.3594

Chaturvedi, R. and Karri, A. (2021) "Entrepreneurship in the Times of Pandemic: Barriers and Strategies:" *https://doi.org/* [Preprint]. .DOI: 10.1177/23197145211043799

Chauhan, G. S., Meena, Y. K., & Gopalani, D.. (2020). A two-step hybrid unsupervised model with attention mechanism for aspect extraction. *Expert Systems with Applications*, 161, 113673. DOI: 10.1016/j.eswa.2020.113673

Cheney, M. (2011). *Tesla: Man Out of Time*. Simon & Schuster.

Cheng, S., Jianfu, S., Alrasheedi, M., Saeidi, P., Mishra, A. R., & Rani, P. (2021). A New Extended VIKOR Approach Using q-Rung Orthopair Fuzzy Sets for Sustainable Enterprise Risk Management Assessment in Manufacturing Small and Medium-Sized Enterprises. *International Journal of Fuzzy Systems*, •••, 1–23.

Choi, S., & Park, C. (2014). Glass ceiling in Korean Civil Service: Analyzing barriers to women"s career advancement in the Korean government. *Public Personnel Management*, 43(1), 118–139. DOI: 10.1177/0091026013516933

Chong, M. Y., Wang, W. C., Hsieh, W. C., Lee, C. Y., Chiu, N. M., Yeh, W. C., & Chen, C. L. (2004). Psychological impact of severe acute respiratory syndrome on health workers in a tertiary hospital. *The British Journal of Psychiatry*, 185(2), 127–133.

Cordova, D. I. (2011). Moving the needle on women's leadership. *On Campus with Women, 40*(1).

Coronavirus disease. *(Covid-19) Pandemic.2020. retrive from World Health Organization:*https://www.who.int/emergencies/diseases/novel-coronavirus-2019

Cotter, D. A., Hermsen, J. M., Ovadia, S., & Vanneman, R. (2001). The Glass Ceiling Effect. *Social Forces*, 80(2), 655–681. DOI: 10.1353/sof.2001.0091

Creswell, J. W. (2007). *Qualitative Inquiry & Research Design: Choosing Among Five Approaches* (2nd ed.). Sage Publications.

Crotty, M. (1998). *The Foundations of Social Research: Meaning and Perspective in the Research Process*. Sage Publications.

Dainty, A. R., Bagilhole, B. M., & Neale, R. H. (2000). A grounded theory of women's career under-achievement in large UK construction companies. *Construction management & economics, 18*(2), 239-250.Kolade, O.J. and Kehinde, O. (2013), "Glass ceiling and women career advancement: Evidence from Nigerian construction Industry. *Iranian Journal of Management Studies*, 6(1), 79–99.

Davis, F. D. (1991). *Perceived Usefulness, Perceived Ease of Use, and User Acceptance of Information Technology*. MIS Quarterly.

Demerouti, E., Bakker, A. B., & Bulters, A. J. (2004). The loss spiral of work pressure, work–home interference and exhaustion: Reciprocal relations in a three-wave study. *Journal of Vocational Behavior*, 64(1), 131–149.

Dezso, C. L., & Ross, D. G. (2012). Does female representation in top management improve firm performance? A panel data investigation. *Strategic Management Journal*, 33(9), 1072–1089. DOI: 10.1002/smj.1955

Didimo, W., Grilli, L., Liotta, G., Menconi, L., Montecchiani, F., & Pagliuca, D. (2020). Combining network visualization and data mining for tax risk assessment. *IEEE Access : Practical Innovations, Open Solutions*, 8, 16073–16086. DOI: 10.1109/ACCESS.2020.2967974

Diehl, A. B., & Diehl, A. B. (2014).Navigating Adversity, Barriers, and Obstacles. *Women and leadership in higher education*, 135..

Dimovski, V., Skerlavaj, M., & Man, M. M. K. (2010). Comparative analysis of mid-level women managers" perception of the existence of „glass ceiling"in Singaporean and Malaysian organizations. *The International Business & Economics Research Journal*, 9(8), 61–78. DOI: 10.19030/iber.v9i8.613

Du, Y., Kochenberger, G., Glover, F., Lu, Z. P., Liu, D. H., & Hulandageri, A. (2020) “Optimal Solutions to the Minimum Sum Coloring Problem: A comparison of Alternative Models”, Working paper, University of Colorado Denver.

Eagly, A. H., & Carli, L. L. (2003). The female leadership advantage: An evaluation of the evidence. *The Leadership Quarterly*, 14(6), 807834. DOI: 10.1016/j.leaqua.2003.09.004

Eagly, A. H., & Carli, L. L. (2007). *Through the Labyrinth: The Truth About How Women Become Leaders*. Harvard Business School Press.

Eagly, A. H., Eagly, L. L. C. A. H., & Carli, L. L. (2007). *Through the labyrinth: The truth about how women become leaders*. Harvard Business Press.

Eagly, A. H., & Johnson, B. T. (1990). Gender and leadership style: A meta-analysis. *Psychological Bulletin*, 108(2), 233–256. DOI: 10.1037/0033-2909.108.2.233

Edwards, J., & Rothbard, N. P. (2000). Mechanisms linking work and family: Clarifying the relationship between work and family constructs. *Academy of Management Review*, 25(1), 178. DOI: 10.2307/259269

Einstein, A. (1905). Zur Elektrodynamik bewegter Körper [On the Electrodynamics of Moving Bodies]. *Annalen der Physik*, 17(10), 891–921. DOI: 10.1002/andp.19053221004

Enid Kiaye, R., & Maniraj Singh, A. (2013). The glass ceiling: A perspective of women working in Durban. *Gender in Management*, 28(1), 28–42. DOI: 10.1108/17542411311301556

Eremeev, M. A., & Zakharchuk, I. I. (2020). A Procedure for Improving Information System Audit Quality by Enhancing Cyberthreat Simulation in Practice. *Automatic Control and Computer Sciences*, 54(8), 854–859. DOI: 10.3103/S0146411620080118

Essays, U. K. (2018). Reliability and Validity in Research. Retrieved 5 February, 2019, from https://www.ukessays.com/essays/psychology/the-reliability-and-validity-psychology-essay.php?vref=1

Esterberg, K. G. (2002). *Qualitative Methods in Social Research*. McGraw-Hill.

Ezzedeen, S., & Ritchey, K. (2009). Career advancement and family balance strategies of executive women. *Gender in Management*, 24(6), 388–411. DOI: 10.1108/17542410910980388

Factors affecting work-life balance. Retrive from Innerhour: https://www.theinnerhour.com/corp-work-life-balance#:~:text=Some%20organisational%20factors%20that%20interfere,and%20lack%20of%20job%20security

Fang, Y., Zhang, C., Huang, C., Liu, L., & Yang, Y. (2019). Phishing email detection using improved RCNN model with multilevel vectors and attention mechanism. *IEEE Access : Practical Innovations, Open Solutions*, 7, 56329–56340. DOI: 10.1109/ACCESS.2019.2913705

Fan, Q. (2019). An exploratory study of cross-border e-commerce (CBEC) in China: Opportunities and challenges for small to medium-size enterprises (SMEs). [IJEEI]. *International Journal of E-Entrepreneurship and Innovation*, 9(1), 23–29. DOI: 10.4018/IJEEI.2019010103

FAO. (2017) Country Profile-Bangladesh, the Food and Agricultural Organization of the United Nations (FAO), Rome, Italy.

Farooq, M., & Raju, V. (2019a). Want to Stay the Market Leader in the Era of Transformative Marketing? Keep the Customers Satisfied! *Global Journal of Flexible Systems Managment*, 20(3), 257–266. DOI: 10.1007/s40171-019-00213-w

Farooq, M., Raju, V., Khalil-Ur-Rehman, F., Younas, W., Ahmed, Q. M., & Ali, M. (2019). Investigating relationship between net promoter score and company performance: A longitudinal study. *Global Journal of Emerging Sciences*, 1(1), 1–10.

Fisher, B. D., Motowidlo, S., & Werner, S. (1993). Effects of gender and other factors on rank of law professors in colleges of business: Evidence of a glass ceiling. *Journal of Business Ethics*, 12(10), 771–778. DOI: 10.1007/BF00881309

Fitzpatrick, L. (2019) "A Complete Beginner's Guide to Atomic Swaps," *Forbes*, Sept 2, 2019 https://www.forbes.com

Fitzpatrick, L., Fulkerson, D.R., Ford Jr., L.R. (1962) *Flows in Networks*, Rand Corporation.

Forbes. (2016). *Which industries has the most women in senior management?* Retrieved from https://www.forbes.com/sites/niallmccarthy/2016/ 03/08/which-industries-have-the-most-women-in[REMOVED HYPERLINK FIELD]senior-management-infographic/#3917ea6f5cc4[REMOVED HYPERLINK FIELD]

Forbes, D. (2019). Artificial Intelligence in the Workplace. *Harvard Business Review*.

Gale, A. W. (1994). Women in non-traditional occupations: The construction industry. *Women in Management Review*, 9(2), 3–14. DOI: 10.1108/EUM0000000003989

Gallhofer, S., Paisey, C., Roberts, C., & Tarbert, H. (2011). Preferences, constraints and work. *Accounting, Auditing & Accountability Journal*, 24(4), 440–470. DOI: 10.1108/09513571111133054

Gao, Y., & Ruan, Y. (2021). Interpretable deep learning model for building energy consumption prediction based on attention mechanism. *Energy and Building*, 252, 111379. DOI: 10.1016/j.enbuild.2021.111379

Gayani Fernando, N., Amaratunga, D., & Haigh, R. (2014). The career advancement of the professional women in the UK construction industry: The career success factors. *Journal of Engineering. Design and Technology*, 12(1), 5370. DOI: 10.1108/JEDT-04-2012-0018

Geertz, C. (1973). *The Interpretation of Cultures: Selected Essays*. Basic Books.

GEM.(2010). *Global Entrepreneurship Monitor 2010 Global Report.* Global Entrepreneurship Research Association: Boston. a.Gender in Management: An International Journal, Vol. 28 No. 1, pp. 28-42.

Global consumer confidence index 2018-2020 | Statista (no date). Available at: https://www.statista.com/statistics/1035883/global-consumer-confidence-index/ (Accessed: January 30, 2022).

Glover, F., & Rego, C. (2006). Ejection chain and filter-and-fan methods in combinatorial optimization. 4OR, 4, 263-296.

Glover, F., Kochenberger, G., Du, Y., Hennig, R., Wang, H., Mniszewski, S., & Hulandageri, A. (2020) "Experience with the QUBO Model for Solving Large Scale Set Partitioning Problems," *12th INFORMS Conference on Information Systems & Technology (CIST),* Virtual 2020 INFORMS Annual Meeting, November 7 - 13, 2020.

Glover, , FLewis, , MKochenberger, , G. (2018). Logical and inequality implications for reducing the size and difficulty of quadratic unconstrained binary optimization problems. *European Journal of Operational Research, 265*(3), 829-842.

Glover, F. (1996). Ejection Chains, Reference Structures and Alternating Path Methods for Traveling Salesman Problems. *Discrete Applied Mathematics*, 65(1-3), 223–253. DOI: 10.1016/0166-218X(94)00037-E

Glover, F., Glover, R., & Klingman, D. (1986). The Threshold Assignment Algorithm. In Gallo, G., & Sandi, C. (Eds.), *Mathematical Programming Study* (Vol. 26, pp. 12–37).

Glover, F., Klingman, D., & Phillips, N. (1992). *Network Models in Optimization and their Applications in Practice*. Wiley Interscience, John Wiley and Sons. DOI: 10.1002/9781118033173

Glover, F., Kochenberger, G., & Du, Y. (2019). "A Tutorial on Formulating and Using QUBO Methods," *4OR Quarterly Journal of Operations Research. Invited Survey*, 17, 335–371.

Glover, F., Kochenberger, G., & Du, Y. (2021). Applications of the QUBO and QUBO-Plus Models. In Punnen, A. P. (Ed.), *The quadratic unconstrained binary optimization problem*. Springer.

Glover, F., & Laguna, M. (1997). *Tabu Search*. Kluwer Academic Publishers, Springer. DOI: 10.1007/978-1-4615-6089-0

Glover, F., Phillips, N., & Klingman, D. (1990). Netform Modeling and Applications. *Special Issue on the Practice of Mathematical Programming, Interfaces*, 20(1), 7–27.

Gomez-Herrera, E., Martens, B., & Turlea, G. (2014). - The drivers and impediments for cross-border e-commerce in the EU. *Information Economics and Policy*, 2014(28), 83–96. DOI: 10.1016/j.infoecopol.2014.05.002

Goodfellow, I., Bengio, Y., & Courville, A. (2016). *Deep Learning*. MIT Press.

Grant Thornton. (2017a). *Malaysia has the least senior business roles held by women in ASEAN at 24%*. Retrieved from https://www.grantthornton.com.my/press/press[REMOVED HYPERLINK FIELD]releases-20162/Malaysia-has-the-least-senior[REMOVED HYPERLINK FIELD]business-roles-held-by-women-in-ASEAN/[REMOVED HYPERLINK FIELD]

Grant Thornton. (2017b). *Women in Business: New Perspectives on Risk and Reward*. Retrieved from http://grantthornton.pl/wp[REMOVED HYPERLINK FIELD]content/uploads/2017/03/Grant-Thornton_Women[REMOVED HYPERLINK FIELD]in-Business_2017-FINAL_Digital.pdf[REMOVED HYPERLINK FIELD]

Greene, B. (2000). *The Elegant Universe: Superstrings, Hidden Dimensions, and the Quest for the Ultimate Theory*. W. W. Norton & Company.

Griffiths, D. J. (2016). *Introduction to Quantum Mechanics*. Pearson.

Grover, D., Bauhoff, S., & Friedman, J. (2019). Using supervised learning to select audit targets in performance-based financing in health: An example from Zambia. *PLoS One*, 14(1), e0211262. DOI: 10.1371/journal.pone.0211262 PMID: 30695057

Guemri, O., Nduwayoa, P., Todosijevic, R., Hanafi, S., & Glover, F. (2019, September 19). Probabilistic Tabu Search for the Cross-Docking Assignment Problem. *European Journal of Operational Research*, 277(3), 875–885. DOI: 10.1016/j.ejor.2019.03.030

Guest, C. (2016). Advantages and Disadvantages of Online Surveys. Retrieved 5 February 2019, from https://blog.cvent.com/events/advantages-disadvantages-online-surveys/IWH (2015). At Work 82 (Fall). Retrieved 5 February 2019, from https://www.iwh.on.ca/newsletters/at-work/82

Gui, G., Liu, F., Sun, J., Yang, J., Zhou, Z., & Zhao, D. (2019). Flight delay prediction based on aviation big data and machine learning. *IEEE Transactions on Vehicular Technology*, 69(1), 140–150. DOI: 10.1109/TVT.2019.2954094

Halliday, D., Resnick, R., & Walker, J. (2014). *Fundamentals of Physics*. Wiley.

Hammad, M., Pławiak, P., Wang, K., & Acharya, U. R. (2021). ResNet-Attention model for human authentication using ECG signals. *Expert Systems: International Journal of Knowledge Engineering and Neural Networks*, 38(6), e12547. DOI: 10.1111/exsy.12547

Hanggraeni, D., Ślusarczyk, B., Sulung, L. A. K., & Subroto, A. (2019). The impact of internal, external and enterprise risk management on the performance of micro, small and medium enterprises. *Sustainability (Basel)*, 11(7), 2172. DOI: 10.3390/su11072172

Harris, C., Ravenswood, K., & Myers, B. (2013). Glass slippers, Holy Grails and Ivory Towers: gender and advancement in academia. *Labour& Industry: a journal of the social and economic relations of work, 23*(3), 231-244.

Hasan, R., Islam, M. M., & Rahman, M. (2022). Modernizing Agricultural Extension in Bangladesh: Shifting Focus from Farmers to Products. *Journal of Agrarian Studies*, 15(3), 45–60.

Hasina, S. (2019). *Agricultural Development in Bangladesh: Achievements and Future Directions*. Government of Bangladesh Press.

Hawking, S., & Mlodinow, L. (2010). *The Grand Design*. Bantam Books.

Helsgaun, K. (2000). An Effective Implementation of the Lin-Kernighan Traveling Salesman Heuristic. *European Journal of Operational Research*, 126(1), 106–130. DOI: 10.1016/S0377-2217(99)00284-2

Helsgaun, K. (2009). General k-opt submoves for the Lin-Kernighan TSP heuristic. *Mathematical Programming Computation*, 1(2-3), 119–163. DOI: 10.1007/s12532-009-0004-6

Hershcovis, M. S., Cameron, A. F., Gervais, L., & Bozeman, J. (2018). The effects of confrontation and avoidance coping in response to workplace incivility. *Journal of Occupational Health Psychology*, 23(2), 163–174. DOI: 10.1037/ocp0000078 PMID: 28191998

He, Y., & Wang, J. (2019). A Panel Analysis on the Cross Border E-commerce Trade: Evidence from ASEAN Countries. *The Journal of Asian Finance, Economics, and Business*, 6(2), 95–104. DOI: 10.13106/jafeb.2019.vol6.no2.95

Hmedan, M., Chetty, V. R. K., & Phung, S. P. (2018). Malaysian tourism sector: Technical review on policies and regulations. *Eurasian Journal of Analytical Chemistry*, 13(6), 114–120.

Holden, J., & McCarthy, H. (2007). *Women at the Top – A Provocation Piece*. City University.

Hoobler, J. M. (2016). Domestic Employment Relationships and Trickle-Down Work–Family Conflict: The South African Context. *Africa Journal of Management*, 2(1), 31–49. DOI: 10.1080/23322373.2015.1126499

Hoobler, J. M., Lemmon, G., & Wayne, S. J. (2014). Women's managerial aspirations: An organizational development perspective. *Journal of Management*, 40(3), 703–730.

Hoobler, J. M., Wayne, S. J., & Lemmon, G. (2009). Bosses" perceptions of family-work conflict and women"s promotability: Glass ceiling effects. *Academy of Management Journal*, 52(5), 939–957. DOI: 10.5465/amj.2009.44633700

Hooks, B. (1984). *Feminist Theory: From Margin to Center*. South End Press.

Hoos, H. (2012). Programming by Optimization. *Communications of the ACM*, 55(2), 70–80. DOI: 10.1145/2076450.2076469

Hossain, M. A., & Ahmed, S. (2021). *Strengthening Agricultural Extension Services in Bangladesh: A Need for Structural Reforms*. Bangladesh Agricultural Research Institute.

Howe-Walsh, L., & Turnbull, S. (2016). Barriers to women leaders in academia: Tales from science and technology. *Studies in Higher Education*, 41(3), 415–428. DOI: 10.1080/03075079.2014.929102

Huang, Y., Chai, Y., Liu, Y., & Shen, J. (2018). Architecture of next-generation e-commerce platform. *Tsinghua Science and Technology*, 24(1), 18–29. DOI: 10.26599/TST.2018.9010067

Hurn, B. (2013). Are cracks now appearing in the boardroom glass ceiling. *Industrial and Commercial Training*, 45(4), 195–201. DOI: 10.1108/00197851311323475

Hu, T. C. (1963). *Multi-commodity network flows*. INFORMS PubsOnline., DOI: 10.1287/opre.11.3.344

Islam, M. A., & Jantan, A. H. (2017). The glass ceiling: Career barriers for female employees in the readymade garments (RMG) industry of Bangladesh. *SSRN*, 16(3), 1–11. DOI: 10.2139/ssrn.3414583

Islam, M. M., & Ahmed, S. U. (2018). *Transformation of Agriculture in Bangladesh: Role of Education and Extension*. Bangladesh Agricultural Research Council.

Islam, M. S., Rahman, A., & Khan, M. H. (2020). *Challenges and Opportunities in Agricultural Extension in Bangladesh*. Ministry of Agriculture.

Ismail, M., & Ibrahim, M. (2008). Barriers to career progression faced by women. *Gender in Management*, 23(1), 5166. DOI: 10.1108/17542410810849123

Ismail, R., Wye, C.-K., Palel, M., & Sabrina, N. (2017). Analysis of Glass Ceiling and Sticky Floor Effects for Gender Wage Gap in Malaysian Labour Market. *Jurnal Ekonomi Malaysia.*, 51(2), 131–142.

Jafarey, S., & Maiti, P. (2015). Migration, Remittances, and Real Exchange Rate in the Long Run. *World Economy*, 38(1), 19–27.

Jahan, I. (2018). Breaking the Glass Ceiling. ICE Business Times. Retrieved 5 March, 2019, from https://ibtbd.net/breaking-the-glass-ceiling/

Jandeska, K. E., & Kraimer, M. L. (2005). Women's Perceptions of Organizational Culture, Work Attitudes, and Role-modeling Behaviors. *Journal of Managerial Issues*, 17(4), 461–478.

Jaykumar, P. B. (2021). *Covid pandemic alert! India short of 4.3 million nurses*. Fortune India.

Jiang, J., & Chen, J. (2021). Framework of Blockchain-Supported E-Commerce Platform for Small and Medium Enterprises. *Sustainability (Basel)*, 13(15), 8158. DOI: 10.3390/su13158158

Jogulu, U., & Wood, G. (2011). Women managers' career progression: An Asia Pacific perspective. *Gender in Management*, 26(8), 590–603. DOI: 10.1108/17542411111183893

Joseph, G. (2007). *Grzywacz.; Dawn S. Carlson., "Conceptualizing work- family balance: implications for practice and research"*. Sage Journals.

Kabir, M. (2016). Islamic Banking in Bangladesh: Past, Present, and Future. *Journal of Islamic Banking and Finance*, 33(4), 12–24.

Kagan, J. (2018). *Psychology: Cognitive Development*. Encyclopedia Britannica.

Kanagaraj, R., Rajkumar, N., & Srinivasan, K. (2021). Multiclass normalized clustering and classification model for electricity consumption data analysis in machine learning techniques. *Journal of Ambient Intelligence and Humanized Computing*, 12(5), 5093–5103. DOI: 10.1007/s12652-020-01960-w

Kang, J., Liu, L., Zhang, F., Shen, C., Wang, N., & Shao, L. (2021). Semantic segmentation model of cotton roots in-situ image based on attention mechanism. *Computers and Electronics in Agriculture*, 189, 106370. DOI: 10.1016/j.compag.2021.106370

Kelly, H. H. (1967), "Attribution theory in social psychology", *Nebraska Symposium on Motivation*, University of Nebraska Press.

Kiaye, R. and Singh, A. (2013), "The glass ceiling: a perspective of women working in Durban",

Kittel, C. (2005). *Introduction to Solid State Physics*. Wiley.

Kochenberger, G., & Ma, M. (2020) "Quantum Computing Applications of QUBO Models to Portfolio Optimization," White paper, University of Colorado, Denver, July, 2020.

Kohls, R. L., & Uhl, J. N. (2002). *Marketing of Agricultural Products* (9th ed.). Prentice Hall.

Krishna, D. G. R., & Lakshmypriya, K. (2016). Work Life Balance and Implications Of Spill Over Theory–A Study on Women Entrepreneurs. *International Journal of Research in IT and Management*, 6(6), 96–109.

Kuroda, N. (2021). Editorial Comment to False-positive 123 I-metaiodobenzylguanidine scan in a patient with renal cell carcinoma: A case of chromophobe renal cell carcinoma oncocytic variant with a complicated clinical course. *IJU Case Reports*, 4(1), 42–43. DOI: 10.1002/iju5.12244 PMID: 33426496

Kwilinski, A., Volynets, R., & Berdnik, I.. (2019). E-Commerce: Concept and Legal Regulation in Modern Economic Conditions. Journal of Legal. *Ethical and Regulatory Issues*, 22, 1–6.

Lai, J. (2020). *Simeng Ma.; Ying Wang., "Factors Associated wWith Mental Health Outcomes Among Healthcare Workers Exposed to Coronavirus Disease 2019"*. JAMA Network.

Lakshmi, K. N., Neema, N., Muddasir, N. M., & Prashanth, M. V. (2020). Anomaly Detection Techniques in Data Mining—A Review. Inventive Communication and Computational Technologies, 799-804.

Lathabhavan, R., & Balasubramanian, S. A. (2017). Glass Ceiling and women employees in Asian organizations: A tri-decadal review. *Asia-Pacific Journal of Business Administration*, 9(3), 232246. DOI: 10.1108/APJBA-03-2017-0023

Lawton, R. (2018). It Ain't What You Do (But the Way That You Do It): Will Safety II Transform the Way We Do Patient Safety?: Comment on" False Dawns and New Horizons in Patient Safety Research and Practice. *International Journal of Health Policy and Management*, 7(7), 659–661. DOI: 10.15171/ijhpm.2018.14 PMID: 29996586

Leonard, L. N., & Jones, K. (2021). Trust in C2C electronic commerce: Ten years later. *Journal of Computer Information Systems*, 61(3), 240–246. DOI: 10.1080/08874417.2019.1598829

Lewis, J. J. (2019, January 29). Women's Rights Movements: A Historical Overview. ThoughtCo.

Li, H., Duan, H., Zheng, Y., Wang, Q., & Wang, Y. (2020). A CTR prediction model based on user interest via attention mechanism. *Applied Intelligence*, 50(4), 1192–1203. DOI: 10.1007/s10489-019-01571-9

Li, J., Liu, X., Zhang, W., Zhang, M., Song, J., & Sebe, N. (2020). Spatio-temporal attention networks for action recognition and detection. *IEEE Transactions on Multimedia*, 22(11), 2990–3001. DOI: 10.1109/TMM.2020.2965434

Linehan, M., Scullion, H., & Walsh, J. S. (2001). Barriers to women"s participation in international management. *European Business Review*, 13(1), 10–19. DOI: 10.1108/09555340110366444

Lin, N. (2001). *Social Capital: A Theory of Social Structure and Action*. Cambridge University Press. DOI: 10.1017/CBO9780511815447

Liou, J. J., Chang, M. H., Lo, H. W., & Hsu, M. H. (2021). Application of an MCDM model with data mining techniques for green supplier evaluation and selection. *Applied Soft Computing*, 109, 107534. DOI: 10.1016/j.asoc.2021.107534

Lips, H. M., & Keener, E. (2007). Effects of gender and dominance on leadership emergence: Incentives make a difference. *Sex Roles*, 56(9-10), 563–571. DOI: 10.1007/s11199-007-9210-8

Liu, X., Xu, Y. C., & Yang, X. (2021). Disease profiling in pharmaceutical E-commerce. *Expert Systems with Applications*, 178, 115015. DOI: 10.1016/j.eswa.2021.115015

Li, Y., Yan, C., Liu, W., & Li, M. (2018). A principle component analysis-based random forest with the potential nearest neighbor method for automobile insurance fraud identification. *Applied Soft Computing*, 70, 1000–1009. DOI: 10.1016/j.asoc.2017.07.027

Li, Z., & Liu, Y. (2017). A differential game-theoretic model of auditing for data storage in cloud computing. *International Journal on Computer Science and Engineering*, 14(4), 341–348.

Lorentz, H. A. (1895). *The Ether and the Relative Motion of Matter. Collected Papers*. Springer.

Lu, H. (2020). *Yang Zhao.; Alison While., "Job satisfaction among hospital nurses: a literature review"*. Researchgate.

Lunn, M. (2007). *Women academicians: Gender and career progression*. Jurul.

Lu, S., Lu, Z., & Zhang, Y. D. (2019). Pathological brain detection based on AlexNet and transfer learning. *Journal of Computational Science*, 30, 41–47. DOI: 10.1016/j.jocs.2018.11.008

Lv, Z., Qiao, L., & Singh, A. K. (2020). Advanced machine learning on cognitive computing for human behavior analysis. *IEEE Transactions on Computational Social Systems*, 8(5), 1194–1202. DOI: 10.1109/TCSS.2020.3011158

Malaysia Employment Act. 1955. Retrieved 5 February 2019, from https://www.ilo.org/dyn/natlex/docs/WEBTEXT/48055/66265/E55mys01.htm

Malaysiakini News. (2017). Empowering women, empowering Malaysia.Retrieved from www.malaysiakini.com/letters/368977

Malik, S. (2011). A Portrayal of Women Educational Leadership in Pakistan. *Journal of Educational Psychology*, 5(2), 37–44.

Mattis, M. C. (2004). Women entrepreneurs: Out from under the glass ceiling. *Women in Management Review*, 19(3), 154–163.

Mavin, S. (2001). Women"s career in theory and practice: Time for change? *Women in Management Review*, 16(4), 183–192. DOI: 10.1108/09649420110392163

Merriam, S. B. (2002). *Qualitative Research in Practice: Examples for Discussion and Analysis*. Jossey-Bass.

Meyerson, D. E., & Fletcher, J. K. (2000). A Modest Manifesto for Shattering the Glass Ceiling. *Harvard Business Review*, 78(1), 126–136.

Mia, A. (2016). *Sustainable Development in Emerging Markets: Challenges and Solutions*. Routledge.

Ministry of Agriculture. (2020). *Agricultural Extension Policy: A Framework for Sustainable Agricultural Development*. Government of Bangladesh.

Ministry of Fisheries and Livestock. (2021). *Annual Report on Agricultural Extension Services*. Government of Bangladesh.

MoA. (2016-17) Annual *Report*. Government of Bangladesh (www.moa.gov.bd)

Mohd Adnan, S. N. S., & Valliappan, R. (2019). Communicating shared vision and leadership styles towards enhancing performance. *International Journal of Productivity and Performance Management*, 68(6), 1042–1056. DOI: 10.1108/IJPPM-05-2018-0183

Morrison, A. M., & Von Glinow, M. A. (1990). Women and minorities in management. *The American Psychologist*, 45(2), 200–208. DOI: 10.1037/0003-066X.45.2.200

Mujeri, M. K. (2014). Vision 2030: What lies Ahead for Bangladesh in a post-MDGs World. 1st Conference organized by the Bangladesh Economist Forum at RadisonBlu, Water Garden on 21- 23June.

Mullen, K. (2015). 21. Barriers to Work-life Balance for Hospital Nurses. *Sage (Atlanta, Ga.)*.

Müller, J. C., Pokutta, S., Martin, A., Pape, S., Peter, A., & Winter, T. (2017). Pricing and clearing combinatorial markets with singleton and swap orders. *Mathematical Methods of Operations Research*, 85(2), 155–177. DOI: 10.1007/s00186-016-0555-z

Mun, E., & Jung, J. (2017). Change above the glass ceiling: Corporate social responsibility and gender diversity in Japanese firms. *Administrative Science Quarterly*, (May), 0001839217712920.

Myers, C. E. (2010). *Perceptions of the glass ceiling effect in community colleges*. University of New Orleans.

National Academies. (2019). *The National Academies of Sciences, Engineering and Medicine, 2019. Quantum Computing: Progress and Prospects*. The National Academies Press., DOI: 10.17226/25196

Nauman, A., Qadri, Y. A., Amjad, M., Zikria, Y. B., Afzal, M. K., & Kim, S. W. (2020). Multimedia Internet of Things: A comprehensive survey. *IEEE Access : Practical Innovations, Open Solutions*, 8, 8202–8250. DOI: 10.1109/ACCESS.2020.2964280

Nawaiseh, A. K., Abbod, M. F., & Itagaki, T. (2020). Financial Statement Audit using Support Vector Machines, Artificial Neural Networks and K-Nearest Neighbor: An Empirical Study of UK and Ireland. International Journal of Simulation—Systems. *Science & Technology*, 21(2), 1–8.

Nelson, T., Maxfield, S., & Kolb, D. (2009). Women entrepreneurs and venture capital: Managing the shadow negotiation. *International Journal of Gender and Entrepreneurship*, 1(1), 5776. DOI: 10.1108/17566260910942345

Nevill, G., Pennicott, A., Williams, J., & Worrall, A. (1990). *Women in the workforce: the effect of demographic changes in the 1990s*. The Industrial Society.

Nguyen, T. L. H. (2013). Barriers to and facilitators of female Deans" career advancement in higher education: An exploratory study in Vietnam. *Higher Education*, 66(1), 123–138. DOI: 10.1007/s10734-012-9594-4

Nolan, T. (2013) "Alt chains and atomic transfers," *Bitcointalk*https://bitcointalk.org/index.php?topic=193281.0

Northouse, P. G. (2013). *Leadership: Theory and practice* (6th ed.). Sage.

OECD. (2014). *Innovation Policies for Inclusive Growth*. OECD Publishing.

Ogbonna, E., & Harris, L. C. (2000). Leadership style, organizational culture and performance: Empirical evidence from UK companies. *International Journal of Human Resource Management*, 11(4), 766–788. DOI: 10.1080/09585190050075114

Pal, A. K., Rawal, P., Ruwala, R., & Patel, V. (2019). Generic disease prediction using symptoms with supervised machine learning. *Int. J Sci. Res. Comput. Sci. Eng. Inf. Technol*, 5(2), 1082–1086. DOI: 10.32628/CSEIT1952297

Pandey, S. (2019). Importance of Online Survey and How to Set Up One. Retrieved 5 February 2019, from https://wpmanageninja.com/importance-online-survey/

Patton, M. Q. (2002). *Qualitative Research and Evaluation Methods* (3rd ed.). Sage Publications.

Phung, S. P., & Valliappan, R. (2018). Conceptualizing the Application for Ethereum Blockchains: Front End Application Development. *Eurasian Journal of Analytical Chemistry*, 13(6), 105–113.

Ping, P., Qin, W., Xu, Y., Miyajima, C., & Takeda, K. (2019). Impact of driver behavior on fuel consumption: Classification, evaluation and prediction using machine learning. *IEEE Access : Practical Innovations, Open Solutions*, 7, 78515–78532. DOI: 10.1109/ACCESS.2019.2920489

Polas, M. R. H. *et al.* (2021) 'Rural women characteristics and sustainable entrepreneurial intention: a road to economic growth in Bangladesh', *Journal of Enterprising Communities*. .DOI: 10.1108/JEC-10-2020-0183

Polas, M. R. H.. (2020). Customer's revisit intention: Empirical evidence on Gen-Z from Bangladesh towards halal restaurants. *Journal of Public Affairs*. Advance online publication. DOI: 10.1002/pa.2572

Pompper, D. (2011). Fifty years later: Midcareer women of color against the glass ceiling in communications organizations. *Journal of Organizational Change Management*, 24(4), 464486.

Post, C., & Byron, K. (2015). Women on boards and firm financial performance: A meta-analysis. *Academy of Management Journal*, 58(5), 1546–1571. DOI: 10.5465/amj.2013.0319

Powell, G. N., & Butterfield, D. A. (2015). The glass ceiling: What have we learned 20 years on? *Journal of Organizational Effectiveness: People and Performance*, 2(4), 306–326. DOI: 10.1108/JOEPP-09-2015-0032

Preuss, L. (2016). *Corporate Social Responsibility: Voluntary Codes of Conduct in the Mining Industry*. Springer.

Qi, N., Wang, W., Xiao, M., Jia, L., Jin, S., Zhu, Q., & Tsiftsis, T. A. (2021). A learning-based spectrum access Stackelberg game: Friendly jammer-assisted communication confrontation. *IEEE Transactions on Vehicular Technology*, 70(1), 700–713. DOI: 10.1109/TVT.2021.3049653

Quote by Warren Buffett: "Opportunities come infrequently. When it rains ..." (no date). Available at: https://www.goodreads.com/quotes/952671-opportunities-come-infrequently-when-it-rains-gold-put-out-the (Accessed: January 30, 2022).

Rahaman, M.R. & Jahan, N. (2015). Sexual Harassment in Workplace in South Asia: A Comparative Study on Bangladesh, India, Nepal, and Sri Lanka. IOSR Journal of Business and Management (IOSR-JBM). 17(6). 49-57.

Rahman, M. A. (2016). *Bangabandhu and the Agricultural Revolution of Bangladesh*. University Press Limited.

Rahman, M. A., & Akter, N. (2019). *Assessing the Impact of Project-Based Approaches in Agricultural Extension: A Case Study of Bangladesh*. University Press Limited.

Raju, V. (2021). Implementing Flexible Systems in Doctoral Viva Defense Through Virtual Mechanism. *Global Journal of Flexible Systems Managment*, 22(2), 127–139. DOI: 10.1007/s40171-021-00264-y PMID: 38624609

Raju, V., & Phung, S. P. (2018). Production of methane gas from cow's residue: Biogas as alternative energy in transportation and electricity. *Eurasian Journal of Analytical Chemistry*, 13(6), 121–124.

Raju, V., & Phung, S. P. (2020). Economic dimensions of blockchain technology: In the context of extention of cryptocurrencies. *International Journal of Psychosocial Rehabilitation*, 24(2), 29–39. DOI: 10.37200/IJPR/V24I2/PR200307

Rani, L. N., Defit, S., & Muhammad, L. J. (2021). Determination of Student Subjects in Higher Education Using Hybrid Data Mining Method with the K-Means Algorithm and FP Growth. *International Journal of Artificial Intelligence Research*, 5(1), 91–101. DOI: 10.29099/ijair.v5i1.223

Rauf, F. H. A., Khalid, F. M., Zulkifli, A. M., Manaf, N. J. F. A., Sulaiman, N. F. A., Hanim Abdul Rauf, F., ... & Fatin Amirah Sulaiman, N. (2018). Individual Factors, Work-Family Conflict And Organisational Structure Towards Malaysian Women Career Progress. European Proceedings of Social and Behavioural Sciences, 44.

Rego, C., Gamboa, D., & Glover, F. (2016). Doubly-Rooted Stem-and-Cycle Ejection Chain Algorithm for the Asymmetric Traveling Salesman Problem. *Networks*, 68(1), 23–33. DOI: 10.1002/net.21676

Ren, Q., Li, M., Li, H., & Shen, Y. (2021). A novel deep learning prediction model for concrete dam displacements using interpretable mixed attention mechanism. *Advanced Engineering Informatics*, 50, 101407. DOI: 10.1016/j.aei.2021.101407

Resende, M. G. C., Ribeiro, C. C., Glover, F., & Martí, R. (2010) "Scatter Search and Path Relinking: Fundamentals, Advances and Applications," *Handbook of Metaheuristics: International Series in Operations Research & Management Science,* Volume 146, pp 87-107.

Reskin, B. F., & Ross, C. E. (1992). Jobs, Authority, and Earnings among Managers: The Continuing Significance of Sex. *Work and Occupations*, 19(4), 342–365. DOI: 10.1177/0730888492019004002

Russell, S., & Norvig, P. (2022). *Artificial intelligence: A modern approach* (4th ed.). Pearson.

Ryan, M. K., & Haslam, S. A. (2005). The glass cliff: Evidence that women are over. *British Journal of Management*, 16(2), 81–90. DOI: 10.1111/j.1467-8551.2005.00433.x

Sabharwal, M. (2013). From glass ceiling to glass cliff: Women in senior executive service. *Journal of Public Administration: Research and Theory*, 25(2), 399–426. DOI: 10.1093/jopart/mut030

Sadeeq, M., Abdulla, A. I., & Abdulraheem, A. S.. (2020). Impact of electronic commerce on enterprise business. *Technol. Rep. Kansai Univ*, 62(5), 2365–2378.

Sahoo, D. K., & Lenka, U. (2016). Breaking the glass ceiling: Opportunity for the organization. *Industrial and Commercial Training*, 48(6), 311–319. DOI: 10.1108/ICT-02-2015-0017

Saigopal, V. V. R. G., & Raju, V. (2020a) 'IIoT Digital Forensics and Major Security issues', *2020 International Conference on Computational Intelligence, ICCI 2020*, pp. 233–236. DOI: 10.1109/ICCI51257.2020.9247685

Saigopal, V. V. R. G., & Raju, V. (2020b) 'IoT based Secure Digital Forensic Process according to Process Management', in *2020 International Conference on Computational Intelligence, ICCI 2020*. DOI: 10.1109/ICCI51257.2020.9247710

Samorani, M., Wang, Y., Lu, Z., & Glover, F. (2019) "Clustering-driven evolutionary algorithms: an application of path relinking to the QUBO problem," *Special Issue on Intensification, Diversification and Learning* of the *Journal of Heuristics*, F. Glover and M. Samorani, eds., Volume 25, Issue 4–5, pp 629–642

Sandberg, S. (2013). Lean. In *Women, Work, and the Will to Lead*. Knopf.

Sanders, T. (1982). *Sociological Perspectives on Aging*. Cambridge University Press.

Savitsky, B., Radomislensky, I., & Hendel, T. (2021). Nurses' occupational satisfaction during Covid-19 pandemic. *Applied Nursing Research*, 59, 151416.

SBA. (2011a). *Frequently Asked Questions*. Small Business Administration.

Schein, V. E. (2007). Women in management: Reflections and projections. *Women in Management Review*, 22(1), 6–18. DOI: 10.1108/09649420710726193

Schwartz, D. B. (1996). The impact of workfamily policies on women"s career development: Boon or bust? *Women*, 11(1), 5–19.

Schwartz, J. (2020). *Chwan-Chuen King.; Muh-Yong Yen., "Protecting Healthcare Workers During the Coronavirus Disease 2019 (COVID-19) Outbreak: Lessons From Taiwan's Severe Acute Respiratory Syndrome Response"*. Academic.

Serway, R. A., & Jewett, J. W. (2018). *Physics for Scientists and Engineers*. Cengage Learning.

Shabbir, H., Shakeel, M. A. & Zubair, R. A. (2017). Gender Stereotype, Glass Ceiling, and Women's Career Advancement: An Empirical Study in Service Sector of Pakistan. City University Research Journal. Special Issue: AIC, Malaysia PP 236-246.

Shad, M. K., Lai, F. W., Fatt, C. L., Klemeš, J. J., & Bokhari, A. (2019). Integrating sustainability reporting into enterprise risk management and its relationship with business performance: A conceptual framework. *Journal of Cleaner Production*, 208, 415–425. DOI: 10.1016/j.jclepro.2018.10.120

Shah, S. J. (2010). Re. *International Journal of Leadership in Education*, 13(1), 27–44. DOI: 10.1080/13603120903244879

Sharif, M. (2014). *Economic Growth and Development in South Asia. Oxford University Press. Gupta, S. (2018). Introduction to Financial Markets*. McGraw-Hill.

Shein, E. (2004). *Organizational culture and leadership*. Jossey-Bass.

Shivaprasad, A. h. (2013). 19. Work related stress of nurses. *Journal of Psychiatric Nursing*.

Simpson, R., & Altman, Y. (2000). The time bounded glass ceiling and young women managers: career progress and career success – evidence from the UK. *Journal Of European Industrial Training, 24*(2/3/4), 190-198.

Smith, R. A.. (2012). Glass Ceilings and Glass Escalators: Hidden Barriers or Hidden Advantages to Women in the Workplace? *Social Problems*, 59(3), 373–394.

Snaebjornsson, I. M., & Edvardsson, I. R. (2013). Gender, nationality and leadership style: A literature review. *International Journal of Business and Management*, 8(1), 89.

Socratous, M. (2018). Networking: A male dominated game. *Gender in Management*, 33(2), 167–183. Advance online publication. DOI: 10.1108/GM-11-2016-0181

Stripling, J. (2012). With Tilghman"s resignation, another pioneer female president moves on. *Chronicle of Higher Education.Retrieved from*http://chronicle.com/article/Another-PioneerFemale/134600

Subramaniam, G., Khadri, A. N. M., Maniam, B., & Ali, E. (2016). The glass ceiling phenomenon-does it Really affect Women's career advancement in Malaysia? Journal of Organizational Culture. *Communications and Conflict.*, 20, 81.

Sujan, M. (2018). A Safety-II Perspective on Organisational Learning in Healthcare Organisations: Comment on" False Dawns and New Horizons in Patient Safety Research and Practice. *International Journal of Health Policy and Management*, 7(7), 662–666. DOI: 10.15171/ijhpm.2018.16 PMID: 29996587

Süßenbacher, S., Amering, M., Gmeiner, A., & Schrank, B. (2017). Gender-gaps and glass ceilings: A survey of gender-specific publication trends in Psychiatry between 1994 and 2014. *European Psychiatry*, 44, 90–95. DOI: 10.1016/j.eurpsy.2017.03.008 PMID: 28550785

Swandt, T. A. (2001). *Dictionary of Qualitative Inquiry* (2nd ed.). Sage Publications.

Talent Corp Malaysia. (2016). *Diversity and Workforce Composition for Top 100 PLCs*. Retrieved from https://www.talentcorp.com.my/clients/TalentCorp_2016_7A6571AE-D9D0-4175-B35D-99EC514F2D24/contentms/img/publication/Divers ityArtcard_v2.0.pdf[REMOVED HYPERLINK FIELD]

Terjesen, S., & Singh, V. (2008). Female presence on corporate boards: A multi-country study of environment context. *Journal of Business Ethics*, 83(1), 55–63. DOI: 10.1007/s10551-007-9656-1

The Sun Daily. (2017). *Govt will name and shame PLCs with no women on their boards in 2018*. Retrieved from http://www.thesundaily.my/news/2017/07/25/govt[REMOVED HYPERLINK FIELD]will-name-and-shame-plcs-no-women-their[REMOVED HYPERLINK FIELD]boards-2018[REMOVED HYPERLINK FIELD]

Thornton, G. (2015). *The Economic Impact of Digitalization*. Grant Thornton LLP.

Thurasamy, R., Lo, M., Yang Amri, A., & Noor, N. (2011). An analysis of career advancement among engineers in manufacturing organizations. *International Journal of Commerce and Management*, 21(2), 143–157. DOI: 10.1108/10569211111144346

Timmers, T. M., Willemsen, T. M., & Tijdens, K. G. (2010). Gender diversity policies in universities: A multi-perspective framework of policy measures. *Higher Education*, 59(6), 719735. DOI: 10.1007/s10734-009-9276-z

Tlaiss, H., & Kauser, S. (2011). The impact of gender, family, and work on the career advancement of Lebanese women managers. *Gender in Management*, 26(1), 8–36. DOI: 10.1108/17542411111109291

Tomas, M., Lavie, J. M., Duran, M. D. M., & Guillamon, C. (2010). Women in academic administration at the university. *Educational Management Administration & Leadership*, 38(4), 487–498. DOI: 10.1177/1741143210368266

Tukonic, S. & Harwood, D. (2015). The Glass Ceiling Effect: Mediating Influences on Early Years Educators' Sense of Professionalism. Journal of Childhood Studies. 40(1) 36 to 54.

U.S. Department of Labor. (1995). *Good for business: Making full use of the nation's human capital*. Federal Glass Ceiling Commission.

Van Manen, M. (1990). *Researching Lived Experience: Human Science for an Action Sensitive Pedagogy*. State University of New York Press.

Vasić, N., Kilibarda, M., Andrejić, M., & Jović, S. (2021). Satisfaction is a function of users of logistics services in e-commerce. *Technology Analysis and Strategic Management*, 33(7), 813–828. DOI: 10.1080/09537325.2020.1849610

Wadud, M. M., Maniruzzaman, F. M., Satter, M. A., Miah, M. A. A., Paul, S. K., & Haque, K. R. (2001). *Agricultural research in Bangladesh in the 20th century. BARC*. Bangladesh and Bangladesh Academy of Agriculture.

Wan Liyana, W.. (2016). The Impact of Organizational Culture on Knowledge Management in Higher Education Institutions. *International Journal of Business and Management*, 11(9), 123–132.

Wang, C., Han, D., Liu, Q., & Luo, S. (2018). A deep learning approach for credit scoring of peer-to-peer lending using attention mechanism LSTM. *IEEE Access : Practical Innovations, Open Solutions*, 7, 2161–2168. DOI: 10.1109/ACCESS.2018.2887138

Wang, K., Shawl, R. Q., & Neware, R.. (2021). Research on immersive interactive experience of content e-commerce live users in the era of computer digital marketing. *International Journal of System Assurance Engineering and Management*, •••, 1–11.

Wang, Y., Jia, F., Schoenherr, T., Gong, Y., & Chen, L. (2020). Cross-border e-commerce firms as supply chain integrators: The management of three flows. *Industrial Marketing Management*, 89, 72–88. DOI: 10.1016/j.indmarman.2019.09.004

Wang, Y., Lu, Z., Glover, F., & Hao, J.-K. (2012). Path relinking for unconstrained binary quadratic programming. *European Journal of Operational Research*, 223(3), 595–604. DOI: 10.1016/j.ejor.2012.07.012

Wang, Z., Zheng, X., Li, D., Zhang, H., Yang, Y., & Pan, H. (2021). A VGGNet-like approach for classifying and segmenting coal dust particles with overlapping regions. *Computers in Industry*, 132, 103506. DOI: 10.1016/j.compind.2021.103506

Weiler, S., & Bernasek, A. (2001). Dodging the glass ceiling? Networks and the new wave of women entrepreneurs. *The Social Science Journal*, 38(1), 85–103. DOI: 10.1016/S0362-3319(00)00111-7

WHO. (2020). Keep health workers safe to keep patients safe.

Winter, T., Rudel, M., Lalla, H., Brendgen, S., Geißler, B., Martin, A., & Morsi, A. (2011) “System and method for performing an opening auction of a derivative.” URL https://www.google.de/patents/US20110119170, Pub. No.: US 2011/0119170 A1. US Patent App. 12/618,410.

Wu, M., & Moon, Y. (2018). DACDI (Define, Audit, Correlate, Disclose, and Improve) framework to address cyber-manufacturing attacks and intrusions. *Manufacturing Letters*, 15, 155–159. DOI: 10.1016/j.mfglet.2017.12.009

Xiao, H. (2020). *Yan Zhang.; Desheng Kong.; Shiyue Li.; Ningxi Yang.,* "The Effects of Social Suffort on Sleep Quality of Medical Staff Treating Patients with Coronavirus Disease 2019(Covid-19) in January and February 2020 in China". *Medical Science Monitor*. Advance online publication. DOI: 10.12659/MSM.923549

Xu, J., Chiu, S., & Glover, F. (1997). Tabu Search for Dynamic Routing Communications Network Design. *Telecommunication Systems*, 8(1), 1–23. DOI: 10.1023/A:1019149101850

Xu, Y., Du, B., Zhang, L., Cerra, D., Pato, M., Carmona, E., Prasad, S., Yokoya, N., Hansch, R., & Le Saux, B. (2019). Advanced multi-sensor optical remote sensing for urban land use and land cover classification: Outcome of the 2018 IEEE GRSS data fusion contest. *IEEE Journal of Selected Topics in Applied Earth Observations and Remote Sensing*, 12(6), 1709–1724. DOI: 10.1109/JSTARS.2019.2911113

Yagiura, M., Ibaraki, T., & Glover, F. (2006). A path relinking approach with ejection chains for the generalized assignment problem. *European Journal of Operational Research*, 169(2), 548–569. DOI: 10.1016/j.ejor.2004.08.015

Yagiura, M., Komiya, A., Kojima, K., Nonobe, K., Nagamochi, H., Ibaraki, T., & Glover, F. (2007). *A path relinking approach for the multi-resource generalized quadratic assignment problem* (Vol. 4638). Lecture Notes in Computer Science. Springer. DOI: 10.1007/978-3-540-74446-7_9

Yang, B., & Liao, Y. M. (2021). Research on enterprise risk knowledge graph based on multi-source data fusion. *Neural Computing & Applications*, •••, 1–14.

Yang, J. C., Chuang, H. C., & Kuan, C. M. (2020). Double machine learning with gradient boosting and its application to the Big N audit quality effect. *Journal of Econometrics*, 216(1), 268–283. DOI: 10.1016/j.jeconom.2020.01.018

Yizhou, Z., Simeng, Z., & Raj, V. (2020) 'A Discussion of the Application of Artificial Intelligence in the Management of Mass Media Censorship in Mainland China', *ACM International Conference Proceeding Series*, pp. 79–84. DOI: 10.1145/3407703.3407719

Younus, A. M., & Raju, V. (2021). Resilient Features of Organizational Culture in Implementation of Smart Contract Technology Blockchain in Iraqi Gas and Oil Companies. *International Journal of Qualitative Research*, 15(2), 435–450. DOI: 10.24874/IJQR15.02-05

Yousaf, R., & Schmiede, R. (2016). Underrepresentation of Women at Academic Excellence and Position of Power: Role of Harassment and Glass Ceiling. *Open Journal of Social Sciences*, 4(2), 173–185. DOI: 10.4236/jss.2016.42023

Yousaf, R., & Schmiede, R. (2017). Barriers to women"s representation in academic excellence and positions of power. *Asian Journal of German and European Studies*, 2(1), 2–13. DOI: 10.1186/s40856-017-0013-6

Yu, X., Feng, W., Wang, H., Chu, Q., & Chen, Q. (2020). An attention mechanism and multi-granularity-based Bi-LSTM model for Chinese Q&A system. *Soft Computing*, 24(8), 5831–5845. DOI: 10.1007/s00500-019-04367-8

Zaragas, C. K. (2021). The Psychodrama and its Contribution to The Children's Competitive manifestation. Case Study. *Cultural-historical Psychology*, 17(3), 143–151. DOI: 10.17759/chp.2021170318

Zhang, F., & Yang, Y. (2021). Trust model simulation of cross border e-commerce based on machine learning and Bayesian network. *Journal of Ambient Intelligence and Humanized Computing*, •••, 1–11.

Zhang, K., Guo, Y., Wang, X., Yuan, J., & Ding, Q. (2019). Multiple feature reweight DenseNet for image classification. *IEEE Access : Practical Innovations, Open Solutions*, 7, 9872–9880. DOI: 10.1109/ACCESS.2018.2890127

Zhang, X., Yang, F., & Hu, Y.. (2021). RANet: Network intrusion detection with group-gating convolutional neural network. *Journal of Network and Computer Applications*, •••, 103266.

Zhao, J., Lu, Y., Ban, H., & Chen, Y. (2020). E-commerce satisfaction based on synthetic evaluation theory and neural networks. *International Journal on Computer Science and Engineering*, 22(4), 394–403.

Zhou, Y., Li, J., Chen, H., Wu, Y., Wu, J., & Chen, L. (2020). A spatiotemporal attention mechanism-based model for multi-step citywide passenger demand prediction. *Information Sciences*, 513, 372–385. DOI: 10.1016/j.ins.2019.10.071

Zhu, Z., Xu, S., Wang, H., Liu, Z., Wu, J., Li, G., . . . Wang, W. (2020). COVID-19 in Wuhan: immediate psychological impact on 5062 health workers. MedRxiv, 2020-02.

Zhu, K., Wang, R., Zhao, Q., Cheng, J., & Tao, D. (2019). A cuboid CNN model with an attention mechanism for skeleton-based action recognition. *IEEE Transactions on Multimedia*, 22(11), 2977–2989. DOI: 10.1109/TMM.2019.2962304

Zhu, L. (2020). Analysis and Research of Enterprise Information System Security Based on e-Commerce. *Academic Journal of Computing & Information Science*, 3(3), 1–9.

Zhu, W., Mou, J., & Benyoucef, M. (2019). - Exploring purchase intention in cross-border E-commerce: A three-stage model. *Journal of Retailing and Consumer Services*, 2019(51), 320–330. DOI: 10.1016/j.jretconser.2019.07.004

Zuo, X., Chen, Z., Dong, L., Chang, J., & Hou, B. (2020). Power information network intrusion detection based on data mining algorithm. *The Journal of Supercomputing*, 76(7), 5521–5539. DOI: 10.1007/s11227-019-02899-2

About the Authors

Adrian David Cheok is Full Professor at i-University Tokyo, Director of the Imagineering Institute, Malaysia, Visiting Professor at Raffles University, Malaysia, Visiting Professor at University of Novi Sad-Serbia, on Technical faculty "Mihailo Pupin", Serbia, and CEO of Nikola Tesla Technologies Corporation.

Rose Marie Azzopardi is an economist with a research focus on the labour market. She has presented and published work on several related areas such as women in the labour market, entrepreneurship, the gender pay gap, skills, migration, and also on small states, economic development and social policy. Her current commissioned research is on the future of skills. She has collaborated on research projects with national, regional and international organizations such as the EU, ILO, Commonwealth, UNRISD and the World Bank. Prof Azzopardi has read for degrees at the University of Malta, and the University of Sussex UK, and also participated in courses at the University of Victoria, Australia and Harvard Business School, US

Index

www.ingramcontent.com/pod-product-compliance
Lightning Source LLC
LaVergne TN
LVHW080638011026
849160LV00014B/1252